THE CAMBRIDGE COMPANION TO AMERICAN FICTION AFTER 1945

Each generation revises literary history and this is nowhere more evident than in the post-World War II period. This Companion offers a comprehensive, authoritative, and accessible overview of the diversity of American fiction since World War II. Essays by nineteen distinguished scholars provide critical insights into the significant genres, historical contexts, cultural diversity, and major authors during a period of enormous American global political and cultural power. This power is overshadowed, nevertheless, by national anxieties growing out of events ranging from the Civil Rights Movement to the rise of feminism; from the Cold War and its fear of communism and nuclear warfare to the Age of Terror and its different yet related fears of the Other. American fiction since 1945 has faithfully chronicled these anxieties. An essential reference guide, this Companion provides a chronology of the period, as well as guides to further reading.

JOHN N. DUVALL is the Margaret Church Distinguished Professor of English at Purdue University. He has published nine previous books on modernist and contemporary American fiction, most recently *Race and White Identity in Southern Fiction* (2008), *The Cambridge Companion to Don DeLillo* (2008), and *Faulkner and His Critics* (2010).

D0151073

THE CAMBRIDGE COMPANION TO

AMERICAN FICTION AFTER 1945

EDITED BY

JOHN N. DUVALL

Purdue University, Indiana

CAMBRIDGE
UNIVERSITY PRESS

CONTRIBUTORS

VICTORIA AARONS is the O. R. and Eva Mitchell Distinguished Professor of Literature and Chair of the English Department at Trinity University. She is the author of *A Measure of Memory: Storytelling and Identity in American Jewish Fiction* (1996) and *What Happened to Abraham? Reinventing the Covenant in American Jewish Fiction* (2005), both recipients of a CHOICE Award for Outstanding Academic Books.

LAURA BARRETT is Professor of English and Dean of the College of Liberal Arts at Armstrong Atlantic State University in Savannah, Georgia. Her work on nineteenth- and twentieth-century American fiction has appeared in such journals as the *Journal of Modern Literature*, *MFS*, *Papers on Language and Literature*, *Studies in the Novel*, and *Western American Literature*.

MARTYN BONE is Associate Professor in the Department of English at the University of Mississippi. He is the author of *The Postsouthern Sense of Place in Contemporary Fiction* (2005) and the editor of *Perspectives on Barry Hannah* (2007). His articles have appeared in *American Literature*, *Journal of American Studies*, *Comparative American Studies*, *New Centennial Review*, *Mississippi Quarterly*, and other journals.

KEITH BYERMAN is Professor of English at Indiana State University. His books include *Fingering the Jagged Edge: Tradition and Form in Recent Black Fiction* (1985), *John Edgar Wideman: A Study in Short Fiction* (1998), and *Remembering the Past in Contemporary African American Fiction* (2008).

JOHN N. DUVALL is the Margaret Church Distinguished Professor of English and the editor of *MFS: Modern Fiction Studies* at Purdue University. He has published nine previous books on modernist and contemporary American fiction, most recently *Race and White Identity in Southern Fiction* (2008) and *Faulkner and His Critics* (2010).

AMY J. ELIAS is Associate Professor of English at the University of Tennessee. She is the author of *Sublime Desire: History and Post-1960s Fiction* (2001), winner of the Perkins Prize from the International Society for the Study of Narrative, and numerous articles concerning post-1960s literature, digital media, and narrative theory. She is the founder of ASAP: The Association for the Study of the Arts of the Present. Her second book project focuses on the ethics and import of dialogics to the contemporary arts.

JANE ELLIOTT is Senior Lecturer in the Department of English and Related Literature at Kings College London. She is the author of *Popular Feminist Fiction as American Allegory: Representing National Time* (2008), and, with Derek Attridge, co-editor of *Theory after "Theory"* (2011). She is currently at work on a book entitled *The Prison-House of Interest: Neoliberalism, Popular Aesthetics and the Agonies of Agency*.

BRIAN JARVIS is Senior Lecturer in American Literature and Film at Loughborough University. He is the author of *Postmodern Cartographies: The Geographical Imagination in Contemporary American Culture* (1998) and *Cruel and Unusual: A Cultural History of Punishment in America* (2004), the co-author of *The Contemporary American Novel in Context* (2011), and has written essays on topics that include Vietnam War fiction, 9/11, globalization, US TV prison dramas, and horror film.

A. ROBERT LEE, previously of the University of Kent at Canterbury, until 2011 was Professor of American Literature at Nihon University, Tokyo. His recent publications include *Designs of Blackness: Mappings in the Literature and Culture of Afro-America* (1998), *Multicultural American Literature: Comparative Black, Native, Latino/a and Asian American Fictions* (2003), which won the American Book Award, and *Modern American Counter Writing: Beats, Outriders, Ethnics* (2010).

SUSAN LOHAFER is Professor Emeritus in the Department of English at the University of Iowa. Her books include *Coming to Terms With the Short Story* (1983) and *Reading for Storyness: Preclosure Theory, Empirical Poetics, and Culture in the Short Story* (2003). She also has co-edited *Short Story Theory at a Crossroads* (1989) and *The Tales We Tell: Perspectives on the Short Story* (1998). She has published numerous essays on particular short stories and on the genre.

ALAN NADEL, William T. Bryan Chair in American Literature and Culture at the University of Kentucky, is the author of several books on post-World War II American literature and culture, including *Containment Culture* (1995) and, most recently, *Television in Black-and-White America: Race and National Identity* (2005). He is co-editor with Susan Griffin of *The Men Who Knew Too Much: Alfred Hitchcock and Henry James* (forthcoming).

STACEY OLSTER is Professor of English at the State University of New York at Stony Brook. She is the author of *Reminiscence and Re-Creation in Contemporary American Fiction* (1989) and *The Trash Phenomenon: Contemporary Literature, Popular Culture, and the Making of the American Century* (2003), and the editor of *The Cambridge Companion to John Updike* (2006) and *Don DeLillo: Mao II, Underworld, Falling Man* (2011).

LINDEN PEACH is Dean of Arts and Humanities at the University of Wales, Cardiff. His books include *Toni Morrison* (2000), *Masquerade, Crime and Fiction* (2006), *Contemporary Irish and Welsh Women's Fiction* (2007), *Angela Carter* (2009), and *Emyr Humphreys* (2011). He has also published recently on the relatively neglected area of African American women's crime writing. He is a Fellow of the English Society, a member of the Welsh Academy, and an Honorary Fellow of Swansea University.

NANCY J. PETERSON, Professor of English at Purdue University, focuses on contemporary American literature and culture in her research and teaching, with particular interests in ethnic literatures and Native studies. She has published two books and two edited collections, along with essays on Sherman Alexie, Louise Erdrich, and other Native writers, as well as on Toni Morrison.

JESSICA PRESSMAN is Assistant Professor of English at Yale University. She specializes in twentieth- and twenty-first-century American literature, digital literature, and media theory. Her articles on experimental literature have appeared in *MFS*, *Studies in American Fiction*, and *Dichtung-Digital*. She is completing a manuscript titled *Digital Modernism: Making It New in New Media*, which charts a genealogy between modernist literature and electronic literature.

ROBERT REBEIN is the author of *Hicks, Tribes, and Dirty Realists: American Fiction after Postmodernism* (2001). Other work has appeared in *The Mourning After: Attending the Wake of Postmodernism*, *The Blackwell Encyclopedia of Twentieth-Century Fiction*, *Ecotone: Reimagining Place*, *Georgia Review*, *Cream City Review*, and other journals. He directs the graduate program in English at Indiana University–Purdue University Indianapolis.

NICOLE A. WALIGORA-DAVIS is Assistant Professor of English at Rice University and specializes in African American and American literature and culture. She is the author of *Sanctuary: African Americans and Empire* (2011). Her essays have appeared in *Centennial Review*, *African American Review*, *MFS*, *Mississippi Quarterly*, and the *Cambridge History of African American Literature*.

JAY WATSON is Howry Professor of Faulkner Studies at the University of Mississippi, where he teaches in the English Department. His books include *Forensic Fictions:*

The Lawyer Figure in Faulkner (1993), *Conversations With Larry Brown* (2007), and *Faulkner and Whiteness* (2011), and he is the author of numerous essays on Southern literature and culture.

PHILLIP E. WEGNER is University Research Foundation Professor in the Department of English at the University of Florida. He is the author of *Life Between Two Deaths, 1989–2001: U.S. Culture in the Long Nineties* (2009); *Imaginary Communities: Utopia, the Nation, and the Spatial Histories of Modernity* (2002); and the forthcoming *Periodizing Jameson; or, the Adventures of Theory in Post-contemporary Times* and *Ontologies of the Possible: Utopia, Science Fiction, and Globalization.*

CHRONOLOGY

1969   July 20, first moon landing

Saturday Evening Post ceases publication because of declining
    readership

Kurt Vonnegut, Slaughterhouse-Five; or The Children's
    Crusade

1970   Toni Morrison, The Bluest Eye

Joan Didion, Play It as It Lays

1971   E. L. Doctorow, The Book of Daniel

John Updike, Rabbit Redux

1972   Ishmael Reed, Mumbo Jumbo

1973   October: Arab oil embargo causes gas prices to rise

Thomas Pynchon, Gravity's Rainbow

1974   Richard Nixon resigns his Presidency on August 8

1975   In April, the United States ends all military and financial support
    to South Vietnam. South Vietnam falls to communist North
    Vietnam

William Gaddis, J R

1976   America celebrates its Bicentennial on July 4

Jimmy Carter elected President

Maxine Hong Kingston, The Woman Warrior

1977   Robert Coover, The Public Burning

Toni Morrison, Song of Solomon

Leslie Marmon Silko, Ceremony

1978   Michael Herr, Dispatches

John Irving, The World According to Garp

1979   Joan Didion, The White Album

Norman Mailer, The Executioner's Song

1980   Ronald Reagan elected President

Marilynne Robinson, Housekeeping

Joyce Carol Oates, You Must Remember This

John Kennedy Toole, A Confederacy of Dunces

1981   John Updike, Rabbit is Rich

1982   Alice Walker, The Color Purple

1983   Raymond Carver, Cathedral

William Kennedy, Ironweed

1984   Sandra Cisneros, The House on Mango Street

William Gibson, Neuromancer

Louise Erdrich, Love Medicine

1985   Don DeLillo, White Noise

Bobbie Ann Mason, In Country

1986   Kathy Acker, *Don Quixote*
        Richard Ford, *The Sportswriter*
1987   Paul Auster, *The New York Trilogy*
        Toni Morrison, *Beloved*
1988   Raymond Carver dies on August 2
        George Bush elected President
        Gloria Naylor, *Mama Day*
1989   Amy Tan, *The Joy Luck Club*
1990   Tim O'Brien, *The Things They Carried*
        Charles Johnson, *Middle Passage*
        John Updike, *Rabbit at Rest*
1991   January–February: US-led coalition invades Iraq
        December: the Soviet Union officially dissolves
        Gish Jen, *Typical American*
1992   William Jefferson Clinton elected President
        Dorothy Allison, *Bastard out of Carolina*
        Cormac McCarthy, *All the Pretty Horses*
        Denis Johnson, *Jesus' Son*
1993   Toni Morrison is awarded the Nobel Prize for Literature
        Annie Proulx, *The Shipping News*
        Philip Roth, *Operation Shylock*
1994   William Gaddis, *A Frolic of His Own*
        David Guterson, *Snow Falling on Cedars*
1995   Sherman Alexie, *Reservation Blues*
        Chang-rae Lee, *Native Speaker*
1996   Joyce Carol Oates, *We Were the Mulvaneys*
        David Foster Wallace, *Infinite Jest*
1997   Don DeLillo, *Underworld*
1998   President Clinton impeached by US House of Representatives
        Toni Morrison, *Paradise*
        Thomas Pynchon, *Mason & Dixon*
        Barbara Kingsolver, *The Poisonwood Bible*
1999   Ralph Ellison dies on April 16
        Ha Jin, *Waiting*
2000   December 12, US Supreme Court decides five to four in *Bush v. Gore* to stop the Florida vote recount; George W. Bush elected to the Presidency
        Michael Chabon, *The Amazing Adventures of Kavalier & Clay*
        Mark Z. Danielewski, *House of Leaves*

2001	September 11: terrorists attack the World Trade Center towers and the Pentagon, killing 2,996; United States begins bombing Afghanistan in October
	Jonathan Franzen, *The Corrections*
2002	Jeffrey Eugenides, *Middlesex*
2003	United States invades Iraq on March 23
	Edward P. Jones, *The Known World*
2004	Marilynne Robinson, *Gilead*
	Philip Roth, *The Plot Against America*
2005	Saul Bellow dies on April 5
	William T. Vollman, *Europe Central*
2006	Richard Ford, *The Lay of the Land*
	Thomas Pynchon, *Against the Day*
2007	Norman Mailer dies on November 10
	Don DeLillo, *Falling Man*
	Junot Díaz, *The Brief Wondrous Life of Oscar Wao*
2008	Barack Obama elected President
	Toni Morrison, *A Mercy*
2009	John Updike dies on January 27
	Colson Whitehead, *Sag Harbor*
	Sherman Alexie, *War Dances*
2010	According to AWP, 336 graduate programs in creative writing exist in the United States (116 MA, 184 MFA, and 36 PhD)
	Jonathan Franzen, *Freedom*

JOHN N. DUVALL

Introduction: A story of the stories of American fiction after 1945

This may well be the last volume ever to survey American fiction from 1945 to the present. That is not because scholarship on this body of narrative is waning. Far from it. There is a more pragmatic reason for my prediction: the period is getting a little long in the tooth. The Victorian Era will never exceed sixty-four years. Modernism is often dated from 1890 to 1945 (a solid fifty-six-year run), but the post-1945 period (which until recently we simply called "postmodernism"), if a person, could now be collecting Social Security. It is only a matter of time before the profession decides that, if for nothing more than curricular reasons (after all, there is only so much one can teach in a semester), we need to close off the postwar period in some definitive fashion. Certainly, no one in 2045 will be teaching a course in contemporary American fiction from 1945 to the present.

Not surprisingly, because the postwar period has been left openended for so long, there have been generational shifts, so that post-1945 fiction looks quite different now than for earlier critics. One of the earliest attempts to make sense of American fiction following World War II occurs in John Aldridge's *After the Lost Generation* (1951), which saw contemporary novelists falling short of the achievement of American modernist writers. Except for Norman Mailer, Truman Capote, and Gore Vidal, however, the postwar novelists on whom Aldridge bases his assessment have largely been relegated to the ash heap of history: Robert Lowry, John Horne Burns, Alfred Hayes, Merle Miller, and Vance Bourjaily. In 1971, Tony Tanner published his magisterial study of postwar American fiction, *City of Words*, one that was certainly among the dominant narratives of this period when I began my graduate studies in 1978. Tanner tells a compelling story about postwar fiction, arguing that American novelists thematize a paranoid fear of deterministic systems, problematize identity, use language in a unique way that calls attention to itself, but are often trapped by their own verbal performances. For Tanner the typical fictional hero searches for a freedom that is not amorphous and wants "to establish an identity that is not a prison."

The protagonist's quest is in a sense a double for the author's: "Can he find a *stylistic* freedom which is not simply a meaningless incoherence, and can he find a stylistic form which will not trap him inside the existing forms of previous literature?"[1]

Tanner based his study on twenty-two writers: Ralph Ellison, Saul Bellow, Joseph Heller, James Purdy, William S. Burroughs, Thomas Pynchon, Kurt Vonnegut, John Hawkes, John Barth, Walker Percy, Sylvia Plath, Susan Sontag, William H. Gass, John Updike, Philip Roth, Frank Conroy, Bernard Malamud, Norman Mailer, Ken Kesey, William Gaddis, Donald Barthelme, and Richard Brautigan. Of Tanner's novelists, only nine remain relevant to the conversation today, if we base our sense of the canonical on that venerable institution of American pedagogy, the seventh edition of the *Norton Anthology of American Literature*, vol. E (Literature since 1945): Malamud, Ellison, Bellow, Vonnegut, Gass, Barthelme, Updike, Roth, and Pynchon. Plath appears in the anthology but only for her poetry. Gass perhaps should not fully count because he is represented only by an essay he wrote about fiction, not by any of his fiction.

In terms of who matters in contemporary American fiction, 1971 was a very different world from ours. Some of the omissions from Tanner's list can easily be explained by this date. Toni Morrison and Don DeLillo were unknown: DeLillo's first novel was published the same year as Tanner's study, while Morrison's first had appeared just a year earlier. But more striking from a contemporary perspective is the gender and racial imbalance: twenty men, two women, one African American. Tanner wrote his book before the rise of academic feminism and African American (as well as other ethnic) studies.

A scholar of contemporary American fiction today reads multiculturally or not at all, and in the world of literature anthologies (which can only contain so many pages and cost only so much), John Barth must make way for Toni Cade Bambara; Joseph Heller for Amy Tan; Ken Kesey for Sherman Alexie. But such decisions by anthology editors necessarily reduce the complexity of literary history. One purpose of this volume is to tell a fuller story of the breadth and nuance of American fictional production since 1945.

One story that explains part of the post-1945 landscape has been told by people as various as the Marxist critic Fredric Jameson and the metafictionist John Barth. It is the story of postmodernist experimentation, which Amy Elias explores more fully in Chapter 1. As Jameson puts it, postmodernism "is most often related to notions of the waning or extinction of the hundred-year-old modern movement (or to its ideological or aesthetic repudiation)"; for fiction, this means that "final forms of representation in the novel" have been spent and the new forms of fiction are aggressively nonmimetic.[2]

Fiction, as indeed all forms of cultural production, for Jameson, has become an expression of the cultural logic of late capitalism and therefore has lost its ability to think historically and to comment critically on the culture. From the point of view of a practicing novelist, Barth sees that the modernist thematics of alienation and the failure of language as a medium of expression have come to the end of the road in Samuel Beckett's late fiction. If nothing more can be accomplished in that arc of modernist experimentation, what is to be done? Barth's answer is to follow in the footsteps of Jorge Luis Borges and to produce metafiction: "novels that imitate the form of the Novel, by an author who imitates the role of the Author."[3] While Barth admits that such self-conscious and self-reflexive fiction runs the risk of becoming a contemporary form of art for art's sake, he insists that metafiction could be "serious and passionate despite its farcical aspect."[4]

In the late 1980s, Linda Hutcheon, critiquing Jameson's pessimistic view of postmodernism, would develop Barth's sense of the serious possibilities of ludic narration in her conception of postmodern fiction as historiographic metafiction. For Hutcheon, contemporary fiction, by blending the reflexivity of metafiction with a sense of historiography, could still create a critical purchase on the culture by taking us where the official archives of history were either silent or repressed. Where Jameson sees only apolitical pastiche (artists simply recycling and dehistoricizing previously articulated styles), Hutcheon sees parody, which has the power to produce a complicit critique. While Hutcheon's is a more hopeful theoretical model than Jameson's, in the hands of practicing critics just about any post-1945 novel can be identified as historiographic metafiction. When texts as different as Robert Coover's *The Public Burning* (1977), with every other chapter narrated by then Vice President Richard M. Nixon and which climaxes with a mass orgy during the execution of the Rosenbergs in Times Square, and Toni Morrison's *Beloved* (1977), a serious narrative of the trauma of slavery and the need to recover stories of historical abuse, can both be termed historiographic metafiction, the concept loses a good deal of its usefulness. Whatever its theoretical limitations, Hutcheon's concept allowed more women and minority writers to be considered postmodern, broadening a canon that had previously been composed largely of white men.

By the turn of the twenty-first century, the story of postmodernist fiction was beginning to unravel. The problem is that debates within postmodern theory and discussions of postmodernist experimentation do not adequately account for the full range of fictional production after 1945. As Michael Bérubé so pithily put it in his essay "Teaching Postmodern Fiction without Being Sure That the Genre Exists," while the theory he teaches is unquestionably postmodern, "The problem is with the fiction: It just isn't postmodern enough. And that, I've gradually come to realize, is because there really isn't any such thing as postmodern fiction – at least not in terms that most literary critics have proposed so far."[5] As Bérubé goes on to elaborate: "there's nothing especially postmodern about most critically acclaimed writers of 'quality fiction' ... Richard Ford, E. Annie Proulx, Mary Carr, Madison Smartt Bell, Oscar Hijuelos ... can't plausibly be called postmodernists. For the most part, they seem to be capable, mimesis-minded chroniclers of contemporary life."[6]

If the canonization of the high modernist formal experiments pushed writers of the 1950s through the 1980s to different narrative forms, to a writer starting out today, the metafictional and nonmimetic moves of the high postmodernists (Barth, Pynchon, Coover, and Barthelme) must now feel like the dead hand of history, much as modernism did to Barth when he published "The Literature of Exhaustion" in 1967. What is next when the solution to the problem of modernism's exhaustion, metafiction, itself seems to have reached the point of exhaustion? Very often it is the re-emergence of mimesis-minded chroniclers of contemporary life, a topic Robert Rebein explores in Chapter 2. But beyond a backlash to postmodernism, what else might account for the rise of contemporary realism?

One promising way to begin responding to this question is recent work done on the institutionalization of creative writing programs in the United States after World War II. American modernist novelists, such as F. Scott Fitzgerald, Sherwood Anderson, and Ernest Hemingway, found a congenial meeting spot in Gertrude Stein's salon – a place for conversation and poetics. Stein famously provided Hemingway with a critique of a draft of his *The Sun Also Rises*. Aspiring American writers no longer have to go Paris for camaraderie and critique. Instead, they may go to just about anywhere in the hinterland of America – Iowa City, Iowa; Lincoln, Nebraska; West Lafayette, Indiana. That is because whether famous (as the Iowa Writers' Workshop is) or obscure, just about any university worth its salt has an MFA program, even my home institution, Purdue, which markets itself almost exclusively for its strength in the STEM disciplines.

As Mark McGurl has recently argued, the rise of creative writing in the university goes a long way toward explaining the landscape of American fiction after World War II:

> The handful of creative writing programs that existed in the 1940s had, by 1975, increased to 52 in number. By 1984 there were some 150 graduate degree programs ... and as of 2005 there were more than 350 creative writing programs in the United States, all of them staffed by practicing writers, most of whom, by now, are themselves holders of an advanced degree in creative writing.[7]

This specialization has had a profound impact on the culture of university-sponsored quarterlies and little magazines that grew to prominence from the late 1930s to the early 1950s. Magazines such as the *Southern Review*, first series (1935–1942); the *Kenyon Review*, first series (1939–1970); and the *Sewanee Review* (1892–) all published seminal mixes of literary and cultural criticism, as well as poetry and fiction. The foundational theoretical essays that shaped New Critical formalism appeared side-by-side with fiction by such writers as Eudora Welty, Flannery O'Connor, and Peter Taylor. That is because these journals were edited by men of letters who wrote fiction and poetry, as well as literary criticism and theory: Robert Penn Warren was one of the editors of the *Southern Review*; John Crowe Ransom edited the *Kenyon Review* from 1939 to 1959; Andrew Lytle and Allen Tate edited the *Sewanee Review* during its zenith from 1943 to 1946. Both the *Southern Review* and the *Kenyon Review* were revived during the 1970s, but now as journals edited by and for "creative writers," the term of choice for faculty members affiliated with MFA programs. There is very little crossover readership among English professors today. Professors who teach literature (to say nothing of general readers) do not, by and large, read the highly competent, well-crafted poetry and fiction published in literary reviews, and professors who teach in MFA programs do not read the essays on modernist and contemporary fiction published in journals like the one I edit, *MFS: Modern Fiction Studies*, because these essays have nothing to say about craft.

The changes in mass-market magazines have been even more profound. If the growth of magazine culture following the Civil War allowed writers to earn a living through their fiction, many of these magazines, such as the *Saturday Evening Post*, begin to lose their cultural force with the advent of electronic media (radio, film, television) and eventually disappear. While there are still a few mass-market magazines that publish fiction, notably *The New Yorker*, these venues create insufficient opportunities for most writers to make a living. Prior to the eighteenth century, writers worked under a patronage system, supported by the largess of the aristocracy. Since 1945, American fiction has returned by and large to a patronage system, one that is underwritten by state governments. Like academic quarterlies, literary magazines published by universities, for the most part, pay contributors nothing. The eighteenth-century writer Samuel Johnson famously said that "No man but a blockhead ever wrote, except for money." Today's university creative writers, though, are not blockheads for publishing their work in venues that pay nothing because such publication can help advance their careers.

Starting with Flannery O'Connor, who honed her craft at the Iowa Writers' Workshop, if we look at the writers discussed in the various chapters that follow, the majority were nurtured and sustained by the university. This is not to say that the man or woman of letters, someone who supports themselves solely by the products of their pen or PC, has disappeared, but simply that the Updikes, Pynchons, and DeLillos of the world are becoming increasingly rare. Even for the generation of writers who came of age prior to the rise of MFA programs, many have taught in the American university. Barth taught at Penn State University in the 1960s before moving on to the State University of New York at Buffalo. Nobel Laureate Toni Morrison taught for years at various universities before ending her academic career at Princeton.

One result of the growth of creative writing programs has been the institutionalization of Hemingway's version of modernist experimentation, his minimalism. The neo-realist minimalism of Raymond Carver (who attended the Iowa Writers' Workshop for a year) and other writers of the 1980s, as Eric Bennett has argued, "did not simply arise as a protest against the wooly experimental fiction of the 1960s."[8] Rather, along with the exponential growth of MFA programs in the last sixty years, Hemingway's minimalism took hold as the unacknowledged hegemony of creative writing programs. In the 1950s, Hemingway was central to both New Critical pedagogy and the New Humanists' development of creative writing at Iowa and Stanford.[9] As graduates of these early MFA programs went on to found new MFA programs, modernist minimalist aesthetic increasingly became institutionalized. This is not to say that MFA programs suppress all difference. They do not. Even the metafictional novelist David Foster Wallace earned an MFA from the University of Arizona.[10] But such formal experimenters are the exceptions that prove the minimalist rule. To write a text like Pynchon's *Gravity's Rainbow* today would not get one to a thesis defense at most MFA programs.

Another reason for the unraveling of the story of postmodernism is the growing recognition of the full range of writing in a multicultural America. Fiction by Native American, African American, Latino/a, Asian American, and other ethnic groups have both challenged the presumption of a white canon of American literature and made clear the colonial impulses of the United States. Leaving aside the many foreign interventions and adventures of the US military and American corporations, the long history of colonial appropriation of land and labor within America – from the displacement of the Native population and the slave trade (as well as the subsequent development of quasi-apartheid of Jim Crow until the post-Civil Rights period), to the interment of Japanese Americans during World War II – indicates how America has repeatedly scared the racial Other and produced a discourse about race and identity that may be critiqued from the perspective of postcolonial theory. In the post-1945 period, many ethnic and minority writers have plumbed this history, as Chapters 6 through 9 by Keith Byerman, Nancy Peterson, A. Robert Lee, and Victoria Aarons make clear.

Although best known as a Nobel Prize-winning novelist, Toni Morrison in her study of whiteness in *Playing in the Dark: Whiteness and the Literary Imagination* (1992) begins to make clear the way toward a rapprochement between ethnic and postcolonial studies. Influenced by Edward Said's classic postcolonial study *Orientalism* (1978), Morrison develops her concept of the Africanist presence in American literature. Just as Said sees British colonial understanding of the Oriental Other as telling us more about white colonial identity than about Islamic people, Morrison details the way the representation of the Africanist Other tells us much more about white American identity than it does about actual black people. And the relation between Morrison and postcolonial theorist Homi Bhabha is a two-way street of influence. If Morrison's thinking has been influenced by Bhabha's work on mimicry and hybridity, Bhabha acknowledges the importance of Morrison's fiction in shaping his understanding of narrative.[11] Morrison's explicit embrace of postcolonialism helps us better recognize the way that earlier African American writers of the post-1945 period, such as Ralph Ellison, were themselves critics of American colonialism.

A more historical reason for still considering the period from 1945 to the present as a coherent unit for literary study is that the United States continues to play out the cultural logic of its failure to fully claim or process the act of dropping atomic bombs on Hiroshima and Nagasaki at the end of World War II. For Donald Pease, that failure constitutes the latest form of exceptionalism governing American political life. A sense that America is exceptional is as old as Puritan America, first articulated in 1630 by Jonathan Winthrop in his sermon "A Model of Christian Charity" which, quoting Jesus' Sermon on the Mount, declared that their new community would be a "city upon the hill." During the Cold War, America denied its responsibility for using atomic weapons through fantasy: "In that fantasy, the United States always successfully liberated other nations from the nuclear threats posed by Soviet imperialism"; thus, as a signifier, "Hiroshima" "became a purely symbolic referent for the merely possible event, which was reassigned the duty to predict what 'will have happened' had not the United States already mobilized the powers of nuclear deterrence against the Soviets."[12]

America's first Gulf War, for Pease, becomes a way in 1992 to provide the literal war (in defense of Kuwait but also to ensure that Iraq's nuclear capability was neutralized) that the Cold War never provided but always feared (an all-out nuclear war) to assure Americans that the Cold War was indeed over.[13] With the terrorist attacks of 9/11, however, America's Cold

War fantasy became reborn, energized by a born-again Christian, President George W. Bush. The shorthand way of understanding this Cold War resurgence is that the site where the destroyed World Trade Center towers once stood is referred to as Ground Zero, a term that in the late 1940s through the 1990s would have been understood to refer primarily to the point on the surface of the Earth closest to the detonation of the atomic bombs at Hiroshima and Nagasaki. The destruction of the WTC towers, then, serves as the fulfillment of the fantasy logic of the Cold War, thus initiating a new version of Us versus Them, substituting a forty-five-year struggle with the Soviet Union with what, it seems, may be an equally lengthy War on Terror. The paranoid style of right-wing American politics that Richard Hofstader wrote about in 1964 was reincarnated during the eight-year Bush administration (2001–2008), when any criticism of the government was labeled un-American. And as the administration of President Barack Obama faces the worst economic crisis since the Great Depression, the paranoia from the political Right and cultural conservatives continues unabated with fears about the Ground Zero mosque and with the anti-intellectualism of the tea party movement, which backs political candidates who do not believe that the First Amendment to the US Constitution provides any rationale for the separation of church and state.

In this symbolic logic of history, the attempts of novelists who have tried to make sense of the 2,752 deaths at America's Ground Zero and of post-9/11 America may ultimately lead us to a better understanding of the initiating moment of this volume: an America of 1945 as the atomic power that brought about the end of World War II at the price of 200,000 civilian deaths at Japan's two Ground Zeros – Hiroshima and Nagasaki.

The chapters that follow are divided into three parts: "Poetics and genres," "Historical and cultural contexts," and "Major authors." I have noted the work of many of the chapters throughout the course of this introduction but should briefly mention now those that were not embedded in my previous comments. The first part, in addition to the chapters on postmodern metafiction and contemporary realism, explores a number of generic developments. In Chapter 3 Stacey Olster surveys two related hybrid narrative forms, the nonfiction novel and the new journalism, that came to prominence in the 1960s and that have blurred the boundaries of fiction, history, and reportage. Looking at a range of writing from Truman Capote and Norman Mailer to Joan Didion and Hunter S. Thompson, Olster examines the way this work can be read as a skeptical response to the supposed objectivity of mass media – newspaper and television accounts of current events. Next, Phillip Wegner in Chapter 4 looks at the reasons why a global form of narrative, science fiction, came to be dominated by American writers after 1945. Relating this dominance to both publishing practices and Cold War politics, Wegner takes the reader through a decade-by-decade history ending with the post-Cold War period, arguing that the period of American hegemony is ending as the genre returns to its global roots. Part I concludes with Susan Lohafer's chapter on the short story. For Lohafer, the post-1945 American short story is fiction's truest workshop, continually in the vanguard of trends that play out more slowly in the more expansive worlds of the novel, whether 1960s experimentalism or 1980s neo-realism, or multiculturalism in the 1990s.

Over and above the chapters devoted to racial and ethnic identity in Part II (Chapters 6–9), other historical and cultural contexts are represented in Chapters 10 through 13. Jane Elliott explores the emergence of fiction written by women for women with an overtly feminist perspective, particularly since the mid-1960s. While acknowledging women's writing between 1945 and 1965 as a kind of feminist fiction *manqué*, Elliott unpacks the theoretical and critical debates within feminist criticism and theory of the 1980s that allows women's fiction to be understood as feminist. In this context, many writers who are claimed by others in the name of multiculturalism (Alice Walker, Maxine Hong Kingston) are viewed more for their perspectives on gender than for the specificity of their race or ethnicity.

In Chapter 11, Martyn Bone explores the ways in which Southern writers after World War II struggled to step out of the long shadow cast by William Faulkner. These post-Southern Renaissance writers of the 1950s and 1960s – Flannery O'Connor, William Styron, and Walker Percy – nevertheless prepare the way for the truly postsouthern writers who began writing in the aftermath of the Vietnam War and the Civil Rights Movement. Postsouthern is a term Bone uses to express the racial and class diversity of contemporary Southern writers, whether African American (Alice Walker, Ernest Gaines) or working class (Ray Brown, Dorothy Allison), who previously would have fallen outside the parameters of Southern literature as conceived by the Southern Agrarian/New Critical founders of the field.

Alan Nadel in Chapter 12 contextualizes the Cold War fiction of the 1950s and 1960s through David Riesman's 1950 popular sociological study, *The Lonely Crowd*, that identified the problem with contemporary America as the rise of the Other-directed individual (which represented a falling-off from older societies that had been tradition-directed or individual-directed) susceptible to the manipulations of the (communist) Other. While identifying Reisman's generalizations as Cold War fantasy, Nadel nevertheless sees *The Lonely Crowd* as providing a scheme that allows one to connect the dots between texts as various as J. D. Salinger's *Catcher in the Rye*, Ralph Ellison's *Invisible Man*, and Saul Bellow's *Herzog*. In Nadel's mapping of Cold War fiction, paranoia is repositioned from being a psychological disorder to being instead a social condition.

My contribution concludes Part II by looking at the ways in which fiction after the terrorist attacks of September 11, 2001 has addressed the resulting individual and collective trauma. Because authors have produced such a variety of mimetic, metafictional, and allegorical narratives to explore this trauma, attempts to tell the bigger story of the cultural work of this body of fiction, whether identifying it as a failure for foregrounding domesticity or claiming that it signals the end of irony, typically exclude certain novels that would complicate such claims.

Part III provides overviews of the writing careers of five of the most significant writers of the post-1945 period, writers who appear frequently on syllabi of American literature surveys and courses on contemporary American fiction. Chapters by Nicole Waligora-Davis, Jay Watson, Brian Jarvis, Linden Peach, and Laura Barrett provide overviews of the lives and careers of, respectively, Ralph Ellison, Flannery O'Connor, Thomas Pynchon, Toni Morrison, and Don DeLillo. The volume concludes with Jessica Pressman's reflections on the future of American fiction in a world where the printed word is increasingly being displaced by digital and Web-based technologies.

No course in fifteen weeks can tell the full story of American fiction since 1945. I hope that readers will turn to these chapters for grounding in areas that may have been underrepresented or excluded from their previous introductions to this period.

NOTES

1 Tony Tanner, *City of Words* (New York: Harper & Row, 1971), p. 19.
2 Fredric Jameson, *Postmodernism, or, The Cultural Logic of Late Capitalism* (Durham, NC: Duke University Press, 1991), p. 1.
3 John Barth, "The Literature of Exhaustion," in *The Friday Book: Essays and Other Nonfiction* (Baltimore: Johns Hopkins University Press, 1984), p. 72.
4 Ibid.
5 Michael Bérubé, "Teaching Postmodern Fiction without Being Sure That the Genre Exists," *Chronicle of Higher Education* (May 19, 2000): 159.
6 Ibid.
7 Mark McGurl, *The Program Era: Postwar Fiction and the Rise of Creative Writing* (Cambridge, MA: Harvard University Press, 2009), p. 24.
8 Eric Bennett, "Ernest Hemingway and the Discipline of Creative Writing, or, Shark Liver Oil," *MFS*, 56.3 (2010): 563.
9 Ibid., pp. 545–9.

10 McGurl, *The Program Era*, p. 17.
11 Homi K. Bhabha, *The Location of Culture* (London: Routledge, 1994), p. ix.
12 Donald Pease, *The New American Exceptionalism* (Minneapolis: University of Minnesota Press, 2009), p. 49.
13 Ibid., pp. 50–1.

PART I

Poetics and genres

I

AMY J. ELIAS

Postmodern metafiction

Metafiction is fiction that calls attention to its representational techniques and knowledge claims. However, metafiction is something neither new nor inherently American. As Gerald Prince has noted, the novel, as a genre, harbors a range of possible narrative strategies that include metanarrative constructions such as self-reflexivity,[1] and this accounts for why novels with metafictional elements appear at different historical moments, well before the second half of the twentieth century. Citing fiction from numerous literary periods, Robert Alter defines metafiction within the larger category of "self-conscious fiction,"[2] as does Brian Stonehill, who defines metafiction as "an essentially ludic art form" that includes books in which narrators are clearly engaged in the act of composition or which point to the author behind a succession of narrators, or novels that feature ostentatious and nonmimetic style, conspicuous structural architecture, flat characters often aware of their status as characters, or self-parody and skepticism concerning the satirical efficacy of language.[3] For instance, Laurence Sterne's *Tristram Shandy* (1759–1767), with its self-conscious eponymous narrator and comically digressive disruptions of linear plot, is an exemplary work of metafiction. But one can turn to even earlier prose fiction for other examples. Cervantes's *Don Quixote* (1605, 1615) plays with notions of authorship in ways that have inspired twentieth-century metafictionists such as Jorge Luis Borges and Vladimir Nabokov. And American postmodernist John Barth has made it clear that his use of tale-within-tale structure derives in part from his fascination with the storyteller Scheherazade in Richard F. Burton's 1885 translation of the tenth-century Persian epic, *The Book of One Thousand and One Nights*.

Yet while postmodernism did not invent metafiction as a novelistic practice, it did invent the term and theory of the form. The term "metafiction" is generally attributed to the American author William Gass[4] and has been used to describe much of the experimental, anti-realist fiction produced since 1945. Patricia Waugh notes that if literary Realism celebrated the integration of the individual into the social structure, and literary Modernism revealed the individual at odds with, and alienated from, social institutions and conventions, then postmodernism or post-1945 fiction had nowhere to go but inward, to focus on its own medium of expression. Waugh contends that metafiction arises at the postmodern moment when the novel is attacked and undermined by other media forms: after World War II mass media is the dominant mode of mimesis, and the novel reacts by relinquishing representation of the real to that media and turning to the philosophical and ethical questions of what representation essentially *is*.[5]

A number of critics also have argued that metafiction surfaces in the postmodern period because this is when critical and cultural theories arise that radically question traditional systems of meaning such as realism, empiricism, and philosophies of identity. Writers started to see language as a problem and a puzzle, and the novel became a vehicle of investigation into the efficacy and ethics of language. As early as 1970 Robert Scholes claimed that metafiction "assimilates all the perspectives of criticism into the fictional process itself."[6] Building from her argument in *Narcissistic Narrative* (1980), which showed metafiction to be essentially ironic, Linda Hutcheon argued in *A Poetics of Postmodernism* (1988) that history writing is one such system of meaning questioned by metafiction. Metafiction thus invites criticism to consider itself as fiction, and fiction to consider itself as theory and criticism.

Theories such as these that define post-1945 metafiction use many examples drawn from international fiction to support their claims. A question thus arises: is metafiction produced in the United States in any way unique within this mode of storytelling?

Metafiction is unquestionably ubiquitous in mid-twentieth-century American fiction to the point that at least from the 1960s through the 1970s, metafiction seemed to characterize "postmodernism" and define generally what American fiction had become. At this time, the United States was undergoing a cultural revolution (including the creation of the New Left, the hipster/beat/hippie/Yippie movements, and a new Green revolution); it was reeling from political upheaval, including political assassinations, a number of controversial wars and police actions, and government scandals such as Watergate; it saw civil rights revolutions (including African American, gay, and women's liberation movements) challenge the nation's political and economic majority to reconsider its values and surrender its hegemony; and it was transformed economically and culturally as consumer capitalism and technological advancement shifted into high gear. After World War II, the United States became the world's major producer and exporter of mass culture; more than any other nation it became the empire of the unreal, the country with the economic resources to develop cultural products such as novels and films and export them throughout the world. The United States also emerged at this time as one of the world's superpowers, and, as Dwight D. Eisenhower himself noted, the country entered an era dominated by a military-industrial complex linked in labyrinthine ways to systems of media distribution. The term "postmodernism" as a result came increasingly to be, de facto, a term related to Americanness, a term that could not be divorced from, and was connected in fundamental ways (but not exclusively) to, the US culture industry.

The new 1960s Pop Art aesthetic championed by Andy Warhol and others in the United States ironized and exposed the values and dominance of US mass culture after 1945, and like America's cultural revolution it directly influenced some forms of post-1960s American metafiction. This "Pop" metafiction often targeted mass culture as part of its metafictional critique, even as it structured itself on genres previously identified as "low" or popular art forms, such as science fiction, comics, fairy tales, and the detective story. This metafiction tends to revel in the emptiness of aesthetic forms, seeing a correlation between Baudrillardian simulation, consumerism, and ennui in contemporary life.

As John Barth makes clear in his preface to the 1987 Anchor reprint of *Lost in the Funhouse*, the combined force of post-1945 cultural and epistemological crises in the United States, poststructuralism in high theory, and postcolonial and race politics outside the academy, together with the success of the US culture industry, was enough, perhaps, to fundamentally unhinge American authors' faith in mimesis and what a "reality" unmediated by images, language, and ideology could be. Therefore, when we talk about post-1945 American metafiction, we must look in two directions. Certainly, writers of American metafiction were in conversation with artists producing metafiction in Central and South America, France, Italy, the United Kingdom, and other parts of the world. They also inflected metafiction with an American cultural sensibility. This sensibility turned the critique of language and representation inward toward America's cultural revolution as well as its culture industry – the massive production of popular market culture influencing American life and letters after World War II.

What I hope I have conveyed thus far is that metafiction is multifaceted and can be viewed from a number of critical angles, such as its epistemological claims, its formal strategies, or its cultural politics. Tracing a general pattern of historical development in American metafiction from 1945 to the present is also complex, but we may begin to do so by dividing this tradition into three categories reflecting the definitions presented above: (1) novels that exemplify formal metafiction reflecting poststructuralist theories of language; (2) novels that exemplify Hutcheon's "historiographic metafiction"; and (3) novels that deploy metafictional techniques but seem to stand outside these other two categories.

The work as text machine

When people talk about metafiction, they often refer to fiction whose themes and narrations focus on the death of fiction; that presents overtly fictional story elements, motifs, and archetypes as reality or realistic actors and existents; and that employs techniques of installation, Happening, and street theater to break the "fourth wall" and insert real-life authors directly into the fictional construct as narrators or characters. These are what Alter would term "self-conscious novels." The immediate forebears of these post-1945 American texts are novels by James Joyce, Samuel Beckett, Vladimir Nabokov, and Jorge Luis Borges.

In American literature, a strong statement of this view that metafiction is "self-conscious fiction" is John Barth's famous essay "The Literature of Exhaustion." Published to some controversy in 1967, the essay posits that "the novel, if not narrative literature generally, if not the printed word altogether, has by this hour of the world just about shot its bolt."[7] However, Barth turns to the metafictional writing of the Argentinian Borges as a way to revive a moribund genre: great fabulists such as Borges can use this perceived exhaustion of narrative as the very subject matter for creating new fiction. Barth implies that Borges's work can model a new, postmodern American fiction since his stories' self-reflexive word puzzles – particularly those in *Labyrinths* (1964) – introduced not only the thought-problem technique but also themes central to metafiction: the relation between text and world; the death of the author's authority; the impotence (or infinite multiplicity) of narrative reference; language as a labyrinth, a self-contained system that nevertheless eludes authorial control; and the text as world. Similarly, Barth maintains that metafiction can explore essentially post-structuralist ideas such as the problem of infinite regress, *mise en abyme*, metalepsis, and the relation between reality, perception, and writing. If the time of mimetic realism is over, then the novel can turn back to itself as an art form and interrogate its own first principles. The resulting novel form may be ironic but also a serious and passionate epistemological investigation rather than an attempt to imitate the world in the manner of an old-fashioned, and exhausted, literary mimesis.

This theory is compatible with an existentialist philosophy informing all of Barth's work that posits human beings as essentially alone in a meaningless universe, but engaged through art both in the world and with philosophical speculation about the meaning of their own lives. His early novels, such as *The End of the Road* (1958), were realist explorations of these ideas, which remain as his fiction becomes more game-like and allegorical – as in *The Sot-Weed Factor* (1960) and *Giles Goat-Boy (The Revised New Syllabus of George Giles Our Grand Tutor)* (1966). The former tells the story of the English virgin poet Ebenezer Cooke and his adventures in eighteenth-century Maryland. The long and complex picaresque novel is a historical farce, based on an actual historical personage and poem but constructing a ribald fabulation around meager historical details. The latter features a protagonist who is raised by goats but seems destined by fate to become university Grand Tutor, and the book is an allegorical "campus novel" that satirically transforms the university into a world model: the Chancellor has the powers of UN president, squabbles between campus factions are allegories of the Cold War, the control of campus functions by WESCAC computer satirizes science fiction conventions and the development of NASA and technological branches of the military-industrial complex after World War II. Barth's *Lost in the Funhouse* (1968) is a further move away from realism into the territory of poststructuralist metafictional play. The stories in the collection play with intertextuality, retelling Greek and Arabic myths; with narrative structure (one story, "Menelaiad," has seven metaleptic levels, which Barth masterfully leads the reader into and then back out of by the end of the story); with ironic commentary about art; with aesthetic forms (we are told that "Autobiography" is "meant for monophonic tape and visible but silent author");[8] and with the heroic nature of the artist (the narrator of "Night Sea Journey" is a sperm cell). However, Barth's novel *Letters* (1979) is cited as his metafictional tour de force. An epistolary novel, it presents correspondence between seven characters from, or associated with characters in, Barth's previous novels. The letters on the title page spell out a kind of acrostic that sums up the game: "an old-time epistolary novel by seven fictitious drolls & dreamers each which imagines himself factual."[9] The title "Letters" has seven letters, the novel has seven characters, the novel itself is epistolary (consisting of letters), and one of the "drolls & dreamers" is the Author, Mr. John Barth, Esq. Barth's characters are from different historical times (in their original novelistic contexts) yet gather in a metafictional zone. These novels enact Barth's thesis in "The Literature of Exhaustion" that an exhausted realism can be revitalized through metafictional play.

If Barth's influences were the avant-garde and countercultural social currents, Ronald Sukenick's Fiction Collective – an independent publisher of experimental fiction started in 1974 – aligned itself with continental poststructuralism. In "The New Tradition" (1972), Sukenick writes that American letters needs a way of thinking about novels that acknowledges their technological character,[10] and he experimented with tape-recorded stories and "shaped" or physical text (in the manner of concrete poetry). Like Jacques Derrida in *Glas*, he breaks page text into columns; like street art, his novel *Mosaic Man* (1999) containing hand-drawn pictures and symbols; *Doggy Bag* (1994) presents stories contains strings of punctuation marks, like Barth's play with quotations. His novels, such as *UP* (1968), include the breaking of the fourth wall to include a character named Ronnie Sukenick who himself is writing a novel. Another American writer, Raymond Federman, was famously associated with FC2, and his novel *Double or Nothing* (1971) is often cited as a prime example of physical writing, influenced by poststructuralism, the spatial form of the modernist avant-garde, the "writing under constraint" of Oulipo, and shaped poetry. In 1975, Federman presented a manifesto that advocated this type of writing and coined a new term for metafiction:

> For me, the only fiction that still means something today is that kind of fiction that tries to explore the possibilities of fiction; the kind of fiction that challenges the tradition that governs it; the kind of fiction that constantly renews our faith in man's imagination and not in man's distorted vision of reality – that reveals man's irrationality rather than man's rationality. This I call SURFICTION.[11]

Double or Nothing exemplifies this aesthetic. Like Sukenick, Federman experiments with narrative as improvisational performance rather than static and revered art object.

The 1960s and 1970s in fact were a heyday for this kind of Barthian self-reflexive metafiction that deflated the heroic nature of the author and playfully argued that we should enjoy the pleasures of the text. This focus characterizes the work of William H. Gass, who is known as much for his criticism as his novels (his Cornell dissertation in philosophy was titled "A Philosophical Investigation of Metaphor"). Gass's *Willie Masters' Lonesome Wife* (1968) is a frolic of a novella and a classic metafiction, rife with wordplay. It presents the thoughts of an ex-stripper, the wife of said Willie Masters, as well as pictures of her nude body romping through a text whose pages change color with her moods. She herself is a metaphor for writing and repeatedly supports the poststructuralist notion that erotics and language are linked ("You, the world; and I, the language," she says).[12]

Donald Barthelme's *Snow White* (1965), a brilliant parody of Disney's *Snow White and the Seven Dwarfs* (1937), is also in this metafictionist camp. But in addition to its sparkling and witty transpositions of poststructuralist theory into a fairy-tale story frame, this zany parody exemplifies a kind of Pop Aesthetic, using elements and language of popular culture to construct a critique of power. The novel transports Snow White to the 1960s, where she is a bored liberal arts major who takes showers with seven little men (all born in national parks and all working as vat tenders in a baby-food factory). "Oh I wish there were some words in the world that were not the words I always hear," she cries.[13] The novel pointedly satirizes a sexist culture that reduces women to "horsewives" and replaceable parts ("as new classes of girls mature you can always get a new one," says the evil Hogo de Bergerac); where education has been reduced to pose; where production is centered on useless goods; and where the president is a moron waging a war on poetry. The role of the wicked witch is taken by Jane Villiers de l'Isle-Adam, who understands the power not of spells but of language. In a famous passage, Jane writes a note to a Mr. Quistgaard (a parodic portrayal of Kierkegaard) in which she tells him she now has his phone number and threatens to call and penetrate his universe of discourse. She concludes,

> The moment I inject discourse from my u. of d. into your u. of d., the you-ness of yours is diluted. The more I inject, the more you dilute. Soon you will be presiding over an empty plenum, or rather, since that is a contradiction in terms, over a former plenum, in terms of your yourness. You are, essentially, in my power. I suggest an unlisted number.[14]

One might also include in this Pop camp a novel such as Vonnegut's *Breakfast of Champions, or Goodbye Blue Monday!* (1973). The novel's main character is a science fiction writer invited to a Midwest town to participate in its local arts festival and includes characters from Vonnegut's other novels as well as an author character. The main title itself is taken from a slogan for Wheaties, a popular American breakfast cereal; the book's colloquial tone, irony, frequent references to elements of mass culture, and "hand-drawn" sketches of vaginas and anuses make it seem casual and offhand, like popular culture itself. Yet the novel constructs a scathing indictment of stupidity and corruption in small-town American life. Interestingly, some twenty years after this novel's publication, Larry McCaffery published *After Yesterday's Crash* (1995), which introduced the term "avant-pop" to describe a combination of "Pop Art's focus on consumer goods and mass media with the avant-garde's spirit of subversion and emphasis on radical formal innovation."[15] The term was meant to replace "postmodernism," which had by then become emptied of meaning through overuse and, ironically, commercialization. One can see, perhaps, the origins of the "avant-pop" in novels such as *Snow White*, *Willie Masters*, and *Breakfast of Champions*.

In addition to poststructuralist-informed and Pop-Aesthetic writing, American self-conscious metafiction is also frequently characterized by intertextuality and intermediality. Such metafiction self-consciously parodies themes and story elements of other texts or may be a hybrid text that physically incorporates elements of other art forms. This category blends into others discussed at more length in the current volume, but here it is important to note the metafictional elements that are central to these novels.

Self-consciousness merges with intertextuality in a number of ways. First may be that exemplified by post-1945 African American fiction, if seen through the lens of Henry Louis Gates's and, later, Madelyn Jablon's arguments that self-consciousness is built into African American fiction and includes polyphony and dialogism linked to double consciousness, call-and-response patterns that equate reading and writing, signifying on and repetition of past writers' themes, and metafictional tropes (such as the trope of the talking book).[16] Jablon specifically contrasts black metafiction's referencing of literary antecedents to Barth's interest in *regressus ad infinitum* (and the idea of a lost original).[17] For example, she discusses Leon Forrest's massive *Divine Days* (1995) as a self-conscious movement toward a self-authenticating voice – noted by Robert Stepto as a key trajectory in African American literature. One might in fact understand Percival Everett's *Erasure* (2002), a book Jablon does not discuss, in this context. *Erasure* is an acerbic satire incorporating a novel-within-a-novel (that itself parodies a real-life novel that was turned into a real-life award-winning Hollywood film) as well as numerous theory references (the main character at one point gives a talk at a conference on avant-garde fiction about deconstruction). The highly metafictionalized novel specifically "talks back" to Ralph Ellison's 1952 novel *Invisible Man* (the protagonist is named Monk Ellison) as well as contemporaneous novels about "black life" lauded by popular culture.

Self-consciousness merges with intertextuality in another way in "guerrilla plagiarism," a pragmatic strategy utilized by feminist, postcolonial, and other writers that aims to subvert dominant ideology.[18] According to Randall, guerilla plagiarism shows narrators clearly engaged in the act of composition, uses ostentatious and nonmimetic style, constructs conspicuous structural architecture and flat characters often aware of their status as characters, and integrates self-parody and skepticism concerning the efficacy of language – the very characteristics of the self-conscious novel according to Alter. Kathy Acker's *Don Quixote* (1986), for instance, retains many of the themes of Cervantes's original while completely rewriting elements of the story: here, Quixote is a woman knight in Nixon's America with her companion dog Sancho Panza, traveling in a kind of hallucinogenic nightmare. One might include Shelley Jackson's *Patchwork Girl* (1995) as an example of "guerrilla plagiarism" as well: the hypertext novel is a brilliant parody of

Mary Shelley's *Frankenstein* (1818) and a meditation on female identity, and includes direct quotations from Shelley's novel as well as from Derrida and French feminist writers. Jackson's CD-ROM novel also includes the author as character and centrally equates the human body with the body of the text in the manner of other self-conscious metafiction.

Intertextual metafictions might include Susan Daitch's *L.C.* (1986), a self-conscious epistolary novel, or Paul Auster's *The New York Trilogy*. The trilogy's first novel, *City of Glass* (1985), for example, blends the detective novel genre with a "metacommentary" on logic and the scientific method that is central to the genre, and we see the appearance of a character named "Paul Auster" who is both author and detective in the text. (The book's intermediality was extended in 1994 when it was made into a graphic novel by Paul Karasik and David Mazzucchelli.) Intermedial as well as intertextual, Mark Z. Danielewski's cult classic *House of Leaves* (2000) extended self-conscious metafiction into a new century. The novel is a haunted house story that parodies the horror film genre: it is the supposed transcript/compilation of a blind critic's notes about a film made about a malevolent house that is larger on the inside than on the outside. The novel is also a "house of leaves" (the book "houses" its pages) that plays with typography and shaped prose, includes extensive footnotes (with embedded footnotes) as alternative storylines, works with textual color-coding, and has elements of *roman-à-clef* (its protagonist is modeled on a famous photographer). Covert references to Borges as well as famous films and directorial techniques intertextually lace the novel.

Similarly intermedial, Percival Everett's *I Am Not Sidney Poitier* (2009) embeds myriad references to the movies of Sidney Poitier as well as characters named "Professor Percival Everett" and "Jane Fonda" in a scathing but hilarious irrealistic metacommentary on racism in contemporary American society. The novel tells the story of a fatherless black man named "Not Sidney Poitier" (his very name is *sous rature*) who looks exactly like Sidney Poitier and ends up living out the actor's movie plots. He inherits a fortune from his mother's investments in Ted Turner's broadcasting network, lives with Turner for a time, and then attempts to locate himself through the miasma of pop-cultural and racist signifying systems that seem to define him. In a less satiric vein, but also concerning a protagonist's search for father and identity, Art Spiegelman's intermedial graphic novels *Maus: My Father Bleeds History* (1986) and *Maus II: Here My Troubles Began* (1991) embed a novel within a novel as well as photographs and "drawings," and in the manner of the beast fable present peoples of different ethnic and national groups as different kinds of animals (the French as frogs, for example). Like Everett's *I Am Not Sidney Poitier*, the book has many of the characteristics of both the self-conscious novel and historiographic metafiction: the author "Art" is embedded at multiple levels of a text that continually interrogates its own ethics and methods of storytelling while it constructs a serious commentary on evil and on Holocaust history. These post-1980s intertextual and intermedial metafictions illustrate the range of self-conscious metafiction based in poststructuralist assumptions, and all prove Barth's claim that metafiction is a regenerative form, always able to turn a parodic lens upon current art to generate new fiction.

Historiographic metafiction

A second group of metafiction exemplifies the characteristics of Hutcheon's "historiographic metafiction," centralizing questions about what history is and complicating the entire notion of historical knowledge. Hutcheon argues that historical practices need to be revised to include a pluralist view of historiography "consisting of different but equally meaningful constructions of past reality."[19] Historiographic metafiction has distinct characteristics: it questions the notion of individualism and the stable self/subject that form our notions of historical agency, it is ironic, it is self-reflexive about language and suspicious of political power, it shows all values as context-dependent and ideological, and it highlights the artificiality of historical explanations of reality. Historiographic metafictions are deeply politicized texts that claim that history – material history played out on bodies, or written history transcribed into history books – is always ideological and the tool of power. If Hutcheon is correct, and historiographic metafiction characterizes all of the international fiction that we might call "postmodernist," then there are too many examples to discuss here. However, in post-1945 American fiction, I would argue that "historiographic metafiction" is a subgrouping of a larger category of metafictional novels and includes works such as: William Demby's *The Catacombs* (1965); Robert Coover's *The Public Burning* (1977); William Kennedy's *Legs* (1973); Max Apple's *The Propheteers* (1984); Jonathan Safran Foer's *Extremely Loud and Incredibly Close* (2005); Thomas Pynchon's *Mason & Dixon* (1997); Ana Castillo's *The Mixquiahuala Letters* (1986); Toni Morrison's *Beloved* (1987); Maxine Hong Kingston's *Tripmaster Monkey: His Fake Book* (1989); Charles Johnson's *Middle Passage* (1990) and *Dreamer* (1998); William T. Vollmann's Seven Dreams series, beginning with *The Ice Shirt* in 1990; Gerald Vizenor's *Griever: An American Monkey King in China* (1987); Don DeLillo's *Underworld* (1997); and Mark Z. Danielewski's *Only Revolutions* (2006).

Many of these texts were central to discussions of American postmodernism in late twentieth-century criticism, when metafictionality was understood to be an important strategy for attacking the historical and social metanarratives being spun by the majority culture. Even for a Marxist theorist such as Fredric Jameson, who has dedicated many books to exposing the political vacuity of postmodernist art forms, historiographic metafiction of a type written by E. L. Doctorow has the potential to defamiliarize the naturalness of historical narratives and possibly provoke readers to question the seamless political narratives about history and culture central to the ideological functioning of post-industrial capitalism. Jameson's tempered enthusiasm for Doctorow is not surprising, since the latter is a great writer of the Left and inheritor of a realist historical novel tradition.[20] Doctorow's novels do not incorporate the antics of Pop Aesthetic metafictionists or the irrealistic satire of guerilla plagiarists. *The Book of Daniel* (1971), for example, is a fictional retelling of the nuclear espionage trial of Ethel and Julius Rosenberg, told in the journal of their adult son Daniel, who with his sister is heavily involved in 1960s counterculture and antiwar protests. *Ragtime* (1974) is set in turn-of-the-century New York City, and like classic historical fiction it includes real historical personages such as J. P. Morgan, Sigmund Freud, and Booker T. Washington and depends heavily on period markers to create an aura of historical authenticity. However, Doctorow's novels frequently deviate from the accepted historical record, assigning unverified actions to, and creating alternative historical paths for, well-known historical characters and events, thereby underscoring the emplotment – ideological and narratological – at the core of all historical narrative.

Like his novel *Flight to Canada* (1976), Ishmael Reed's *Mumbo Jumbo* (1972) is an example of historiographic metafiction that has more of the flavor of self-conscious, irrealistic metafiction than does Doctorow's work. Reed's novel is set in the 1920s, and it blends Juvenalian satire on racist American society with Haitian hoodoo references, parody of numerous art forms (the detective story, African trickster tales, film noir, ragtime, and jazz), and mixed-media format (the text includes photographs, footnotes, and a bibliography). Telling the tale of Jew Grew (a dance virus) unleashed in 1920s New York, it presents an alternative history of the West since the Egyptian empire, a history that pits white Apollonian logicians (The Wallflower Order), intent upon monological thought and social control, against Dionysian impulses (Jew Grew), representing blackness, freedom, improvisation, and art. Within this wild re-mythologization of history, however, historical references and commentaries proliferate: Marcus Garvey, the US occupation of Haiti, the Harlem Renaissance art world, Warren Harding, and other historical referents are central to the text's political commentary. The novel asserts that the Atonist/White/Western/Christian history is a political narrative, in dialectical relation with another narrative and way of being linked to personal and social freedom.

Historiographic metafiction with an allegorical edge is represented in Thomas Pynchon's *Gravity's Rainbow* (1973), which likewise constructs a paranoid critique of the West by focusing on a specific historical moment, World War II. The massive intertextual and historically informed novel tells, at least in part, the story of Tyrone Slothrop, a GI who was sold to Pavlovian scientists as a baby and hence now has a penis that can predict rocket hits because it reacts to a substance used in rocket construction. It also hints at a larger tale about a historical struggle of power between forces of control (government, military-industrial complex, colonialism) and forces of freedom and play. "Somewhere, among the wastes of the World," says Enzian, a Herero who has formed a counter-military unit among the German rocket troops, "is the key that will bring us back, restore us to our Earth and to our freedom."[21] Parodying the detective story, drug novel, erotica, picaresque, love story, dream vision, Orpheus tale, Hollywood movie, and *bildungsroman*, the novel thwarts narrative closure, presents allegorical characters, incorporates limericks and typographical effects, and intertextually references contemporaneous culture theories as well as scores of religious and scientific concepts. Beginning in Advent and ending at Pentecost on the Christian calendar, it also begins near the end of World War II as Germany is bombing Britain and ends immediately after the bombing of Hiroshima. The novel presents a picture of the West as a society of "suicidal energy addicts," decadent and in love with technology and death.

As noted above, the category of historiographic metafiction is vast, but its chief characteristic is the uneasy blending of metafictional storytelling strategies and overt political and social commentaries in the manner of the traditional historical novel. Combining the two categories of self-conscious, poststructuralist-inflected metafiction and historiographic metafiction illustrates the wide range of options and examples of American metafiction after 1945.

The last wave of metafiction?

Certainly, metafictionality and metafictional elements preceded postmodernism and inevitably post-date it. Yet whether metafiction was primarily a mid-twentieth-century phenomenon that has now, in Barth's terms, "just about shot its bolt" is a critical question.

David Foster Wallace's monumental novel *Infinite Jest* (1996) and the author's published essays, for example, bring this question to the fore. Often compared to the novels of Joyce, Barth, and Pynchon, the 1079-page *Infinite Jest* weaves in and out of stories of Hal Incandenza and his family, the recovering addict Don Gately, and a huge cast of other characters. Playing off the conventions of the horror story, dystopian science fiction, the literary hoax, and the detective novel is a plot concerning the search for Infinite Jest, a video produced by Hal's father that turns viewers into catatonic imbeciles. In this alternate reality, corporations own time itself (calendar years have been replaced by corporate "sponsorship" tags, so 2009 is officially the Year of the Depend Adult Undergarment); television has been replaced by the Interlace system that allows people to view media "cartridges" at any time via a network grid; the United States has colonized all of North America and turned New England into a toxic waste dump; addicts wander the streets in a lawless search for a new fix; and media addicts are glued to Interlace screens, divorced from active life and one another.

It would be easy to put this novel into the category of "self-conscious fiction" and perhaps even historiographic metafiction. Foster Wallace was vocal about the authors who were "a patriarch for my parricide,"[22] the novelists who influenced him: Pynchon, DeLillo, Coover, Donald Barthelme, Nabokov, Cortazar, Vollmann, Puig – experimental writers linked to metafiction. Barth was a particular influence: he appears overtly and covertly in a number of Foster Wallace's fictions and essays. However, Foster Wallace consistently distanced himself from ironic metafiction and argued that its time in American literature was over. In essays and interviews he aligned metafiction with a praiseworthy 1960s and 1970s "fiction of image" that was sympathetic to the countercultural revolution and used irreverent irony productively to defamiliarize a repressive everyday reality.[23] But by the mid-1970s, he claims, this art was dying, a victim of its own success, and by the 1990s, TV had co-opted metafiction's self-reflexivity, absurdity, sardonic fatigue, iconoclasm, and irony. The answer, writes Foster Wallace in an oft-quoted passage, is that US writers may have to move away from institutionalized irony: "The next real literary 'rebels' in this country might well emerge as some weird bunch of 'anti-rebels' ... Who eschew self-consciousness and fatigue."[24]

Foster Wallace's writings raise important questions concerning the future of metafiction. Can metafictionists survive in a world where television and the Internet have co-opted irony for the purposes of lemming-like group-think, narcissistic display, and uncivil (if not oppressive) discourse – precisely what metafiction originally attacked? Or will, as Barth hoped, the American novelist continue to turn "the felt ultimacies of our time into material and means for his work – *paradoxically* because by doing so he transcends what had appeared to be his refutation"?[25]

FURTHER READING

Currie, Mark. *Metafiction*. London: Longman, 1995

Gates, Henry Louis. *The Signifying Monkey: A Theory of African American Literary Criticism*. Oxford University Press, 1989

Hutcheon, Linda. *Narcissistic Narrative: The Metafictional Paradox*. New York: Methuen, 1980

McCaffery, Larry. *The Metafictional Muse: The Works of Coover, Gass and Barthelme*. University of Pittsburgh Press, 1982

McHale, Brian. *Postmodernist Fiction*. New York: Methuen, 1987

NOTES

1 Gerald Prince, *Narratology* (Berlin, New York, and Amsterdam: Mouton De Gruyter, 1982).

2 Robert Alter, *Partial Magic: The Novel as a Self-Conscious Genre* (Berkeley: University of California Press, 1975), pp. x–xi.

3 Brian Stonehill, *The Self-conscious Novel: Artifice in Fiction from Joyce to Pynchon* (Philadelphia: University of Pennsylvania Press, 1988), p. 13.

4 William H. Gass, "Philosophy and the Form of Fiction," in *Fiction and the Figures of Life* (New York: Alfred A. Knopf, 1970).

5 Patricia Waugh, *Metafiction: The Theory and Practice of Self-conscious Fiction* (London: Routledge, 1984), p. 2.

6 Robert Scholes "Metafiction," *The Iowa Review*, 1 (1970), reprinted in *Metafiction*, ed. Mark Currie (London: Longman, 1995), p. 29.

7 John Barth, "The Literature of Exhaustion," *The Atlantic Monthly*, 220.2 (1967), reprinted in *Metafiction*, ed. Mark Currie (London and New York: Longman, 1995), p. 167.

8 John Barth, *Lost in the Funhouse* (New York: Anchor, 1988), p. 35.

9 John Barth, *Letters* (Normal, IL: Dalkey Archive Press, 1994), title page.

10 Ronald Sukenick, *In Form: Digressions on the Act of Fiction* (Carbondale: Southern Illinois University Press, 1985).

11 Richard Federman, "Introduction," in Federman (ed.), *Surfiction: Fiction Now ... and Tomorrow* (Chicago: Swallow Press, 1975), p. 7.

12 William H. Gass, *Willy Masters' Lonesome Wife*, supplement #2 to *TriQuarterly* (1968), white section, 4th page.

13 Donald Barthelme, *Snow White* (New York: Scribner, 1972), p. 6.

14 Ibid., p. 46.

15 Larry McCaffery, *After Yesterday's Crash: The Avant-pop Anthology* (New York: Penguin, 1995), pp. xvii–xviii.

16 See Jablon's introduction in *Black Metafiction: Self-consciousness in African-American Literature* (University of Iowa Press, 1997).

17 Ibid., p. 114.

18 This term is taken from Marilyn Randall, *Pragmatic Plagiarism: Authorship, Profit, Power* (University of Toronto Press, 2001).

19 Linda Hutcheon, *A Poetics of Postmodernism* (New York: Routledge, 1988), p. 89.

20 Fredric Jameson, "Postmodernism and Consumer Society" (1988), reprinted in *The Norton Anthology of Theory and Criticism*, Gen. Ed. Vincent B. Leitch (New York: W. W. Norton, 2001), p. 1967.

21 Thomas Pynchon, *Gravity's Rainbow* (New York: Viking, 1973), p. 525.

22 David Foster Wallace, "*E Unibus Pluram*: Television and U.S. Fiction," *Review of Contemporary Fiction*, 13 (1993): 146.

23 Ibid., p. 171.

24 Ibid., pp. 192–3.

25 Barth, "The Literature of Exhaustion," pp. 167–8.

2

ROBERT REBEIN

Contemporary realism

Despite the formal innovations of the high postmodernists, the vast majority of American fiction published since 1945 has made no pretense of being avant-garde or experimental, but rather has remained unabashedly realist in its rendering of character, setting, and time. This is not surprising. As Raymond Carver once remarked, true formal innovation in fiction, while "cause for rejoicing," is exceedingly rare.[1] Too often what has been proclaimed innovative has proven on closer examination to be little more than the repetition of certain postmodernist devices (self-reflexivity in narration, for example) that long ago lost their ability to surprise. Indeed, during the period in question, realism has proven to be far more resilient and adaptable to change than "metafiction," "surfiction," "fabulism," or any of the other -isms subsumed under the umbrella of literary postmodernism. The fact is, realism continued to be practiced by major writers throughout the period of high postmodernism, and the years since 1980 have witnessed the emergence of a renewed or revitalized realism marked by its variety and wide range of effects. Because of this it makes sense to speak not of a monolithic realism, but rather of a number of different, at times overlapping, realisms, all of them making use of a common core of techniques and exhibiting the same belief in the power of language to accurately represent life "as it really is." Taken together, this body of work exhibits a number of shared aims and identifying traits, including a recognition of character as the sine qua non of the fictional enterprise, a tendency to focus on material drawn from the margins of society, a concern with the accurate representation of region or place, and a preoccupation with matters of race and ethnic (Native American, Asian American, Hispanic American) identity. Perhaps because of this variety and range, contemporary realism exhibits another trait as well: an unselfconscious mixing of the realist mode with other complementary (and in some cases even some antithetical) modes, including a few borrowed from postmodernism itself.

Character

Realism in the arts is traditionally defined as the accurate representation of nature or of life, particularly contemporary life, without embellishment, abstraction, or idealization. Although the second half of the nineteenth century is often called the Age of Realism, as a mode of representation, realism is not limited to a single literary period but rather is present in a variety of literary works from Homer to the present. Realism is often associated with the Enlightenment-inspired belief that humans can use language to accurately reproduce both the world external to them and their own subjective responses to that world in ways that will be recognized and understood by others. Another cognitive dimension of realism has been the subject of an ongoing debate since at least the end of the French Revolution. During the period of high postmodernism in the 1960s and 1970s, this debate found its way into European and American literary theory and from there into manifestos written by postmodernist authors, who began to ask, along with the critic Jerome Klinkowitz, "If the world is absurd, if what passes for reality is distressingly unreal, why spend time representing it?"[2] This critique of realism's foundational assumptions did not stop at its representation of the outer world. Following the lead of the French novelist Alain Robbe-Grillet, the postmodernists sought to empty the notion of character itself of its claims of fullness and continuity, indeed of its "humanness." The novelist Jonathan Franzen once described this radical distrust by noting that in his understanding of postmodern fiction, "Characters, properly speaking, weren't even supposed to exist. Characters were feeble, suspect constructs, like the author himself, like the human soul."[3]

For their part, realist authors have taken a more pragmatic approach. "Should art follow culture?" the novelist Saul Bellow asked in his 1976 Nobel Prize lecture, which exists, in part, as an answer to Robbe-Grillet and the postmodernists. Should intellectuals, Bellow continued, when they read novels, "find nothing in them but the endorsement of their own opinions? Are we here on earth to play such games?"[4] For Bellow, the purpose of literary art is not to parrot the conclusions of theology, philosophy, or social theory, but rather to provide "a broader, more flexible, fuller, more coherent, more comprehensive account of what we human beings are, who we are, and what this life is for."[5]

The search for meaning in human life, particularly the individual life as viewed against the backdrop of an indifferent, mechanical, or oppressive society, is the great theme of Bellow's fiction. In a series of brilliant novels, beginning with *Dangling Man* (1944) and *The Victim* (1947), and continuing through the masterworks of his middle period, *The Adventures of Augie March* (1953), *Seize the Day* (1956), *Henderson the Rain King* (1959), *Herzog* (1964), *Mr. Sammler's Planet* (1971), and *Humboldt's Gift* (1975), Bellow balances a closely observed representation of the social world (particularly the world of the modern city) with an equally compelling rendering of his characters' interior states. He is interested in character as it is revealed under pressure or strain, isolated from others, frustrated, on the verge of financial ruin or emotional collapse. Male and middle-aged, the typical Bellow protagonist soon descends into a slough of despair; the physical world, with its demands and entanglements, blankets him; the mistakes of the past haunt him; and his relations with other people become frayed or completely undone. It is only after reaching this point of crisis that the protagonist's true journey, either outward into a larger field of experience, or inward toward a recognition of his true relation to his fellow men, can begin. Thus Eugene Henderson at the beginning of *Henderson the Rain King*:

> What made me take this trip to Africa? There is no quick explanation. Things got worse and worse and worse and pretty soon they were too complicated.
>
> When I think of my condition at the age of fifty-five when I bought the ticket, all is grief. The facts begin to crowd me and soon I get a pressure in the chest. A disorderly rush begins – my parents, my wives, my girls, my children, my farm, my animals, my habits, my money, my music lessons, my drunkenness, my prejudices, my brutality, my teeth, my face, my soul! I have to cry, "No, no, get back, curse you, let me alone!" But how can they let me alone? They belong to me. They are mine. And they pile into me from all sides. It turns to chaos.[6]

The list of people and things crowding Henderson belongs to him and him alone; their particularity ("my drunkenness, my prejudices, my brutality, my teeth") mark him for who and what he is. However, like Bellow's other protagonists, especially Tommy Wilhelm and Moses Herzog, Henderson is also an Everyman whose function is to dramatize and explore universal aspects of the condition of modernity, such as alienation from the environment and the search for identity and purpose in a lonely, mechanical world. Despite operating in a mechanical world, Bellow's characters do not fall prey to determinism, as do the characters in naturalist fiction. Like the realism advocated by William Dean Howells in the late nineteenth century, Bellow's fiction allows characters agency or the capacity for change, dramatizing their struggle toward recognition and release, as in the famous final scene of *Seize the Day*, in which Tommy Wilhelm, having lost nearly everything, stumbles into a stranger's funeral and is finally unburdened of the troubles that have been choking him, achieving a kind of "great and happy oblivion of tears."[7]

John Updike attempts a similar balancing of the internal and external in his Rabbit Angstrom novels, *Rabbit, Run* (1960), *Rabbit Redux* (1971), *Rabbit Is Rich* (1981), and *Rabbit at Rest* (1990), only here the recording of the contemporary social world has been taken to its logical extreme. In these books, each focused on a specific decade in the life of Harry "Rabbit" Angstrom, Updike operates almost like a photorealistic painter, building up layer upon layer of observed and researched detail in the form of headlines, snatches of popular songs, and water-cooler talk about problems of the day, creating in the process a compendium of postwar suburban life. Here, for example, is the opening of *Rabbit Is Rich*, a novel set amid the inflation-era/ gas crisis/Skylab-is-falling hysteria of 1979:

> Running out of gas, Rabbit Angstrom thinks as he stands behind the summer-dusty windows of the Springer Motors display room watching the traffic go by on Route 111, traffic somehow thin and scared compared to what it used to be. The fucking world is running out of gas. But they won't catch him, not yet, because there isn't a piece of junk on the road gets better gas mileage than his Toyotas, with lower service costs. Read *Consumer Reports*, April issue. That's all he has to tell the people when they come in. And come in they do, the people out there are getting frantic, they know the great American ride is ending. Gas lines at ninety-nine point nine cents a gallon and ninety per cent of the stations to be closed for the weekend.[8]

The point of all this fine-grained detail is not to hold a mirror up to small-town Pennsylvania circa 1979, but rather to alert the reader that Rabbit's thoughts and actions (many of them tinged with small-mindedness, misogyny, even racism) must be understood as responses to this particular time and place, as well as to his position in it as a middle-aged, middle-class, white Protestant male.

This focus on a singular (usually white male) point of view is both the strength and an obvious weakness of Everyman realism of the kind we see in Bellow and Updike, as well as other novelists in this tradition, including Philip Roth and the Richard Ford of *The Sportswriter* (1986), *Independence Day* (1995), and *The Lay of the Land* (2006). Unlike previous realists like Tolstoy or Henry James, or later practitioners like Tom Wolfe, Louise Erdrich, or Franzen, the Everyman realists make no attempt to capture a wider swath of experience by multiplying the vantage points from which the social world is perceived and judged. While this adds uncommon depth to their portrayal of a single, embattled protagonist (especially when the portrayal is drawn out across decades of writing about the same character, as in the case of Updike and Ford), it necessarily forestalls the kind of multi-faceted, wide-angled representation of society we find in more unruly and ambitious works of realism like Joyce Carol Oates's *We Were the Mulvaneys*

(1996), Franzen's *The Corrections* (2001), Jeffrey Eugenides' *Middlesex* (2002), or indeed a raft of neo-realist novels and story collections published since 1990.

Dirty Realism

In the late 1970s and early 1980s, a different kind of realism began to emerge on the American literary scene. The first to give it a name was Bill Buford, the expatriate American editor of the British quarterly *Granta*, who in 1983 devoted an entire issue of the magazine to a new vein of American writing he called "Dirty Realism." "These are strange stories," Buford wrote in his introduction to the volume, "unadorned, unfurnished, low-rent tragedies about people who watch day-time television, read cheap romances or listen to country and western music. They are … drifters in a world cluttered with junk food and the oppressive details of modern consumerism."[9] According to Buford, Dirty Realism differed significantly from both the traditional realism of an Updike or William Styron, which was "ornate, even baroque by comparison," and the "consciously experimental" writing of the literary postmodernists, which "seemed pretentious in comparison."[10] Dirty Realism focused on the small rather than the large, and the stories it told were so spare that it took some time before the reader realized how completely "a whole culture and a whole moral condition" were being represented.[11] *Granta 8: Dirty Realism* included stories by Raymond Carver, Richard Ford, Jayne Anne Phillips, Frederick Barthelme, Tobias Wolff, Bobbie Ann Mason, Elizabeth Tallent, and Angela Carter, but from the first, the acknowledged master of this kind of writing was Carver, whose stories about working-class characters struggling to make sense of their stunted, chaotic lives did much to spark a renaissance in the American short story in the 1980s and 1990s.

In terms of both philosophy and practice, Carver is the quintessential realist: focused on character, earnest in his use of language, distrustful of experimentation for its own sake. Carver absorbed these lessons from his mentor and first teacher, the novelist John Gardner, whose theory of fiction calls for the creation and maintenance of a "fictional dream" in the mind of the reader and precludes any maneuver on the part of the writer that might endanger or disrupt this dream.[12] In "On Writing," a 1981 essay, Carver expresses many of the same concerns about writing as Gardner, complaining of the literary postmodernism then in ascendancy: "Too often such writing gives us no news of the world, or else describes a desert landscape and that's all – a few dunes and lizards here and there, but no people; a place uninhabited by anything recognizably human, a place of interest to only a

few scientific specialists."[13] In a series of widely read and discussed stories –
collected in *Will You Please Be Quiet, Please?* (1976), *What We Talk about
When We Talk about Love* (1981), *Cathedral* (1983), and *Where I'm Calling
From* (1988) – Carver almost singlehandedly reversed that trend, refocusing
American fiction on a tersely expressed and concisely rendered version of
human affairs that looked nothing at all like realisms of the past.

In a tribute published ten years after Carver's death, Richard Ford offers
a vivid account of the impact Carver's work had on writers and readers in
the late 1970s. The two were at a writers' conference at Southern Methodist
University in the fall of 1977, and Carver was reading from the story that
would later be known as "Are These Actual Miles?"

> His voice was typically hushed, seemingly unpracticed, halting almost to the
> point of being annoying. But the effect of voice and story upon the listener
> was of actual life being unscrolled in a form so distilled, so intense, so *chosen*,
> so affecting in its urgencies as to leave you breathless and limp when he was
> finished … Life was this way – yes, we already knew that. But *this* life, *these*
> otherwise unnoticeable people's suitability for literary expression seemed new.
> One also felt that a consequence of the story was seemingly to intensify life,
> even dignify it, and to locate in it shadowed corners and niches that needed
> revealing so that we readers could practice life better ourselves.[14]

Ford isolates here several important aspects of Carver's realism, including
its verisimilitude ("actual life being unscrolled"), its appeal to emotion ("so
affecting … as to leave you breathless and limp"), its focus on ordinary
("otherwise unnoticeable") people, and, finally, its moral purpose ("so we
readers could practice life better ourselves"). However, Ford does not stop
there. "And yet the story itself," he continues, "in its spare, self-conscious
intensity, was such a *made* thing, not *like* life at all." The writing contained
"no ponderous naturalism," indeed "barely the rudiments of realism."
Instead it represented a "highly stylized, artistic writing with life, not art, as
its subject."[15]

In the years following the success of *What We Talk about When We Talk
about Love*, Carver's brand of "highly stylized," stripped-to-the-bone realism took the American literary scene by storm. Quarterlies like *Ploughshares*
and the *Missouri Review*, mainstream periodicals like *Harper's* and *The New
Yorker*, anthologies like *The O. Henry Awards* and *Best American Short
Stories* were all overflowing (or so it seemed) with tersely written stories
about ordinary people going about their ordinary, undramatic lives. As was
inevitable, a reaction set in. Writing in *Harper's* in April 1986, the novelist
Madison Smartt Bell, himself a realist, castigated the "minimalist school"
of Carver, Barthelme, Amy Hempel, and others for what he considered its

"obsessive concern for surface detail," its "tendency to ignore or eliminate distinctions among the people it renders," and its "deterministic, at times nihilistic, vision of the world."[16] For Bell the accomplishments of so-called minimalist fiction were purely technical and stylistic; beneath its cool surfaces and lean prose lurked a terrible estimation of human possibility. "The characters come to resemble rats negotiating a maze the reader can see and they cannot," he wrote of Carver's story "The Bridle."[17] Of one of Hempel's minimal works, he wrote: "It is an admirably well-made story, as tidily constructed a bit of nastiness as anyone could wish for."[18]

While Bell's criticism certainly applies to a story like "The Bridle" – and, more to the point, to entire collections by some of Carver's lesser imitators – it misses the mark in the case of stories like "Gazebo," "What We Talk About When We Talk About Love," "A Small, Good Thing," "Cathedral," and "Where I'm Calling From," all of which display a complex and nuanced handling of human character. This, along with his openness to realism more generally, is the legacy Carver passed on to the next generation of story writers, including Lorrie Moore, Denis Johnson, Thom Jones, T. C. Boyle, George Saunders, Mary Gaitskill, Alice Adams, and Robert Olen Butler. Whereas at the beginning of the 1980s, writers like Bellow and Updike felt obliged to defend the humanistic underpinnings of their craft, by the end of the decade such a defense no longer seemed necessary. "As of 1992," Robert Stone wrote in his introduction to the *Best American Short Stories* anthology for that year, "American writers seem ready to accept traditional forms without self-consciousness in dealing with the complexity of the world around them."[19]

The realism of place

A corollary of contemporary realism's interest in the margins of society is its preoccupation with region or place. Even a short list of contemporary writers for whom this is a vital concern would include not only Carver and the other Dirty Realists, but also Bell, Erdrich, Cormac McCarthy, Annie Proulx, Richard Russo, Anne Tyler, William Kennedy, John Edgar Wideman, Larry McMurtry, Thomas McGuane, Ernest J. Gaines, Rudolfo Anaya, Dorothy Allison, Reynolds Price, Lee Smith, Peter Taylor, and Barbara Kingsolver. That a majority of these writers focus on mythic regions of the country like the South or West is no accident, for what is often at stake in the realism of place is the replacement of stereotype and myth with a more informed, concrete, and accurate representation.

In a series of novels set on a fictional Ojibwa reservation in eastern North Dakota, most notably *Love Medicine* (1984), *The Beet Queen* (1986), *Tracks*

(1988), *The Bingo Palace* (1994), and *Tales of Burning Love* (1996), Erdrich has created the deepest and most sustained portrait of a fictional place since William Faulkner's Yoknapatawpha County. Like Faulkner, to whose work she owes an obvious debt, Erdrich views the representation of place as a high-stakes enterprise in which the meaning of history itself hangs in the balance. However, as a Native American, Erdrich is equally interested in a more localized interpretation of what it means to occupy a particular locale. "In a tribal view of the world," she has written, "where one place has been inhabited for generations, the landscape becomes enlivened by a sense of group and family history. Unlike most contemporary writers, a traditional storyteller fixes listeners in an unchanging landscape combined of myth and reality. People and place are inseparable."[20]

If Erdrich is a writer who approaches place from a nativist, insider perspective, Proulx is the opposite, a writer who comes at her subject from a decidedly non-nativist, outsider perspective. Starting with *The Shipping News* (1993), set in Newfoundland, and continuing through the peripatetic *Accordion Crimes* (1996), a novel set in Oklahoma (*That Old Ace in the Hole* [2002]), and three story collections set in Wyoming (*Close Range* [1999], *Bad Dirt* [2004], and *Fine Just the Way It Is* [2008]), Proulx has made a career of discovering and mastering new territory in her fiction. While in graduate school in Canada in the early 1970s, Proulx admired the work of the French Annales school of historiography, which eschews the study of large historical movements in favor of a detailed examination of the lives of ordinary people as evidenced in account books, wills, court records, and the like. This influence is readily apparent in Proulx's fiction, which relies for its authenticity on the kind of meticulous research and reporting Wolfe called for in his 1989 essay "Stalking the Billion Footed Beast." In preparation for writing *The Shipping News*, for example, Proulx visited Newfoundland eight times over a six-year period, staying for a month or longer on each visit. "One doesn't just absorb it," she has said of her process of coming to know a place. "I must have read 50 or 60 sociological, folkloristic and historical studies of Newfoundland before I sat down to write a single word."[21] For Proulx and writers like her, the accumulation of observed and researched detail is one part of a process that ultimately is aimed at depicting change itself. "There's a particular kind of personality and social situation I'm attracted to," Proulx once remarked, "and that is the individual, or group, or region, or place, or time that's caught in change, that's caught in flux, that balances on some kind of edge that's either disintegrating or coming together or both."[22]

McCarthy's Border Trilogy of novels, *All the Pretty Horses* (1992), *The Crossing* (1994), and *Cities of the Plain* (1998), is a work of contemporary realism that attempts to capture a time and place caught in precisely this kind of flux. Set in West Texas and Mexico in the years during and immediately following World War II, the trilogy operates as an extended meditation on the fate of the American West as a place. In volume one of the trilogy, we are introduced to John Grady Cole, the dispossessed son of ranchers, whom we follow on a doomed quest to turn back the clock to a time before the closing of the western range left men like him no option but to ride off beneath a blood-red sunset "into the darkening land, the world to come."[23] The final two volumes in the trilogy carry this image of a "blood meridian" to its logical conclusion: *The Crossing* ending with its young hero Billy Parham witnessing a blinding light that turns out to be the Trinity, New Mexico nuclear test explosion of July 1945, while *Cities of the Plain* closes with John Grady Cole's death in Juarez and the transformation of the range where he once worked into a Cold War military base.

Erdrich's North Dakota series and McCarthy's Border Trilogy – as well as novels by Jane Smiley, Richard Russo, William Kennedy, and James Wilcox – present the reader with a researched, detail-oriented realism of place that attempts to tell the often tragic story of man's relationship with the environment; a story, these authors imply, that is inseparable from the larger narrative of American history. For this reason, these works cannot be pigeonholed as "regional" in the pejorative sense, but instead must take their place alongside earlier novels in the tradition like Twain's *The Adventures of Huckleberry Finn* (1884), Steinbeck's *The Grapes of Wrath* (1939), and Faulkner's *Go Down, Moses* (1942).

Multicultural realism

Their status as works of contemporary realism aside, Bellow's novels of the 1950s, 1960s, and 1970s are also examples of ethnic American literature; indeed, they belong to a distinguished line of Jewish American novels that includes work by Henry Roth, Bernard Malamud, Norman Mailer, Philip Roth, E. L. Doctorow, and others. As such, they operate as forerunners of a sort for a number of other ethnic or identity-based traditions in American literature, including Native American, Asian American, and Hispanic American varieties. (Realism is also an important mode of representation in post-1945 African American fiction [see Chapter 6], which has also conditioned the possibilities of multicultural fiction.) That each of these literatures is realist at its core should not surprise us. The authentication of experience is an important goal of any emerging literature, and realism provides a tried and true program for such authentication.

Among writers whose work fits the paradigm of multicultural realism, the most celebrated are N. Scott Momaday, Leslie Marmon Silko, Erdrich, James Welch, and Sherman Alexie (Native American); Maxine Hong Kingston, Amy Tan, Ha Jin, and Jhumpa Lahiri (Asian American); Rudolfo Anaya, Sandra Cisneros, Julia Alvarez, and Junot Díaz (Hispanic American); and, more recently, Edwidge Danticat (Haitian American). Inspired by the example of Toni Morrison in particular, these writers have striven to represent their respective cultures and communities with honesty and a researcher's attention to detail. Like most contemporary fiction, their work is a hybrid phenomenon, grafting elements drawn from folklore, mythology, and other traditions onto a recognizably realist base.

Tan's *The Joy Luck Club* (1989) is a good example of such hybridity. The book tells the story of four Chinese American immigrant families through a series of vignettes narrated by three of the mothers and four of the daughters (one of the mothers has died before the novel opens). Drawing its structure from the Chinese game of Mahjong, the novel has four parts divided into four sections each, for a total of sixteen chapters. Each part is prefaced by a brief, parable-like tale with some bearing on the novel's primary themes. These elements, together with Tan's weaving of transliterated Chinese words into the overall fabric of the text, give the novel its hybridized, vaguely exotic feel. Underneath this surface, however, the novel works as a straightforward, character-driven work of realism. For example, in a late section of the novel, "Double Face," Lindo Jong's daughter plans a trip to China but worries that she might be mistaken as a Chinese citizen and not allowed to return:

> "Aii-ya," I said. "Even if you put on their clothes, even if you take off your makeup and hide your fancy jewelry, they know. They know just watching the way you walk, the way your carry your face. They know you do not belong."
>
> My daughter did not look pleased when I told her this, that she didn't look Chinese. She had a sour American look on her face. Oh, maybe ten years ago, she would have clapped her hands – hurray! – as if this were good news. But now she wants to be Chinese, it is so fashionable. And I know it is too late … the only Chinese words she can say are *sh-sh*, *houche*, *chr fan*, and *gwan deng shweijyau*. How can she talk to people in China with these words! Pee-pee, choo-choo train, eat, close light sleep. How can she think she can blend in? Only her skin and her hair are Chinese. Inside – she is all American-made.[24]

Authenticity in this passage is generated in two separate but related ways. First there is Tan's use of scene, or dramatization, which carries us from the beginning of the vignette to its end with no disruptions of Gardner's fictional dream to slow us down or make us doubt the story we are being told. Laced throughout this, however, is another aspect of the passage's authenticity, supplied by the narrator's bilingual voice, her odd syntax and diction, and her cultural attitudes as an immigrant to America. These, too, feel real to us – real because they are convincingly "foreign" and yet also recognizably American.

Other works of multicultural realism, for example Sandra Cisneros's *The House on Mango Street* (1985), Julia Alvarez's *How the Garcia Girls Lost Their Accents* (1991), and Junot Díaz's *The Brief Wondrous Life of Oscar Wao* (2007), repeat this strategy with varying degrees of complexity and success. So, for that matter, does Robert Olen Butler's *A Good Scent from a Strange Mountain* (1992), a Pulitzer Prize-winning collection of stories about Vietnamese immigrants in Louisiana written not by a Vietnamese or an immigrant, but rather by a white man, a former Army linguist who has found in the strategies of multicultural realism a powerful way to tell a particularly American story.

Turncoat realism

Perhaps the greatest testament to realism's continuing relevance in American fiction is the number of writers once identified wholly or in part with literary postmodernism who in recent years have produced major works in the realist mode. Even a short list of these writers would include Russell Banks (*Affliction* [1989]), Joyce Carol Oates (*We Were the Mulvaneys* [1996]), Don DeLillo (*Underworld* [1997]), Phillip Roth (*American Pastoral* [1997]), William T. Vollmann (*The Royal Family* [2000]), and Jonathan Franzen (*The Corrections* [2001]). Franzen's very public transition from young, hip postmodernist to "purveyor of tragic realism" is a case in point, providing us an opportunity to consider some of the reasons why American fiction returned to its roots so definitively in the last two decades of the twentieth century.[25]

Franzen began his career with two long novels, *The Twenty-Seventh City* (1988) and *Strong Motion* (1992), both very much designed to take their place alongside such masterworks of literary postmodernism as William Gaddis's *The Recognitions* (1955) and Thomas Pynchon's *Gravity's Rainbow* (1973). Both novels were well received, and soon after the second was published, Franzen began work on a third novel designed to bring postmodernist technique (self-conscious narration, deconstructed character, temporal disorientation, externalized absurdist plot) to bear on a number of preselected social issues, including race, drugs, prison life, insider trading, and so on. However, a couple of years into work on the novel, Franzen became hopelessly stalled. In an angst-ridden essay published in *Harper's* in 1996, Franzen diagnosed the problem as a willful imposition of postmodernist theory on subject matter it did not suit and could not contain. "At the heart of my despair about the novel," he recalled, "had been a conflict between my feeling that I should Address the Culture and Bring News to the Mainstream, and my desire to write about the things closest to me, to lose myself in the characters and locales I loved."[26] As soon as he abandoned this "perceived obligation to the chimerical mainstream," the new novel took off in a number of promising and unexpected directions, leaving him amazed that he had "felt such a crushing imperative to engage explicitly with all the forces impinging on the pleasure of reading and writing: as if, in peopling and arranging my little alternative world, I could ignore the bigger social picture even if I wanted to."[27]

As it happened, Franzen's turning away from postmodernist theory and practice regarding character and plot eventually led him to precisely the kind of critique of society he had hoped to achieve in the first place. Nowhere is this more evident than in the changes Franzen made in his handling of character between his first and third novels. Here, for example, is his description of Martin Probst in *The Twenty-Seventh City*:

> Born in the very pit of the Depression, he had groped and bullied his way into some kind of light, demolishing and steam-rolling and building higher, building the Arch, building developments of the most youthful and prosperous nature, the golden years of Martin Probst. Inside, though, he was sick, and the city was sick on the inside too, choking on undigested motives, racked by lies. The conspiracy invaded the city's bloodstream while leaving the surfaces unchanged, raged around him and in him while he sat apparently unseen, uncounted, uninvolved, and it was right here, in this identity of his life with the city's life, that he could see himself disappearing. The more he was a figure, the less he was a person.[28]

That last sentence says it all – *The more he was a figure, the less he was a person*. The entirety of the characterization is insisted upon or, worse, imposed by the author. Even the thematic linking of Probst with St. Louis is handled in this way – from the outside and above. Compare this with Franzen's characterization of Alfred Lambert, a man afflicted with Parkinson's struggling to eat a plate of food prepared by his daughter, in *The Corrections*:

> His affliction offended his sense of ownership. These shaking hands belonged to no one but him, and yet they refused to obey him. They were like bad children. Unreasoning two-year-olds in a tantrum of selfish misery. The more sternly he gave orders, the less they listened and the more miserable and out of control they got. He'd always been vulnerable to a child's recalcitrance and refusal to behave like an adult. Irresponsibility and undiscipline were the bane of his existence, and it was another instance of that Devil's logic that his own untimely affliction should consist of his body's refusal to obey him.
> If thy right hand offend thee, Jesus said, cut it off.[29]

In this characterization, every word and image arises from the specific situation and is seen from a particularized point of view, that of a lonely disciplinarian who secretly longs to connect with his adult children. Because of this attention to situation and detail, we come to know Alfred Lambert in a way we cannot hope to know Martin Probst – from the inside out.

The strategy is employed throughout *The Corrections*. As readers, we first experience the characters in all their particularity – Alfred and his hallucinations, Enid and her Christmas obsession, Chip and his confused relationships with women, Gary and his determination not to become his father, Denise and her workaholic's repression of self-awareness – and only later do we begin to ask the big, universal questions. What are the burdens we pass on to our children without even knowing we are doing it? Should a person be medicated just because he is unhappy or feels a sense of shame? How do large economic movements impact the lives of the people who are caught up in them? Questions such as these are not forced on the material or lowered from above on a string of abstract rhetoric. Rather they are *evoked*, brought to life first within the characters, and then, through them, within us as readers. This is the great achievement of *The Corrections* as well as the reason why it is not only Franzen's best work to date but, arguably, the first great work of twenty-first-century American fiction.

FURTHER READING

Furst, Lilian R. *All Is True: The Claims and Strategies of Realist Fiction*. Durham, NC: Duke University Press, 1995

Leypoldt, Gunter. "Recent Realist Fiction and the Idea of Writing 'After Postmodernism'." *Amerikastudien/American Studies*, 49.1 (2004): 19–34

Morris, Pam. *Realism (The New Critical Idiom)*. New York: Routledge, 2003

Rebein, Robert. *Hicks, Tribes, and Dirty Realists: American Fiction after Postmodernism*. Lexington: University Press of Kentucky, 2001

Versluys, Kristiaan (ed.). *Neo-Realism in Contemporary American Fiction*. Amsterdam and Atlanta: Rodopi, 1992

Wolfe, Tom. "Stalking the Billion-Footed Beast: A Literary Manifesto for the New Social Novel." *Harper's*, November 1989: 45–56

NOTES

1 Raymond Carver, "On Writing," in *Fires: Essays, Poems, Stories* (New York: Vintage, 1989), p. 23.

2 Jerome Klinkowitz, *Literary Disruptions: The Making of a Post-contemporary American Fiction* (Urbana: University of Illinois Press, 1975), p. 32.

3 Jonathan Franzen, "Mr. Difficult," *New Yorker*, September 30, 2002: 103.

4 Saul Bellow, "Nobel Lecture," in Tore Frangsmyr and Sture Allen (eds.), *Nobel Lectures in Literature 1968–1980* (London: World Scientific Publishing, 1993), p. 133.

5   Ibid., p. 138.
6   Saul Bellow, *Henderson the Rain King* (New York: Viking, 1959), p. 3.
7   Saul Bellow, *Seize the Day* (New York: Penguin Classics, 1996), p. 114.
8   John Updike, *Rabbit Angstrom: The Four Novels* (New York: Everyman's Library, 1995), p. 623.
9   Bill Buford, "Introduction" to "Dirty Realism: New Writing from America," *Granta* 8 (1983): 4.
10 Ibid.
11 Ibid.
12 John Gardner, *The Art of Fiction: Notes on Craft for Young Writers* (New York: Vintage, 1991), pp. 31–3.
13 Carver, "On Writing," pp. 23–4.
14 Richard Ford, "Good Raymond," *New Yorker*, October 5, 1998: 72.
15 Ibid.
16 Madison Smartt Bell, "Less Is Less: The Dwindling of the American Short Story," *Harper's*, April 1986: 65.
17 Ibid., p. 67.
18 Ibid., p. 64.
19 Robert Stone, Introduction to *Best American Short Stories 1992* (New York: Houghton-Mifflin Press, 1992), p. xviii.
20 Louise Erdrich, "Where I Ought to Be: A Writer's Sense of Place," *New York Times Book Review*, July 28, 1985: 23–4.
21 Geraldine Baum, "A Mind Filled with Stories," *Los Angeles Times*, November 15, 1993: E1.
22 Suzanne L. MacLaughlin, "The Life of an Author in Demand," *Christian Science Monitor*, July 22, 1994: 14.
23 Cormac McCarthy, *All the Pretty Horses* (New York: Alfred Knopf, 1992), p. 302.
24 Amy Tan, *The Joy Luck Club* (New York: Vintage Contemporaries, 1991 [1989]), pp. 253–4.
25 For more detail, see my "Turncoat: Why Jonathan Franzen Finally Said 'No' to Po-Mo," in Neil Brooks and Josh Toth (eds.), *The Mourning After: Attending the Wake of Postmodernism* (Amsterdam: Rodopi, 2007).
26 Jonathan Franzen, "Perchance to Dream: In the Age of Images, a Reason to Write Novels," *Harper's*, April 1996: 54.
27 Ibid.
28 Jonathan Franzen, *The Twenty-Seventh City* (New York: Farrar, Straus, and Giroux, 1988), pp. 216–17.
29 Jonathan Franzen, *The Corrections* (New York: Farrar, Straus, and Giroux, 2001), p. 67.

3

STACEY OLSTER

New journalism and
the nonfiction novel

When John Hersey ended the first chapter of *Hiroshima* (1946) by describing the burial of Toshiko Sasaki beneath the rubble of the East Asia Tin Works, his decision to focus "principally and first of all" on the bookcases that collapsed upon her on August 6, 1945, signaled his feelings about the collapse of available literary forms, all of which proved inadequate to convey the devastation of the atom bomb that he was trying to recreate.[1] In this recognition of the limitations of existing narrative forms, Hersey anticipated by two decades one of the primary impulses behind the emergence of new journalism and the nonfiction novel, twin phenomena whose birth date, as John Hellmann argues, can be given as 1965, the year that saw the publication of Tom Wolfe's first essay collection, *The Kandy-Kolored Tangerine-Flake Streamline Baby*, and the serialization of Truman Capote's *In Cold Blood* in *The New Yorker*.[2] The other primary impulse comes by way of a story Hunter S. Thompson tells about standing beside a Lear Jet that Richard Nixon is about to board during his 1968 presidential election campaign and being frantically thrust aside when a Nixon aide realizes he is smoking one Marlboro after another over the fuel tank. Thinking he can defend himself by reminding the advance man that he is a "sane, responsible journalist" who, otherwise, might have hurled his flaming Zippo into the tank, Thompson is exposed for the precise kind of journalist he is by the man who easily sees through the (il)logic of his reasoning: "Egomaniacs don't do that kind of thing ...You wouldn't do anything you couldn't live to write about."[3]

By 1965, of course, a series of articles had steadily made clear the frustrations with the novel as a vehicle for expressing the nature of contemporary reality. Philip Roth famously depicted the mid-century American fiction writer as having "his hands full in trying to understand, and then describe, and then make *credible*" implausible actualities that were "continually outdoing our talents."[4] Norman Mailer saw those talents stymied by a society "resistant (most secretly) to an objective eye,"[5] which left the novelist unable either to extrapolate from minute observation and "fill in unknown colors in the landscape" in the manner of Balzac or write the panoramic novel of Tolstoy due to the overwhelming "plethora of detail in each joint of society."[6] The result, in Wolfe's somewhat hyperbolic assessment, was a fiction that replaced characters of manners and milieu with variations of the "Prince of Alienation ... sailing off to Lonesome Island on his Tarot boat with his back turned and his Timeless cape on, reeking of camphor balls," an abdication of social realism that produced a gap "big enough to drive an ungainly Reo rig like the New Journalism through."[7]

Wolfe traced that interloper writing back to the "feature," or human interest, story, often relegated to the Sunday supplements, that liberated lumpenprole journalists such as Jimmy Breslin and Dick Schaap at the *Herald Tribune*, Gay Talese and Robert Lipsyte at the *New York Times*, and Michael Mok at the *Daily News* from both the inverted pyramid and beige neutrality of conventional journalism. Faced with the gun-toting bikers and mechanics assembled for the Fourth Annual Las Vegas "Mint 400," Thompson, for instance, quickly realized that the "idea of trying to 'cover this race' in any conventional press-sense" was "like trying to keep track of a swimming meet in an Olympic-sized pool filled with talcum powder instead of water."[8] Faced with the "freakyfluky" war that was Vietnam,[9] Michael Herr dismissed "[c]onventional journalism" as "no more [able to] reveal this war than conventional firepower could win it,"[10] for conventional journalism could no more convey "what Vietnam looked like" than it could convey "how it smelled."[11]

The democratizing of subject matter to which this freedom from convention lent itself often exposed readers to segments of society far outside their usual frames of reference: demolition derby racers, twenty-three-year-old record tycoons, custom car manufacturers in *The Kandy-Kolored Tangerine-Flake Streamline Baby*; Pentecostal churches whose members await the destruction of the world by earthquake, Gamblers Anonymous meetings, the Operations Control Center for the California State Water Project in Joan Didion's *The White Album* (1979). At times, these subjects dwarfed even the writers' imaginative frames of reference: Lucille Maxwell Miller setting her sleeping husband on fire in a Volkswagen could be made comprehensible by Joan Didion because the act prompted by a tawdry love triangle derived from "the novels of James M. Cain, the movies of the late 1930's, all the dreams in which violence and threats and blackmail are made to seem commonplaces of middle-class life";[12] Betty Lansdown Fouquet placing her five-year-old daughter out to die on the center divider of Interstate 5, by contrast, had no such analogues, leaving Didion with apprehension as the most she could hope to transmit.[13] At best, however, subjects possessing traits with deeper historical and cultural resonance enabled writers to turn them into the kind of national emblems that novelists had, out of despair, relinquished. The laconic Junior Johnson, who races stock cars at speeds of 180 miles per hour and prefers dirt-track races that depend on a driver's skill and not a car's outfitting, has all the "right stuff" of the single-combat warrior with which Wolfe later would glorify the Edwards Air Force Base pilots and, eventually, the Project Mercury astronauts; what makes him "The Last American Hero" of Wolfe's 1965 essay is the fact that the early moonshine runs that were, in effect, his first races extended a century-and-a-half-old tradition of country folk rebelling against federal oppression (e.g., Shays' Rebellion [1786], the Whiskey Rebellion [1794]) and developing through their isolation a kind of courage "that became extinct in most other sections of the country by 1900."[14]

Looked at in such iconographic terms, the achievement of Capote's *In Cold Blood* has little to do with its "true account of a multiple murder and its consequences," as the subtitle asserts. Its brilliance derives instead from Capote's use of that murder to portray the decline of the American West, the death of the small town, and the ease with which American dreams can turn into American nightmares – issues not even remotely hinted at in the scant 291-word *New York Times* article of November 16, 1959 ("Wealthy Farmer, 3 Of Family Slain"), hidden on page 39, that first piqued the author's interest. With dazzling economy, Capote's opening sentences establish Holcomb, Kansas, as more "Far Western than Middle West,"[15] its darkened dance hall, shut-down bank, peeling train depot, and crumbling post office giving the lie to all beliefs – such as Mr. Clutter maintains – that just an extra inch of rain would turn the country into an "Eden on earth."[16] This paradise has already been lost – only the residents no more acknowledge it than they do the frequency of Mrs. Clutter's trips to Wesley Medical Center for psychiatric treatment. The oracular details that punctuate the book's first section (the bookmark of Bonnie Clutter embroidered with a reminder to "heed, watch and pray";[17] the velvet dress her daughter Nancy lays out for church that serves as her burial dress),[18] by contrast, refuse the reader any such comfort. So does information later gleaned about the "terrible destinies that seemed promised the four children of Florence Buckskin and Tex John Smith,"[19] which turns what initially might be dismissed as Perry Smith's crackpot superstition in fate ("once a thing is set to happen, all you can do is hope it won't")[20] into a form of fatalism that this son born into a family of alcoholics and suicides cannot escape. Such inevitability exposes the pathos behind even the most banal aspirations of the characters, killers and victims alike, whose introduction by way of cinematic cross-cutting (Herb Clutter refusing stimulants and Perry Smith refraining from coffee; Perry and Dick

Hickock admiring their automotive work and Nancy Clutter and a young protégé admiring their bakery work) only heightens their similarities. Much like Nancy Clutter, who plans to study art in college, Perry draws portraits, yearns for an education, and even imagines "a college graduate" as his ideal sweetheart,[21] only to end up with a life of "ugly and lonely progress toward one mirage and then another."[22] Dick, an "American-style 'good kid' with an outgrown crew cut,"[23] gets a football scholarship to study engineering in college but opts instead for the life of wife, children, house, and car he thinks "a man ought to have,"[24] only to start passing bad checks when his life of conspicuous consumption cannot be supported by his job as a mechanic. Rudely awakened to the carnage to which envy and displaced anger can lead, to that recoil predicted by Frederick Jackson Turner a half-century earlier, Holcomb residents no longer question when they can return to "living an ordinary life" even after the killers are executed;[25] they know all too well that "something around here had come to an end," notably, their faith in God and innate human goodness.[26]

To be sure, much that defined these examples of new journalism and the nonfiction novel was hardly "new." Wolfe traced many of the characteristics of the former back to the travel literature of the late eighteenth and early nineteenth centuries and to Boswell's reporting on Samuel Johnson in particular. Daniel Defoe's *A Journal of the Plague Year* (1722) was noted frequently as a prototype of the latter. But contributing greatly to the debate over the novel in the 1960s was the growth of new communications technologies that provided so many disparate views of reality that no single competing interpretive frame could be deemed capable of containing them all: in contrast to the ten thousand television sets in use in America at the time of Pearl Harbor, and the ten million sets in use at the start of the Korean War, for instance, nearly one hundred million sets were in use by January 1968.[27] Already skeptical of journalistic objectivity (recognized as a mere convention that developed in tandem with the teletype and radio), writers became increasingly suspicious of the synergistic interests that were both manufacturing news as well as deciding which news was "fit" for distribution. "By the time Eisenhower was first elected," wrote Mailer, "the Media was beginning to make history as well as report it,"[28] which included, in his view, the replacement of facts with "factoids," or "facts which have no existence before appearing in a magazine or newspaper."[29] Thompson concurred, offering what he termed the "Hell's Angels Saga" as proof of the "awesome power of the New York press establishment": specifically, the *New York Times*, which attached a completely bogus lead to a condensed attorney general's report from Monterey, and *Time* and *Newsweek*, which picked up the story and ran with it.[30]

Reacting against such powerful interests, new journalists and nonfiction novelists increasingly drafted themselves as the primary figures of their works. This was not only to bypass the filters of the media. Having frequently become participants (intentionally or not) through their immersion in the events they were covering, who better to convey the feel of the experiences in question than they? In *Dispatches* (1978), for example, Michael Herr describes himself coming to Vietnam in 1967 "to watch";[31] as *Esquire* correspondent – a "peculiarity" who is "extremely privileged" in having no daily deadlines to meet or bureau to answer to[32] – he watches airstrikes across the river while sipping drinks on the roof of the Caravelle Hotel and battles at the front knowing that volleyball games and steaks await him at the press center afterwards. But remaining "as close to" the infantry grunts as he can "without actually being one of them" becomes impossible during the 1968 Tet Offensive, when he finds himself having "slid over to the wrong end of the story, propped up behind some sandbags at an airstrip in Can Tho with a .30-caliber automatic in my hands, firing cover for a four-man reaction team trying to get back in,"[33] forcing him to admit that "I wasn't a reporter, I was a shooter," and later, after working in the Can Tho hospital, "not a reporter or a shooter but a medic, unskilled and scared."[34] And, ultimately, a persona, distinguished from the writer, as a transcribed conversation that follows an "Editor's Note" at the end of *Fear and Loathing: On the Campaign Trail '72* (1973) makes clear. Asked, after a year of covering the 1972 presidential campaigns, whether politics constitutes the "greatest Edge" he has ever experienced,[35] "Dr. Hunter S. Thompson" – the name that appears on the book's title page – has no doubts about the difference between the experience of the journalist and the experience of the man who once ran for Sheriff of Aspen on the Freak Power ticket: "That actually isn't much fun, writing about it … the High is in the participation."[36] Yet the inclusion of metafictional devices such as Author's Note and Epitaph, frequent Editor's Notes, transcribed tapes ("98 percent verbatim"),[37] and "actual" manuscripts (complete with crossed-out passages and hand-written emendations)[38] reminds us that the journalist repeatedly missing deadlines and suffering nervous breakdowns is as much a persona and as little to be trusted as the participant who admits to having become "a flack for McGovern," thus granting the reader, in the end, the final say in the determination of the book's accuracy.[39]

And what an array of personae emerged, with no necessary consistency from text to text or within even the same text! In *Slouching towards Bethlehem* (1968), Didion cites her slight bodily stature – "I am so physically small, so temperamentally unobtrusive, and so neurotically inarticulate" – as key to the invisibility that grants her reportorial entrée;[40] in *The White Album*, she employs her bodily infirmities – migraines, multiple sclerosis – as "offering a precise physiological equivalent to what had been going on in my mind,"[41] evidence of which already has been supplied by the psychiatric report that depicts that mind as breaking under the strain of the environmental and social chaos now deemed "*normal stress.*"[42] In the first part of *Fear and Loathing in Las Vegas* (1971), Thompson christens himself Raoul Duke, a high-octane "[g]onzo journali[st]"[43] unnoticed in a "town full of bedrock crazies,"[44] switches to infiltrating "spy" when assigned to cover the National District Attorneys' Conference on Narcotics and Dangerous Drugs in the second part,[45] and switches one last time from "Special Investigator" (modeled on Kennedy assassination investigator James Garrison)[46] to "Doctor of Divinity," certified "Minister of the Church of the New Truth," when purchasing a box of amyls at the Denver airport in the book's last pages.[47] Perhaps most dramatically, Mailer alternates between libertine *manqué* and doting father of six, Marxist anarchist and Left Conservative, in *The Armies of the Night* (1968), all the while grandstanding as the "Participant," "Ruminant, " "Critic," "Beast," "General," "Historian," and, finally, "Novelist" as the spirit moves him.

Mailer explains the value of these personae when shifting from the lengthy description of his own escapades that forms Book One of *Armies of the Night*, "History as a Novel," to the far shorter "The Novel as History" that is Book Two, in which the climactic moments of the 1967 March on the Pentagon are finally rendered. Having proposed that the best way of viewing the horizon from a forest comes from the building of a tower, Mailer goes on to admit that the tower is invariably "crooked" and its telescopes, like the instruments of all sciences, "history so much as physics," are "warped." But, as he continues, "what supports the use of them now is that our intimacy with the master builder of the tower, and the lens grinder of the telescopes (yes, even the machinist of the barrels) has given some advantage for correcting the error of the instruments and the imbalance of his tower. May that be claimed of many histories?"[48] Certainly not Capote's, which, while missing an authorial persona, is nonetheless suffused from start to finish with its author's manipulations: multiple written accounts of Perry Smith's life (his father's, his sister's, his jail mate's, his own) that both complicate, and create sympathy for, him in ways not granted the one-dimensional thug that is Dick; pre-trial confessions made to fit psychiatric evaluations of diminished capacity precluded at trial by the M'Naghten Rule. Mailer, by contrast, does not follow the slick *Time* piece, with its emphasis on bourbon slurped and obscenities spewed, that opens his text with anything that purports to be a definitive account; when he "leave[s]" *Time* "to find out what happened,"[49] it is to present an alternative version – biases on display, failings in full view – not the "real" version.

Behind such modesty – however disingenuous (for if Mailer refrains from pitching his account as a "true" account, he undoubtedly casts it as a "truer" account than *Time*'s) – is the simple fact that, in Book One, Mailer does not witness the most climactic events of the March because he is not present when they occur. Arrested without incident and taken to spend the night at a workhouse in Occoquan, Virginia, he does not witness the brutal beatings that take place on the steps of the Pentagon Mall later that evening; released from Occoquan the next day and back in New York in time for dinner, he does not witness the effects of dehydration and malnutrition on the Quakers from Voluntown, Connecticut, who choose to remain in jail and refuse to eat, drink, or co-operate in any way. Having bound himself in the subjective history that is Book One to events that involve him personally – refusing to embellish them for dramatic purposes (not adding a lady to share his bed at the Hay-Adams Hotel) or impose upon them the selectivity of hindsight (not excising a pointless conversation with a man holding a clipboard), Mailer comes up against the limits of the written history. Forced to conclude "that an explanation of the mystery of the events at the Pentagon cannot be developed by the methods of history – only by the instincts of the novelist," he asserts: "the novel must replace history at precisely that point where experience is sufficiently emotional, spiritual, psychical, moral, existential, or supernatural to expose the fact that the historian in pursuing the experience would be obliged to quit the clearly demarcated limits of historic inquiry."[50] And so he speculates wildly throughout the "collective novel" that he terms Book Two (the dryness of its tone punctuated by frequent reminders of its conjectural status). He imagines a dialogue between organizers David Dellinger and Jerry Rubin. He locates a frontier on the Mall between demonstrators and MPs. He pictures the Quakers wandering across their isolation cells, deprived of sanity as much as sleep.

Such forays into fiction enable Mailer in Book Two to assess the March in ways that elude him in Book One, and, more to the point, situate it with respect to longstanding American traditions. His early misgivings about the protestors (their use of drugs, their banal language, their dismissal of the past) notwithstanding, Mailer portrays their decision to stay overnight on the Mall as a "rite of passage" that evokes "all the great American rites of passage when men and women manacled themselves to a lost and painful principle and survived a day, a night, a week, a month, a year, a celebration of Thanksgiving – the country had been founded on a rite of passage."[51] The Voluntown Quakers who offer "some small penance for the sins of the nation" he casts as Puritan "saints."[52] The final image of America "heavy with child"[53] of as yet unknown traits he takes from the emerging larva that ends *Walden* (1854); the "[r]ush to the locks" for safe delivery/deliverance are the same "locks" whose "unscrew[ed]" doors form the "sign of democracy" in "Song of Myself" (1881).[54]

Extended resonance of this kind is predicated on two factors, however. One, Mailer can extrapolate from the particular to the general. Having earlier justified his persona of "monumental disproportions" with the remark, "Once History inhabits a crazy house, egotism may be the last tool left to History,"[55] the rite of passage he experiences during his overnight stay at the Occoquan workhouse enables him to invoke the rite of passage on the Pentagon Mall, just as the fast he begins at the Lincoln Memorial grants him psychological access to the hunger strike undertaken by the Voluntown Quakers. Two, the material with which he works lends itself to deeper reverberation. The Pentagon in *Armies of the Night* in which Mailer symbolizes "the military might of the Republic" can sustain the weight he ascribes it (despite its Virginia location) because it does house the Department of Defense.[56] The 1967 March can acquire "quintessentially American" status because the city in which it occurs is capital to the American Republic.[57] Protestors dressed as Wyatt Earp, Kit Carson, and Daniel Boone can evoke a series of battles from Valley Forge through Normandy and Pusan because the clothing they literally wear on their backs attests to a historical continuum. Much the same occurs in *The Executioner's Song* (1979), a "*true life story*" presented "as if it were a novel."[58] Utah – in which, as an ACLU lawyer quips, "The Church *was* the State"[59] – can recall the theocratic principles upon which the nation was founded and, with an exchange of Mormons for Puritans, illustrate those kinds of principles in action. Gary Gilmore, the book's central figure, can serve as a "quintessentially American" example of what Mailer had been saying about the nation for years because his various poses – twenty-seven according to the journalist who counted them – constitute a cross-section of American society: "racist Gary and Country-and-Western Gary, poetic Gary, artist manqué Gary, macho Gary, self-destructive Gary, Karma County Gary, Texas Gary," and, last but not least, Gary "the movie star, awfully shit-kicking large-minded aw-shucks."[60] In contrast, the Chicago portrayed in *Miami and the Siege of Chicago* (1968) has little ready-made mythical import. The "Massacre of Michigan Avenue" cannot bring to mind "the old Indian raids" of the past, much less evoke the current war in Vietnam, when Mailer must concede that "no one was killed."[61] And describing the televised violence at the convention as breaking the Democratic Party "in two before the eyes of a nation like Melville's whale charging right out of the sea" only highlights the lesser authority of Mailer's voice by reminding the reader of the greater authority of his predecessor's.[62]

Alert for years to the falsehoods that attend any framing of experience in language – an army that traffics in "transmittals" instead of death certificates,[63] lifeguards that discuss "operations" and "functions" but shirk at "bodies"[64] – Didion in a 1990 essay warned of the falsehoods that can emerge when historical events are framed as narratives that misconstrue their meaning. The vexed issues they raise trumped by an urge for clear-cut resolution, events so rendered become "merely illustrative, a series of set pieces, or performance opportunities."[65] The actual performances to which Didion refers in this essay are those of New York City politicians, who spin crimes in such a way that they offer "however erroneously, a story, a lesson, a high concept":[66] the 1986 "Preppy Murder" becomes a cautionary tale of unrestricted teenage extravagance; the 1989 "Central Park Jogger" case a triumph of the best and brightest rising like a Phoenix along with the distressed city she personified.[67] Yet Didion's term applies equally well to the performances of writers, driven by the allure of the Great American Novel (their version of the Great White Whale) and seduced by historical events they think will finally place that elusive beast within their grasp.

Nothing better illustrates that misguided approach than the career of Lawrence Schiller. Introduced in *The Executioner's Song* as a checkbook journalist and often compared to various scavengers of the animal kingdom, Schiller also functions as Mailer's surrogate (on the scene in Utah when Mailer, once again, is absent). As such, Schiller as surrogate-participant is given a metafictional sub-plot of his own that traces the efforts of an Academy Award-winning film producer and made-for-TV movie director to become the one thing he is not: a writer. He fails, of course; gastrointestinal moments of moral clarity that convince him "you can't fictionalize, you can't make it up, you can't *embroider*"[68] confirm an outmoded model of historiography based on the transparency of the written product, and so he ends the book a "writer without hands."[69] But even in the tomes that bear his name as author, he fares no better. *American Tragedy* (1996), obviously written with Dreiser's 1925 masterpiece in mind, reveals little about the pivotal issues of race, class, and celebrity in America that the O. J. Simpson trial raised. With the victims reduced to abstractions, as empty as the stripped Bundy condo crime scene, and Simpson, who tried to block the book's publication, completely fragmented if not disembodied by Schiller's decision to portray the defendant through the voices of third parties, the book never makes clear just whose American tragedy it seeks to chronicle. And because the killing of JonBenét Ramsey that forms the center of *Perfect Murder, Perfect Town* (1999) has scant resonance to begin with, all Schiller can do to assert its importance is situate "*the Ramsey thing*" as successor to "*the Simpson thing*" and "*the Susan Smith thing*," which only backfires since pitching each "thing" as the latest in a series of destabilizing criminal "things" only reduces in significance the status of any one of them.[70]

If new journalism and the nonfiction novel were born in the 1960s, it is tempting to look at these works written three decades later, driven by an urge for literary respectability, as attesting to the arteriosclerosis of middle age, especially when one recalls how much the urge to explode literary forms was, in the work of the first practitioners, fueled by equal parts rage and remorse. One thinks of Thompson's elegiac realization that the San Francisco of the mid-1960s, where people rode "the crest of a high and beautiful wave," assured of "inevitable victory over the forces of Old and Evil," is visible from a steep hill in Las Vegas five years later as "that place where the wave finally broke and rolled back."[71] Or one thinks of the excoriation Mailer unleashes on those "princelings on the trail of the hip," including himself, who end the decade "an army of outrageously spoiled children who cooked with piss and vomit while the Wasps were quietly moving from command of the world to command of the moon."[72] Appalled at changes in the nation, and accepting their own neglect as contributing factors, these veteran scribes do not know the meaning of the phrase "off the record" and write "as close to the bone" as they can get, "to hell with the consequences."[73] We may not emerge with truth, or anything resembling truth, from our travels with them. But the ride on which we have been taken in search of that other White Whale (and, if we are lucky, maybe in that white Coupe de Ville that Thompson drives around Vegas) is one that is not to be missed. Who knows? Next time someone might just throw that Zippo into the fuel tank.

FURTHER READING

Hollowell, John. *Fact and Fiction: The New Journalism and the Nonfiction Novel.* Chapel Hill: University of North Carolina Press, 1977

Underwood, Doug. *Journalism and the Novel: Truth and Fiction, 1700–2000.* Cambridge University Press, 2008

Weber, Ronald. *The Literature of Fact: Literary Nonfiction in American Writing.* Athens: Ohio University Press, 1980

Zavarzadeh, Mas'ud. *The Mythopoeic Reality: The Postwar American Nonfiction Novel.* Urbana: University of Illinois Press, 1976

NOTES

1 John Hersey, *Hiroshima* (New York: Bantam, 1975), p. 20.
2 John Hellmann, *Fables of Fact: The New Journalism as New Fiction* (Urbana: University of Illinois Press, 1981), p. 1.
3 Hunter S. Thompson, *Fear and Loathing: On the Campaign Trail '72* (New York: Grand Central Publishing, 2006), p. 45.
4 Philip Roth, "Writing American Fiction," *Commentary*, March 1961: 224.
5 Norman Mailer, "Some Children of the Goddess," *Esquire*, July 1963: 69.

6 Ibid., p. 105.
7 Tom Wolfe, "The New Journalism," in Tom Wolfe and E. W. Johnson (eds.), *The New Journalism* (New York: Harper & Row, 1973), pp. 30–1.
8 Hunter S. Thompson, *Fear and Loathing in Las Vegas: A Savage Journey to the Heart of the American Dream* (New York: Vintage, 1998), p. 38.
9 Michael Herr, *Dispatches* (New York: Knopf, 1978), p. 14.
10 Ibid., p. 218.
11 Ibid., p. 93.
12 Joan Didion, *Slouching towards Bethlehem* (New York: Touchstone, 1979), p. 17.
13 Joan Didion, *The White Album* (New York: Pocket, 1980), p. 13.
14 Tom Wolfe, *The Kandy-Kolored Tangerine-Flake Streamline Baby* (New York: Bantam, 1999), p. 156.
15 Truman Capote, *In Cold Blood: A True Account of a Multiple Murder and Its Consequences* (New York: Signet, 1980), p. 13.
16 Ibid., p. 23.
17 Ibid., p. 42.
18 Ibid., p. 71.
19 Ibid., p. 209.
20 Ibid., p. 109.
21 Ibid., p. 116.
22 Ibid., p. 277.
23 Ibid., p. 43.
24 Ibid., p. 117.
25 Ibid., p. 241.
26 Ibid., p. 137.
27 Don Oberdorfer, *Tet!: The Turning Point in the Vietnam War* (New York: Da Capo, 1984), p. 159.
28 Norman Mailer, *St. George and the Godfather* (New York: Signet, 1972), p. 93.
29 Norman Mailer, *Marilyn* (London: Coronet-Hodder, 1974), p. 18.
30 Hunter S. Thompson, *Hell's Angels: A Strange and Terrible Saga* (New York: Ballantine, 1996), pp. 34–5.
31 Herr, *Dispatches*, p. 20.
32 Ibid., p. 212.
33 Ibid., p. 67.
34 Ibid., p. 68.
35 Thompson, *Fear and Loathing: On the Campaign Trail '72*, p. 471.
36 Ibid., p. 473.
37 Ibid., p. 267.
38 Ibid., p. 429.
39 Ibid., p. 423.
40 Didion, *Slouching towards Bethlehem*, p. xiv.
41 Didion, *The White Album*, p. 46.
42 Ibid., p. 14.
43 Thompson, *Fear and Loathing in Las Vegas*, p. 12.
44 Ibid., p. 24.
45 Ibid., p. 81.

46 Ibid., p. 201.
47 Ibid., p. 203.
48 Norman Mailer, *The Armies of the Night: History as a Novel/The Novel as History* (New York: Signet, 1968), p. 245.
49 Ibid., p. 14.
50 Ibid., p. 284.
51 Ibid., p. 311.
52 Ibid., p. 319.
53 Ibid., p. 320.
54 Walt Whitman, "Song of Myself" (1881), in Sculley Bradley and Harold W. Blodgett (eds.), *Leaves of Grass (1891–1892)* (New York: Norton, 1973), pp. 501–2, 506.
55 Mailer, *The Armies of the Night*, p. 68.
56 Ibid.
57 Ibid., p. 241.
58 Norman Mailer, *The Executioner's Song* (New York: Warner, 1980), p. 1022.
59 Ibid., p. 755.
60 Ibid., p. 806.
61 Norman Mailer, *Miami and the Siege of Chicago: An Informal History of the Republican and Democratic Conventions of 1968* (New York: Signet, 1968), p. 159.
62 Ibid., p. 172.
63 Didion, *The White Album*, p. 141.
64 Ibid., pp. 210–11.
65 Joan Didion, "Sentimental Journeys" (1990), reprinted in *After Henry* (New York: Vintage, 1993), p. 297.
66 Ibid., pp. 255–6.
67 Ibid., pp. 259–60.
68 Mailer, *The Executioner's Song*, p. 833.
69 Ibid., p. 1013.
70 Lawrence Schiller, *Perfect Murder, Perfect Town: JonBenét and the City of Boulder* (New York: HarperCollins, 1999), p. 214.
71 Thompson, *Fear and Loathing in Las Vegas*, p. 68.
72 Norman Mailer, *Of a Fire on the Moon* (New York: Signet, 1971), pp. 385–6.
73 Thompson, *Fear and Loathing: On the Campaign Trail '72*, p. 4.

4

PHILLIP E. WEGNER

Science fiction

Science fiction represents, along with film, one of the most significant global forms to emerge in the twentieth century, its estranging visions of other worlds bringing into focus the dramatic transformations that define modernity. Thus, as Pascale Casanova argues in the case of the novel more generally, it is difficult to constrain its history to one nation.[1] However, by the end of World War II, the United States had come to dominate science fiction. The story of how this came to pass is a fascinating one. While there were major American precursors – including Edgar Allan Poe and Edward Bellamy – what we think of as science fiction emerged at the close of the nineteenth century in the "scientific romances" of the British author, H. G. Wells. Wells's work paved the way for a dramatic global production of the genre in a diverse group of writers, many of whom treat science fiction as a form of modernist experimental literature.

However, a number of developments in the 1920s helped conclude this opening chapter in the genre's history. First, the increasing intolerance within the Soviet Union for artistic experimentation put one fecund tradition on hold until the 1950s. Second, as Roger Luckhurst maintains, the use of Wells's work as "a negative foil in aesthetics" by the British modernist writing establishment meant that those "who continued with the scientific romance did so in conditions of marginality and insularity."[2] Finally and most significantly, the emergence of science fiction pulp magazines, beginning in 1926 with *Amazing Stories* under the editorship of Hugo Gernsback (who also coined the term "science fiction"), set the genre's agenda for the coming decades.

Gary Westfahl argues, "What Gernsback provided was not simply a set of marketing slogans or slick promotions; he offered a complete theory of science fiction which readers, editors, and writers understood and responded to."[3] While reprinting some of the genre's earliest writers, Gernsback's *Amazing Stories* also published melodramatic "space operas," including E. E. "Doc" Smith's *The Skylark of Space* saga and Philip Francis Nowlan's

Anthony "Buck" Rogers stories, and fantasy adventure by Edgar Rice Burroughs, creator of Tarzan and John Carter of Mars. These works (the *Stars Wars* films are among their descendants) offered tales of adventure in intergalactic space and on exotic worlds and epic struggles between good and evil, with the experimental dimensions of an earlier transnational science fiction kept to a minimum. Equally significantly, Gernsback helped create the first "fan" communities, primarily young men and boys interested in science and technology and intent on producing their own cultural argot.

The full flourishing of magazine science fiction took place under the direction of another editor, John W. Campbell. Campbell's *Astounding Science-Fiction* inaugurated in the 1930s what is referred to as science fiction's "Golden Age." The writers Campbell brought to prominence – Isaac Asimov, Robert Heinlein, L. Ron Hubbard, Murray Leinster, Theodore Sturgeon, A. E. Van Vogt, and others – continued to produce significant work in the postwar period, and still remain some of the genre's most well known. Campbell demanded a more rigorous grounding in scientific knowledge (also thereby creating the basis for the subgenre of "hard science fiction," exemplified by such US writers as Hal Clement and Larry Niven and, more recently, Gregory Benford and Kim Stanley Robinson). Moreover, these writers expressed a tremendous faith in science, rationality, and technology as "the privileged solution to the world's ills."[4] Two examples of this view are evident in, first, Van Vogt's short story "Black Destroyer" – published as the cover story for the July 1939 issue of *Astounding* that is considered to be the watershed moment of the Golden Age – wherein an apparently unstoppable alien menace is overcome only through humanity's superior knowledge. Similarly, Asimov's epic *Foundation* trilogy, published in book form between 1951 and 1953 by combining stories that appeared earlier, presents a future history in which a scientific elite helps humanity move out of an interplanetary Dark Age.

Dystopia, apocalypse, and the Cold War (1950s)

After the war the landscape of US science fiction changed in significant ways. A leading factor lay in changes in publishing practices: although science fiction magazines continued to flourish after the war – including, beginning in 1950, *Galaxy Science Fiction*, which first published such significant work as Heinlein's classic of Cold War paranoia, *The Puppet Masters* (1951) – the growing market for cheap paperback fiction shifted more and more work back into the novel form. Another, more literary, catalyst for change was the British writer George Orwell's *Nineteen Eighty-Four* (1949). Following Orwell's lead, the 1950s witnessed a resurgence of dystopian fiction – what

Kingsley Amis in an early influential study called the "new maps of hell" – exemplified by Ray Bradbury's *Fahrenheit 451* and Frederick Pohl and C. M. Kornbluth's *The Space Merchants* (both from 1953). Both novels offered visions of an anti-intellectual consumer society along the lines of Aldous Huxley's *Brave New World* (1932).[5]

Two other writers who are central to American letters in the postwar decades published dystopias: Vladimir Nabokov's *Bend Sinister* (1947) was his second English-language book, while *Player Piano* (1952) was Kurt Vonnegut's first novel. Vonnegut would later publish other science fiction, including *The Sirens of Titan* (1959), *Cat's Cradle* (1963), and *Slaughterhouse-Five* (1969). In these writers, we see the earliest signs of a development that would be crucial to postmodern fiction, as the boundaries separating this popular form and high art become increasingly blurred, something also evident in the work of William Burroughs, Thomas Pynchon, and Jonathan Lethem. Moreover, if we consider North America more broadly, the Canadian writer Margaret Atwood has written significant works of science fiction, including the dystopias *The Handmaid's Tale* (1985) and *Oryx and Crake* (2003).

The re-emergence of dystopian science fiction bore out the ways that both World War II and the Cold War, with its threat of an even more devastating global conflict, had deeply shaken the confidence in progress, science, and technology that had been a hallmark of Golden Age science fiction. Another development that signaled this changed landscape was the increasingly influential post-apocalypse novels. An early masterpiece, *Earth Abides* (1949), was written by George R. Stewart, an English professor at the University of California at Berkeley. In following the adventures of a survivor of a devastating plague, Stewart's novel revives the apocalyptic sensibility that had been prominent in the late nineteenth century, in works such as J. A. Mitchell's *The Last American* (1899). Also significant is Richard Matheson's *I Am Legend* (1954), which treats the theme of a biological catastrophe in a more spectacular vein.

Other notable works in this subgenre include Andre Norton's *Daybreak 2250 A.D.* (1952), Leigh Brackett's *The Long Tomorrow* (1955), and Walter M. Miller's *A Canticle for Leibowitz* (1959). These novels imagine worlds that in the aftermath of a devastating nuclear war regress to earlier historical cultures – nomadic tribes, Mennonites, and European medieval monastic communities. Miller's novel was also one of the few works, along with James Blish's *A Case of Conscience* (1958), to deal in this period directly with religion. Others, like Pat Frank's *Alas, Babylon* (1959), portray nuclear war in a more positive vein, as clearing away a debilitating contemporary culture. Similarly, while Judith Merril's "That Only a Mother" (1948) emphasized the destructive aspects of radiation-induced mutations, Sturgeon's moving *More Than Human* (1953) reframes mutations as part of human evolution, a trope that would be taken up a decade later in the superhero renaissance begun by Stan Lee's *Marvel* comics.

Transitions: Bradbury, Bester, and Dick

During the same early Cold War period, more attention was paid to the social and psychological impact of modernity and to the development of complex character psychology, giving rise to what would be known as "soft" science fiction. One of the first masterpieces was Bradbury's *The Martian Chronicles* (1950), a novel detailing the consequences for humanity of the colonization of the red planet. Of the significance of Bradbury's work, David Pringle notes, "He put far more emphasis on style and mood than he did on technical detail or scientific plausibility, thus offending the already hardening sensibilities of editors and writers who had grown up with the American sf magazines … despite opposition from certain quarters, his work became an example to many younger writers."[6]

Another author who would deeply influence postwar science fiction was Alfred Bester. Bester's two science fiction novels of the 1950s, *The Demolished Man* (1953) and *The Stars My Destination* (1956), mark his greatest influence on the genre. The first winner of the Annual Science Fiction Achievement Award (better known as the Hugo Award), *The Demolished Man* tells a tale of twenty-fourth-century corporate intrigue in a world where telepathy has become a significant part of everyday life. Even more dramatically diverging from conventional pulp formulas, Bester's *The Stars My Destination* – set in a future Earth where teleportation, or "jaunting," has become a common practice – comes to "a spectacular synaesthetic climax in which towers of drunken typography totter across the page," a formal experiment that recalls earlier surrealist efforts (or more directly in science fiction, those of the Czech author Karel Čapek's *The War with the Newts* [1936]) and looks forward to the experimentalism that becomes prevalent again in subsequent decades.[7] Bester's contributions to the genre were cut short by his decision to abandon the form for the more lucrative markets of magazine nonfiction and television.

The writer considered to be the most important to emerge in the 1950s, Philip K. Dick, unlike Bester published the majority of his output in science fiction. Dick – whom Fredric Jameson names "the Shakespeare of Science Fiction" (making Bester the genre's Christopher Marlowe) and who is the only science fiction writer included in the Library of America – wrote hundreds of short stories and dozens of novels ranging widely across the genre's forms.[8] For example, *The Penultimate Truth* (1964), an expansion of his early short story "The Defenders" (1953), and *Dr. Bloodmoney* (1965) are set in the aftermath of nuclear wars. His Hugo Award-winning *The Man in the High Castle* (1962) is a marvelous example of the alternate history, or "what if" story, that depicts a United States divided between German and Japanese occupation forces after the nation's defeat in World War II. However, it was Dick's rich and diverse visions of near-future worlds dominated by corporations and the state – *Martian Time-Slip* (1964), *The Three Stigmata of Palmer Eldritch* (1965), *Do Androids Dream of Electric Sheep?* (1968), *Ubik* (1969), and *Flow My Tears, the Policeman Said* (1974), among others – that would most influence both the genre's development and, especially through film adaptations such as Ridley Scott's *Blade Runner* (1982), Paul Verhoeven's *Total Recall* (1990), Steven Spielberg's *Minority Report* (2002), and Richard Linklater's *A Scanner Darkly* (2006), popular culture at large. Moreover, Dick's blurring of the boundaries between the human and the machine, and the real and virtual worlds, would be foundational to later cyberpunk fiction and theorizations of postmodernism.

New Wave and new directions (1960s–1970s)

The work of these postwar writers set the stage for the next great period in science fiction history, upon which another group of British authors, the so-called "New Wave," championed in North America by the editor Judith Merril, would have a major influence. The New Wave included such figures as Brian Aldiss, John Brunner, Michael Moorcock, Norman Spinrad, and, most importantly, J. G. Ballard, who, as Rob Latham notes, articulated "a program of renovation that would shift the genre's focus from the soaring vistas of interstellar space to the convoluted mental landscapes of an encroaching modernity."[9] Although older practices would continue in the jumbled and uneven non-synchronicity characteristic of any period, these years witnessed a revolution in the genre as writers became more willing to experiment with form and to tackle the period's political turbulence, offering brilliant critiques of bureaucracy, consumerism, environmental spoilage, gender and racial inequality, the Vietnam War, and a host of other previously taboo issues. As a result the genre's audience grew, encompassing many in the burgeoning youth movements. Even well-established writers were "rediscovered" by a countercultural audience, as was Heinlein with the publication of *Stranger in a Strange Land* (1961). Heinlein's libertarian political views are even more evident in his gripping *The Moon Is a Harsh Mistress* (1966), a narrative concerning a supercomputer-assisted rebellion of a moon colony.

Some of the writers who rose to prominence as part of the New Wave in the United States include Harlan Ellison, who penned the short story, "I Have No Mouth, and I Must Scream" (1967), and scripts for the science fiction television series *The Outer Limits* (1963–1965) upon which the *Terminator* films were based, as well as the script for what is considered the best episode of the *Star Trek* series (1966–1969), "The City on the Edge of Forever." Ellison also edited the landmark *Dangerous Visions* anthologies (1967, 1972) showcasing the work of many New Wave writers. Frank Herbert's *Dune* (1965), and its various sequels, placed ecological concerns centrally within the genre's purview, while also introducing its readers to the Islamic term "jihad." Thomas Disch's *Camp Concentration* (1968), set in a world where a Robert McNamara-led United States has declared global war, is, along with Ursula K. Le Guin's *The Word for World Is Forest* (1972) and Joe Haldeman's *The Forever War* (1974), one of the great science fiction allegories of the Vietnam War. Robert Silverberg's career entered a renaissance after he was given free rein to experiment by magazine editor Pohl, resulting in three novels in three years: a retelling of Joseph Conrad's *Heart of Darkness* in *Downward to Earth* (1970); *A Time of Changes* (1971); and a telepathy novel, *Dying Inside* (1972). Barry N. Malzberg's *Beyond Apollo* (1972) offered a satirical take on the US space program. Finally, Gene Wolfe's *The Fifth Head of Cerberus* (1972) lyrically reflected on anthropological and colonial relationships with the Other.

Another significant writer to emerge from the New Wave was Samuel R. Delany, Jr. Delany both continues many of the genre's classic practices, as in his space opera, *Nova* (1968), and advances the formal experimentation and challenging themes of New Wave science fiction, as in his Nebula Award-winning *Babel-17* (1966) and *The Einstein Intersection* (1967), the former drawing upon the Sapir–Whorf hypothesis in a story about intergalactic war and the latter retelling the Orpheus myth in a far-future Earth inhabited by an alien species. Moreover, Delany is a scholar well versed in contemporary theory, and he often incorporates these ideas into his work. For example, his utopia, *Triton* (1976), is subtitled, after Michel Foucault, "an ambiguous heterotopia." Equally importantly, as the first major African American and later one of the few openly gay science fiction writers – the latter made explicit in his brilliant and complex *Stars in My Pocket Like Grains of Sand* (1984) – Delany helped open the door for a new diversity in the genre.

It was in this period, too, that women writers began to have increasing influence. Although a handful of women – including Merril, C. L. Moore (whose story "Greater Than Gods" also appeared in the July 1939 issue of *Astounding*), Brackett, Carol Emshwiller, Andre Norton (Alice Mary Norton), and James Tiptree, Jr. (Alice Sheldon) – did publish memorable work early on, it would not be until the later 1960s that women writers would take up prominence in the genre, often with works that dealt directly with gender and sexuality.[10] Some of these writers include Anne McCaffrey, Vonda McIntyre, Suzy McKee Charnas, Marge Piercy, and Joanna Russ.

The most important writer from this group was Le Guin. The daughter of anthropologists Arthur and Theodora Kroeber, Le Guin brought a new depth of attention to the portrayal of alien cultures. Jameson names Le Guin's central technical device, *world reduction*, as "based on a principle of systematic exclusion, a kind of surgical excision of empirical reality."[11] *The Left Hand of Darkness* (1969) is exemplary in this regard, as it tells of a species whose sexual biology is radically different from our own, and who lack our fixed gender divisions. Le Guin also wrote *The Dispossessed* (1974), one of the significant new science fiction utopias to appear in this period. Some of the other important American contributions to this revival include Mack Reynolds's *Looking Backward, from the Year 2000* (1973), Russ's *The Female Man* (1975), Ernest Callenbach's *Ecotopia* (1975), and Piercy's *Woman on the Edge of Time* (1976), as well as Le Guin's later *Always Coming Home* (1985).[12] Both *The Left Hand of Darkness* and *The Dispossessed* are part of Le Guin's interplanetary Hainish cycle, which also encompasses her earliest published novels, *The Word for World Is Forest*, stories reprinted in the collection *The Wind's Twelve Quarters* (1975), and, more recently, *Four Ways to Forgiveness* (1995) and *The Telling* (2000).

A number of these writers also helped reform the genre of heroic fantasy, brought to prominence by the British writer J. R. R. Tolkien in his *Lord of the Rings* trilogy (1954–1955). Tolkien explicitly posited fantasy as antithetical to science fiction, stating that the genre "may, almost certainly does, proceed from a considered disgust for ... the Robot Age."[13] These later writers both blurred the distinctions between fantasy and a harder science fiction and opened the often conservative form to other ends. Some of the most significant new fantasy fiction of this period includes McCaffrey's *Dragonriders of Pern* works, Le Guin's *Earthsea* novels, Delany's *Return to Nevèryon* series, Charles R. Saunders's *Imaro* novels, Roger Zelazny's *Chronicles of Amber* series, and Wolfe's far future, *Book of the New Sun*. The far-future narrative is also the purview of one of the most idiosyncratic postwar short-story writers, Cordwainer Smith, beginning with his haunting "Scanners Live in Vain" (1950).

Finally, it was in this moment that a serious and sustained scholarly attention to science fiction emerged. The first courses devoted to the genre appeared on US college campuses, important early studies were published, and the two most significant journals devoted to the genre, *Extrapolation* (1959) and *Science-Fiction Studies* (1973), began their long runs. The latter in particular, under the editorship of Darko Suvin (whose definition of the genre as the "literature of cognitive estrangement" remains a touchstone of all discussions of the form), helped bring a new rigor and sophistication to science fiction's study.[14]

Postmodernism, cyberpunk, critical dystopia, and post-Cold War science fiction (1980s–present)

By the end of the 1970s, the energies of the New Wave moment had been spent, and the conservative counter-assault of the 1980s created an environment less hospitable to formal experimentations and dangerous visions. This was the context from which emerged "cyberpunk" fiction. Although Bruce Sterling, author of *Schismatrix* (1985) and *Islands in the Net* (1988), took on the role of spokesperson, it was the US–Canadian writer William Gibson who emerged as cyberpunk's leading practitioner. Gibson's place in the science fiction canon was secured with his debut novel, *Neuromancer* (1984), the first part of a trilogy that also includes *Count Zero* (1986) and *Mona Lisa Overdrive* (1988). These novels presented urbanized worlds where corporations have displaced nation-states, thriving black markets trade in biotechnologies, and hip freelance data "cowboys" sell their services to the highest bidder. A similar vision of the near future is evident in *Blade Runner*; however, Gibson goes beyond the film in envisioning a digitally constructed "cyberspace" existing alongside the physical environment. Rejecting the optimism of pre-World War II science fiction – something made explicit in Gibson's "The Gernsback Continuum" (1981) (the lead story in the Sterling-edited *Mirrorshades: The Cyberpunk Anthology* [1986]) – and equally cool on New Wave radicalism, cyberpunk proved to be a perfect fit for a Thatcher–Reagan-era sensibility. (Other science fiction writers would become directly involved in conservative politics as members of Reagan's Citizens' Advisory Panel on National Space Policy, which helped formulate the infamous Strategic Defense Initiative [SDI], or "Star Wars" policy.)[15] Moreover, in its brilliant figurations of information technologies, its suspicion of welfare-state policies, and its poaching from a wide range of genres, most prominently *noir*, cyberpunk emerged as exemplary postmodernist fiction more generally.[16]

Other writers associated with the movement include Pat Cadigan, John Shirley, Lewis Shiner, Rudy Rucker, and Neal Stephenson, the latter's *Snow Crash* (1992) and *The Diamond Age* (1996) representing some of the most interesting science fiction of the early 1990s. Gibson's own work continued in new directions, as he first co-authored with Sterling a Victorian-era alternate history, *The Difference Engine* (1990), which popularized the subgenre of "steampunk" and then another near-future trilogy drawing upon the urban commentaries of Mike Davis.

Less recognized at the time, a rejoinder to cyberpunk emerged in the later 1980s, in novels Tom Moylan names "critical dystopias": these include Piercy's *He, She, and It* (1991) and works by the two most important US writers to rise to prominence in this period, Kim Stanley Robinson and Octavia Butler (and to Moylan's list we might also add Kathy Acker, whose experimental *Empire of the Senseless* [1988] offers an explicit critique of Gibson's work).[17] Moylan focuses on Robinson's *The Gold Coast* (1988), the second novel – framed by *The Wild Shore* (1984) and *Pacific Edge* (1990) – in his "Three Californias" trilogy, which portrays different possible futures for Robinson's home in Southern California. However, it was his next trilogy, *Red Mars* (1992), *Green Mars* (1993), and *Blue Mars* (1996) – an exploration of the terraforming and settlement of the red planet – that established Robinson as one of the most important contemporary science fiction writers. Robinson's work is unique in that it combines a hard science fiction sensibility with the complex plotlines of Dick and the radical sensibilities of 1960s science fiction. Robinson's outlook is shaped in part by his experiences as a student at the University of California, San Diego, where he studied with Jameson and later wrote a dissertation entitled "The Novels of Philip K. Dick" (1984). Robinson's concerns with ecology, begun in the Three Californias and Mars trilogies, continue in both *Antarctica* (1997) and his "Science in the Capital" trilogy, *Forty Signs of Rain* (2004), *Fifty Degrees Below* (2005), and *Sixty Days and Counting* (2006); and his exploration of intellectuals is further developed in his rich alternate history, *The Years of Rice and Salt* (2002) and *Galileo's Dream* (2009). (The latter novel also recalls R. A. Lafferty's unjustly forgotten *Past Master* [1968].) Other writers who emerge in this moment and take up ecological concerns are Sheri Tepper, author of the brilliant *Grass* (1989), and Terry Bisson, author of "Bears Discover Fire" (1990), *Voyage to the Red Planet* (1990), and the alternate history, *Fire on the Mountain* (1988).

Butler, the first science fiction writer to receive a MacArthur Genius Grant, was also a child of Southern California. Butler's debut novel, *Patternmaster* (1976), would serve as the final volume in her "Patternist" series, preceded chronologically by *Wild Seed* (1980), *Mind of My Mind* (1977), *Clay's Ark* (1984), and *Survivor* (1978). Already evident are many of Butler's major themes, including African American experience, the disorienting effects of wide-scale social change, and biological and genetic engineering. Her novel, *Kindred* (1979), uses the science fiction device of time travel to explore the crippling effects of slavery. Similarly, her most celebrated trilogy, "Lilith's Brood" or "Xenogenesis" – *Dawn* (1987),

Adulthood Rites (1988), and *Imago* (1989) – tells the story of the encounter of the human survivors of a nuclear war with an alien species that initiates the genetic exchanges they deem necessary for humanity's survival. The trilogy offers a complex allegory of the Civil Rights struggle, and also influenced Donna J. Haraway's theorization of the cyborg.[18] (A different contemporary treatment of the alien-encounter theme occurs in Orson Scott Card's Enders series, beginning with *Ender's Game* [1985], a work that revives the militaristic science fiction of Heinlein's *Starship Troopers* [1959] and Larry Niven and Jerry Pournelle's *The Mote in God's Eye* [1974].) Butler's critical dystopias, *Parable of the Sower* (1993) and *Parable of the Talents* (1999), offer devastating critiques of neoliberal violence and religious fundamentalism while also exploring the formation of alternative kinship structures.[19] This last theme is also central to Butler's final novel, *Fledgling* (2005).

Science fiction in the post-Cold War 1990s becomes one of the most effective ways for coming to grips with what commentators increasingly refer to as globalization. Some of the works that take up this task are Haldeman's multiple-award-winning *Forever Peace* (1997); Robinson's *The Years of Rice and Salt* and Steven Barnes's alternate histories *Lion's Blood* (2002) and *Zulu Heart* (2003); the so-called New Space Operas, of which Dan Simmons's *Hyperion* (1989) and its sequels are exemplary; and Gibson's *Pattern Recognition* (2003), a novel that also was among the first to treat explicitly the events of September 11, 2001. The Jamaican-born Canadian writer Nalo Hopkinson – author of *Brown Girl in the Ring* (1998), *Midnight Robber* (2000), and the folk fantasy *The Salt Roads* (2003), as well as the editor of a number of significant collections – and the Granada-born Tobias S. Buckell – who has written *Crystal Rain* (2006), *Ragamuffin* (2007), and *Sly Mongoose* (2008) – further expand the genre's range by incorporating elements from Caribbean cultures.

Contemporary science fiction also continues to investigate the impact of new media technologies on our world. Vernor Vinge's early *True Names* (1981) offered the first fully realized portrait of cyberspace, and his later works, *A Fire Upon the Deep* (1992), *A Deepness in the Sky* (1999), and *Fast Times at Fairmont High* (2002), speculate on the Singularity, the "moment at which the creation of a superhuman, machine-based intelligence will result in 'a regime as radically different from our human past as we humans are from animals'."[20] Vinge's earlier *Marooned in Real Time* (1986) is a prominent example of the "small but growing SF subgenre" of the post-Singularity novel, more recently represented by Rucker's *Postsingular* (2007) and *Hylozoic* (2009) and the Canadian author and digital-rights activist, Cory Doctorow's *Down and Out in the Magic Kingdom* (2003).[21]

Hopkinson and Doctorow are part of an increasingly influential group of younger Canadian science fiction writers, which also includes Peter Watts and Karl Schroeder. Similarly, the last two decades have witnessed another renaissance in British science fiction. These developments signal the ways that, while exceptional science fiction is still being produced in the United States, the postwar American hegemony over the genre has come to an end. Contemporary science fiction thus not only represents one of the most important cultural forms for thinking about globalization, but also serves as a significant aspect of an emerging global culture.

FURTHER READING

Barr, Marleen S. *Afro-Future Females: Black Writers Chart Science Fiction's Newest New Wave Trajectory*. Columbus: Ohio State University Press, 2008
  Feminist Fabulation: Space/Postmodern Fiction. University of Iowa Press, 1992
Booker, M. Keith and Anne-Marie Thomas. *The Science Fiction Handbook*. Oxford: Wiley-Blackwell, 2009
Freedman, Carl. *Critical Theory and Science Fiction*. Hanover, NH: Wesleyan University Press, 2000
McCaffery, Larry (ed.). *Storming the Reality Studio: A Casebook of Cyberpunk and Postmodern Science Fiction*. Durham, NC: Duke University Press, 1992
Moylan, Tom. *Demand the Impossible: Science Fiction and the Utopian Imagination*. London: Methuen, 1986
Seed, David (ed.). *A Companion to Science Fiction*. Oxford: Blackwell, 2005
Suvin, Darko. *Positions and Presuppositions in Science Fiction*. Kent, OH: Kent State University Press, 1988
Wegner, Phillip E. *Ontologies of the Possible: Science Fiction, Utopia, and Globalization*. Oxford: Peter Lang, forthcoming

NOTES

1 Pascale Casanova, *The World Republic of Letters*, trans. M. B. Debevoise (Cambridge, MA: Harvard University Press, 2004).
2 Roger Luckhurst, *Science Fiction* (Cambridge: Polity Press, 2005), p. 46.
3 Gary Westfahl, *The Mechanics of Wonder: The Creation of the Idea of Science Fiction* (Liverpool University Press, 1998), p. 28.
4 Peter Fitting, "The Modern Anglo-American SF Novel: Utopian Longing and Capitalist Cooptation," *Science Fiction Studies*, 17 (1979): 60.
5 Kingsley Amis, *New Maps of Hell: A Survey of Science Fiction* (London: Gollancz, 1961).
6 David Pringle, *Science Fiction, The 100 Best Novels: An English-Language Selection, 1949–1984* (London: Xanadu, 1985), pp. 25–6.
7 Ibid., p. 60.
8 Fredric Jameson, *Archaeologies of the Future: The Desire Called Utopia and Other Science Fictions* (New York: Verso, 2005), p. 345.

9   Rob Latham, "The New Wave," in David Seed (ed.), *A Companion to Science Fiction* (Oxford: Blackwell, 2005), p. 209.

10 Lisa Yaszek, *Galactic Suburbia: Recovering Women's Science Fiction* (Columbus: Ohio State University Press, 2008).

11 Jameson, *Archaeologies of the Future*, p. 271.

12 Tom Moylan, *Demand the Impossible: Science Fiction and the Utopian Imagination* (London: Methuen, 1986).

13 Luckhurst, *Science Fiction*, p. 11.

14 Darko Suvin, *Metamorphoses of Science Fiction: On the Poetics and History of a Literary Genre* (New Haven: Yale University Press, 1979), p. 4.

15 Luckhurst, *Science Fiction*, pp. 199–200.

16 Brian McHale, *Constructing Postmodernism* (London: Routledge, 1992).

17 Tom Moylan, *Scraps of the Untainted Sky: Science Fiction, Utopia, Dystopia* (Boulder, CO: Westview Press, 2001).

18 Donna J. Haraway, *Simians, Cyborgs, and Women: The Reinvention of Nature* (New York: Routledge, 1991), pp. 179 and 225–30.

19 I treat Butler's *Parable* novels in more detail in Wegner, Phillip E., *Life Between Two Deaths, 1989–2001: U.S. Culture in the Long Nineties* (Durham, NC: Duke University Press, 2009), ch. 8.

20 Steven Shaviro, *Connected: Or What It Means to Live in a Network Society* (Minneapolis: University of Minnesota Press, 2003), p. 120.

21 Steven Shaviro, "The Singularity is Here," in Mark Bould and China Miéville (eds.), *Red Planets: Marxism and Science Fiction* (London: Pluto Press, 2009), p. 103.

5

SUSAN LOHAFER

The short story

In Paris, on August 25, 1944, a trim, dark-eyed survivor of the Utah Beach landing sat down for a drink with a burly war correspondent who had written very famously about an earlier world war.[1] At the time of this meeting, Jerome David Salinger was twenty-five years old, struggling to break into the exclusive pages of *The New Yorker*. At forty-five, Ernest Hemingway had already immortalized the psychic wounds of war and, along with James Joyce and Sherwood Anderson, had reinvented the short story as a modernist art form: spare and concrete, yet riddled with meaning. On the popular front, the slick magazines were publishing upbeat, neatly turned consumable fiction well into the 1940s. Salinger's clever potboilers, closer in spirit to F. Scott Fitzgerald's society sketches than to Hemingway's "Lost Generation" tales, had appeared in venues like *Collier's*. Hemingway knew of Salinger and praised a story the younger man showed him. Perhaps he caught a glimpse of the fallout to come.

In 1948 Salinger's gently explosive story, "A Perfect Day for Bananafish," appeared in *The New Yorker*. Its hero, Seymour Glass, showing signs of what today would be called post-traumatic stress disorder, is on his honeymoon in Florida. Through an introductory conversation between the nail-polishing wife and her badgering mother, Salinger deftly characterizes the superficiality of postwar America. Seymour delights in puncturing complacency with antic non sequiturs. Alienated from a world that finds him mentally unstable, he strikes up an alliance with a six-year-old on the beach. Her innocent candor and responsive curiosity are balm to his soul. Together they search for the imaginary "bananafish," which dies from gorging itself on the yellow fruit – a fanciful analogy for a bloated society. He is charmed and bemused, but the escape is short-lived. When Seymour once again meets reality in the form of his dozing wife – "Miss Spiritual Tramp of 1948" – he calmly and deliberately shoots himself in the head.

Unlike Hemingway's "Big Two-Hearted River," a 1925 story about another fragile veteran, Salinger's tale offers no healing return to nature, no code of male fellowship. Instead it captures a yearning attraction to the incorruptible, the quirkily imaginative, that would dominate his first collection, *Nine Stories* (1953). Schooled in the light fiction of his day, Salinger had learned how to spin clever dialogue, zero in on a telling moment, and finger a heartstring. However, it was his blend of dead-on satire and lovable eccentricity – a tangy ache of the spirit – that gave his most memorable stories ("Uncle Wiggily in Connecticut," "For Esmé – With Love and Squalor," and "Pretty Mouth and Green My Eyes") a tonal synergy that was new and inimitable. Later readers might charge him with romantic self-indulgence and eventual single-mindedness. Nevertheless, "A Perfect Day for Bananafish" remains a seminal document in the history of the American short story in the second half of the twentieth century.

To understand why, it is convenient to look at another, more famous story also published by *The New Yorker* in the same year – Shirley Jackson's "The Lottery." Arguably the most anthologized story in the twentieth-century American canon, this less-than-3400-word tale is one of the most streamlined and resonant in modern-day English. Earlier in the century, nearing the heyday of the wide-circulation weeklies where many of Jackson's stories would be published, the short-story form had sometimes been regarded as a cheap bag of tricks. In 1923 N. Bryllion Fagin deplored "O. Henryism," associated then as now with the manipulative "surprise ending" favored by William Sydney Porter. Fagin hoped someone would save the genre from impending death-by-formula. Sherwood Anderson and Ernest Hemingway had already stepped up, but it was probably their contemporary, F. Scott Fitzgerald, vacillating between commercial fiction and lasting art, who proved the vitality of the magazine culture from which, in the late 1940s, "A Perfect Day for Bananafish" and "The Lottery" could emerge. Each tale builds with deceptive mildness to a violent conclusion that would have stunned Mr. Porter. Both stories signal the future role of *The New Yorker* as the premier venue for the genre; both tales move a "popular" genre into a more ambitious orbit where it would remain – with important exceptions – a satellite of the novel; and both are shadowed, as were the times themselves, by the mid-century Holocaust.

Jackson's story is set in a nameless, New England-style village. With implacable ordinariness, arrangements begin for an annual event that is an ancient tradition in the rural community. A busy housewife is the last straggler to join the assembled villagers for a yearly lottery to ensure a good harvest. Rereading the tale, one spots the innocuous details that should have seemed strange, but the guile of the story is its neighborly air. By the time the true nature of the lottery is revealed and its victim identified, Jackson's readers, like the generations of quiescent townspeople in the story (and, in the real world, those who normalize evil), have been swept into the primal darkness of ritualized human sacrifice.

Although both Salinger's and Jackson's stories end in a death that sends a message, they are strikingly different in style and sensibility. In retrospect, they are the yin and yang of the American short story after World War II. In Salinger's lament for a tender soul with nowhere to go but oblivion, there is a precedent for the story as an imprint of personality, an unspooling of impressions and reactions that are their own validation, inseparable from the focal character. Salinger is the guru of wounded self-expression, where form renders feeling. By contrast, Jackson's hard-edged narrative projects a confidence in the artist's power to wrest meaning from chaos, to shape and exhibit a paradigm of truth. Hers is the genius of profound simplicity, of gnomic design. As the years undo the century, the short story can be seen in the forefront, veering at times toward the urgency of the lyric, at times toward the polish of the riddle, but cognizant of both.

Important as *The New Yorker* would be to the status of short fiction, the development of the genre was really fostered by the "little" maga- zines, especially those sponsored by colleges or universities in the South. The *Virginia Quarterly* (1925) was joined by the *Southern Review* (1935), edited by Southern realist Robert Penn Warren with Cleanth Brooks, one of New Criticism's foundational theorists. The *Kenyon Review* (1939) was overseen by another key figure in New Criticism, John Crowe Ransom, who had taught Brooks and Warren at Vanderbilt. Self-consciously liter- ary, the editors of these quarterlies had a taste for the intricate imagery, strong sense of locality, subtly managed tone, looser plot structure, and embedded meaning that the New Critics would valorize from the 1940s through the 1960s. Not surprisingly, the writers they championed were mostly from the South.

Oldest among these was Katherine Anne Porter (1890–1980), who appeared in the first issue of the *Southern Review*. In 1941, she would write the introduction to a collection of short stories by her protégée, Eudora Welty, whose stories were "discovered" by that magazine and would appear seven times in its pages. In another manifestation of her influence, Porter's short novel *Noon Wine* impressed fellow Southerner Flannery O'Connor during her student days at the Iowa Writers' Workshop. The younger woman's stor- ies began appearing in another Southern periodical, the *Sewanee Review*, edited in the mid-1940s by another two students of Ransom – Andrew Lytle and Allen Tate. These men, like Salinger, were nay-sayers, retreating from the shoddiness of the modern urban world after the war, turning also toward Eastern mysticism but much more importantly toward the South's agrarian past, tightly knit communities, and traditions of oral storytelling.

Porter, in her elbow-length gloves, was a holdover from High Modernism. Briefly an expatriate in Mexico, she later reclaimed her Southern past. "The Grave," first published in the *Virginia Quarterly* in 1935, became part of a sequence of early stories reappearing as "The Old Order" in the Pulitzer Prize-winning *Collected Stories* of 1965. In terms of influence if not chronology, this deft, sensitive vignette about a Texas girl's childhood belongs to the postwar resurgence of the genre.

A similar lyricism can be found in a number of Eudora Welty's stories in *The Curtain of Green* (1941), *The Wide Net* (1943), and *The Golden Apples* (1949). She was alert to the eccentricities of her regional culture but often embedded Greek mythology as well as the local folklore of the Natchez Trace into the allusive descriptions, exuberant dialogue, and small-town drama of her place-conscious stories. They range widely in subject matter and style, across boundaries of age and race, to include the dreamily lyrical ("A Memory," "The Wide Net"), the rigorously anecdotal ("Why I Live at the P. O."), the amusingly grotesque ("Petrified Man"), and the jazzily experimental ("Powerhouse" – about a black pianist whose music and life are a dual lament transcribed into prose). Invited readings, deferential interviews, short-term teaching positions, and frequent anthologizing turned Welty, like Porter before her, into a one-woman literary establishment founded on an oeuvre of short fiction.

The same path awaited Flannery O'Connor, had she not died at thirty-nine. Leaning more toward the paradigmatic and tough-minded form of Jackson's "The Lottery," O'Connor's stories combined a devastatingly accurate ear and eye for the comedy of local manners with a scouring outlook on modern society from the unusual perspective of a Southern Catholic. Typically, her Protestant characters are mired in the everyday but illusory world of the rational and the physical, only to be shocked into an awareness of divine grace when it arrives in the form of a violent blow, forcibly revealing the transcendence of spirit.

In "A Good Man Is Hard to Find," an average family, with delightfully banal parents, misbehaving children, and a heritage-proud grandmother, sets out on a car trip. Selective details pin each character to his or her shallow essence with entertaining panache, but this family is on a serious journey. News of an escaped criminal, "The Misfit," titillates their fears, but they are oblivious to their danger – as are all complacent souls in O'Connor's world – until a concatenation of human frailties and sudden accidents lands their car in a ditch. The Misfit and his companions seize the car for their getaway, first disposing of the family. With chilling efficiency, the dazed parents and children are led off into the woods to be shot. Left alone with The Misfit, the grandmother remains locked in assumptions of privilege and a sentimentally redemptive Christianity that the killer fiercely challenges. Then a premonition overtakes her and she reaches out, mistaking The Misfit for her son. Reflexively, he shoots her, mildly concluding, with a harsh wisdom beyond his understanding, that she "would of been a good woman … if it had been somebody there to shoot her every minute of her life."[2] Death is often the accompaniment of grace in O'Connor's stories.

This shocked-awakening plot is reincarnated in many of the stories, making for the sort of end-directed and message-bound structure associated with the parable or exemplum. Long before the 1971 publication of *The Complete Stories*, O'Connor had repositioned the short story as a major literary genre with ties to the local-color regionalism of the nineteenth century and to the postwar disaffection with materialism. Southern writers Carson McCullers and Peter Taylor (with a steady output of high-quality short fiction into the 1990s) deserve mention too, as does the more northerly spinner of more forgiving Catholic tales, J. F. Powers.

While the South was responding to the postwar era by re-examining its heritage, the mid-Atlantic and Northern portions of the country were discovering a new American dream: the suburban life of commuter trains and cocktail parties. The reality of spiritual confusion, marital dysfunction, and the new consumerism fueled the work of two artists initially identified with the understated, nuanced, "slice-of-life" norms of *New Yorker* fiction: John Cheever and John Updike. Cheever's métier is the small family group (parents, children, maid, and the babysitter who frees the parents for social activity) within an upper-middle-class neighborhood like Shady Hill (a recurring locale), or a rabbit-warren apartment building in the city from which the tenants might hope to migrate to a home with a lawn. Drawing upon the moral anxieties of an enervated Puritan tradition, the elemental naturalism of a buried pagan instinct, and the wry objectivity of a social realist, Cheever created stories in which pathos and humor blend in bemused irony. Unlike J. D. Salinger (whose *Nine Stories* upstaged Cheever's first significant collection, also published in 1953), Cheever found no anchor in a surrogate family like the mythical Glass clan. Unlike Flannery O'Connor (whose first collection, *A Good Man Is Hard to Find*, came out in 1955), he had religious yearnings without a firm and sustaining religion. Instead, he found inspiration in ambivalence, and, in each story, set his teeth anew into the flesh of the apple.

His best-known early story, "The Enormous Radio," is a surreal, Hawthornesque parable revealing the hidden sordidness of outwardly respectable lives in a Manhattan apartment building. In his skepticism about middle-class values, Cheever is as critical of pretension as Salinger, and many of his stories, like "The Housebreaker of Shady Hill," are open-ended explorations of conflicting impulses; however, in his most famous story – "The Swimmer" (*New Yorker*, July 18, 1964) – he tends toward the paradigmatic form of "The Lottery." At a party with hungover friends, Neddy Merrill, a self-deluded former athlete, decides to "swim" his way home through the swimming pools of the neighborhood, but soon notices uncanny signs that seasons have changed and years have passed since he took the first plunge. The story has a taut and evocative journey-structure, an ingeniously fast-forwarded time-frame, and eerily symbolic details. Cheever's tragicomic hero ends his journey looking into the window of his own foreclosed and empty home, a 1950s version of *nada*. In 1979, *The Stories of John Cheever* won the Pulitzer Prize for Fiction (one of the few books of *short* fiction to win since the genre became eligible in 1948), finding a new audience for his chronicles of dislocation, rendered in prose that is formal, supple, buoyant, wry, meditative, and shot through from time to time with a rhapsodic vein of pageantry, a glint of archaically pure sensuousness. Here is the last line of "Goodbye, My Brother," about two middle-aged people on a dour New England beach: "and I saw that they were naked, unshy, beautiful, and full of grace, and I watched the naked women walk out of the sea."[3]

Verbal felicity is the hallmark of John Updike, the writer most often paired with Cheever, both in the pages of *The New Yorker* and in literary history. Characteristically leaving no insight to chance, Updike, in the "Foreword" to *The Early Stories: 1953–1975* (2003), noted his debt to Salinger, who, in the transitional 1950s, had shaken his hand as the two writers waited to join their *New Yorker* editors for lunch, and to Cheever, whose paths into suburbia left markers for Updike: receding faith, lost dreams, embattled loves. In his longer and more prolific career (twelve volumes of short stories), Updike used the short story to create a panorama of ordinary American life, primarily in Pennsylvania and New England – its small-town high schools, interstate motels, suburban cocktail parties – with the micro-dot precision of a pointillist painting. In his later work, foreign venues appear more often and old themes are revisited with novel ingenuity (a divorce reconsidered through the history of a swimming pool in "The Orphaned Swimming Pool"; a wryly humorous updating of the Tristan-and-Iseult foursome in "Four Sides of One Story"). Some of the stories, like the relentlessly anthologized "A & P," have the classic outline of the initiation story: boy, mocking bourgeois banality of resort town, is entranced by confidently lovely young girl violating dress-code of the store where he clerks for the summer; boy, roused to gesture of courtly defense when she is reprimanded, quits job unbeknownst to departing girl; boy, facing uncaring world, exits store and adolescence. Many other stories, like "The Music School," expand a forgettable snippet of routine – divorce-bound father waits for daughter to conclude music lesson – into a replete rendering of what it means to be caught in that web of circumstance.

What Cheever and Updike passed on to Ann Beattie, one of their best-known successors in the *New Yorker* "stable," was the short story's adequacy for reporting the social as well as the inner life. Both men were accomplished novelists as well, but it is in the cumulative impressions of decades of short takes that these writers painted their most expansive portrait of the American family emerging in the 1950s: self-conscious, sex-troubled, well-meaning, and clinging, as it aged, to a baffled and belea-guered faith in its normalcy. Meanwhile, the influence of New Criticism on pedagogy (especially Brooks and Warren's *Introduction to Fiction* [1943], which taught a generation how to view literary gems through a jeweler's loupe) solidified the place of the short story in college literature classes. Generations of students learned to identify tone, track down an image, interpret a symbol, and characterize "voice" – that is to say, learned the rudiments of literary criticism – through intensive analysis of "The Swimmer" and "A & P." Both Updike and Cheever mastered a doughty realism critical of, yet appropriate to, a society proud of its labor-saving devices, college-educated veterans, and country-club memberships. Yet both artists, here and there, experimented with surreal and stylized defor-mations of the "slice of life" story, giving a backhanded blessing to the coming attack on their fortress.

The onslaught came in the mid-to-late 1960s. Often considered the most important year in American history since the end of World War II, 1968 is forever associated with political unrest, and more generally with a sea-change in American society: the tide turned against the Vietnam War, against the institutionalized authority of the military-industrial complex, against the bourgeois values of the 1950s, and – in the work of four or five literary protestors – against the perceived tyranny and banality of realism. In 1968 the following books appeared: *In the Heart of the Heart of the Country*, by William H. Gass; *Unspeakable Practices*, by Donald Barthelme; and *Lost in the Funhouse*, by John Barth. *Pricksongs and Descants*, by Robert Coover, followed in 1969. The incorporation of self-reflexive commentary on the creative process; the fragmenting (and often rearranging) of normative sequence; the foregrounding of fiction's mechanisms – its devices, tropes, and conventions; and the insistence on the medium as the message: these are the distinguishing characteristics of metafiction or fabulism, and of its signature story, Barth's "Lost in the Funhouse."

This tale, ostensibly dwelling on a thirteen-year-old boy's anxieties about sex, identity, and vocation, is also a text continually interrupting itself with instructions from grammar books and fiction-writing manuals. Set in the wartime 1940s, during a day-trip to Ocean City, Maryland, the narrative is wittily deconstructed through the funhouse devices of infinite regressions, aborted sequences, and uncanny echoes. Readers, left with the impression of an author trammeled by the conventions of a decomposing art-form, are paradoxically swept up into the moving predicament of a sensitive writer-in-the-making, a city under U-boat surveillance, a literature both stymied and propelled by its own artificiality, and a clearly autobiographical author still committed to the burgeoning power and indestructible allure of human consciousness and desire.

For many years, Barth directed the Writing Seminars at Johns Hopkins University. Gass is still known as the philosopher of the group, Coover as the author of "The Babysitter," and *Sixty Stories* (1981) by Barthelme continues to influence antic dissections of popular culture in an absurd, post-industrial society. Inevitably, however, there was a reaction against experimental stories inaccessible to readers not trained to appreciate them. Reality pressed in: the Vietnam War, women's liberation, the Civil Rights Movement, the sexual revolution, and the generational gap tore the country apart. Swarms of young men and women – in or out of a uniform, a job, a "relationship," a bottle – drifted through the pages of the neo-realists, seeing few choices, their fictional lives an endless round of malaise, compulsion, and escapism. The experimentalism of the 1960s had shown that the short story had brains. The 1970s showed that it had grit.

Ironically, though not surprisingly, this was the first generation of writers to graduate, in overwhelming numbers, from university writing programs, and to support themselves by teaching in similar programs or by applying for grants, fellowships, and residencies in academia. It would be far too simple to explain the boom in short fiction during the 1970s as a confluence of antiwar interest in the underdog, pedagogical emphasis on conveniently short genres, academic privileging of artfully crafted language, and university-sponsored reviews and quarterlies in the market for stories. Nevertheless, all of these factors played a part.

Those who began publishing stories in small literary magazines in the 1970s were returning to the classic subject matter of Gogol and Chekhov: the frustrations of the "little man," of those whom Frank O'Connor (in his famous 1963 meditation on the genre) called the "submerged populations" of nations in turmoil, those who, in the academic argot, were "disempowered" – economically, socially, and spiritually.[4] Never mind that, in many cases, the disaffected were exiles from the middle class, down-and-out graduate students – not so much fighters in the trenches as dropouts in the library. The emptiness was real. So was the talent, and from it came the second renaissance of the short story in the twentieth century.

Collections appearing in the mid-to-late 1970s include Andre Dubus's *Separate Flights* (1975), Ann Beattie's *Distortions* (1976), Raymond Carver's *Will You Please Be Quiet, Please?* (1976), Barry Hannah's *Airships* (1978), and Jayne Anne Phillips's *Black Tickets* (1979). Hannah's degree was from Arkansas, but Dubus, Carver, and Phillips were all connected with the Writers' Workshop at the University of Iowa. All five explored, in stylistically innovative ways, a disquieted demographic far from the classroom – New England's troubled couples (Dubus), the East Coast's disaffected Baby Boomers (Beattie), the stalled and dispirited in the West (Carver), Alabama's eccentrics (Hannah), and a migrant band of the abused, addicted, and violent (Phillips). In 1983, the British periodical *Granta* heralded Carver, Richard Ford, Bobbie Ann Mason, and Tobias Wolff as practitioners of a new kind of writing. The editor, Bill Buford, gave it a name: "Dirty Realism."[5] That term – along with "minimalist" – has been hard to dislodge, although scholars have continually challenged it. All of the showcased writers had illustrious careers, yet it is Carver who stands out. He is credited with doing, in the last quarter of the century, what Hemingway did in the first: reinventing and elevating the genre of the short story, spawning decades of imitators.

Until the last years of his life, as Carol Sklenicka's biography makes clear, this was a man who could not stay employed, sober, faithful, or solvent. He was an alcoholic, a recreational drug-user, an irresponsible employee and father. He had a long, provocative, intense, stimulating, and ultimately failed marriage to a woman who believed in his art, took day-jobs to support it, fought hard for his survival, yet enabled his weakness. All of the above was grist for his mill. His life was his "Workshop," and in it (with the help, early on, of his friend and editor, Gordon Lish), he fashioned spare yet haunting tales of stunted lives, a glint of "menace" (as he called it) in the air.[6] He was famous for transposing the shambles of his marriage into taut stories vibrating with yearning beneath a matter-of-fact delivery. Obviously, he had learned from Hemingway as well as Chekhov.

A few early reviewers complained about all that is missing from stories devoted to a few autobiographical themes, to men and women without grace, culture, depth, self-awareness, or richness of any sort in their lives. Scholars now celebrate what is there: a homing instinct for radiant sore-spots that – more than any conventional plot – shapes messy anecdotes into plangent narratives; an ear for the hardscrabble lyricism of the American idiom, the vernacular reborn as a lean-but-layered medium, freighted with meaning; a feel for the uncanny that gives the most ordinary tale of bad faith or ineptitude an afterglow of poignancy, an aura of fatality that reveals – as Elizabeth Bowen thought all great stories must – our universal loneliness. Others had tapped these resources, but in Carver's work they came together, annealed by a lightning strike (his own image) of genius and luck.

His career divides easily into stages: the early stories stripped to the bone by Lish, notoriously dubbed "minimalist" despite their depth of resonance; the stories of the sober period, retrieving and expanding the sensibility most famously expressed in "Cathedral"; and the late-period stories, like "Chef's House," with their wryly tender perspective on fatal dysfunction (the first of his stories to breach the citadel of *The New Yorker*), or the more intricate, formally inventive, rather postmodern stories like "Blackbird Pie" and "Errand," Carver's last story before his death, in 1988, of complications from lung cancer.

In 1978, at the University of Iowa, those who heard him read "Why Don't You Dance?" saw a tall, newly sober, bearish yet fragile man, around whom a mythology was already forming. In this famous story, a husband living alone (divorce is implied) has moved his furniture out onto his front lawn, arranging it into "rooms" that echo the home's interior. Perhaps it is a clever yard-sale. Perhaps a bitter joke. Perhaps a psychic purge. Returning from the grocery store, he finds a young couple examining the layout, fiddling with the appliances, testing the bed, role-playing at the domestic life the owner has vacated. The boy is uncertain, the girl aggressive. They're in the market for furniture. Sitting down, the man offers whiskey, takes any bid offered, and finally puts music on the record-player. At his invitation, the young couple dance. When the boy becomes dizzy, the girl changes partners, dancing with the man. She intuits his desperation. Weeks later, she is still trying to tell people what happened; she's trapped in her own banality, but knows she has missed something. The story expires in a failure of articulation. Although Carver's stories in general have the more open form associated with Salinger (among others), this one leans toward the paradigmatic side of the short story's lineage, pairing inner and outer worlds, older and younger couples, real and surreal ambience. It is a parable that represses as much as it displays.

Amy Hempel, one of Gordon Lish's students, shares the "minimalist" label, with a dead-pan treatment of heart-wrenching sadness in pop-culture America, where best friends die of cancer and the grief zooms, with chilling accuracy, through the humor ("In the Cemetery Where Al Jolson Is Buried," in *Reasons to Live* [1985]). It is difficult to think of this story without remembering Lorrie Moore's "People Like That Are the Only People Here: Canonical Babbling in Peed Onk," first published in *The New Yorker*, then in *Birds of America*, 1998: a young mother faces the horror of her child's stay in a pediatric cancer ward, brandishing an armor of black humor that cracks with agony and outrage. Moore became known, early on, for her wise-cracking, girl-talking, sophisticated stories about rudderless young women presented with liberation and unsure what to do with it, or whether they even wanted it. Like Hempel, she belongs to a transitional period in the social history of the country, no longer battling institutionalized oppression, but struggling in a vacuum of values. What to do? Does it matter? The short story, capable of tonal extremes and narrative compression, could turn the trigger into the bullet *and* the target. Writers like Mary Robison, another "minimalist," could turn fragments of banal speech into grace-notes of befuddlement ("Coach," in *An Amateur's Guide to the Night* [1983]).

Many of the writers who emerged in the 1970s mellowed in the following decade, often producing more expansive, emotionally rich, and in some cases redemptive stories of a maturing generation. One of Carver's friends, Tobias Wolff, got his start in the early 1980s. Well known as a memoirist, he is a fine short-story writer. *In the Garden of the North American Martyrs* (1981) was followed by *Back in the World* (1985), *The Night in Question* (1996), and *Our Story Begins: New and Selected Stories* (2008). A prominent neo-realist, Wolff shares with Carver a focus on everyday experience, with evolving situations rather than plotted resolutions, and a low-keyed, conversational tone. No one, however, would confuse the two writers. Wolff's prose is engagingly unforced, naturally rhythmic, idiomatically deft with tuning-fork clarity. His wry common sense, likable humor, and remarkable empathy are all grounded in his view of life as a moral problem. In a Wolff story, "true" matters. Decisions are tough and actions have consequences. Paradoxical motives, conflicting desires – these are the fault-lines of his narratives. His most famous stories include "Hunters in the Snow" (a cruel twist on Bruegel's comradely scene), "Bullet in the Brain" (a surreal reinvention of Ambrose Bierce's "Occurrence at Owl Creek"), and "A White Bible" (a tale of mutual prejudice in post-9/11 America). For a time the director of Stanford University's graduate writing program, he continues to teach, give readings, and write. For many, he is, today, the dean of the American short story.

Conventional wisdom still says that publishers prefer novels, that television has replaced the mass-market weekly as the purveyor of sliced fiction, and that the literary short story can be found only in entry-level English courses, small-distribution "quarterlies," and the pages of *The New Yorker*. Offsetting that claim is the undeniable proliferation of short fiction in the 1990s and the twenty-first century: stories from minority and/or marginalized communities, post-Updike studies of marriage in suburbia and small towns (Richard Bausch comes to mind, and Charles Baxter), and new interest in hybrid forms and interdisciplinary source material. Legatees of Guy Davenport's learned parables (*Tatlin!* [1974]; *Da Vinci's Bicycle: Ten Stories*

[1979]) include Andrea Barrett, whose lapidary use of scientific data can be seen in *Ship Fever* (1996) and *Servants of the Map* (2002), or Steven Millhauser, whose mock-antiquarian tales of life-like automata appear, along with other curiosities, in *The Knife Thrower and Other Stories* (1998). Harsher voices can be heard, too: Thom Jones (*The Pugilist at Rest* [1993]; *Cold Snap* [1995]; *Sonny Liston Was a Friend of Mine* [1999]) is a descendant of Hemingway, and Robert Stone (*Bear and His Daughter* [1997]) travels deep into black-humor territory in an amoral universe, looking for sanctity. Stephen Dixon, in more than ten volumes of stories, offers a darkly comic, Kafkaesque twist on life.

Another storyteller in his prime, T. Coraghessan Boyle is worth mentioning for his sheer Dickensian vitality, acuity as a social critic, and comedic ingenuity. Rick Moody is notable for his understated anguish and formal inventiveness (his premier collection, *Demonology* [2000], offers "Surplus Value Books; Catalogue Number 13," organized as its title suggests). Other writers of interest today include Stuart Dybek, George Saunders, Joy Williams, Mary Gaitskill, ZZ Packer, and Yiyun Li.

Collections of stories may be harder to sell than novels, but anthologies are money-makers. Ever since the era of New Criticism, stories have been bundled into textbooks. Anthologies also serve niche markets. Examples are single-theme collections and "prize-winner" digests (*Best American Short Stories*; *O. Henry Prize Stories*). All such publications have responded to the call for diversity. Every textbook now includes stories by racial, ethnic, and other minorities, while insisting on a balance of male and female authors.

Largely because of the expanding canon, college students are now familiar with the stories of Cherokee German Louise Erdrich, Chinese American Gish Jen, Latina Sandra Cisneros, African American John Edgar Wideman, Native Americans Leslie Marmon Silko and Sherman Alexie, Indian Americans Bharati Mukherjee and Jhumpa Lahiri, as well as a host of other writers who speak from (but not necessarily for) identifiable subcultures. The new inclusiveness underscores the long (often oral) history and global presence of short fiction. The short-story cycle, with origins in ancient cultures, has attracted new attention as it weaves the fate of individuals into the fabric of their communities.

Yet the emphasis on diversity should not obscure the fact that some "minority" writers have been steadily at work since the 1960s. Ernest Gaines is a good example, with his often nostalgic stories of rural Louisiana in the 1940s and onward (*Bloodline* [1968]), dealing with issues of race and family in realistic prose while metafiction stole the spotlight. Even more widely known are Bernard Malamud, spinner of moral parables and tragicomic fairy tales, mostly of Jewish life, and Grace Paley, sounding-board of the New York Jewish wife and mother, sorting out love, politics, and female empowerment in a juicy, off-kilter syntax entirely her own. Her first collection, *The Little Disturbances of Man*, appeared in 1959; the last new one, *Later the Same Day*, in 1985; *The Collected Stories*, in 1994. Both Malamud and Paley drew on their ethnicity, its characteristic speech-patterns and urban history, yet both were writing about the same topic as the author of "The Lottery": the maze of the human heart.

Today, a new experimentalism often raids non-narrative systems of information: stories sifting through the cracks of expository forms. Robert Olen Butler, bursting on the scene with his Pulitzer Prize-winning collection of stories about Vietnamese immigrants (*A Good Scent from a Strange Mountain* [1992]), is Barthelme's descendant as the genius of "found art": a collection of stories spun from bizarre headlines (*Tabloid Dreams* [1996]), reconstructed from messages on old postcards (*Had a Good Time* [2004]), projected from the severed heads of famous people (*Severance* [2006]), or formed in the lonely minds of conjoined couples (*Intercourse* [2008]). The last two books are collections of short takes, prose poems, or "flash fictions," taking minimalism to the limit.

Past the turn of the new century, the very idea of genre seems unnecessary. Fiction and nonfiction, narrative and anti-narrative, verbal and graphic media combine in hybrid texts that, in brief, tell a tale. Yet, as a literary form, the short story survives. More important than any hierarchy of authors, any shift in fashion or popularity, is the dynamic of the genre itself. That is why its history after 1945 can be imagined as the legacy of Salinger and Jackson, a sentimental cult figure and a minor fabulist with one masterpiece. Between the lyricism and the logic are the many ways of filtering experience in a powerful, fast-moving, and increasingly divided country. Distilling old and new concerns, pinpointing the stakes, foreshortening the perspective, this genre is constantly reinventing itself. An elastic form, it always rebounds, from mandarin polish to visceral punch, from laced-up paradigm to loose-limbed confession. Experiments in narrative technique, inclusion of new voices, responses to social change, all can be tested in the workshop of the short story.

FURTHER READING

Gretlund, Jan Nordby. "Architexture in Short Stories by Flannery O'Connor and Eudora Welty," in Per Winther, Jakob Lothe, and Hans H. Skei (eds.), *The Art of Brevity: Excursions in Short Fiction Theory and Analysis*. Columbia, SC: University of South Carolina Press, 2004, pp. 151–62

Nagel, James. *The Contemporary American Short-Story Cycle: The Ethnic Resonance of Genre*. Baton Rouge: Louisiana State University Press, 2001

Parks, John G. (ed.). *American Short Stories Since 1945*. Oxford University Press, 2002

Sklenicka, Carol. *Raymond Carver: A Writer's Life*. New York: Scribner, 2009

Weaver, Gordon (ed.). *The American Short Story, 1945–1980: A Critical History*. Boston: Twayne Publishers, 1983

NOTES

1 Ian Hamilton, *In Search of J. D. Salinger* (New York: Random House, 1988), pp. 85–6.

2 Flannery O'Connor, "A Good Man Is Hard to Find," in *The Complete Stories* (New York: Farrar, Straus, and Giroux, 1971), p. 133.

3 John Cheever, "Good-bye, My Brother," in *The Stories of John Cheever* (New York: Vintage International, 2000), p. 21.

4 Frank O'Connor, *The Lonely Voice* (Cleveland: The World Publishing Company, 1963), p. 18.

5 Bill Buford (ed.), "Dirty Realism: New Writing From America," *Granta* 8 (1983).

6 Raymond Carver, "On Writing," in *Fires* (New York: Vintage Contemporaries, 1989), p. 26.

PART II

Historical and cultural contexts

6

KEITH BYERMAN

African American fiction

African American fiction of the last seventy years has largely been defined by dichotomies: ideological/aesthetic, male/female, traditional/experimental. While there is some relevance to these categories, the deeper reality is that there has been a remarkable range of themes, styles, and techniques displayed in this body of work. Despite pressures at various times to make black writing fit a rigid definition or to expel authors from the race for their work, authors have consistently produced narratives that defy easy categorization. Much of the debate about black narrative has been carried out in essays and articles that extend back to the early twentieth century, when W. E. B. Du Bois contended that black writing should serve as propaganda for the advancement of the race and attacked Claude McKay, among others, for his failure to do so.[1] Langston Hughes responded with his declaration of artistic freedom that rejected either black or white proscriptions on the black writer.[2] We see variations on this conversation in the critiques of Richard Wright by Ralph Ellison and James Baldwin; in the Irving Howe/Ellison debate; in the denunciations of Ellison by participants in the Black Arts Movement; in Clarence Major's responses to his work; in Ishmael Reed's assaults on white critics, feminism, and black women writers; and finally in the manifesto by Trey Ellis on a New Black Aesthetic.[3] All the while, writers were going about the business of producing an array of fictions that always exceeded the arguments about what they were doing.

Rather than reinscribing these binaries or constructing new ones, this chapter emphasizes the diversity of fictive production over several literary generations. Ultimately, I would argue, the individual artistic vision is more important than race, class, gender, or ideology. Nonetheless, there are patterns of theme, technique, and movement that allow for some useful groupings, even if these are primarily heuristic. Thematically, fiction writers have concerned themselves with history (national, regional, local, personal, folk, literary, and academic), with identity, with the relationship of the individual to the community, with religion and spirituality, with gender, sexuality, and sexual orientation, with inter- and intra-racial relationships, with urban and rural environments, with violence, whether domestic or social, and with families and personal relationships. As should be clear, such a list suggests many of the universal themes of literature: love, hate, life, and death. Writers use the techniques of satire, parody, melodrama, autobiography, tragedy, and the picaresque, as well as versions of mimesis. We find elements of the *bildungsroman*, the *künstlerroman*, the travel narrative, and the epistolary novel. Work is done in the modes of naturalism, realism, magic realism, modernism, and postmodernism. What these lists point to is the lack of something we can call "African American fiction" in any very meaningful sense. Rather, the term is a construction that enables marketing, reviewing, and academic career-building. But given the continuing failure of the nation to achieve a postracial condition, it is useful as a device to call public attention to the visions, methods, and stories of a large group of writers often neglected or misread because of their "race."

The story of modern and contemporary black writing begins with Richard Wright, not because of his direct influence but rather because he casts such a large shadow. Both *Native Son* (1940) and *Black Boy* (1945) were best-sellers. Their success largely defined expectations for African American fiction. They pushed to the side the folk-based narratives of Zora Neale Hurston, published around the same time, and the middle-class novels of the Harlem Renaissance. In their place, Wright offered naturalistic narratives that revealed the violent effects of racism and poverty. He was willing to risk having his characters associated with racial stereotypes in order to make clear what the nation was doing to its black citizens.

Although Wright himself would go into exile after World War II and produce somewhat different fiction as a result, he left behind a group of writers who constituted "the Wright school." While it is simplistic to suggest that these authors mechanically followed Wright's lead, they did generally create naturalistic narratives based in urban spaces that incorporated deprivation and violence. Ann Petry's *The Street* (1946) tells the story of Lutie Johnson, a young mother whose effort to find a safe life for herself and her son leads ironically to ever-greater trouble. While the story results in an act of violence as a predictable outcome, much like *Native Son*, Petry offers the complication of gender; in addition, Lutie is granted significantly more agency in responding to her situation. In contrast, the works of Chester Himes, William Gardner Smith, and Lloyd Brown written in this mode tend to be more fatalistic. Himes's *If He Hollers Let Him Go* (1946) and *The Lonely Crusade* (1947) are in the proletarian tradition of the 1930s in that they concern black workers in the defense industry. In both cases, however, it is race rather than corporate oppression that is the source of suffering for the protagonists. Similarly, Smith's *The Last of the Conquerors* (1948) describes the racism experienced by African American soldiers in occupied Germany after the war. He suggests through the story that blacks are better treated in post-Nazi Germany than in the United States. Brown's *Iron City* (1950) points to the racism inherent in the American judicial system in a narrative of a falsely accused African American man who seeks the aid of black communists imprisoned for their organizing activities. Even though Brown worked for the leftist publication *New Masses* at the time his novel was released, his novel's focus is more on racial than class issues. While all of these works point to the powerful effects of racial oppression, they never quite accept either the total passivity or dehumanization of their characters.

Some of the same authors are also part of an effort to transcend racial subject matter altogether. In 1952 Himes published *Cast the First Stone*, a naturalistic story of prison life, which, although based on his own experience, features a white protagonist who must endure brutality from the prison system; it is also one of the first works to explore homosexual relationships in a prison context. Smith published *Anger at Innocence* (1952), which describes the sexual desires and frustrations of a group of white outsiders. None of them ever achieve anything approaching happiness and the result, as in naturalistic works, is violence. Petry took on life in a small New England town in *Country Place* (1947), in which the narrowness of life and the frustration of desires and ambitions are central. In their depictions of white life, these writers continue the naturalistic tradition. Willard Motley followed in this vein with his first novel, *Knock on Any Door* (1947), which portrays a young Italian whose environment leads him inevitably to a life of crime. Unlike other writers in this discussion, Motley never portrayed black life in his fiction.

Two otherwise antagonistic writers, Wright and Hurston, also contributed to this category. Wright's *Savage Holiday* (1954) tells a story similar to that of his other fiction, in which social stresses lead to a violent reaction on the part of the protagonist. Hurston's *Seraph on the Suwanee* (1948) continues her interest in Southern life, but creates a poor white woman as its central character. Like Hurston's most famous figure, Janie of *Their Eyes Were Watching God* (1937), Arvay Henson seeks happiness and selfhood and ultimately succeeds. By undertaking the so-called raceless novel, a number of black writers attempt to reconstruct their literary identities by generating stories that reveal their grasp of American issues and experiences rather than merely African American ones. While some of these works were artistically successful, they generally did not have public appeal, which indicates the ongoing racialization of the American literary marketplace.

Another approach is taken by writers who neither avoid race nor see it as the primary cause of black identity or problems. These writers – William Demby, Owen Dodson, Dorothy West, and Gwendolyn Brooks – instead focus on a critique of the values of society generally, including racism. In *Beetlecreek* (1950), Demby moves his young protagonist from Pittsburgh to a small West Virginia town to live with relatives. What he finds is a provincial community in which both blacks and whites cannot tolerate any deviation from their mores. The chief victim in this case is a white man who has chosen to live near the African American part of town and who, though mostly a recluse, communicates primarily with his black neighbors. His greatest mistake, however, is to attempt to bring black and white children together. For this he is verbally attacked by both races, and his home is destroyed by the protagonist as a gang initiation. Demby's theme might be said to be a version of the banality of evil in that resistance to difference and change, in the name of community values, permits attacks on humanity.

Similarly, Dodson's *Boy at the Window* (1951) exposes the selfishness at the core of most human society through his story of a boy who must move in with his uncle when his beloved mother dies. Though the child is only ten, the uncle is much more concerned with alcohol and women than with the rearing of a child. While racism plays a role in the narrative, it is clear, through the stream-of-consciousness telling, that it is the boy's need for and pursuit of love that is central. Unlike Demby and the naturalists, Dodson implies at the end that such a quest can be successful.

West turns to satire as a way of attacking the misplaced values of the black bourgeoisie. *The Living Is Easy* (1948) examines the pretensions and distorted values of upper-class blacks in Boston. They use their economic power and social status to distance themselves as much as possible from their Southern and poverty-ridden pasts. They embrace as fully as possible the values, styles, and possessions of wealthy whites. They turn their backs on the issues still facing the race generally, not out of fear, but out of indifference. In this sense, they are just as venal as the characters in *Beetlecreek* and *Boy at the Window*.

A somewhat different approach is taken by Brooks in *Maud Martha* (1953); this difference is important, as shall be seen, for the later development of women's fiction. While race in many ways circumscribes Maud's life, the key issue is survival in an unloving world. She has to deal with the disadvantage of her dark skin color in both black and white communities, with conflicts between her parents, with financial difficulties, and with an indifferent husband. Her story is told in brief, slice-of-life episodes that depict an ordinary life in 1940s Chicago. It veers between realism and impressionism as it records Maud's refusal to surrender to despair or bitterness. It reveals the everydayness of life for a black woman that will later become important for Alice Walker, Toni Morrison, Toni Cade Bambara, and others.

The transition to a truly modern African American fiction is often seen as occurring when Ellison and Baldwin published their first novels within a few months of each other in 1952–1953. However, what should be evident at this point is that the ground was prepared for them over the previous decade. What they succeeded in doing was moving the black novel into the American mainstream, though in different ways. Both brought African American traditions into the practice of modernism, though Ellison's method was more experimental. In *Invisible Man* (1952), he quite deliberately brings the techniques of T. S. Eliot, William Faulkner, and Ernest Hemingway to bear on black folklore, history, and social and political life. Through the genre of the *bildungsroman*, he is able to present a tragicomic vision of American society with a primary, though not exclusive, focus on race. He attacks Southern racism, the black bourgeoisie, black nationalist movements, Northern liberals, capitalism, and left-wing politics through a combination of satire, parody, and surrealism. He incorporates performative elements of speech, song, ritual, and impersonation. Through his first-person, often naive, narrator, he is able to expose both the superficiality of social practices and the depth of African American folk traditions, which he consistently links to basic American values of liberty, equality, and human dignity. He claims all of American literary and cultural history for his materials. In essence, he sets aside the naturalistic and protest tradition in favor of his version of the great American novel.

Baldwin, who, like Ellison, felt it necessary to repudiate Wright in order to create a space for himself, offers a different approach. He eschews the "big," social novel in favor of the tighter stories of families and closely linked individuals. He takes as a model Henry James and his commitment to psychological realism. In his first work, *Go Tell It on the Mountain* (1953), he tells the story of the Grimes family, struggling to make a life in Harlem. They are headed by Gabriel, an embittered, would-be preacher who uses his self-righteousness as a weapon against his family, especially his wife and her son John from a previous relationship. The story is told in a Faulknerian manner, using a variety of focal characters to reveal the emotional significance of the action narrated. The novel is also important for its engagement with African American religion, as the storefront church becomes the stable center of lives that struggle with frustrations caused by racism, poverty, and tensions within the family. Like *Maud Martha* in its representation of everyday urban life among the poor, *Go Tell It* raises the level of intensity as disappointments turn to hatreds and open hostility. The novel is also noteworthy for introducing elements of the homoerotic in the black community, a subject Baldwin will engage more directly in later work.

Fiction from the decade of the Civil Rights Movement (1954–1965) in some ways returns to the protest tradition, though with less of the overt violence of earlier work. John O. Killens's *Youngblood* (1954) tells the story of a Southern black family that struggles against the oppressive environment of the region in the era between post-Reconstruction and the Depression. By adding this historical perspective, Killens moves the protest novel from a focus on current problems to the larger national experience. Smith reveals the efforts of a family trying to reshape race relations in Philadelphia in *South Street* (1954). Frank London Brown, like his fellow Chicagoan Lorraine Hansberry, depicts efforts to integrate housing in *Trumbull Park* (1959). John A. Williams shifts ground somewhat in his semi-autobiographical *The Angry Ones* (1960), which explores issues of race in the postwar corporate world. His second work, *Night Song* (1961), which is attentive to problems of race, follows Ellison in seeing the potential of black music as an element of fiction; Williams creates a protagonist suggestive of Charlie Parker, who uses his talent to attempt to break through racial barriers. Kirstin Hunter's *God Bless the Child* (1964) complicates the protest narrative not only by telling the story of the struggles of a young woman and her mother and grandmother to emerge from the ghetto, but also by critiquing the black community for its contribution to the protagonist's failure. Himes uses an interracial relationship in *The End of a Primitive* (1955) to critique American liberal attitudes on race. Protest takes a symbolic turn in William Kelley's *A Different Drummer* (1962), in which a sharecropper named Tucker Caliban buys land that he then destroys before moving to the North. His action leads to the emigration of all African Americans from that state. In effect, he carries out the logic of racism by erasing the black presence, but leaves the racists to contemplate the implications of having their desires fulfilled.

While protest continued to be central to African American fiction, a number of writers began moving in directions that have influenced later developments in the fiction. Baldwin, Demby, Charles Wright, and Paule Marshall produce narratives that involve race, but are centrally concerned with other aspects of their characters. Baldwin turns his attention to sexual orientation in his fiction of this period. *Giovanni's Room* (1956) offers an all-white cast in order to explore homosexual identity. His American narrator struggles with notions of masculinity in his attraction to and then abandonment of Giovanni, a gay Italian. As in much other black fiction of the modern period, the inability to embrace otherness, whether based on race, class, gender, or sexual orientation, leads to violence. In *Another Country* (1962), Baldwin brings together racial and sexual issues to tell the story and repercussions of the suicide of Rufus Scott. The narrative brings into play a variety of racial, regional, national, and sexual identities. Baldwin challenges any fixed notions of the self by suggesting that such notions limit the possibility of love and human connection. Only those characters who can transcend such boundaries are able to enter "another country." While the novel can be considered a form of protest, its target is social and cultural narrow-mindedness rather than racial or sexual oppression. Its structure also points to postmodernist writing by breaking with temporal and spatial conventions.

Marshall saw herself in the context of Baldwin in her desire to trace family tensions and link them to cultural identity. In *Brown Girl, Brownstones* (1959) she tells the story of Selina Boyce, the daughter of parents who have moved to New York from Barbados. This *bildungsroman* follows the pattern of a number of immigrant narratives in putting the child in the middle of a struggle between Americanization and nostalgia for the old country, in this case represented by the mother and father, respectively. Like Rufus Scott, Deighton Boyce commits suicide, although his death results from the thwarting of his desire to return. Marshall brings to the modern African American novel a diasporic sensibility that will become ever more prominent in contemporary writing.

Charles Wright and Demby move the genre into an experimental phase with works that challenge the boundaries of narrative fiction. In his first novel, *The Messenger* (1963), Wright blends autobiography and fiction in an otherwise realistic and almost naturalistic story. His second work, *The Wig* (1966), breaks with that tradition entirely by telling a futuristic tale of Lester Jefferson, a young man pursuing the promise of the Great Society by working in an electrified chicken suit on the streets of New York. Demby takes a different direction in *The Catacombs* (1965) by constructing a narrative based on principles of modernist painting. It is a *künstlerroman* focusing on an African American writer named Bill Demby living in Rome and trying to create a novel based on the love life of another expatriate. Into this narrative, which is repeatedly broken up spatially and temporally, the author interjects news items or passages from books or his own thoughts about the story.

Such methods were being developed by white metafictionists such as John Barth and Donald Barthelme, but were not deemed appropriate for African American writers. The reason for this effort at literary control was the Black Arts Movement, which emerged as a response to the perceived limited achievements of the Civil Rights Movement. Amiri Baraka, Larry Neal, and other artists and critics of this persuasion, returning to a much older notion of black writing, insisted that it must have a clear political function.[4] Literature should serve the needs of "the people," and be written in a style that they could easily apprehend. For this reason, the works of Baldwin and Ellison, with their modernist techniques and their "dependence" on white predecessors, were considered irrelevant and insufficiently "black." The movement produced virtually no fiction, in part, it could be argued, because narrative does not lend itself to the declamatory mode favored by nationalists. The one exception is Baraka's own *The System of Dante's Hell* (1965), which by its very title suggests a necessary link to European literary tradition. The text itself is fragmentary and autobiographical, an experimental work that seeks to break down assumptions of the Western culture it engages. Its ideological purpose is served through critiques of forms of black identity that remain dependent on white values.

What African American novelists of the post-civil rights period did, in place of constructing political narratives, was to move toward a recognition of black identity without reducing it to either victimization or essentialism. Beginning in the late 1960s, a new generation, born during the Great Depression and college-educated, started producing work that engages African American history and folk culture, but combines that material with a commitment to a high level of artistry, learned from whatever sources work best for them. Some are realists, others modernists, and yet others postmodernists. Some are cosmopolitan, while others, following Faulkner, cultivate their "own little postage stamp of native soil."[5] Some work is in satiric or humorous modes, while others are deadly serious. Some focus on issues of gender, others on sexuality, and still others on spirituality. Some of the authors became celebrities, while others died without a significant reputation. What is noteworthy about this generation is its diversity, even its individuality. The discussion that follows will undertake to reveal commonalities, while noting that few of the writers can be contained within any one category.

One aspect that many of them share is the employment of African American folk culture for both content and structure. While this is a pattern that goes back to Charles Chesnutt, Hurston, and more recently Ellison, it became especially prominent in the post-civil rights period with such writers as Ernest Gaines, Toni Morrison, Leon Forrest, Alice Walker, and Toni Cade Bambara. They construct fictions that employ folk characters, music, tales, rituals, and verbal expression (signifying, dozens, sermons). More important, they articulate a folk sensibility that embraces both survival and resistance. They go beyond merely offering a contemporary version of local color narrative; instead, they engage in social and cultural critique through the device of the worldview of the oppressed. They reject a binary of victim and hero, avoid the rhetoric of nationalism, protest, or accommodation, examine the positive and negative aspects of black community, and construct sophisticated and artistically successful fictions.

A prominent example is Walker's *The Color Purple* (1982), narrated primarily in the semi-literate voice of Celie, who is compelled by her abusive father to tell "nobody but God" what she has suffered from him.[6] In an act that is both obedient and subversive, she writes letters to God, meaning that her indictments of male violence exist as concrete documents potentially available to any reader. The text also employs women's blues as a means of giving expression to more general claims against male domination. Similarly, Bambara, especially in *Gorilla, My Love* (1972), uses a variety of urban black female voices, from little girls to older women, to narrate everyday life in the inner city. In the process, she challenges the social and racial silencing that has prevented the articulation of their experiences. The most elaborate of these folk voices is found in Gaines's *The Autobiography of Miss Jane Pittman* (1971). A 108-year-old illiterate woman recounts the local history of rural Louisiana from slavery through Reconstruction and Jim Crow to the Civil Rights Movement. In doing so, she captures the importance of black religion and music, of black cowboys, of conjure, and of black sports heroes such as Joe Louis and Jackie Robinson. In addition, she embodies the values of the folk that emphasize survival over open resistance, but also a desire for true freedom.

Morrison and Forrest shape some of their early fiction on folk principles. In both *Sula* (1974) and *Song of Solomon* (1977), Morrison demonstrates how folk practices can create narrative. In *Sula*, the author invents folk beliefs and practices, such as National Suicide Day, to reveal how communities give meaning to those events and experiences over which they have little control. The title character becomes a scapegoat so that the community can displace its defects and live self-affirming lives. *Song of Solomon* is structured around a man's quest for his family history that specifically includes a children's song that, when decoded, reveals his African genealogy.

In contrast, Forrest consciously constructs modernist texts that use elements of folk material in conjunction with biblical and literary allusions to create his vision of African American life. He employs sermons, legends (both borrowed and invented), family stories, jazz, blues, and spirituals motifs, "superstitions," and folk storytelling practices and links them to references to Melville, Dostoevsky, Joyce, Eliot, Faulkner, and Ellison, as well as material from Genesis through Revelations. In *There Is a Tree More Ancient Than Eden* (1973), *Bloodworth Orphans* (1977), and *Two Wings to Veil My Face* (1984), Forrest produces highly rhetorical narratives that explore not only the psychic costs of slavery and racism, but also the cultural resources available to African Americans.

Tied to this use of traditional materials is a commitment to recuperation of the past, in both its positive and negative aspects. In addition to those works that Ashraf Rushdy has designated "neo-slave narratives,"[7] there are also narratives of the post-Civil War period, of the Harlem Renaissance, the Civil Rights era, and the Black Power period. A neo-slave narrative is one that reconstructs in some form the experience of slavery. It can be one that follows the conventions of the historical novel, such as Margaret Walker's *Jubilee* (1966), Sherley Anne Williams's *Dessa Rose* (1986), or Morrison's *Beloved* (1987), all of which attempt to capture a sense of the period and its impact on those who lived through it. Such narratives make use of historical events and persons, but adapt that material to the purposes of fiction. Other works in the genre establish a contrast between the present and the past so as to suggest the continuation of the past into the present. These versions can include historiography, as in David Bradley's *The Chaneysville Incident* (1981), in which a professional historian traces his own family back to a fugitive slave; or science fiction, such as Octavia Butler's *Kindred* (1979), wherein a contemporary young woman is pulled back in time to the plantation of her black and white ancestors; or Gloria Naylor's *Mama Day* (1988), in which present-day characters must come to terms with the legends and beliefs associated with the slavery past on one of the Sea Islands. Yet a third variation is the postmodern slave narrative, seen in fictions by Charles Johnson, Ishmael Reed, and John Edgar Wideman. Johnson, in *Oxherding Tale* (1984) and *Middle Passage* (1990), offers tales that incorporate a range of discourses and literary allusions, as well as anachronisms in first-person narratives revealing the spiritual and psychological meanings of slavery and race. Reed, in *Flight to Canada* (1976), employs satire and parody to subvert the conventional wisdom about American history, especially the antebellum period. In *Cattle Killing* (1996), Wideman fractures time to show how those in power have manipulated race from eighteenth-century America to the present to justify dehumanizing the oppressed.

Some authors have explored later periods, including the 1920s. Morrison and Reed have produced very different versions of the Harlem Renaissance. Morrison's *Jazz* (1992) takes a serious look at the lives of participants in the Great Migration from the rural South to Northern cities. She emphasizes the stresses on her characters as they adjust to new economic, political, and interpersonal dynamics. In contrast, Reed uses jazz and African American culture generally in *Mumbo Jumbo* (1972) to parody the assumptions and values of Western culture. He plays with the structure of the detective novel to reveal a vast conspiracy, originating in ancient Egypt, designed to suppress the life-affirming principles of African-derived cultures.

The post-World War II period has been a key era for a number of novelists seeking to describe the meaning of modern American society. Ernest Gaines has produced several works that engage the setting of Louisiana backwaters where ancient racial beliefs and practices only gradually evolve into new perspectives. In *Catherine Carmier* (1964), *Of Love and Dust* (1967), *Bloodline* (1968), *A Gathering of Old Men* (1983), and *A Lesson Before Dying* (1993), he describes the tensions among blacks, whites, and black and white creoles as mechanization, education, and shifting attitudes force everyone to confront modernity, often with tragic consequences. Walker in *Meridian* (1976) and Johnson in *Dreamer* (1998) reveal many of the underlying stresses embodied in the Civil Rights Movement. Morrison's *Song of Solomon* (1977), Forrest's *Divine Days* (1993), Reed's *The Last Days of Louisiana Red* (1974), and Wideman's *The Lynchers* (1973) all offer significant critiques of the black nationalist movement, as it developed in the late 1960s and early 1970s.

Women's writing during the 1970s and 1980s provided a major challenge to the dominance of male authors. Much of this work, including Morrison's *The Bluest Eye* (1970), Walker's *The Third Life of Grange Copeland* (1970), Gayl Jones's *Corregidora* (1975) and *Eva's Man* (1976), and Gloria Naylor's *Women of Brewster Place* (1982), *Linden Hills* (1985), and *Bailey's Café* (1992), focuses on the abuse suffered by black women at the hands of black men. This body of fiction and material like it, by such popular writers as Terri McMillan, shifted the ground of African American writing through its popular and critical success. Male writing generally was eclipsed as the work of Morrison, Walker, Naylor, and McMillan not only climbed bestseller lists but also was made into feature films and made-for-television movies.

An often overlooked category of black writing is the experimental work of Clarence Major, Nathaniel Mackey, and Samuel R. Delany. Mackey's fiction is an ongoing series of jazz works collectively titled *From a Broken Bottle Traces of Perfume Still Emanate*. The series includes *Bedouin Hornbook* (1986), *Djbot Baghostus's Run* (1993), *Atet A.D.* (2001), and *Bass Cathedral* (2008). They follow the epistolary tradition and comprise letters from a jazz musician and composer named N., who writes to the Angel of Dust. The works follow the lives of a group of musicians, but primarily concern the creation of art. Delany's second-wave science fiction is clearly postmodern in its self-reflexivity, its construction of heterotopias, and its play with form. In *Dahlgren* (1975) and *The Tides of Lust* (1980; also known as *Equinox*), he engages issues of sexuality to such an extent that his work has been associated with pornography. The role of the erotic also gives shape to some of Major's early, experimental fictions. *All-Night Visitors* (1969) was published by Olympia Press, which made its profits through a pornography series, money that was used to support experimental writing by Henry Miller, J. P. Donleavy, and others. Major's fragmented narratives in *NO* (1973), *Reflex and Bone Structure* (1975), and *Emergency Exit* (1979) reflect his view that art is less a representation of reality than a creation of new reality; it also manifests his interest in developing techniques derived from cubist and surrealist painting in order to write fiction.

A younger generation of artists has emerged since the Civil Rights Movement that has expressed little interest in issues of racial identity or racial conflict per se. Variously labeled "cultural mulattos" or "post-soul," they tend to engage race solely as a social construction that may be the subject of satire or of serious investigation of cross-racial life in America. Though he is somewhat older than this group, Percival Everett shares its perspective. After undertaking classic narratives in *Suder* (1983), a baseball novel, and *Walk Me to the Distance* (1985), the story of a returning Vietnam veteran, Everett turned to parodies and variations of western genre fiction and Greek mythology. His frustrations with the categorization of writers by race led to the writing of *Erasure* (2006), which explores the career of a sophisticated but little-known African American author (named Thelonius Monk Ellison) who angrily writes a simple-minded ghetto novel that satirizes Wright's *Native Son* and Sapphire's *Push* (1996). The work becomes extremely popular, and the author finds himself in a series of awkward situations as he tries to disguise his identity behind the gangsta persona he has generated.

A similar situation is created in Trey Ellis's *Platitudes* (1988), in which an unsuccessful male experimental novelist seeks help in a publishing world that has come to be dominated by women writers. Similar to Reed's *Reckless Eyeballing*, published two years earlier, *Platitudes* uses the dilemma of its protagonist to comment on the racial politics of contemporary literature. In both cases, help is sought from women artists, with what the authors saw as hilarious results, though both books were criticized for their attacks on black feminism. The current edition of *Platitudes* is bundled with "The New Black Aesthetic," Ellis's articulation of the post-soul aesthetic.

Any list of post-soul artists includes Paul Beatty, Colson Whitehead, and Danzy Senna. The first two of these have followed in the Everett–Ellis practice of satire. Beatty, in *White Boy Shuffle* (1996), *Tuff* (2000), and *Slumberland* (2008), engages various aspects of contemporary American society and its flawed efforts to deal with matters of race. Whitehead shows the influence of Thomas Pynchon in *The Intuitionist* (1999), a novel about elevator inspectors and secret texts, as well as race and gender issues. In *John Henry Days* (2002), he takes on the commercial exploitation of African American culture, and in *Apex Hides the Hurt* (2006), looks at the power of modern marketing.

Senna, in contrast, joins two other recent authors in undertaking a serious examination of issues often considered on the margins of African American literature and culture. In *Caucasia* (1998), she tells the story of a biracial family driven apart by the racial tensions of 1970s Boston. It is the tale of a daughter's search for an identity that can bridge the racial gap. Similarly, Randall Kenan, in *A Visitation of Spirits* (1989), narrates the brief life of a teenager trying to define a self that is both black and gay in the homophobic and racially enclosed world of his small Southern town. Finally, Edward P. Jones, in *The Known World* (2003), returns to the interest in history through the story of an African American family who become slaveowners; in doing so, he offers the ultimate challenge to Du Bois's assertions of the political function of black writing.

FURTHER READING

Bell, Bernard W. *The Contemporary African American Novel: Its Roots and Modern Literary Branches.* Amherst: University of Massachusetts Press, 2004

Byerman, Keith E. *Fingering the Jagged Grain: Tradition and Form in Recent Black Fiction.* Athens: University of Georgia Press, 1986

   Remembering the Past in Contemporary African American Fiction. Chapel Hill: University of North Carolina Press, 2005

Christian, Barbara. *Black Women Novelists: The Development of a Tradition, 1892–1976.* Westport, CT: Greenwood Press, 1980

Coleman, James W. *Black Male Fiction and the Legacy of Caliban.* Lexington: University Press of Kentucky, 2001

Dickson-Carr, Darryl. *African American Satire: The Sacredly Profane Novel.* Columbia: University of Missouri Press, 2001

Dubey, Madhu. *Black Women Novelists and the Nationalist Aesthetic.* Bloomington: Indiana University Press, 1994

Fox, Robert Elliot. *Conscientious Sorcerers: The Black Postmodernist Fiction of LeRoi Jones/Amiri Baraka, Ishmael Reed, and Samuel R. Delany.* New York: Greenwood Press, 1987

Schraufnagel, Noel. *From Apology to Protest: The Black American Novel.* Deland, FL: Everett Edwards, 1973

NOTES

1 See W. E. B. Du Bois, "The Criteria of Negro Art," *Crisis*, 32 (October 1926): 290–7.

2 See Langston Hughes, "The Negro Artist and the Racial Mountain," *Nation*, 122 (June 23, 1926): 692–4.

3 See Ralph Ellison, "The World and the Jug," *Shadow and Act* (New York: Vintage, 1973 [1964]), pp. 107–43; James Baldwin's "Everybody's Protest Novel," in *Notes of a Native Son* (New York: Bantam, 1968 [1955]); and Trey Ellis's "The New Black Aesthetic," *Callaloo*, 12 (Winter 1989): 233–43.

4 Amiri Baraka, "Black Art," in *Selected Poetry of Amiri Baraka/LeRoi Jones* (New York: William Morrow, 1979), pp. 106–7; Larry Neal, "And Shine Swam On," in *Visions of a Liberated Future: Black Arts Movement Writings*, ed. Michael Schwartz (New York: Thunder's Mouth Press, 1989), pp. 7–23.

5 Jean Stein, "William Faulkner: The Art of Fiction, No. 12," *Paris Review*, 12 (Spring 1956): 26.

6 Alice Walker, *The Color Purple* (New York: Harcourt Brace Jovanovich, 1982), p. 3.

7 Ashraf H. A. Rushdy, *Neo-slave Narratives: Studies in the Social Logic of a Literary Form* (New York: Oxford University Press, 1999).

7

NANCY J. PETERSON

American Indian fiction

While World War II offers a convenient dividing point for mainstream American literature and is often used as a breaking point between modernism and postmodernism, 1945 does not have the same import in the history and development of American Indian fiction. For American Indian literature, the most important milestone comes in 1969, the year that N. Scott Momaday won the Pulitzer Prize for his first novel, *House Made of Dawn* (1968). To be sure, there were accomplished American Indian authors writing in English in the twentieth century who preceded Momaday, and many of those earlier narrative works were not critically recognized until the postwar period (D'Arcy McNickle's 1936 novel *The Surrounded*, for instance, or Ella Cara Deloria's novel *Waterlily*, which was completed in the 1940s but not published until 1988). But this chapter focuses on the outpouring of American Indian fiction since 1968 to provide an overview of some of the key writers and developments of this remarkable period.

In approaching Native literary texts, one must keep in mind that social, cultural, and historical contexts are crucial. Federal policies concerning Indian affairs and indigenous responses to those policies influence the themes and forms of works by American Indian writers. Popular culture matters as well: the antiwar and countercultural movements of the 1960s and 1970s, for instance, led to increased interest in Native peoples and texts as middle-class whites sought out alternative cultures and spiritual lifeways. *Black Elk Speaks*, the famous as-told-to autobiography of the Lakota spiritual leader Nicholas Black Elk edited by John G. Neihardt (originally published in 1932, but reissued in a mass paperback edition in 1977), became a bestseller among nonnatives, and has been referred to as a "North American bible of all tribes."[1] Native fiction since 1968 particularly responds to the Civil Rights struggles of the time, especially the Red Power Movement that led to the occupation of Alcatraz Island in 1969, the founding of the American Indian Movement, and the takeover of the town of Wounded Knee, South Dakota in 1973. American Indian fiction of the late twentieth and early twenty-first centuries demonstrates that Native peoples, nations, cultures, and traditions not only have survived but have been reinvigorated.

This chapter outlines three phases in American Indian fiction published since 1968 by discussing key figures from each era. It begins with writers associated with the "Native American Renaissance,"[2] a term that scholar Kenneth Lincoln coined to describe the development and flourishing of literature written by American Indians sparked by Momaday's 1969 Pulitzer Prize. These writers, who achieved critical recognition in the 1960s and 1970s, were often influenced by literary modernism and effectively adapted such modernist tactics as an emphasis on culture, its exploration of alienation, and an aesthetics of fragmentation to foreground their Native protagonists and subject matter in compelling narratives. The group of Native writers that followed became critically recognized during the 1980s and early 1990s at a time when postmodern theories and cultural analysis prevailed, and many of the Native writers of this era critically engage postmodernism. They do so to articulate the contradictions and opportunities of living indigenously in the contemporary world, to draw complex portraits of Native characters and communities, and often to insist on the relevance of Native traditions in dealing with the debilitating effects of postmodern culture. The Native writers who have come to critical recognition most recently are charting their own course: they are in the process of creating new narrative forms to articulate indigenous ways of knowing and storytelling. This recent group of Native fiction writers is influenced by the importance of claiming sovereignty, a principle that recognizes contemporary tribes as sovereign nations with the right to self-determination.

Native American Renaissance: Momaday, Ortiz, Welch, and Silko

Native writers of Momaday's generation share an interest in making Native protagonists visible and telling stories of their distinct experiences as Indian people. These writers typically present protagonists who are caught between Native traditions and white mainstream expectations, but they reject the typical modernist narrative ending of alienation. In a 1987 essay, scholar William Bevis observed that "coming home" is the predominant motif found in American Indian fiction, in contrast to the "leaving home" journey to find one's identity typical of the Euro-American novel: "coming home," Bevis emphasizes, "is not only the primary story, it is a primary mode of knowledge and a primary good."[3] This central thematic – along with a focus on tribal lands, indigenous languages, and traditional stories and rituals – emerges across fictional texts written by many different authors.

N. Scott Momaday (Kiowa/Cherokee, b. 1934) was raised in Oklahoma among his father's people, the Kiowa, and in Arizona and New Mexico, where his parents worked as teachers on the Navajo Reservation and at Jemez Pueblo. Elements of Kiowa, Navajo, and Pueblo cultures appear in his novels and poems. Momaday, who met William Faulkner while studying law at the University of Virginia in 1956–1957 and who studied at Stanford University with Yvor Winters while earning his MFA and PhD, is clearly influenced by literary modernism. Given the name Tsoai-talee (Rock Tree Boy, the Kiowa name for Devil's Tower) by an elder when he was a baby, Momaday creates literary works infused with the presence of indigenous stories, rituals, and traditions, and a spiritually animate landscape.

His acclaimed first novel, *House Made of Dawn* (1968), tells the story of Abel, an Army veteran who returns from World War II to his pueblo and finds himself alienated. He gets into an altercation with an albino, whom he sees as a witch or evil spirit in accordance with tribal teachings, and so he kills the man, but is sentenced by the mainstream justice system for murder and ends up in prison. Abel thus functions symbolically as the alienated Indian man who struggles to locate himself in very different worlds. Eventually granted parole, Abel is relocated to Los Angeles, where he takes a job in a factory and becomes part of an urban community of exiled Natives, among whom he tries to find a sense of belonging. But he detests his job, and after he is severely beaten by a police officer, he decides to return home to the reservation and to his grandfather, and the last scene of the novel shows him taking his place among the dawn runners to carry out an ancient ritual of racing against death and evil in the world.

Louis Owens (Cherokee/Choctaw) has described *House Made of Dawn* as a "Trojan-horse novel" in its ability to appeal to a white mainstream critical audience while containing "within its shell of modernist sophistication a thoroughly 'Indian' story and discourse."[4] Momaday's success with this novel paved the way for his innovative prose work *The Way to Rainy Mountain*, which was published in 1969, the same year he received the Pulitzer Prize. Part autobiography, part Kiowa history and story, part ethnography, *The Way to Rainy Mountain* traces the migration journey of the Kiowa to their current location near Rainy Mountain in Lawton, Oklahoma, while also narrating moments of personal and family history. The text is accompanied by illustrations from Momaday's father, Al, and the interplay between visual and verbal text reflects Momaday's own accomplishments as a painter and as a writer, and his interest in using multiple modes to tell stories of Native peoples. Indeed, over the course of his career, Momaday has worked in several genres, including poetry, memoir, and children's literature, as well as fiction. *The Man Made of Words* (1997), a remarkable collection of essays and stories spanning Momaday's career, includes the influential essay of the same title, in which Momaday asserts that Indian identity is not solely a matter of ancestry but is also a work of imagination.

Another key writer of the time is Simon Ortiz (Acoma Pueblo, b. 1941), who spent his formative years at Acoma and spoke the Keres language of the pueblo as his mother tongue. He learned English in school, and his bilingualism is readily apparent in his published work. While Ortiz showed academic talent in high school, he did not proceed to college immediately after graduation, but worked in a series of positions as a laborer and did a stint in the US Army, before enrolling in writing programs at the University of New Mexico and the University of Iowa. His early poetry attracted attention for its ability to speak concretely and eloquently about Acoma traditions and values, and to depict vividly the landscape surrounding the pueblo (called "Sky City" by tourists because the old village sits atop a 367-foot sandstone bluff). He is an accomplished fiction writer and a noted activist, in addition to being recognized for his poetry.

Ortiz was among the writers included in *The Man to Send Rain Clouds* (1974), an important anthology of short stories by Native writers edited by Kenneth Rosen. Five of Ortiz's stories appear in this volume, and his prowess in the genre has helped to make the short story a welcoming genre for Native writers. The volume *Men on the Moon* (1999) collects twenty-six of his stories and demonstrates his ability to mix Acoma ways of life with contemporary events, often resulting in wry humor and sobering insight. The story that lends the collection its title, for instance, is set at Acoma, where a grandfather watches the Apollo mission to the moon on a TV set that has just been given to him by his family. Interspersed with descriptions of the blast-off, the landing on the moon, and the walk on the lunar landscape are the grandfather's dreams and memories of Acoma stories; there is no boundary between these different worlds in Ortiz's sense of things. Similarly, "The Killing of a State Cop" is based on an actual incident involving two young Indian men and a racist police officer, but depicts the events from an indigenous perspective as a ritualistic slaying of witchery, and "To Change Life in a Good Way" depicts the dangers of uranium mining and modern warfare as well as espousing traditional healing rituals. Throughout Ortiz's work, indigenous beliefs and stories offer potent ways of making the contemporary world meaningful and of restoring balance. He elaborates on this theme in his 1981 essay, "Towards a National Indian Literature: Cultural Authenticity in Nationalism," in which he describes the ability of indigenous peoples to reckon with outside influences and colonialism through oral traditions and knowledge. For Ortiz, Native literary texts drawing on these traditions articulate a strong "nationalistic character" and are an important cultural resource to advocate for self-determination and sovereignty.[5]

James Welch (Blackfeet/Gros Ventre, 1940–2003), like Ortiz and Momaday, worked in more than one genre as a writer. Welch memorably portrayed the alienation of contemporary Indian men and the continuing presence of oral traditions in his works. He studied creative writing at the University of Montana, where the poet Richard Hugo became an important mentor. His first full-length volume was a poetry collection titled *Riding the Earthboy 40* (1971, exp. edn. 1975), which depicts the Montana landscape he grew up in and represents the deeply embedded sense of place important to all his work. Welch is best known as the author of five novels – *Winter in the Blood* (1974), *The Death of Jim Loney* (1979), *Fools Crow* (1986), *Indian Lawyer* (1990), and *The Heartsong of Charging Elk* (2000). In his novels, Welch unsparingly presents the harsh effects of US policies toward American Indians, as well as presenting compelling protagonists who thoughtfully reflect on the conditions they face, their sense of Indian identity, and their responsibility to their tribal peoples.

Welch's most discussed novel is *Fools Crow*, an ambitious historical novel set in the mid nineteenth century, when the Pikunis (Blackfeet) come into increasingly hostile contact with white settlers. Welch endeavors to recreate the world of the Pikuni by creating a hybrid English prose that features indigenous-inflected rhythms and tribally based terms ("ears-far-apart" for owl, for example; "Many-sharp-points-ground" for fort; or "the white sand that makes things sweet" for sugar).[6] Fools Crow, the title character, eventually becomes the leader of his people, an honor and responsibility he accepts with a heavy heart as, near the end of the novel, he is granted a vision of his people's future, which leads to a horrific massacre, and the knowledge that he must be the one to ensure that the tribe endures.

A similar sense of tribal responsibility affects the protagonist of Leslie Marmon Silko's novel *Ceremony*, which is today perhaps the best-known and most widely studied and taught novel by an American Indian writer. Silko (Laguna Pueblo, b. 1948) grew up hearing the stories of her people and understanding the importance of the Laguna landscape to stories and traditions; she skillfully incorporates oral stories and Laguna beliefs into the contemporary lives of her protagonists. Silko attended the University of New Mexico, where she earned her BA (summa cum laude) in English in 1969. She subsequently enrolled in the American Indian law program, but soon decided to transfer to the Creative Writing program in English. In 1974 the successful publication of her first volume of poetry (*Laguna Woman*) and several of her short stories in Rosen's *The Man to Send Rain Clouds* confirmed that writing should be her primary occupation. Over the years,

Silko has published three novels, *Ceremony* (1977), *Almanac of the Dead* (1991), and *Gardens in the Dunes* (1999); *Storyteller* (1981), a collection of poetry, short fiction, autobiography, and photographs; two collections of essays; and a memoir. In 1981, Silko was recognized with a MacArthur Foundation Prize Fellowship (the "genius grant"), which allowed her to concentrate fully on her writing; this prestigious fellowship, like the Pulitzer Prize awarded to Momaday in 1969, also signaled to a wider critical audience that American Indian fiction had arrived.

While all of her published work has received considerable critical attention, Silko's *Ceremony* and *Almanac of the Dead* are essential to understanding her compelling vision of how stories and traditions from "time immemorial"[7] continue to animate the world today. *Ceremony* tells the story of Tayo, a World War II veteran suffering from post-traumatic stress disorder who returns to Laguna after the war, shattered and in need of healing. As it turns out, it is not only his war experience but other kinds of trauma that haunt him – his abandonment as a child by his mother, his mixedblood status, the deaths of his beloved cousin Rocky and his uncle Josiah, the drought that has left much of the land infertile, as well as the loss of the cattle his uncle chose and cared for so diligently. The first part of the novel develops these interconnected tensions as Tayo accepts help from Ku'oosh, a traditional Laguna healer, which enables him to begin to face his inner turmoil. But it is his encounter with Betonie, an unorthodox mixedblood Navajo medicine man, that proves to be a turning point for Tayo. Betonie sees clearly that Tayo has a larger role to play for his people; his ceremonies and stories enable Tayo to connect his personal turmoil to the troubles afflicting the land and the Laguna people. The second half of the novel unfolds as Tayo enters the world of story come to life and encounters a woman named Ts'eh, who represents Yellow Woman (Kochinnenako), a female figure in traditional stories who ensures orderly transitions, balance, and harmony. Through his relationship with Ts'eh, Tayo is able to face the "Destroyers" who threaten to upset the world, and in the end, order and harmony are beautifully restored to Tayo, the land, and the Laguna people.

Like *Ceremony*, *Almanac of the Dead* connects the health and disease of its characters to the world around them, but carries out this analysis on an epic scale (the novel runs to 763 pages). Acknowledging the legacy of 500 years of colonialism in the Americas, *Almanac* protests capitalist greed, environmental exploitation, and loss of indigenous-held land, among other things, and turns to extreme portraits of drug abuse, pornography, torture, killing, and other kinds of violence to make clear that Western civilization has created a horrible culture of death. The novel takes a hemispheric approach to this problem and depicts two groups of protestors – one marching north from Central America, the other marching south from the United States – to join together in resistance. In the end, *Almanac* conveys a powerful vision of a time when indigenous-inspired revolution will over-turn dominant colonial powers and restore tribal values of healing and life to the Americas.

Postmodern and postcolonial voices: Vizenor, Erdrich, Hogan, and Alexie

The awareness of and resistance to colonialism found in Silko's 1991 novel is explored extensively in fictional works by Gerald Vizenor, Louise Erdrich, Linda Hogan, and Sherman Alexie, writers who gained critical recognition in the 1980s and early 1990s in the context of postmodern media culture. They are acutely aware of popular stereotypes and racist ideas of Native peoples and understand only too well how difficult it is to counter such images. They are also deeply concerned with the pernicious effects of coloni-alism, in the past and the present. In the face of tragedy and trauma, racism and oppression, however, these writers often turn to irony, as well as poign-ant lyricism, to portray Native realities. They craft stories and novels that foreground trickster strategies, Indian humor, and tribal values to reveal the limits of whitewashed histories and the mainstream legal system, while advancing Indian claims for recognition and justice.

Gerald Vizenor (White Earth Ojibwe, b. 1934) is one of the most prolific American Indian authors, and he has published several volumes of poetry, collections of essays, literary criticism, plays, novels, and collections of short fiction. No matter what genre he works in, Vizenor is unique in his approach to writing. Concerned about the way that Indian peoples have been mis-represented in mainstream culture and literature as simulations, Vizenor embraces postmodern theory along with indigenous traditions, especially trickster stories, to create his own critical vocabulary that allows "postin-dian warriors [to] create a new tribal presence in stories."[8]

Born to a white mother and an Ojibwe father, who was killed before Gerald turned two years old, Vizenor was raised among various relatives on his father's side of the family. He did not finish high school and enlisted in the Army when he was eighteen; being stationed in Japan introduced him to Japanese culture, stories, and aesthetics – an influence that can be seen especially in his earliest published works, which innovatively use the haiku form to speak of American Indian realities. As a writer, Vizenor brilliantly combines multifarious influences to create stories of "survivance"; surviv-ance for him goes well beyond mere survival to speak of dynamic ways of resisting colonialism and creating stories of tribal presence and sovereignty.[9]

His work effortlessly and imaginatively blends traditional Ojibwe stories with contemporary events, autobiography, literary theory, stories from other cultures, legal and political realities, and much more. Kimberly Blaeser (White Earth Ojibwe) convincingly demonstrates that Vizenor works in the oral tradition, rather like a traditional trickster in his imaginative manipulations,[10] but many readers and students of Native literature find his work daunting in its leaps of imagination and breadth of reference. *The Heirs of Columbus* (1991), which reimagines the historic explorer as having Mayan ancestry, is perhaps Vizenor's most accessible novel and demonstrates his ability to weave together historical details, Native traditions, and postmodern aesthetics to tell the story of a new America, one where anyone may receive an injection to become "Indian" and where Columbus becomes a figure of healing rather than destruction as his heirs receive healing genes extracted from his bones. Serious play characterizes all of Vizenor's work, and his recent novels have taken a new twist on human remains and repatriation claims (*Chancers* [2000]), the atom bomb and nuclear destruction (*Hiroshima Bugi* [2003]), and sexual abuse by reservation priests (*Father Meme* [2008]).

Reckoning with injustice is a theme that resonates in the work of another prominent Ojibwe writer, (Karen) Louise Erdrich (Turtle Mountain Ojibwe, b. 1954). Erdrich, like Vizenor, has published prolifically in a variety of genres, though it is her fiction that has garnered the most attention from readers and scholars. Erdrich is Ojibwe on her mother's side and German on her father's side; she grew up mostly in Wahpeton, North Dakota, where her parents were employed by the Bureau of Indian Affairs. In 1972, she was in the first class of women to be admitted to Dartmouth College in New Hampshire. In 1979, Erdrich finished an MA in Creative Writing at Johns Hopkins University, where John Barth, the noted postmodern writer, was among the faculty she worked with. Erdrich's fiction innovatively combines indigenous oral traditions, postmodern narrative strategies, and lyrical prose rhythms.

Because of her interest in continuing characters and stories across novels, Erdrich is often likened to William Faulkner and his creation of Yoknapatawpha County. The major families Erdrich focuses on – the Kashpaws, Pillagers, Lamartines, Nanapushes, and Lazarres – are introduced in her acclaimed first novel, *Love Medicine* (1984, rev. 1993), which was followed by *The Beet Queen* (1986), *Tracks* (1988), *The Bingo Palace* (1994), *Tales of Burning Love* (1996), *The Last Report on the Miracles at Little No Horse* (2001), and *Four Souls* (2004). The order of publication does not correspond to the chronology of events in the overall saga, and some readers have found this mix of time, place, and character to be perplexing. But Erdrich's vision is of how past, present, and future flow together in sometimes unexpected ways and how stories from the past become meaningful in new and contemporary contexts. A strong connection to the land pervades Erdrich's fiction, and the loss of Indian-held lands through various acts of legislation and dishonest dealings is an open wound that reappears in her novels, treated most extensively in *Tracks*. All of Erdrich's novels are preoccupied with history, and taken together they create a Native-focused counterhistory to the official mainstream story of the settling of America. Through her interlinked novels, Erdrich is writing her own epic, her own tale of the tribe. Her capacious vision and tangled family trees allow her to emphasize the importance of familial and tribal affiliations even in the midst of disputes and different ways of coping with American bureaucracy and hegemony. Erdrich's ability to draw a full range of Native characters is remarkable. Some of her Indian characters become cruel, or greedy, or dogmatic, or insane in their response to colonialism. Others turn to tribal and inner resources to face devastation and fight back. Others wander, looking for direction. But Erdrich's most compelling characters – Nanapush, Fleur Pillager, Lulu Lamartine, Gerry Nanapush, and Lipsha Morrissey – are rather trickster-like in their ability to use old stories and traditions to resist oppression and seek justice.

Erdrich has also published several novels that are not part of this extended tribal epic and that focus on entirely new characters: *The Antelope Wife* (1998), *The Master Butchers Singing Club* (2003), *The Painted Drum* (2005), *The Plague of Doves* (2008), and *Shadow Tag* (2010). These novels are committed to exploring the lasting effects of painful histories, but often develop Indian and white characters who are equally essential to presenting the whole story. All of her characters – Natives and nonnatives alike – must reckon with tremendous hardships and disappointments, and all experience the profound pull of love and desire. Erdrich's fiction as a whole emphasizes the struggle to survive in this world, revealing that wisdom and compassion may result from the struggle.

Linda Hogan (Chickasaw, b. 1947) shares Erdrich's commitment to conveying both painful truths and joy in an eloquent, lyrical prose style. Hogan is Chickasaw on her father's side, Anglo on her mother's. Moving often as she grew up because her father was in the Army, Hogan came to think of Oklahoma, where her paternal grandparents lived and where the Chickasaw Nation is located, as her homeland. Hogan earned her BA as a nontraditional working-class student from the University of Colorado–Colorado Springs and went on to earn an MA in Creative Writing from the

University of Colorado–Boulder. Like other contemporary Native writers, she first began publishing as a poet and then branched out into other genres. She has published several volumes of poetry, an autobiography, a collection of essays, and four novels: *Mean Spirit* (1990), *Solar Storms* (1995), *Power* (1998), and *People of the Whale* (2008). In all of her novels, ecological concerns take center stage, with *Mean Spirit* focusing on the discovery of oil on Osage lands in Oklahoma in the early twentieth century, while *Solar Storms* alludes to the James Bay hydroelectric power project. *Power* focuses on the endangered Florida panther, and *People of the Whale*, as its title suggests, presents whales as tribally sacred. In contrast to many contemporary Native writers, Hogan writes about Indian tribes and traditions other than her own. In this way, her novels outline an ethical ecocritical consciousness that is an urgent concern not just for a specific tribal nation, but for all human beings.

While Hogan's environmental emphasis might seem to lend itself to stereotypical ideas of American Indians as the true keepers of the land (the first environmentalists, in other words), her fiction does much more than depict simple connections between environmentalism, spirituality, and Native peoples. Hogan's novels also offer a graphic view of the devastating effects of colonialism and the capitalist exploitation of Native peoples and lands that makes ecocritical awareness an urgent survival strategy. *Solar Storms*, for instance, unflinchingly presents the alcoholism, child abuse, poverty, racism, and other ills that afflict the Native inhabitants of the community of Adam's Rib to such a degree that they have almost given up any resistance to the government's plan to create a dam that will flood ancestral homelands. But then Angel, a young Native woman who was adopted out as a child because her mother abused her, returns to the community and to her remaining family members. Angel, as it turns out, is a plant dreamer, and so in incremental steps, this hopeful sign leads to collective action and public acts of resistance to the dams and loss of Indian lands. Hogan's ecocritical focus, then, is not New Age fad, but a carefully conceived ethical and political response to centuries of colonial devastation.

A poignant tension between the harsh realities of contemporary Indian life and a longing for positive direction is also found in the work of Sherman Alexie (Spokane/Coeur d'Alene, b. 1966). Alexie grew up in the town of Wellpinit on the Spokane Indian Reservation in Washington state, amid a loving family that often had to deal with difficult circumstances, including poverty, alcoholism, health crises, and house fires. Alexie's writing draws on these difficulties, and his early work is set on the reservation, creating a new literary mode that he calls "reservation realism."[11] Alexie's work has been acclaimed by Native and nonnative readers and critics for its portrayal of reservation life, its critique of stereotypes and identity politics, and its hard-hitting depiction of Indian–Anglo relations, as well as its brilliant deployment of Indian humor.

The Lone Ranger and Tonto Fistfight in Heaven (1993), a collection of mostly interrelated stories, features three compelling characters – Victor Joseph, Thomas Builds-the-Fire, and Junior Polatkin – who must deal with serious problems such as alcoholism, poverty, and despair on the reservation and who struggle to escape them. (So fascinating are these characters that they reappear in Alexie's 1995 novel *Reservation Blues*.) Alexie draws attention to the situation of young Indian men, caught between wanting to be warriors and heroes but having to face the hopelessness of having few opportunities available to them on the reservation. Conversely, Indian women often turn out to be the source of strength for their families and community in these stories, which has led scholar Patrice Hollrah to analyze the strong Native women in Alexie's fiction as "contemporary female warriors" linked to Alexie's sustained critique of patriarchy and homophobia.[12] The complicated relationships between Indian fathers and sons, a theme that recurs in Alexie's work, forms the central tension of "This Is What It Means to Say Phoenix, Arizona," a story that became the basis for the 1998 feature-length film *Smoke Signals*, which won major awards at the Sundance Film Festival and attracted enthusiastic critical and popular response.

The stories of *The Toughest Indian in the World* (2000), *Ten Little Indians* (2003), and *War Dances* (2009) have earned Alexie recognition for his mastery of the short-story form. Several of Alexie's stories present scenarios in which a character's sense of Native identity is unsettled by class, gender, and sexual identities, as in "The Toughest Indian in the World," in which a journalist, of Spokane ancestry but isolated from his people, has a one-night, same-sex encounter with an Indian hitchhiker as a way of renewing his Indianness. Alexie's humane and sympathetic depiction of characters under duress, a quality that has elicited favorable comparisons to Raymond Carver, is most notable in "What You Pawn I Will Redeem," a story from *Ten Little Indians* that follows a homeless, alcoholic Indian man on a quest to find enough money to reclaim his grandmother's regalia from a Seattle pawnshop.

Alexie's fiction alternates between devastating stories and stories of hope. His bleakest vision emerges in the novel *Indian Killer* (1996), which unsparingly depicts the ravages of racism and presents a grim picture of Indian–white relations. Alexie's first novel targeted toward young-adult readers, *The Absolutely True Diary of a Part-Time Indian* (2007), presents a more affirmative look at some of the difficulties that afflict his characters. The novel, drawing on Alexie's own experiences, features Arnold Spirit, Jr., who decides to leave the reservation to go to high school in a nearby predominantly Anglo town and, through various struggles, learns that it is possible to have two hometowns and to walk in both worlds. As Alexie's career has progressed, then, his fiction has significantly evolved from a focus on reservation-based settings and themes to a depiction of twenty-first-century Indians who are mobile, who leave home to fashion their own sense of Indian identity in new, often urban, mixed-race surroundings.

New voices: Glancy, Howe, and Gansworth

American Indian writers gaining critical recognition in the twenty-first century have been inspired by the fictional works and achievements of those who preceded them. But Owens's description of Momaday's *House Made of Dawn* as a "Trojan-horse novel" no longer seems apropos for today's writers, who have been empowered to create new narrative strategies and novelistic conventions. One of the emerging strains is an interest in transforming genre fiction such as the murder mystery (*The Red Power Murders* [2006] by Thomas King, Cherokee, for instance) or science fiction/fantasy (such as *The Way of Thorn and Thunder* trilogy [2005–2007] by Daniel Heath Justice, Cherokee) to critique the misrepresentation of Native peoples in mainstream culture, while telling a distinctively Indian story from a tribally informed perspective. Other contemporary writers have pursued innovations in narrative perspective and chronology, or have juxtaposed fictional and nonfictional, visual and verbal texts in their novels to tell multilayered stories. These innovations are meaningful: transforming narrative conventions allows for the emergence of a richly complex presentation of tribal history and culture, interracial and crosscultural tensions and connections, as well as indigenous identity and ethics – a new form of indigenous writing that LeAnne Howe has called "tribalography."[13]

Diane Glancy (Cherokee, b. 1941) is a writer well known for her interest in literary experimentation, exploring in her works how language can speak from the gaps of what it means to be Native and/or mixedblood and to inherit a history marked by loss and trauma. In *Pushing the Bear* (1996), for instance, Glancy retells the story/history of the Trail of Tears using more than fifty different narrative voices and incorporating historical documents and traditional Cherokee stories, along with dream-visions and her own fictional narrative. What results is an informative and poignant novel that imaginatively recreates the traumatic experience of removal and relocation for the Cherokee. By focusing on how Maritole and Knobowtee, the central couple of the novel, are pulled apart by the trail but endure to make a new home and a new family in Oklahoma territory, Glancy's novel emphasizes the resilience and sovereignty of the Cherokee people.

LeAnne Howe (Choctaw, b. 1951), like Glancy, is interested in exploring Native history from new angles. One of her most distinctive narrative strategies is to avoid chronological sequence and to use overlapping temporalities to fuse events and stories from the past, present, and future. She has published two full-length novels – *Shell Shaker* (2001) and *Miko Kings: An Indian Baseball Story* (2007) – that alternate between narrating events from previous eras in Choctaw history and events that unfold in the contemporary world. *Miko Kings*, for instance, is a fascinating story about Indian baseball in Oklahoma Territory in the early twentieth century, but it is also a story about boarding schools, the terrors of racism, Choctaw mathematics and time travel, and so much more. The female protagonists in Howe's novels yearn for deeper understanding and for healing, which leads them on a quest for knowledge that animates the past as a vital resource. In the end, the need to deal with their own personal conflicts leads to a reinvigorated sense of the importance of Choctaw history, traditions, and values in connection to crises in the contemporary world, a recognition that has led Craig Womack (Musgogee Creek/Cherokee) to comment that Howe's work valuably shows that "tribally specific approaches have global implications."[14]

The fusion of verbal text and visual image to tell new Native stories is a narrative strategy explored extensively in the work of Eric Gansworth (Onondaga). Gansworth is committed to carrying on Haudenosaunee traditions – such as wampum, the three sisters (corn, beans, squash), traditional dancing, and the lunar calendar of the Iroquois – in his work. An accomplished visual artist and creative writer, Gansworth incorporates his own paintings into his novels and stories to bring tribal traditions into relation with the contemporary world through juxtaposed images. The illuminating effect of his mixed-media approach to fiction can be seen in his acclaimed 2005 novel, *Mending Skins*, as well as the interlinked stories of *Smoke Dancing* (2004). Exploring what it means to live as an Onondaga in today's world requires multiple modalities in Gansworth's fiction.

Glancy, Howe, and Gansworth are three exemplary contemporary writers exploring new ways of telling vital stories of Native history, identity, and sovereignty, but even more important, they are in the company of many other indigenous writers working today to promote Native fiction and indigenous perspectives. The stream of American Indian fiction that has been published since 1945 is remarkable. Despite attempts to decimate, assimilate, and legislate American Indians out of existence over the past hundreds of years, American Indian populations are growing in number, and a strong, dynamic group of indigenous writers thrives today.

FURTHER READING

Allen, Chadwick. *Blood Narrative: Indigenous Identity in American Indian and Maori Literary and Activist Texts*. Durham, NC: Duke University Press, 2002

Cox, James H. *Muting White Noise: Native American and European American Novel Traditions*. Norman: University of Oklahoma Press, 2006

King, Thomas. *The Truth about Stories: A Native Narrative*. Minneapolis: University of Minnesota Press, 2005

Krupat, Arnold. *Red Matters: Native American Studies*. Philadelphia: University of Pennsylvania Press, 2002

Owens, Louis. *Other Destinies: Understanding the American Indian Novel*. Norman: University of Oklahoma Press, 1992

Purdy, John Lloyd. *Writing Indian, Native Conversations*. Lincoln: University of Nebraska Press, 2009

Rainwater, Catherine. *Dreams of Fiery Stars: The Transformations of Native American Fiction*. Philadelphia: University of Pennsylvania Press, 1999

Womack, Craig S. *Red on Red: Native American Literary Separatism*. Minneapolis: University of Minnesota Press, 1999

NOTES

1 Vine Deloria Jr., Foreword to *Black Elk Speaks*, by Nicholas Black Elk and John G. Neihardt (Lincoln: University of Nebraska Press, 2000), p. xv.

2 Kenneth Lincoln, *Native American Renaissance* (Berkeley: University of California Press, 1983).

3 William Bevis, "Native American Novels: Homing In," in Brian Swann and Arnold Krupat (eds.), *Recovering the Word: Essays on Native American Literature* (Berkeley: University of California Press, 1987), p. 582.

4 Louis Owens, *Mixedblood Messages: Literature, Film, Family, Place* (Norman: University of Oklahoma Press, 1998), p. 69.

5 Simon J. Ortiz, "Towards a National Indian Literature: Cultural Authenticity in Nationalism," *MELUS*, 8.2 (Summer 1981): 10.

6 James Welch, *Fools Crow* (New York: Viking Penguin, 1986), pp. 5, 15, 16.

7 Leslie Marmon Silko, *Ceremony* (New York: Viking Penguin, 1977), p. 94.

8 Gerald Vizenor, *Manifest Manners: Postindian Warriors of Survivance* (Hanover, NH: Wesleyan University Press/University Press of New England, 1994), p. 12.

9 Gerald Vizenor, "Aesthetics of Survivance," in Vizenor (ed.), *Survivance: Narratives of Native Presence* (Lincoln: University of Nebraska Press, 2008), pp. 1–23.

10 Kimberly M. Blaeser, *Gerald Vizenor: Writing in the Oral Tradition* (Norman: University of Oklahoma Press, 1996).

11 Sherman Alexie, Introduction to *The Lone Ranger and Tonto Fistfight in Heaven*, exp. edn. (New York: Grove, 2005), p. xxi.

12 Patrice E. M. Hollrah, *"The Old Lady Trill, the Victory Yell": The Power of Women in Native American Literature* (New York: Routledge, 2004), pp. 133, 169.

13 LeAnne Howe, "Blind Bread and the Business of Theory Making," in Janice Acoose, Craig S. Womack, Daniel Heath Justice, and Christopher B. Teuton (eds.), *Reasoning Together: The Native Critics Collective* (Norman: University of Oklahoma Press, 2008), pp. 325–39.

14 Craig S. Womack, Review of *Evidence of Red*, by LeAnne Howe, *SAIL*, 17.4 (Winter 2005): 158.

8

A. ROBERT LEE

Multiethnicities: Latino/a and Asian American fiction

Throughout the years following World War II (and particularly since the 1960s), there have been spectacular advances in the quantity and influence of multicultural American authorship. Just as Latino/a and Asian American populations have grown increasingly prominent in the United States, so a plenitude of new literary fiction – novel and novella, story and story cycle – has emerged to match and indeed engender a rethinking of what "ethnic" and allied notions actually signify. This, to be sure, includes reaffirmation and continuance of the Latino/a literary spectrum, the *Chicanismo* signaled in the fiction of Tomás Rivera, Rudolfo Anaya, and Rolando Hinojosa, and a women's generation to include Sandra Cisneros and Ana Castillo, together with the rosters of new storytelling by *Riqueños/as*, Cuban Americans, Dominican Americans, and others whose origins in the Latin and Caribbean Americas give a hemispheric reach to Hispanic voice. An awakened Asian American literary consciousness equally invites its due; narratives that severally but always uniquely pursue American lives filtered through China, Japan, Korea, Vietnam, the Philippines, and Indo-Pakistan and other South Asian countries, by such writers as Maxine Hong Kingston, Toshio Mori, Theresa Hak Kyung Cha, Lan Cao, Jessica Hagedorn, and Bharati Mukherjee.

How best, then, to situate American literary genealogies, Latino/a, Asian American, or otherwise, and each however diverse in itself, within the "national" American canon? Are the respective texts duty-bound to be representational, some prescribed version of the community from which they arise? Implicit, too, is a further issue. Does a demographic minority always write minority literature? Although each of these questions reflects a broad range of ideological and literary-cultural theory, as well as ongoing and often fierce debates about canon and non-canon, mainstream and peripheries, the context of multiethnicity suggests that American literature, from the outset, is best thought of as a spectrum of lineages rather than a single tradition, and is thereby at once more coexistent, hybrid, and inflected by race and ethnicity (to say nothing of class or gender) than it has been customary to acknowledge.

Relevant anthologies notably refract these developments, whether the widely used *Norton Anthology of American Literature* and its successive "ethnic" inclusions and exclusions since the 1960s, or those given to an explicit multicultural impetus like Ishmael Reed's *The Before Columbus Foundation Poetry Anthology* (1991) and *The Before Columbus Foundation Fiction Anthology* (1992), or yet more to immediate purposes, specific-tradition collections like Lauro Flores's *The Floating Borderlands: Twenty-Five Years of US Hispanic Literature* (1998) and Jessica Hagedorn's *Charlie Chan is Dead: An Anthology of Contemporary Asian American Fiction* (1993). The effect has been to situate any one line of fiction, Latino/a and Asian American among them, within a far more encompassing multicultural literary sightline, yet without losing sight of cultural specificity whatever the overlaps in processes of identity-formation and Americanization. A sense of contextual perspective is not only apt or illuminating but also necessary.

The variety of African American literary fiction spans Ralph Ellison's landmark Dixie-to-Harlem *Invisible Man* (1952), Gloria Naylor's *Mama Day* (1988), a palimpsest of *The Tempest*, Walter Mosley's the Easy Rawlins LA mysteries inaugurated in the *Devil in a Blue Dress* (1990), to Toni Morrison's postsecular exploration of black community in *Paradise* (1998) – her Nobel Prize in 1993 was a historic act of recognition. A major novel like N. Scott Momaday's *House Made of Dawn* (1968), with its Jemez Pueblo *mythus* and self-enacting circle of recovery, reminds of a Native America possessed of its own fiction treasury, whether variously tribe- or city-centered, oral-into-written, or even postmodern, at the hands of Leslie Marmon Silko, Louise Erdrich, James Welch, Gerald Vizenor, and Sherman Alexie. The cosmopolitan virtuosity of Jewish fiction extends from the generation of Saul Bellow, Bernard Malamud, and Philip Roth to such contemporary writers as Michael Chabon, who in *The Mysteries of Pittsburgh* (1988) explores loops of city crime and sexual difference, and Allegra Goodman, who pursues the flow and counterflow of modern Jewish American dynasty in *The Family Markowitz* (1996). Arab and Muslim American fiction has become increasingly visible, from Diane Abu-Jader's *Arabian Jazz* (1993) in its portrait of the Ramoud family's vexed negotiation from Jordanian into Western identity, to Laila Halaby's *Once in a Promised Land* (2007) in its bitter-sweet account of a family of Arab genealogy facing America in the wake of 9/11.

Controversially, the multicultural sightline might also include fiction written from, or at least exploratory of, white America whose supposed racelessness has been the subject of interrogation not only by Toni Morrison in her adroit, greatly incisive *Playing in the Dark: Whiteness and the Literary Imagination* (1992) but also by a trove of whiteness-studies scholarship.[1] To hand are realms of culturally white life, notably suburb or sexuality, whose best-known chroniclers include John Updike in his Rabbit Angstrom quartet (1960–2001), John Cheever in his *New Yorker* stories of Westchester and well-heeled Boston, and Raymond Carver with his honed story-vignettes like "Where I'm Calling From" or "Little Things." Blue-collar white America finds its unyielding laureate in Charles Bukowski, either in his "Henry Chinaski" novel of alcoholism and menial jobs, *Post Office* (1970), or his novel set in the lower depths of Los Angeles, *Factotum* (1975). Across a prodigious oeuvre, Joyce Carol Oates addresses white American family life as both 1950s ethos and battle-ground in *You Must Remember This* (1980) and, as the later twentieth-century, in *We Were the Mulvaneys* (1996). The sense of whiteness as hegemonic social code and insignia, in other words, also invites being parsed under ethnic auspices.

Other ethnicities remind us of the historical contingency of whiteness. (After all, Irish and Italian immigrants were not considered white in the nineteenth century.) William Kennedy's *Ironweed* (1983) portrays a Depression-era Irish American's fall from grace into poverty and alcoholism in New York's Albany, while Edwin O'Connor provides a vintage narrative of Boston political graft in *The Last Hurrah* (1956). *Italianetà* can summon Helen Barolini's *Umbertina* (1999), with its canvas of womanhood and family from Calabria to New York, and contrast with Mario Puzo's popular mafia launched with *The Godfather* (1969). Jeffrey Eugenides' *Middlesex* (2002) not only gives virtuoso fashioning to Greek American immigrant life but in the person of its hermaphroditic protagonist, Callie/Cal, a portrait of sexual borders.

It is important as well not to overlook the implications of mixed-ethnicity authorship, the historic *mestizaje* embodied in virtually every Latino/a novelist, or the eclectic family lines called up in the fiction of a Chinese American like Ruthanne Lum McCunn, author of *Thousand Pieces of Gold* (1981) with its serial life of Lalu Nathoy as stolen China-girl, concubine, and Gold Rush figure, and a Filipina American like Jessica Hagedorn, whose *Dogeaters* (1990) evokes Manila and the Marcos years as both family comedy and political dark cinema. Literary ethnicity, to re-emphasize, invites being given a wider than usual lien, the recognition of a more inclusive register.

At the same time the power of specifics, historical and personal, invites being fully weighed. The two fiction domains in view, Latino/a and Asian American, give their own wholly distinctive particularizations to self, family, the different transitions of identity, migrancy, and immigration, and the push and pull of generational assimilation. Not least has to be the impact of backdrops like the Mexican–American War of 1846–1848 and the ensuing Treaty of Guadalupe Hidalgo, with its US seizure of the Mexican West and Southwest, or the "Yellow Peril" Exclusion Act of 1882 and the 1924 Immigration Act, both reflective of white-nativist politics and discrimination. A presiding sense of locale equally feeds into both traditions, whether under Chicano/a auspices, the Southwest at large, and "East Los" and other *barrios,* or Nuyorriqueño Spanish Harlem and island Puerto Rico, and Cuban Miami's Calle Ocho. Under Asian American auspices that has meant West Coast Chinatowns and Little Japans from Seattle to San Francisco and the "Asias" of Hawaii and New York. Domiciles, even so, are to be encountered outside any or all of these, be it Sandra Cisneros's intimate family and girlhood Chicago in *The House on Mango Street* (1983), Karen Tei Yamashita's soaringly fantastical Brazil ecology in *Through the Arc of the Rainforest* (1990), or Gish Jen's dormitory suburb of Tarrytown in her wry take on assimilation as both dream and pratfall in *Typical American* (1991).

These also often enough share another dimension, namely the coexistence and the code-switches and interplays of language, be it Spanish or any one of a continuum of Asian tongues, with English. As Cisneros in "Ghost and Voices: Writing from Obsession" (1978) and Amy Tan in "Mother Tongue" (1990) both underscore, there has always been an interlingual regime, Spanish-English ("What I'm especially aware of is how the Spanish syntax and word choice occurs in my work even though I write English")[2] or Chinese and other Asian styles of English ("all the Englishes I grew up with ... what language ability tests never reveal").[3] Both observations again underscore the resistance to any one template. How, then, and in this wider multicultural context, to take measure of the emphases, the styles, of postwar storytelling within both traditions, whether the fiction of Hispanic America in its multiple *ficciones, corridos,* and *cuentos* or Asian America's galleries of narrative and talk-story?

Latino/a fiction

Chicano/a fiction, by dint of numbers if nothing else, has become the best-known of Latino/a writing – a wide suite of imagining with shared configurations yet, as always, with its own individual styles and focus. In this respect three texts have deservedly received iconic status: Rivera's *...y no se lo tragó la tierra/And The Earth Did Not Part* (1971) (translated in 1975 by Hinojosa as *This Migrant Earth* and told as a story cycle matching the cycle of a migrant labor year); Anaya's *Bless Me, Ultima* (1972), a reflex-ive first-person fiction set in 1940s New Mexico and conveyed as its own Chicano portrait of the artist; and Hinojosa's *Klail City y sus alrededores* (1976), reissued in English as *Klail City* (1987), and a version of the Río Grande Valley as both Chicano and multiethnic human geography. Each connects mythologies of the culture's American history whose signature phrases include *Aztlan* as memorial homeland, *La Raza* as people or race, *mestizaje* as demography, and a politics stretching from the World War II Zoot Suit riots to Brown Power in the 1960s to the signing and implemen-tation of NAFTA in the 1990s.

Rivera's text has an important antecedent in José Antonio Villarreal's *Pocho* (1959) in which, across a canvas from the Mexican Revolution to World War II, first-generation worker migration into *el norte* leads on to the "strange metamorphosis" of Richard Rubio, English-speaking American son to Spanish-speaking-only parents. Belonging to the pre-1960s, he finds himself caught between two worlds, two human econ-omies, if north-of-the-border-raised citizen then also the designated *pocho* of the title (a usually pejorative term in which Mexicans look down on their Chicano successors). But for Rivera, in the fourteen vignettes that make up *...y no se lo tragó la tierra*, the worker-families are Chicano, Tex-Mex, from pueblos near Austin or the Río Grande and trucked into the Midwest and West as itinerant and seasonal cheap field labor. Each of the stories has a *Dubliners* or *Winesburg, Ohio* ring, a mural of remem-brance from the opening "El Año Perdido/The Lost Year" with its child's sense of blur at the passing drama, through to "When We Arrive/Cuando lleguemos" with its invocation of job-to-job labor, subsistence wage, ram-shackle camp housing, and burnt-out truck caught against the dawn sky, together with the figure of Bartolo as poet-bard of migrant life. In these, as in the title piece's invocation of the boy's seeming apostasy, or in stories of anti-Mexican schoolyard racism, family death by fire, and a mother's Christmas-time breakdown, Rivera constructs his own lyric but unyielding figuration of Chicano migrant experience.

For Anaya in *Bless Me, Ultima*, the rite of passage he tells, that of Antonio Márez ("Tony" to his English-speaking schoolmates), renders the Southwest as a coalescence of different kinds of memory. As storyteller, *cuentista*, Antonio remembers his father's *vaquero* and mother's farmer-cultivator ori-gins, his sisters and absentee GI brothers, the family indigency and splits, and not least the Spanish spoken at home and English at school. Above all he remembers the shaman-figure of Ultima, *anciana* and *curandera* and yet also Catholic believer, from whom he learns the land's rhythm; the Native-indigenous arcana of herbs and flora; the symbolism of deific owl, Aztec eagle, and Christly dove; and the pathway out of his childhood fevers and nightmares (*pesadillas*) and the different community killings and setbacks. New Mexico, thereby, in his subtly self-referential telling, becomes not only the literal Southwest of pueblo or shrub-land but also magic terrain – one of Holy Week belief but also Golden Carp river-god creation mythology. As a result, the novel – history and dream, Ultima's death and Antonio's rebirth – understandably has won its place as a benchmark, Rivera's capturing of New Mexico *Chicanismo* as both quintessential Southwest locale and spiritual heritage.

The third of the so-called big three of Chicano fiction, Hinojosa, in the dozen novels which make up his Río Grande/Belken County series and which he inaugurated with *Klail City y sus alrededores*, creates a Tex-Mex version of Faulkner's Yoknapatawpha. This is further historic Chicano terrain, the south Texas of the valley as narrative storehouse of the power-politics between Anglo Klail and Mexican Klail, "the migrant trail" in the novel's own phrase, and a host of vernacular love affairs, scandals, crime, and police. The cross-border river itself serves as emblem of these shifting eddies as told through the narrators Rafe Buenrostro, Jesus Malacara, and P. Galindo, whether the *Aquí Me Quedo* bar story about the Widow Sóstenes and her Mexican Revolution pension, a Klail City High School reunion and its memory of past relationships, or the history of the town's founding by General Rufus T. Klail. The effect is collagist, self-circling, full of voice. Hinojosa's creation of mores and social texture presses throughout, one of family, railroad, war memorial, barbershop, Catholicism to Pentecostalism, bicultural encounter, even the region's heat, and always the valley as mythical kingdom both past and current.

In Cisneros and her compeers *Chicanismo* has a hugely consequential literary cadre, womanhood and its compass as gathering-points for issues of gender identity and autonomy, family, and self-power. *Woman Hollering Creek and Other Stories* (1991) carries much of Cisneros's own verve, a childhood to womanhood round of stories aptly denominated "*estos cuentitos.*" A vignette like "My Lucy Friend Who Smells Like Corn" captures the small-girl world of word inversion and psychology. "Mericans" depicts a girl's witness to her brother's resistance to Anglo tourist patronage and assumption that the pair does not share her American passport. "Tepeyac" offers the nuance of young girlhood memory of Catholic-Mexican grandparents, Cinco de Mayo, and the family store. Adult womanhood finds its expression in stories like "Never Marry a Mexican" with its chronicle of an artist-teacher's affairs with a father and son, the title story "Woman Hollering Creek" as an account of a failed cross-border marriage and use of the weeping woman/*la llorona* myth, and "*Bien* Pretty," the narrator's exuberant love-encounter with Flavier Michoacán and their different idio-syncrasies of mood and gesture. Viewpoint throughout the cycle is delicately handled, a paradigm of Chicana experience afforded rare imaginative filter-ing on Cisneros's part.

Whatever its roots in Samuel Richardson and Laclos or debt to Julio Cortázar's *Rayuela* (1963) with its select-your-own invitation to sequence, Ana Castillo's *The Mixquiahuala Letters* (1986), wholly contemporary in its storyline, represents a subtlety of achievement comparable to that of Cisneros. In the forty letters and ten-year span that disclose Teresa's friend-ship as a West Coast Chicana with Alicia as a New York designer-artist, and their lives and shared journey to Columbia and Mexico, Castillo uses the epistolary form to create a ready sense of historical present. Each increment takes on vitality, the effect of a live diary, from the visit to Mixquiahuala itself as early-Americas Toltec antiquity, to *brujería* in Veracruz, to Teresa's drug-shadowed love affair with the poet Alexis (and Alicia's with the Native figure of Adán in Acupulco), and to the sexualities on display at a Mexico City drag show. The result is a book of mirrors, a thesaurus, of American femininity, both for Teresa (California and behind it Mexico as *manera de ser*) and for Alicia (Manhattan as an always live but also endangering metropolis). Castillo's savvy and adventurous styling creates a compendious *mise-en-scène*, women's daughter–lover–mother roles, crosscultural intim-acy, career paths, and sorority, in all the very reflection of Chicana (and related) womanhood as life-art.

Chicanismo in fiction has demonstrated not only an increasing volume but also an ambit of theme. Ron Arias takes up the magic realist baton in *The Road to Tomazunchale* (1975), with its footfalls in the dying book-salesman Fausto Tejado of *Don Quixote* and picaresque time-shifts across Los Angeles, Tijuana, and Peru. History as chronicle and repetition features in both Nash Candelaria's trilogy of the New Mexico Rafa family in *Memories of the Alhambra* (1977), *Not by My Sword* (1982), and *Inheritance of Strangers* (1985), and Alejandro Morales's *The Rag Dog Plagues* (1992) as a specula-tive fable spanning nineteenth-century Mexico, AIDS in present-day Orange County, and the futurist world the author calls Lamex. A gay dispensation made its notable bow in John Rechy's *City of Night* (1963), as first-person fiction of fact, sexual picaresque through the edge-cities of gay culture. For Arturo Islas's *The Rain God* (1984), the dynamic is one of dynasty: the Tex-Mex Angel family, with its several-generation cast, son and uncle figures of Miguel Chico and Felix, and imperturbable matriarchal presence of Mama Chona. North–south politics shape Demetria Martinez's *Mother Tongue* (1994), José Luis as Salvadoran refugee and the Albuquerque-based Mary whose role in his life is that of both sanctuary movement activist and lover.

Denise Chávez's *Face of an Angel* (1994) sites its story of four "in service" generations of Chicanas in the person of Soveida Dosamantes as she earns a living waitressing in a blue-collar New Mexican restaurant. Chicano/a fiction continues to exert well justified claims not only to overall strength, but also to diversity of direction.

The need to resist undue agglomeration of Latino/a fiction takes on special force in the face of other dispensations. The line of *Puertorriqueño/a* story could not but take cognizance of a history from Puerto Rico's independence from Spain in 1898, to US Commonwealth status, to each wave of diaspora into mainly East Coast America. A selection of consequential texts would include Piri Thomas's ground-zero, Spanish Harlem self-history as told in *Down These Mean Streets* (1967), Nicolasa Mohr's affecting portrait of New York *barrio* girlhood in *Nilda* (1973), or Ed Vega's story collection of bruised *riqueño*-city lives in the well-named *Casualty Report* (1991). For Judith Ortiz Cofer's *The Line of the Sun* (1989), and its collagist follow-up *The Latin Deli* (1993), that has meant New Jersey, or more precisely, El Building, as emigrant "Rican" house of city tenement family and island memory. Told in the voice of Marisol Vivente, *The Line of the Sun* gives authoritative detail to the contrasts of village Puerto Rico's Salud with its Taíno–Spanish heritage, festival, ease, and foodways, yet also its small scandals and relative poverty, with that of the New Jersey tenement – an America of near-to-hand opportunity (and imported *santería*), yet also threats of rape to herself, the robbery and knifing of her uncle Guzmán, and tough city blight. Two mixed American realms, thereby, are seen to coexist even as they vie with one another. *The Latin Deli* gives further local immediacy to the contrast, El Building as "gray prison" yet "dream palace," the island as full of limits yet "warm, vegetative air."[4]

Cuban American fiction possesses few more exhilarating novels than Oscar Hijuelos's *The Mambo Kings Play Songs of Love* (1989): pre-Fidel Havana and its music and heated sexuality brought to New York in the 1940s-and-after as a near-physical sense of *latinidad*. At winning pace it works forwards from the Cuba of the Batista regime to radio and early TV America through the careers of the musician brothers César and Néstor Castillo and their guiding mentor, Desi Arnaz, of *I Love Lucy* fame. The novel, a lively-sad mambo in itself, as it were, is at once the reflection both of Cuban and Cuban American promise and yet also an act of requiem. Hijuelos writes kaleidoscopically. Havana, Miami, and New York are pitched within both exact lives and the flamboyance of Latin club-lands, rhythm, and song. He also belongs to yet another wide Latino/a storytelling gallery. Be it Virgil Suarez's *Latin Jazz* (1989), with its sequence of *revolución, exilio,* and next-generation American lives, or Cristina Garcia's *Dreaming in Cuban* (1992), with its three-era history of the Puente women, *fidelismo* and anti-*fidelismo*, and revolutionary Havana to New York bakery to art-punk Brooklyn, or Achy Obaja's story collection *We Came All the Way from Cuba So You Could Dress Like This?* (1994) with its "tropical eroticism" of lesbian and other styles of love, fiction written under a Cuban American banner clearly yields its own busy variety of styles and directions.

In Julia Alvarez and Junot Díaz, Dominican American fiction possesses two leading storytellers of island-to-mainland generational transition. In mapping the trajectory of Carlos García MD, his wife Laura, and centrally their daughters Carla, Sandra, Yolanda, and Sofia, from the 1950s politics of the Trujillo dictatorship through the 1990s, Julia Alvarez's *How the Garcia Girls Lost Their Accents* (1991) tackles a presiding trajectory: Americanization. Yolanda's brief return to Dominica in adulthood, the symbolic guava, lived-in landscape, yet also memory of childhood ghost fears and voodoo, plays against the American identity she and her sisters have assumed – full of middle-class appurtenance, yet also variously vexed or broken. Theirs has been an inheritance of love–hate offspring rebellion, marriages and divorces, and a traditional Catholic-etiquette Dominica and an immigrant "open" America of both advantage and disadvantage. Díaz's story-cycle *Drown* (1996) turns on a quite other stratum of Dominican American life, again immigrant and then second-generation, but New Jersey-based, blue-collar, class-affected, and meanly shorn of heroics. His clinical portrayals of the Las Casas family – the bigamous father and Cane and Abel sons Rafa and Ramón – moves between an island remembered as much for its pastoral grace as for its betrayal and an America whose *abundancia* likewise both promises and betrays in the face of marginal labor, drugs, frequent physical cruelty, and near defeat. For all their shared interface of migration and assimilation, nostalgia and reality, Dominica-to-America as told by Alvarez and Junot is to be heard in contrasting versions, alternative resonances of class and gender.

Asian American fiction

Asian passage into America, sojourn and settlement, each different population flow has its own complex evolution: Pacific crossing for the most part, Gum Sahn or Gold Mountain, Hawaii as plantation way-station, a West Coast of Chinese railroad work and turn-of-the-century Angel Island detention, Filipino field labor, Korean and Vietnam War migration, rising South Asian citizenry, and the historic need to counter anti-Asian racism and stereotype (Charlie Chan or Fu Man Chu, Tokyo Rose or Emperor Ming). Orientalism, exoticization, not to say resentment at Asian American ascendancy in fields like IT and the sciences, all have persisted. Within community culture, issues arise of ethnic–political cantonment as against a more visible role in mainstream politics, the ambiguities of Asian patriarchy, or loyalty to clan and language as against "outside" marriage or residence. Popular culture affords its own reflections, Chinese New Year and Japanese lantern festivals, Hong Kong movies and Bollywood, Tai-chi and martial arts, Zen and manga, or sushi and wok cuisine. Each Asian America, whatever the travails or triumphs of origins and landfall, timeline and domicile, calls upon huge filaments of storytelling, a composite variousness of literary fiction whose burgeoning through the postwar era yields both the retrospect and the measure of Asian American modernity.

Among a range of early postwar departure-points, two especially rank: John Okada's *No-No Boy* (1957), with its life-story of Ichiro Yamada as a veteran of Executive Order 9066 that sent 120,000 Japanese Americans to internment camps and imprisoned those who refused to do army service, and Louis Chu's *Eat a Bowl of Tea* (1961), the lively portrait of 1940s "bachelor" New York Chinatown with its different sexual revels from which Ben Loy and Mei Oi embark upon a subsequent Chinese America. The effect, in turn, of the two pioneer collections, *Aiiieeeee! An Anthology of Asian-American Writers* (1974) and *The Big Aiiieeeee! An Anthology of Chinese American and Japanese American Literature* (1991), under the inspired baton of a fists-up literary battler like Frank Chin and his fellow editors Jeffery Paul Chan, Lawson Inada, and Shawn Wong, can hardly be overestimated. Here was Asian America, albeit still selectively, in rare expressive hue and cry, authorship across both fiction and other genres infinitely too little known or valued.

Kingston herself, incontestably, has played a major part, above all in *The Woman Warrior* (1976), as one of the most read and taught novels in the American academic syllabus, and in the successive *China Men* (1980), with its cultural patrimony from Grandfather Ah Goong to the narrator's unnamed brother who enlists for Vietnam, and *Trickmaster Monkey: His Fake Book* (1989), with its 1960s San Francisco Chinatown and Beat ethos and monkey-avatar Wittman Ah Sing. *The Woman Warrior* remains Kingston's enduring contribution, a chronicle of village China to metropolitan California told through five female personae and rich in swordswoman/writer legend and riposte to the question "What is Chinese tradition and what is the movies?" Kingston has "Maxine," literary heir to the warrior-queen Fa Mun Lan, reflexively pledge herself to write this legacy of self and womanhood ("I could not understand 'I'. The Chinese 'I' has seven strokes, intricacies").[5] She is thus able to invoke an aunt ostracized for adultery who in revenge drowns herself in the village well and becomes a water-ghost, Lan as fighter, her mother Brave Orchid (a shaman-doctor) and her aunt Moon Orchid who finds both breakage and peace in America, and the Berkeley-radicalized "Maxine" who, feminist daughter of a California laundry family, is inspirited as tongue-liberated writer by each of these iconic forebears. Despite notorious accusations by Frank Chin that she (along with Amy Tan and the dramatist David Henry Hwang) distorts Chinese myth and panders to Western sinophobia by rendering China an ever un-modern misogynist fiefdom, *The Woman Warrior* delivers a China-in-America full of memory, language, journey, dynasty, and always in a voice uniquely Kingston's own.

Around, and subsequent to, Kingston, Chinese American fiction readily suggests an efflorescence. Tan's *Joy Luck Club* (1989), in the metaphor of *mah jong*, geometrically yet always inventively juxtaposes four mother–daughter pairs, Chinese and Chinese American, a dialogic feast of competing "China" story from Shanghai to San Francisco, Mao to Eisenhower and Kennedy. Shawn Wong's *Homebase* (1979) takes on the bequeathed history within the California narrator-writer's Chan ancestry, and its American identity implications, through a great-grandfather working on the Central Pacific Railway, a grandfather Chinese *vaquero*, and a father who becomes a Guam US airman. Gish Jen's *Typical American* (1991) offers a parody of Chinese American Gatsbyism, the first-generation Ralph Chang's rise and fall (after leaving China in the 1940s) in his bid to become an all-American entrepreneur parlayed into suburban sex and finance comedy. Chin's *Gunga Din Highway* (1995) develops a dense four-panel canvas of storytelling centered on the Kwan dynasty and in its principal incarnation, Longman Kwan. It sets itself to explore the evolving realities and myths of Chinese American identity, from the creation story of Poon Goo and Nur Waw, through 1860s Pacific and railroad migrancy, Chinatown, and on to Oakland–Berkley protest and hippiedom, with Chin's targeting of Charlie Chan in his different film incarnations, Hollywood screen Asians, and Kingston–Tan celebrity. As astute a portrait as almost any is to be found in John Yau's story "How to Become Chinese," published in his *Hawaiian Cowboys* (1995), a surrealist and cunningly ironic dream-parable of how Chineseness in America has often been taken to signify otherness, the alien signature, despite well over a century's inescapable historical presence.

Postwar Japanese American fiction can look to a seminal authorial double in Toshio Mori and Hisaye Yamamoto, *Nisei* World War II camp internees both (Mori at Topaz, Utah, and Yamamoto at Poston, Arizona). Their respective short-story collections bring a quiet but wholly crafted nuance to the triumphs, and also the nagging shadow, within everyday community life. In *Yokohama, California* (1949) Mori's take on that community life is rarely bettered than in "Lil' Yokohama," his vintage portrait of a California township of everyday birth and death, baseball and high school, Benny Goodman on the radio, the *Mainichi News*, and gossip. Other stories confirm Mori's touch, whether "Tomorrow Is Coming, Children" as a deft, oblique take on internment life in the form of a grandmother's monologue, or "The Woman Who Makes Swell Doughnuts" as a portrait of Zen example and spirit, or "Slant-Eyed Americans" with its localization of the impact of Pearl Harbor on a Japanese American flower-nursery business. Yamamoto's *Seventeen Syllables* (1988, revised and expanded 2001) exhibits a different kind of virtuosity, always several inter-choric stories bound into one. It embraces the title-story "Seventeen Syllables," set on a California tomato smallholding, the drama of a failing *Issei* marriage, a Japanese American daughter's generational distance from her mother, and with haiku as organizing leit-motif. "The Legend of Miss Sasagawara" offers another perspective on Executive Order 9066 and the camps through the life of a Buddhist minister's fetch-and-carry daughter, to her fellow internees an oddity but, as it proves, the mask of a poet of autonomous brilliance – rare, pointed scrutiny by Yamamoto of Japanese and Japanese American gender paradigms.

Subsequent fiction has been equally rich in addressing Asian American experience and memory. Milton Murayama's *All I Asking for Is My Body* (1975) turns to an interwar Hawaiian sugar plantation as a site for a migrant Japanese laboring family to labor. Cynthia Kadohata's *The Floating World* (1989) acts as a Salinger-voiced road fable of seasonal employment and ghost memory across Dixie, the Midwest, and the West Coast. Fae Myenne Ng's *Bone* (1993), set in the fictive Salmon Alley of San Francisco's Chinatown, unravels its narrator Leila's heritage of rift and reconciliation, her archives of family and yet Chinatown-leaving. Lois Yamanaka's *Blu's Hanging* (1997) pursues darker fare, the modern Hawaii of Ivah Ogata as she steers through a family corridor of poverty, dysfunction, and, to great controversy on publication, her brother's rape by a Filipino man. Karen Yamashita's *Through the Arc of the Rain Forest* (1990) shifts in scenario to magic-realist Japanese Brazil, another Japan, another America. As with Chinese American fiction, this Japanese American plenty shows little sign of abating.

Other Asian American fiction confirms a shared readiness to remember, and restyle, "ethnic" America as immigrant and generational story. Korean America offers a near-perfect complementarity in Ronyoung Kim's *Clay Walls* (1986) and Theresa Hak Kyung Cha's *Dictee* (1982), both at once journey-to-America stories and accusing refractions of Japanese annexation of Korea (1910–1945), the Korean War (1950–1953), and the 39th Parallel division of the peninsula. The modes of telling, however, could not differ more. Kim's novel offers realist–naturalist chronicle, the Korean past of the high-born or *yangban* mother, Haesu, married to her peasant-stock husband, Chun, their interwar move to Los Angeles, and the Korean American prospect embodied in their daughter Faye. Cha's *Dictee*, collage, full of postmodern narrative gaps and ellipses, seeks to "undictate" each oppressive facet of Korea-to-America history, from Japanese peninsular occupation to American Asia-phobia, a text of startling scriptural as much as politico-cultural liberation.

Other Asian geographies and their impact within Asian American fiction are of shared importance. Filipino/a American has a savvy, at times both magic-realist and Swiftian novel in Hagedorn's *Dogeaters* (1990), the Marcos years ventriloquized from an American vantage-point for all its savage and at times bitterly funny contradictions in the voice of Rio Gonzaga as she writes from her California base. These call up a colonial past both Spanish yet culturally imperial and popular-culture American; fervent Catholicism yet military abuse; Hollywood screen romance yet the Manila street world of drugs, sex trade, and hustle; and always the fund of *tsisis* or gossip, music and foodways, and the presiding figure of Imelda as Madame Galactica. Lan Cao's Vietnamese America in *Monkey Bridge* (1997) acts to connect two broken regimes, that of the narrator Mai Nguyen's mother as she lies stroke-ridden in her Arlington, Virginia, hospital within reach of the national cemetery and that of her family history folded into both Vietnamese and US war casualty and death. The twists of Cao's plotline, both America and Vietnam located, a network of combat, espionage, betrayal, parallel patriotisms and national trauma, Asian gods and TV's *The Bionic Woman*, work one into the other with genuine versatility. In Bharati Mukherjee's *Jasmine* (1989), Indian diaspora, Hasnapur in the Punjab to the Florida Keys, New York to Iowa farmland, takes on far from any roseate hue. This is American immigrant rite of passage as a variorum of often violently transposed identity, the narrator as at once Hindu bride-widow, rape victim on illegal boat arrival in America, lover of a Columbia professor, wife to a wounded, chair-bound agricultural banker, and pending Californian. As Jyoto, Jasmine, Jase, Jane, her serial name changes embody her changing migrant and sexual estate, but she is also the karmic avatar of Kali, goddess both of death and eternal energy and transformation. In this version of immigration, especially its rise and fall across two huge continents, the novel shrewdly ventures as immigrant mantra "the zig-zag route is straightest."[6]

An illuminating place to conclude can be met within Chang-rae Lee's *Native Speaker* (1995). This intriguing cat's cradle of a novel, at once spy and detective fable with an existential patina set in multiethnic Queens, New York makes the very notion of "ethnic identity" itself a mystery to be understood, if not solved. In telling the story of Henry Park, Korean American son of a hugely hardworking immigrant grocery-man father, and of the politician, John Kwang, upon whom he is employed to spy by a murky surveillance corporation, Lee circles brilliantly around issues of true and false namings, public and private American identities, impeded and unimpeded speech, and the loops by which one group "others" another. For as the novel deals in the ways of Korean and Korean American culture – the community economic system of *ggeh*, kimchee and other foodways, the memory of the two Koreas – it also deals in the very politics and ethnicity of language itself. Henry's marriage to the speech therapist Leila, the accidental choking death of their son Mitt who once called his father "*chink*, a *jap*, and a *gook*," and the speech-afflicted children Leila works to heal, becomes a way for the novel to address the very languages of foreign-ness, Asian-ness, and American-ness. In this, both for its own imaginative part and that of other "ethnic" fiction, it makes an immensely valuable contribution to the "speaking," the wherewithal by which multi-ethnic fictions inscribe the differing plies of cultural time and space which continue to be America.

FURTHER READING

Cowart, David. *Trailing Clouds: Immigrant Fiction in Contemporary America.* Ithaca, NY: Cornell University Press, 2006

Lee, A. Robert. *Multicultural American Literature: Comparative Black, Native, Latino/a and Asian American Fictions.* Edinburgh University Press, 2003

Saldívar, Ramón. *Chicano Narrative: The Dialectics of Difference.* Madison: University of Wisconsin Press, 1990

Wong, Sau Ling Cynthia. *Reading Asian American Literature: From Necessity to Extravagance.* Princeton University Press, 1993

NOTES

1 Toni Morrison, *Playing in the Dark: Whiteness and the Literary Imagination* (Cambridge, MA: Harvard University Press, 1992). Relevant studies include Theodore W. Allen, *The Invention of the White Race: Racial Oppression and Social Control* (New York and London: Verso, 1997) and *The Invention of the White Race: The Origins of Racial Oppression in America* (New York and London: Verso, 1997); Mike Hill (ed.), *Whiteness: A Critical Reader* (New York University Press, 1997); Valerie Babb, *Whiteness Visible: The Meaning of Whiteness in American Literature* (New York University Press, 1998); and Nell Irvin Painter (ed.), *The History of White People* (New York: W. W. Norton, 2010).

2 Sandra Cisneros, "Ghosts and Voices: Writing from Obsession," in Nicolás Kanellos (ed.), *Hispanic American Literature* (New York: HarperCollins, 1995), p. 48.

3 Amy Tan, "Mother Tongue," in Joyce Carol Oates (ed.), *The Best American Essays, 1991* (New York: Tickner and Fields, 1991), p. 196.
4 Judith Ortiz Cofer, *The Latin Deli: Prose and Poetry* (Athens: University of Georgia Press, 1993), pp. 14, 22, 81.
5 Maxine Hong Kingston, *The Woman Warrior: Memoirs of a Girlhood Among Ghosts* (New York: Vintage Books, 1977), pp. 5, 166.
6 Bharati Mukherjee, *Jasmine* (New York: Grove Weidenfeld, 1989), p. 101.

9

VICTORIA AARONS

American Jewish Fiction

Irving Howe, in the introduction to the 1977 collection, *Jewish-American Stories*, poses an unsettled and unsettling question: "What is the likely future of American Jewish writing?"[1] Howe's problematical response bears the weight of an anxious history of Jewish exile. American Jewish writing, in the second half of the twentieth century had, Howe contends, "probably moved past its high point,"[2] having found "its voice and its passion at exactly the moment it approache[d] disintegration."[3] The culture of *Yiddishkeit* – the distinctive ethos of a culture derived from the Yiddish-speaking Jews of Eastern and Central Europe – was diminishing from the urban landscapes of American Jewish sensibilities, absorbed and attenuated by the mainstream culture to which it aspired.[4] American Jewish writers, Howe contended, ran out of literary steam, a situation certainly no-good-for-the-Jews, to borrow a phrase from Philip Roth, and counterintuitive given the Jewish penchant for words. For if they do little else, Jewish characters in and out of literature talk. The urban landscape of American Jewish literature has, since the fiction of the immigrant and through the end of the twentieth century, resonated with sound, with characters who talk their way through their self-invented lives.

Most certainly there has continued now beyond the twentieth century a long tradition of Jewish storytelling, established well before the arrival of the immigrant on the shores of America, a tradition of talking lives, a language of memory and desire. This tradition developed out of the rich Yiddish conventions of storytelling, established notably by the Eastern European writers Sholom Aleichem, Mendele Mocher Sforim, and I. L. Peretz and brought to America most prominently by I. B. Singer. These writers drew upon the voices of European Jewry in a collective expression of *Yiddishkeit*, a culture ultimately threatened by the devastation of the Holocaust. *Yiddishkeit* takes root in the dramatic articulation of a collective and unique experience and thus flourishes in the insistent expression of narrative voice. Undeniably resilient, *Yiddishkeit* infused itself into the language and literary imagination of postwar writers such as Bernard Malamud, Herbert Gold, Daniel Fuchs, Tillie Olsen, Grace Paley, and Saul Bellow.

Saul Bellow, in the introduction to *Great Jewish Short Stories*, remarks on the vital and ongoing nature of Jewish storytelling: "For the last generation of East European Jews, daily life without stories would have been inconceivable. My father would say, whenever I asked him to explain any matter, 'The thing is like this. There was a man who lived … There was once a scholar … There was a widow with one son … A teamster was driving on a lonely road."[5] Bellow speaks to the exilic, self-preserving, collective history of the Jews as filtered through storytelling, framing individual lives within a history that both pre-dates them and suggests a future. And surely this penchant for the making of narratives did not dissipate in the wake of American Jewish middle-class ascension, despite Howe's contention that American Judaism is without the kind of binding "shared experience"[6] that creates the urgency necessary for "the making of fictions."[7] If the volume of books published by American Jewish writers since World War II reveals little else, it is that American Jews will not yield to the detached isolation that might be said to characterize American life but rather continue to set loose, as one of Grace Paley's characters insists, the "remembering tongue," the urgent articulation of memory, real or imagined, that continues to enliven American Jewish writing.[8]

The years since 1980 have seen a profusion of new, young Jewish writers, writers for whom the Jewish experience does, indeed, go, in Howe's terms, "deep enough … form[ing] the very marrow of their being."[9] The clamor of Jewish history, "thundering," as the contemporary American Jewish writer Allegra Goodman's Ed Markowitz would have it, is, increasingly, "unmistakable, not to be denied."[10] Yet the recent fiction of American Jews reflects an anxious preoccupation with Jewish identity and history, a tendency among American Jewish writers, as Janet Burstein describes in *Telling the Little Secrets*, to "look back" as they "move forward,"[11] in other words, to seek in a legendary Jewish history the foundations upon which to secure identity, if not place. American Jewish writers at the turn of the twenty-first century, their sensitivities like Grace Paley's narrator poised with her "ears to the ground, listening to signals from long ago," are preoccupied with America and with the expression of American Jewish identities.[12] To this end, one of Thane Rosenbaum's characters ominously portends: "America … Nothing here is what it seems. They show you a statue of a lady holding a lamp when you first arrive. What does that tell you: Look where you're going."[13]

As they have been since the early immigrant literature in America, identity and place – Jewish identity and the ways in which identity is shaped and threatened by place – are the twin antagonists on the fictional stage. And

Jewish identity is derived, in large part, ever since the literature of the 1980s in particular, from the past, as one of Ethan Canin's narrators acknowledges, an "old world gesture,"[14] an old story, in which "faith" – faith in the Hebraic covenant, faith in the future, faith in storytelling – is still, as one of Aryeh Lev Stollman's characters admits, "not an antidote to reality."[15]

Contemporary American Jewish fiction presents a deeply rooted chiastic exchange, an American overlay on Jewish culture, a Jewish comportment on America, the one complicated by the other. While contemporary Jewish writers envision America through a Jewish lens, so too do they perceive Judaism through an American lens, the source of both attachment and antipathy, one inseparable from the other. In response to the question "where are we now?" American Jewish writers since 1945 have set out in new directions as they respond to the changing landscape of both Jewish and American identities. While the overlapping, thematic patterns and preoccupations of American Jewish writing respond to a chronology of political shifts in American thought and culture, place and identity remain the master tropes of American Jewish literature in the second half of the twentieth century. Memory – borrowed, imagined memory – is the connecting tissue that links the one to the other and that, finally, becomes the measure of where we are now.

In the aftermath of World War II

The works of Bernard Malamud (1914–1986), Saul Bellow (1915–2005), and Philip Roth (b. 1933) primarily represent post-World War II American Jewish literary culture, what Andrew Furman refers to as "the golden age of Jewish American fiction."[16] From the 1950s through the 1980s, Malamud, Bellow, and Roth made up the hegemonic trio of American Jewish writers. Their formative influence paved the way for the American Jewish voices that have since emerged. Indeed, although distinct from one another both stylistically and in their construction of character and conceit, the literary destinies of Bellow, Malamud, and Roth have been inextricably connected. But for the accidents of birth, these three formative American writers might not have been linked, for they bring to postwar American fiction predominantly different literary structures, narrative textures, and designs. Since the publication of Bellow's *Dangling Man* (1944), Malamud's *The Natural* (1952), and Roth's *Goodbye, Columbus and Five Short Stories* (1959), these three writers changed the direction not only of Jewish literature, but of American fiction as well. Such consanguineous alignments, though largely accidents of history, capture an extended, defining moment in American Jewish literary history. Along with writers such as Henry Roth and Cynthia

Ozick, Bellow, Malamud, and Roth constitute, as Tresa Grauer suggests, "the Jewish American literary canon."[17] Bellow, Malamud, and Roth, for all their decisive disparateness and deep-seated reluctance to carry the torch of American Jewish letters, together created what in its curiously disjunctive collectivity can only be thought of as a uniquely and brilliantly American Jewish voice and ethos. In doing so, they created a secure place for American Jewish cultural expression at a precariously unstable and therefore malleable time in American and world history following the Nazi attempt to eradicate world Jewry.

In giving voice to a postwar period of cultural and political realignment, especially for Jews, Malamud, Bellow, and Roth prolifically chronicle the struggles, ironies, and calamities of American life and discourse. For all three, the American city is the heart of conflict, its increasing disorder a measure of the psychic unease of their characters, its urban streets, as Bellow would have it, "sweltering ... acres of cement ... the swirling traffic too loud, too swift ... everywhere ... choking crowds."[18] Each writer's characters, however, differ in voice and perspective as they attempt to negotiate the calamities and constraints of modern life. In doing so, all three define, if only contingently, what it means to be Jewish and American. Bernard Malamud is the moralist, the humanist, for whom "what it means to be human" is an acknowledgment of one's incontestable yet always tested responsibility to others.[19] For Malamud, *rachmones*, compassion, is central to the human and Jewish enterprise. For "what it means human," is, in Malamud's universe, what it means to be Jewish. In a pivotal moment in not only Malamud's archetypal novel *The Assistant*, but also in American Jewish literature, Malamud's long-suffering, poverty-stricken grocer Morris Bober will tenaciously assure his assistant, Frank Alpine, an unschooled Catholic orphan who comes to see in Morris the goodness and selflessness of St. Francis of Assisi, "I suffer for you ... I mean you suffer for me."[20] Morris Bober, characteristically self-doubting, but, in the face of his deeply felt moral certainty, at least provisionally confident, will, in a paradigmatically Malamudian moment, acknowledge the intersection of their lives and, in doing so, links "what it means human" to what it means to be Jewish – suffering for others, with all that the ambiguously elliptical preposition "for" implies: both "in place of" and "because of."

In contrast to Malamud, for Philip Roth, what it means to be Jewish is the wary uncertainty, not only of one's connection to others – tenuous under the best of circumstances – but also, in a Kafkaesque way, one's connection to oneself. In Roth's fiction, identity is anxiously and impulsively manufactured and remanufactured, his characters, unguarded and self-exposed, neurotically reinventing themselves. Roth's debut collection, *Goodbye, Columbus: and Five Short Stories* (1959), comically posits characters who are preoccupied with Jewish identity in America. Indeed, Roth's deeply phobic and conflicted protagonist, Eli Peck, in the short story "Eli, the Fanatic," proves to be the nascent prototype for those who follow in Eli's anxiously figured wake. The ironic self-parody, self-indictment, and attempts to reinvent themselves that characterize Roth's protagonists begin with Eli, whose precarious relation to Jewish history and identity is the motivational locus that Roth's protagonists inevitably revisit. In the early stories of *Goodbye, Columbus*, Jewishness seems to impede the possibility of self-invention promised by the rising cultural mobility of postwar America. In Roth's later works, such as *The Counterlife* (1986), *Operation Shylock* (1993), and *Sabbath's Theater* (1995), projected Jewish identity becomes the single most uncompromising antagonist against which Roth's characters must contend. To be Jewish, for Roth's characters, is sometimes beside the point and, at other times, is the focus for anxious projection and hasty retreat. Unlike Malamud's resolute insistence that his characters acknowledge their place as Jews, in Roth's fictive world, identity – Jewish or not – is a made and a troublesomely remade artifact. Moral failures are firm for Malamud; for Roth they are slippery, like identity, traitorously capable of turning on one. There is no moral safety net for Roth, as there is for Malamud, no opportunities for reprieve or redemption.

For Saul Bellow, ironic detachment is the means by which twentieth-century post-industrial man dubiously negotiates American, especially American Jewish, life. Bellow's characters are typically intellectual, self-consciously self-reflexive, humorously self-parodic, and inclined to sarcasm, bitter irony, and complicated scorn. They live internally contained lives, coming out of their reveries only to confront the menacing antagonisms of any external environment that would ensnare them. Bellow's characteristically rough-hewn Chicago neighborhoods, like Malamud's Lower East Side, are peopled with a panoply of immigrant voices – the residue of Yiddish, Hebrew, and Russian-accented English speaking both to cultural difference and to an ascending Jewish American middle class. Bellow's Jewish characters, not unlike those of Malamud and Roth, are as deeply American as they are Jewish, but they are never more displaced than when they are at home in America. In Bellow's novels, their felt sense of exile is always balanced by their absolute sense of belonging. These characters – and by extension their authors – made themselves as Americans and, in doing so, made America, that is, made 1950s America a place for and of Jewish voices.

American Jewish women's voices: feminism, activism, and community

Coinciding with the rise of the Women's Movement, the 1970s saw a prominent rise in fiction by and about American Jewish women. The novels and short stories from the 1950s and 1960s of Bellow, Malamud, and Roth, as well as J. D. Salinger, Edward Lewis Wallant, and Joseph Heller were filtered primarily through male protagonists, whose vision of the world was centered in an ethos of masculine identity. What it meant to be female and Jewish – and thus twice marginalized – became the preoccupation of a rising number of writers for whom feminist issues were linked to those of Judaism in deeply entrenched, conflictual, and defining ways. Earlier Jewish literature, to be sure, did not exclude some prominent women writers. Writing from the turn of the twentieth century into the 1930s and 1940s included such voices as Emma Lazarus, Mary Antin, Edna Ferber, Anzia Yezierska, and Fannie Hurst, who brought to light the tensions between "new" world and "old," between assimilation and tradition. Furthermore, writers such as Tess Slesinger, Leane Zugsmith, Jo Sinclair, and Hortense Calisher anticipated the issues of gendered and ethnic identity later explored by Tillie Olsen, Cynthia Ozick, and Grace Paley, among others.

The work of these women writers responded, both personally and politically, to the dramatically shifting landscape of American cultural identity. This work should be placed, as Jay Halio and Ben Siegel suggest, among "the most significant literary achievements" in American Jewish writing.[21] These writers respond with considerable urgency to what it means to be a Jew and a woman amid a traditional backdrop of institutional dictates and religious practices that marginalized women. They demonstrate, as Lois Ruben suggests, "how the two identities interact – at times supporting each other and at times acting in opposition."[22] To these issues of identity and marginalization, writers such as E. M. Broner, Nessa Rapoport, Joanne Greenberg, Allegra Goodman, Anne Roiphe, Rebecca Goldstein, Marge Piercy, Norma Rosen, Tova Reich, Pearl Abraham, and Lesléa Newman bring an array of competing ideologies and anxieties – feminism, community activism, sexual orientation, maternality – all contributing to an evolving process of defining place and identity in American Jewish writing. These writers, moreover, generally view themselves within a uniquely Jewish context of struggle and survival, community and autonomy.

For Paley, a self-styled antagonist to history, for example, feminism opposes both secular and religious Jewish law and becomes the lens through which individual struggle is viewed. It is, for Paley, women who narrate, navigate, and attempt to bring about change, both personally and collectively. They want to change the life bequeathed to them, to bring about "enormous changes at the last minute," as the title of one of her short-story collections puts it, before it is too late. In Paley's fiction, feminism and Judaism necessarily, if not always easily, coexist. Paley's fiction insists on a regenerative hopefulness that is, for her women characters, a kind of *tikuun olam*, their individual attempts to repair and transform the world. For Paley, such concerns are rooted in a Jewish ethic: the necessity to bear witness to atrocities of the past, both proximate and distant.[23]

It is through women's voices that Paley articulates the dogma of her strongly left-leaning generation. Paley's women characters speak a consanguineous language, one that refuses to be displaced by prejudice, circumstance, or history, including a Jewish history that represents the institutionalized privilege of men over women, but that also calls forth the communal enclosures of women controlling domestic life. The personal and the political are never far apart for Paley. In her fiction, the political emerges as the wider historical and cultural context of an ascendant American Jewish middle class, from steerage to immigrant life to a significantly formative influence on American culture. Here the fictive invention of personal histories is formed within the broader political and historical context of struggle that always exists as an undercurrent in Paley's fiction. The locus of the struggle against oppression and her commitment to an inclusive activism are, for Paley, centered in her mutual concerns with Jewish law and feminism. Paley's writing consciously refashions Judaism through the lens of feminism, both intersecting as ideological points of departure for shared engagements. Set against the backdrop of Judaism, it is thus the women's voices in Paley's fiction that shape and inform the language of the insider, a defining and circumscribing language of shared suffering, shared instincts, and shared histories, a language that is taken up by later American Jewish women writers, such as Nicole Kraus, Dara Horn, Sara Houghteling, and Allegra Goodman.

Exile, displacement, loss, and the paradox of orthodoxy

Increasingly in the literature of contemporary American Jews, there has emerged a conspicuous shift from community to the isolated individual, from a communal sense of a shared identity and past – if only an imagined one – to a disconcerting sense of isolation and fragmentation. Historically, the long-established tradition of Jewish storytelling, scriptural and secular, is marked by ongoing narratives that locate the protagonist within a communal history. But contemporary American Jewish literature increasingly finds little connective cultural tissue to shape the lives of the characters. And this shift from community to isolation in America is revealed largely through the response to a transient culture for which there is no clear ethical measure, no narrative of Jewish identity. And so instead of Bernard Malamud's conviction, uttered with certainty in *The Assistant*, that "I suffer for you … you suffer for me,"[24] the characters in the fiction of contemporary writers like Lev Raphael, Lesléa Newman, Aryeh Lev Stollman, Joseph Skibell, Dara Horn, Nathan Englander, Steve Stern, Nicole Kraus, Jonathan Rosen, and Ethan Canin suffer alone. This preoccupation with isolation and disconnectedness suggests a pronounced unease in response to the compromises of the successfully assimilated American Jew.

As a result, characters emerge who are absorbed with the missing and the lost. Such characters are deeply divided and preoccupied with their place in America and their relation to Judaism. Such ambiguity about identity and place, for example, motivates Canin's narrator, Abba Roth, in the short story "Accountant," to wonder "why, of all the lives that might have been mine, I have led the one I have just described."[25] For Canin, like many other American Jewish writers of his generation, America is both "unimaginable"[26] and "a story without surprises."[27] It is onto the backdrop of this changing cultural landscape that Canin, as well as other writers of his generation, grafts the tangled, often tortuous disposition of middle-class American Jewish life. In his unease about ethical value, America becomes an almost mythic setting for self-invention, a place where, as another of Canin's characters ruefully acknowledges, "he had never known so many people reassessing their lives."[28]

Characters in contemporary American Jewish fiction at once fear and are enticed by contemporary American culture, which is often depicted as a destabilizing threat. Pearl Abraham's Hasidic protagonist, Rachel Benjamin, in *The Romance Reader*, for example, is enticed by the outlawed see-through stockings, bathing suits, and profane novels of her adolescence. But such characters are wary of popular culture as well, since it becomes for them a reminder of what is missing, of what they have all too willingly surrendered. Similarly, Goodman's Ed Markowitz, in the short story "Mosquitoes," guiltily avoids the kosher meal offered to him at the Christian–Jewish symposium, instead "stealthily … load[ing] up with fried chicken, mashed potatoes, peas, and apple pie … eat[ing] like a man rescued from captivity."[29] Here, contemporary America is anxiously figured as a seductively threatening influence on Jewish identity and, in many ways, a measure of loss.

Increasingly, contemporary American Jewish fiction – Debra Spark's novel *Good for the Jews* (2009), Allan Appel's *The Hebrew Tutor of Bel Air* (2009), Dara Horn's *The World to Come* (2006), Jonathan Tropper's *This Is Where I Leave You* (2009), and Joan Leegant's short-story collection *An Hour in Paradise* (2003), for example – has again taken up residence in a faux-suburban urban wilderness, a metaphorical exile, which would not be an unfamiliar landscape to their forebears and where characters make choices in response to the secular, material world. Here America remains the emblem of both unrestrained freedom and a return to captivity. Moreover, the very measure of unimpeded privilege and the sense of familiarity and mobility – economic, psychological, social, cultural – that such autonomy engenders paradoxically heightens the anxiety that so many of the characters in American Jewish fiction experience, creating confusions about place, identity, and time, unresolved tensions among past, present, and future.

Such tensions often present themselves oppositionally in generational terms: orthodoxy and reform, piety and secularism, ancient narratives and modernity, and tradition and change. Goodman's collection of interlocking stories, *The Family Markowitz*, for example, which spans three generations, markedly exposes the ambivalences of American Jewish identity and reveals Goodman's preoccupation with the historical, religious, ideological, and emotional demands of being Jewish in America at the close of the twentieth century.[30] Here the conflict localizes itself between the demands of the orthodoxy – "the original context ... the Jewish people ... God" – and those liberal, secular, and progressive attitudes that would seem to undermine such a heritage, a capitulation to the supposed dissolution of the basic tenets of Jewish faith in contemporary American life.[31]

Reclamation of the past, of Jewish ritual and comportment, has been a recurrent preoccupation in recent American Jewish fiction. For example, in Lynne Sharon Schwartz's short story, "Opiate of the People," an American-born daughter of immigrant parentage, "bred without that ancient history," wants to reclaim into the world of "the fathers."[32] But embracing the past is as seductive to one generation as it is intrusive to the other. As a result, the recurrent voice of orthodoxy reignited, the past refound and embraced, is treated, typically, with a kind of comic and often satiric irony that reflects the antinomies, tensions, and contradictions that come into play when ancient Jewish text meets contemporary American secularism. It is this persistent sense of loss and longing, despite the emendations and amenities that fashion their lives in America, that motivates these characters to recast themselves in what becomes a comic and precarious balance between tradition and change, the intersections of Judaism and contemporary life.

Such tension between orthodoxy and secular life reveals itself, for instance, in Joan Leegant's collection of stories, *An Hour in Paradise*. Here, the past warily meets the present, and one finds a generation in flux, confused by and mistrustful of the religious belief that is at once provisional and unstable and entrenched and excessive. The stories in this collection reveal the uncertain shape of Judaism in the twenty-first century. Here the familiar rituals of Jewish life seem to be losing ground, dispersed among competing generational expectations, both personal and historical. For many of Leegant's characters, Judaism has become, as one character complains, a "claustrophobic preordained life,"[33] a set of laws and restrictions, "the obscure, the arcane," not of this world.[34] Leegant's stories attempt to negotiate what seems at times to be an unbending set of arcane laws and beliefs and the seductions and openness of contemporary life. She, as others, contrives in her fiction a set of circumstances in which a generation coming of age at a tangled and uncertain point in history either temporarily abandons Judaism, runs from it, or fervently embraces it.

So much of the literature by contemporary American Jews is generated by the dissatisfaction of a generation caught between two worlds: the world of their fathers and mothers and the world-in-the-making, that is, a place in which the old rules may no longer apply. This confusion is especially true for a generation whose recurring anxieties of loss, displacement, and discontent take them away from themselves and away from a secure sense of place. Here the past and present collide in uncomfortable ways and the future seems uncertain, both for Judaism and for individuals bound to a Jewish past. With no firm moorings, such characters either reinvent themselves in opposition to Judaism or embrace a reignited sense of Jewish history and communal identity.

Second- and third-generation Holocaust writers

The other "place" in which contemporary American Jewish writers find themselves is in response to the Holocaust. Second- and third-generation Holocaust writers, such as Thane Rosenbaum, Ehud Havazelet, Nathan Auslander, Melvin Jules Bukiet, Art Spiegelman, Aryeh Lev Stollman, Jonathan Safran Foer, and Harvey Grossinger are singularly preoccupied in their work with the specter of the Holocaust. For such writers who have not directly experienced the Holocaust but are compelled to bring it back to imaginative life, memory becomes the master trope, the elusive and cryptically coded narrative figure in their work. For the second and third generation, America serves as the emblematic place of false protection and deceptive security, where the characters' attempts to arm themselves (with the markers of success and supposed freedom) against the ghosts of the past ironically imperil them. Such writers, through a variety of literary forms, attempt to make sense of and articulate the horrors experienced by the victims of the Holocaust. Such inherited memories become the persistent narrative conceit in this literature. No "nice stories" here, as one of Lesléa Newman's Holocaust survivors contends, "no happy endings for a nice girl like you."[35] Revealed in these narratives is the desire not only to communicate the conditions under which Holocaust victims suffered, but also to suggest the ways in which the memory of the Holocaust has come to shape their own identities. Such attempts are further motivated by the haunting sense that Holocaust memory is imperiled, becoming increasingly remote to all but those remaining survivors, whose stories may die with them.

If history is narrative, then the Holocaust breaks the sequential unfolding of time and space, leaping generations, returning reiteratively to the point of traumatic, arresting origin. In, for example, Ehud Havazelet's novel, *Bearing the Body* (2007), the intractable fact of the Holocaust is witnessed anew by subsequent generations for whom the Holocaust, despite the elliptically cryptic silence that often surrounds it, has, from the very beginning, indelibly formed and informed their lives, a past that, as one of Havazelet's characters puts it, "seeped across the walls and floor. It was no longer something to be recalled from a distance – it was there in front of him, to walk into if he dared."[36] These are generations who must bear witness anew to the memory of the Holocaust, and while the loss may be "second hand," a surreptitiously borrowed legacy, it is enough to be indelibly defining.

American Jewish fiction since 1945 has shown itself to adapt to a variety of discursive forms and genres: short stories, novels, graphic narratives, intertwined and interlocking stories, all of which speak to the wealth of a long and enduring culture of Jewish storytelling. These writers draw from a legacy of Jewish history and tradition a unique ethos and backdrop against which they explore what it means to be Jewish and American. Such literature is as indelibly Jewish as it is American, its scope and intensity a faithful depiction of our times.

FURTHER READING

Antler, Joyce (ed.). *America and I: Short Stories by American Jewish Women Writers*. Boston: Beacon Press, 1990

Avery, Evelyn (ed.). *Modern Jewish Women Writers in America*. New York: Palgrave Macmillan, 2007

Halio, Jay L. and Ben Siegel (eds.). *Daughters of Valor: Contemporary Jewish American Women Writers*. Newark: University of Delaware Press, 1997

Parrish, Timothy (ed.). *The Cambridge Companion to Philip Roth*. Cambridge University Press, 2007

Shostak, Debra. *Philip Roth: Countertexts, Counterlives*. Columbia: University of South Carolina Press, 2004

Siegel, Ben and Jay L. Halio (eds.). *Playful and Serious: Philip Roth as a Comic Writer*. Newark: University of Delaware Press, 2010

Wirth-Nesher, Hana. *Call It English: The Languages of Jewish American Literature*. Princeton University Press, 2006

NOTES

1 Irving Howe, "Introduction," in *Jewish-American Stories* (New York: New American Library, 1977), p. 16.
2 Ibid., p. 16.
3 Ibid., p. 3.
4 Ibid.
5 Saul Bellow, "Introduction," in *Great Jewish Short Stories* (New York: Dell, 1963), p. 11.
6 Howe, "Introduction," p. 16.
7 Ibid., p. 17.
8 Grace Paley, "The Loudest Voice," in *The Little Disturbances of Man* (1959; reprinted New York: Penguin, 1985), p. 9.
9 Howe, "Introduction," p. 17.
10 Allegra Goodman, "The Four Questions," in *The Family Markowitz* (New York: Farrar, Straus, and Giroux, 1996), p. 207.
11 Janet Handler Burstein, *Telling the Little Secrets: American Jewish Writing since the 1980s* (Madison: The University of Wisconsin Press, 2006), p. 11.
12 Grace Paley, "Faith in the Afternoon," in *Enormous Changes at the Last Minute* (1960; reprinted New York: Farrar, Straus, and Giroux, 1979), p. 31.
13 Thane Rosenbaum, "The Rabbi Double-Faults," in *Elijah Visible: Stories* (New York: St. Martin's Press, 1996), p. 132.
14 Ethan Canin, "City of Broken Hearts," in *The Palace Thief* (New York: Random House, 1996), p. 141.
15 Aryeh Lev Stollman, *The Dialogues of Time and Entropy* (New York: Riverhead Books/Penguin, 2003), p. 2.
16 Andrew Furman, *Contemporary Jewish American Writers and the Multicultural Dilemma: The Return of the Exiled* (Syracuse University Press, 2000), p. 4.
17 Tresa Grauer, "Identity Matters: Contemporary Jewish American Writing," in Michael P. Kramer and Hana Wirth-Nesher (eds.), *The Cambridge Companion to Jewish American Literature* (Cambridge University Press, 2003), p. 269.
18 Saul Bellow, *The Victim* (1947; reprinted New York: Signet/New American Library, 1965), pp. 14, 96–7.
19 Bernard Malamud, "Idiots First," in *The Stories of Bernard Malamud* (New York: Farrar, Straus, and Giroux, 1983), p. 44.
20 Bernard Malamud, *The Assistant* (1957; reprinted New York: Dell, 1974), p. 150.
21 Jay L. Halio and Ben Siegel (eds.), "Preface," in *Daughters of Valor: Contemporary Jewish American Women Writers* (Newark: University of Delaware Press, 1997), p. 9.
22 Lois E. Rubin (ed.), "Introduction," in *Connections and Collisions: Identities in Contemporary Jewish-American Women's Writing* (Newark: University of Delaware Press, 2005), p. 9.
23 Victoria Aarons, *A Measure of Memory: Storytelling and Identity in American Jewish Fiction* (Athens: University of Georgia Press, 1996), pp. 123–69.
24 Malamud, *The Assistant*, p. 150.
25 Ethan Canin, "Accountant," in *The Palace Thief*, p. 56.
26 Canin, "City of Broken Hearts," p. 151.

27 Ethan Canin, "The Palace Thief," in *The Palace Thief*, p. 155.

28 Canin, "City of Broken Hearts," p. 129.

29 Allegra Goodman, "Mosquitoes," in *The Family Markowitz*, pp. 124–5.

30 Victoria Aarons, *What Happened to Abraham? Reinventing the Covenant in American Jewish Fiction* (Newark: University of Delaware Press, 2005), pp. 104–31.

31 Goodman, "The Four Questions," p. 198.

32 Lynne Sharon Schwartz, "Opiate of the People," in *America and I: Short Stories by American Jewish Women Writers*, ed. Joyce Antler (Boston: Beacon Press, 1990), p. 249.

33 Joan Leegant, "The Lament of the Rabbi's Daughters," in *An Hour in Paradise: Stories* (New York: W. W. Norton & Co., 2003), p. 83.

34 Ibid., p. 79.

35 Lesléa Newman, "A Letter To Harvey Milk," in *America and I*, p. 338.

36 Ehud Havazelet, "To Live in Tiflis in the Springtime," in *Like Never Before* (1998; reprinted New York: Anchor Books, 1999), p. 239.

10

JANE ELLIOTT

Feminist fiction

At the close of 1979, the *New York Times* identified "women's lib" as one of the major and defining publishing phenomena of the previous decade.[1] Yet the novel that *Times* author Ray Walters chose to exemplify this trend, Erica Jong's *Fear of Flying* (1973), was largely disdained by members of the women's liberation movement that it supposedly represented. Despite the fact that journalists like Walters had no trouble discerning feminist content in the novel, by 1985 *Fear of Flying* had come to be viewed by many in the movement as "ultimately 'not feminist'," according to critic Rosalind Coward.[2] In 1998, however, Lisa Maria Hogeland included Jong's novel in her analysis of women's liberation novels, arguing vigorously that previous analyses had overlooked the novel's genuinely feminist critique of the sexual revolution, and, by 2008, some feminist critics at Columbia University felt positively enough about the novel's politics that they organized a symposium celebrating its thirty-fifth anniversary as a "feminist classic."[3] Bringing the process full circle, the pop-feminist website *Jezebel* responded to a report on a family fracas at the conference by debating whether Jong's unsanctioned fictionalization of her sister's marriage in *Fear of Flying* should be considered an anti-feminist act.[4]

In fact this checkered history suggests that *Fear of Flying* may indeed be an exemplary American postwar feminist novel, though not precisely in the way meant by the *New York Times*. Rather, the contentious yet circular trajectory of the discourse surrounding the novel provides a case in point of the myriad literary-critical dilemmas that accompanied the growth of postwar feminist fiction. On the one hand, many agree that something changed in the realm of fiction written by and for women after the mid-1960s, and that this something was related to second-wave feminism; on the other hand, there has been little consensus regarding how to define this transformation, its political consequences, or its literary merit. Of course, debates regarding the parameters of literary-critical categories never really cease, and according to some poststructuralist critiques, such categories are necessarily tautologous in any case. Yet feminist fiction carries the added burden of being defined in relationship to a term, "feminism," that has itself been subject to decades-long contestation. In order to define what feminist fiction is, one must first define what feminism is, and this is an issue even those who have marched under its banner have never been able to settle decisively. As the famous debates regarding Marxist aesthetics in the 1920s and 1930s make clear, such definitional problems plague any category of art with overt political affiliations.[5] However, Marxists at least have the benefit of a single, foundational author as a ground for their competing readings; feminists must first decide who to read in the first place.

Attempting to sidestep such chicken-and-egg dilemmas, Rita Felski's *Beyond Feminist Aesthetics* took as its origin point her concept of a "feminist public sphere," and then subjected literature associated with that sphere to analysis.[6] By making the locus of feminist debate a matter of note, Felski kept this context from being a transparent and naturalized one; in so doing, she helped shift critical focus beyond the question "Is it feminist?" and toward the question, "Feminist *for whom*?" Such a focus on reception and context does not eradicate the necessity of individual value judgments, but it does put those critical value judgments in dialogue with larger questions in both aesthetic and political debates, enabling critics to consider which definitions of feminism circulate in which social arenas and how the particular technologies of the novel propagate or transform those definitions.[7] In what follows I outline an understanding of the field of feminist fiction in this vein, focusing on post-1945 fiction that has either been received as feminist by literary critics or been the subject of significant debate regarding whether it might be considered feminist. Traced over time, I argue, this contested canon is structured by its engagement in literary and political struggles over the representation of historical change itself.

In most descriptions of feminist literary history in the postwar period, the trajectory of feminist fiction is a teleological one, developing from almost-feminist works to fully feminist works and falling off into less-than-feminist works as feminist tropes become disseminated, adulterated, and dissolved into a less politicized "women's literature." Despite marked differences in judgments regarding which periods constitute the apex and decline of this narrative arc, most key accounts of twentieth-century feminist literature pay scant attention to the period 1945–1965 – moving more or less directly from modernist to second-wave literature – or focus on poetry produced by women in this period rather than on fiction. When women's fiction from the 1945–1965 period is subject to significant analysis, it tends to be read as a kind of feminist literature *manqué*. Works frequently noted as producing pre- or partially feminist fictions in this era include Gwendolyn Brooks's

Maud Martha (1953), Paule Marshall's *Brown Girl, Brownstones* (1959), Tillie Olson's short-story collection *Tell Me a Riddle* (1961), and Sylvia Plath's *The Bell Jar* (1963). Gayle Greene's influential *Changing the Story: Feminist Fiction and the Tradition* (1991), for example, includes *The Bell Jar* but finds it falls short as feminist fiction because, while the novel documents the suffering caused by the heroine's confrontation with her limited options as a woman, it still fails to identify patriarchy's oppression of woman as the root cause of these limitations. Similarly, Mary Helen Washington appreciates Brooks's *Maud Martha*, which she notes is an important example of black women's writing; however, Washington argues that Brooks fails to connect her heroine's quest to a larger communal struggle, a failure that leads to a sense of "incompleteness" in the narrative.[8]

As Greene's and Washington's suggestions attest, even critics who might disagree on the status of particular novels often had recourse to the same grounds for dismissal of these texts. Works that failed to measure up as fully feminist fiction were usually indicted for one of two reasons: a failure to connect women's suffering to the patriarchal oppression of women or a failure to register some possibility of transforming this situation. Crucially, the insistence that fiction defined as "feminist" foreground women's gender oppression has interacted in complex ways with feminism's own internal politics regarding other experiences of oppression, including those of class, race, ethnicity, and sexuality. In particular, feminist critics and writers have not always been able to discern feminist content in analyses and activism that focus on women's experience of other axes of oppression, despite the concern of such texts with women's oppression per se. In the collection *The Feminist Memoir Project*, for example, editors Ann Snitow and Rachel Blau DuPlessis responded to Barbara Emerson's contribution about coming of age in the Civil Rights Movement by including a supplementary interview with Emerson, an approach they felt necessary because Emerson's piece "mentioned feminism hardly at all."[9] From another perspective, however, it is possible to view the Civil Rights Movement as inseparable from women's liberation, since it had everything to do with achieving basic civil liberties for a large group of women in the United States.

Although such disputes regarding the relationship between gender and other axes of oppression have never ceased, they had particularly striking effects in the period of second-wave feminism usually associated with the women's liberation movement, roughly from 1965 to 1980. The Women's Liberation Movement expressly positioned being female as the primary ground for women's oppression, and by and large the women's liberation novel reflects this view. From realist novels of housewifery and the gradual "awakening" to feminist consciousness – for example, Sue Kaufman's *Diary of a Mad Housewife* (1967), Alix Kates Shulman's *Memoirs of an Ex-Prom Queen* (1972), Marilyn French's *The Women's Room* (1977), and Marge Piercy's *Small Changes* (1973) – to picaresque romps, such as *Fear of Flying* and Lisa Alther's *Kinflicks* (1976), the most famous women's liberation novels were penned by, and focus on, white women.[10] And this predominance is hardly surprising, given the women's liberation movement's reading of femaleness as the key category of oppression for women – which tended to exclude writers and movements that might have other or more complex priorities. Although there has been a laudable attempt to correct this focus on whiteness retrospectively through the inclusion of work by Alice Walker in newer histories of women's liberation fiction, such attempts overlook the very different form and reception history of Alice Walker's work from the 1970s, which was more experimental and much less widely read than best-selling women's liberation novels such as *Fear of Flying* and *The Women's Room*.[11] While feminist fiction at large in the 1970s included works such as Walker's *Meridian* (1976), the women's liberation genre as it was marketed and consumed – and arguably conceived – did not.

Beyond the confines of the women's liberation novel, however, a host of other feminist fiction was being produced in the 1970s that explored women's simultaneous experience of various categories of identity, including race, ethnicity, sexuality, and class. For example, works by African American women writers, including Walker's *Meridian*, Paule Marshall's *The Chosen Place, The Timeless People* (1969), Toni Morrison's *The Bluest Eye* (1970) and *Sula* (1973), and Gayle Jones's *Corregidora* (1975) have become flag-ship texts in African American feminist literary histories and exemplify the ongoing evolution of forms capable of capturing the complexity of African American women's experience.[12] As part of their attempt to map the complex interaction of forces upon their heroines, these authors frequently adopt a much larger historical scope than do the women's liberation novels, which usually feature a relatively compressed timeline that focuses on the heroine's adult years or deals with childhood in an anecdotal fashion. In contrast, feminist work by women of color in the 1970s often draws on the conventions of historical fiction (*Corregidora*, *The Bluest Eye*) or illustrates the way in which place or location – geographical and social – is implicated in a complex historical frame that covers generations, sometimes even centuries (*Sula*, *Chosen Place*). To the extent that they follow the path of the novel of awakening, these novels often present their heroines as awakening to their position within a long history of suffering and resistance in which they must find their place.

These complex interactions between feminism, race, and novelistic form have led to the production of important feminist literary histories that trace specific traditions for women that attend to particular intersections of gender, race, ethnicity, sexuality, and class.[13] While postwar feminist novels must on the one hand be read in relation to these specific traditions, feminist fiction from across the canon can also be read as united by a struggle to represent some possibility of feminist transformation. Despite the privilege of its most conspicuous exemplars, for example, the women's liberation novel has nevertheless been notable for its almost complete inability to imagine avenues of positive transformation for its heroines. This foreclosed avenue is staged again and again in French's *The Women's Room*, easily the most popular and iconic of the realist women's liberation novels of the 1970s. French's narrator awakens into a world so relentlessly structured by patriarchal oppression that she comes to view her raised consciousness as something of a curse. And certainly if, as the novel suggests, there is no experience not formed by patriarchal oppression, it is difficult to imagine how change might take place – from where would it come? Unable either to deny the extent of patriarchal oppression or to see how to escape it given this scope, *The Women's Room* takes as its primary subject the simultaneous need for and impossibility of change in a totalized landscape of oppression.

Despite very different themes and techniques, a similarly vexed engagement with temporal progression may be traced in texts that fall far outside the confines of the women's liberation novel. In the 1970s, many key novels by women of color addressed the problem of imagining a feminist, anti-racist future through an excavation of individual and collective pasts that might offer some key to the future. In Maxine Hong Kingston's *The Woman Warrior: Memoirs of a Girlhood Among Ghosts* (1975), for instance, autobiography and fiction combine in an experimental form composed of memories of the narrator's childhood, stories her mother imparted to her of her family's history, and retellings of Chinese "woman warrior" legends with herself as a protagonist. Kingston's hybrid approach presages what comes to be a key facet of feminist fiction in the 1980s and 1990s: a retrospective account of familial relationships, usually mother–daughter relationships, that attempts to explain the heroine's inability to progress in the present. For Kingston, this predicament arises from a double bind in which her family demands that she act with fealty toward them and a Chinese village she has never seen, at the same time that they teach her that girls have no value to the family, the community, or the nation. Marked by an experience of identity in which rejection constitutes the very ground of her belonging, the narrator is hostage to competing desires for attachment and escape that make every path the wrong one – a foreclosure of forward motion that is reflected in the tipping of the entirety of the narrative toward the past. The narrator's simultaneous desire to escape this stasis is registered in her repurposing of the woman warrior figure, who seems to offer another, potentially less self-excoriating ground for identification – though the success of this effort at leveraging the past to open the future is left uncertain.

As these descriptions of *The Women's Room* and *The Woman Warrior* suggest, the desire to access feminist futurity inevitably had effects on the way that 1970s feminist writers employed the representational technologies of the novel. Some of these texts focused on reworking traditional forms of plot and genre, in order to access less conventional and imprisoning fates for their heroines, an approach famously encapsulated in DuPlessis's term "writing beyond the ending."[14] For DuPlessis, writing beyond the ending requires inventing transgressive narrative strategies that disrupt the harnessing and channeling of desire within conventional structures, such as the romance plot. Most 1970s feminist novels can be read as part of this attempt to write beyond the ending of conventional narrative forms, producing transgressive feminist revisions of the *bildungsroman* in particular. However, other, more experimental novels attempted to thwart the process of narrative cohesion as a form of oppressive control in its own right. For example, Bertha Harris's *Lover* (1976) has been read as breaking with patriarchal narrative progression in favor of an anarchic representative mode in which characters seem to meet on an interior plane. Frequently compared with the work of Djuna Barnes, Harris's novel expresses its utopian drive not only through its cast of outlandish, sexually adventurous women, but also through its thwarting of the novel's conventional association with discernable plot and cohesive character development.

When even feminist plots come to seem hostage to dangerous forms of epistemological control – that is, when "feminist plot" comes to seem a contradiction in terms – access to the future becomes doubly difficult for feminist fiction: not only is it difficult to imagine and represent the path to a feminist future, but it is also potentially hazardous to do so. Although it takes the shape of a thought experiment rather than a formal deconstruction of narrative, feminist science fiction in the 1960s and 1970s offered its own exploration of these dynamics. Some feminist science fiction classics from this period, including Ursula Le Guin's *Left Hand of Darkness* (1969) and Joanna Russ's *The Female Man* (1975), use the speculative nature of science fiction to catapult the reader into a world with no historical relation to the present, imagining a vastly different way of experiencing gender, while others, such as Octavia Butler's *Kindred* (1979), deploy the science fiction genre to interrogate the intersection of race and gender oppression in the past and the relationship of that past to the present. In Marge Piercy's *Woman on the Edge of Time* (1976), the generic conventions of science fiction become a means of exploring historical causality and individual contributions to the creation of feminist futurity, providing a vision of a utopian feminist future that bears a complex and contingent relationship to the historical present.

Despite very different judgments regarding what constituted the most successful form of 1970s feminist fiction, feminist literary-critical accounts focused on this period frequently end on a mournful note, describing a falling off from a truly feminist form of analysis in novels of the 1980s and 1990s. In part this judgment may be explained by the location of 1970s feminist fiction in a historical moment that for many constituted the highwater mark of second-wave energy and influence. In contrast, the anti-feminist backlash of the 1980s came to be associated with a move toward individualized and depoliticized women's fiction. For example, novels such as Sue Miller's *The Good Mother* (1986) were seen to preserve a focus on women's experience of contemporary gender roles while deleting the structural analysis of these roles that would make such depictions feminist. The appropriation of forms developed by feminist writers for conservative purposes is certainly a trend of note in the 1980s and 1990s, but this period must also be understood as one in which academic feminism's increasing engagements with questions of race and ethnicity were mirrored in a boom in publication of fiction by women of color and a huge demand for some of these novels among nonacademic readers, most notably *The Color Purple* (1982) and *The Joy Luck Club* (1989). If the 1980s produced backlash fictions such as *The Good Mother*, they also produced an incredible variety of important feminist novels, popular and otherwise – including Theresa Hak Kyung Cha's *Dictee* (1982), Marilyn Robinson's *Housekeeping* (1980), and Sandra Cisneros's *The House on Mango Street* (1984).

The varied reception of this body of work is perfectly exemplified by the very different film adaptations of *Housekeeping* and *The Color Purple* – the former very much an independent film, the latter a high-budget extravaganza by one of Hollywood's most successful directors. However, both novels are united by their adaptation and enhancement of forms that came to the fore in 1970s feminist fiction: the novel of the housewife's entrapment and the novel of feminist awakening. From *Housekeeping*'s early image of the train that runs off its tracks into the deep stillness of the town lake, the novel foregrounds the problem of stilled motion, an issue that becomes intricately connected with the feminist trope of enclosure within the domestic sphere as a form of deathly stasis. Giving this trope what is arguably its most nuanced and sophisticated treatment, Robinson's novel explores the notion of "keeping" within the house in relation to dense ethical and philosophical questions regarding the relations between inside and outside, community and individual, rest and motion, pattern and chaos. Yet the trope of housekeeping never becomes merely a metaphor for a more general or generic human experience in the novel; instead, the gendered aspects of these oppositions continually return as the crucial lens through which they may be understood. The novel's conclusion offers a related revision of earlier feminist solutions to these dilemmas: *Housekeeping* ends with two of its central female characters slipping the bonds of all scripted forms of belonging and enclosure, moving at will through the wild world in a way that escapes capture even within narrative form itself.

The Color Purple provides a similarly rich reworking of the 1970s feminist novel of awakening, in the process offering a solution to the sorts of temporalized dilemmas that mark much 1970s fiction, from the dead-end of totalized oppression in *The Women's Room* to the double bind that structures texts such as *The Woman Warrior*, in which desire for feminist futurity wars with fidelity to the familial and community past. Drawing on African American literary tropes regarding writing and the process of coming to voice, *The Color Purple* offers an ingenious solution to such dilemmas: it shares the experience of a feminist present with the pre-feminist past. Set primarily in the decades leading up to World War II, the novel depicts an utterly downtrodden heroine, Celie, who by the end of the novel has gained all the personal and professional fulfillment that the second-wave feminist movement sought for women. While this erasure of historical reality might seem to raise ethical issues in its own right, the novel displaces such problems onto Celie's sister Nettie, a missionary who tries to bring twentieth-century values to remote African villagers. In comparison with Nettie's hubristic and fruitless attempts to graft the ideals of the present onto the past represented by the villagers, the proleptic, feminist fairy-tale awakening that the novel grants to Celie appears both innocent and commendable. In gifting Celie with this trajectory, *The Color Purple* finds a means of achieving the feminist futurity out of reach in most 1970s feminist fiction: it locates totalized oppression in a past so horrendous that the present comes to seem a site of possibility, and then it transports that sense of possibility back into the past.

Both *Housekeeping* and *The Color Purple* also participate in another widespread development in feminist fiction of the 1980s and 1990s: the turn to familial relationships, particularly mother–daughter relationships, prefigured in Kingston's *The Woman Warrior*. From Cisneros's *House on Mango Street* to Lynne Tillman's *Haunted Houses* (1987) to Fae Myenne Ng's *Bone* (1993), a host of feminist fiction in the 1980s and 1990s explored the creation and experience of female oppression as it unfolded in the crucible of the family unit. Drawing on longstanding conventions of the domestic novel, which create complex allegorical relations between family and nation, as well as on psychoanalytic tropes that placed the genesis of gendered subjectivity within the family unit, such novels explored the heroine's relationship to her parents as both a cause of and a metaphor for her experience of oppression as a woman. The allegorical status of such narratives was particularly evident in novels that focused on sexual abuse of daughters by fathers, most notably *The Color Purple*, Jane Smiley's *A Thousand Acres* (1991), and Dorothy Allison's *Bastard out of Carolina* (1993), all of which position the father's abuse of the daughter as a stand-in for patriarchy's oppression of women at large. Smiley's novel, a rewriting of Shakespeare's *King Lear* set on a Midwestern farm, is told from the perspective of one of the two loyal daughters, Ginny, who turns against her father and her upbringing when she recovers memories of her father raping and beating her; Cordelia, having been protected by her older sisters, escapes this history and remains loyal to him. In a complex mirroring of form and content, Smiley's revision of *Lear* becomes analogous to Ginny's recovery of her memories, as both Ginny's past and Shakespeare's play are revealed to harbor the same covert but violent patriarchal drive to dominate women, children, and the landscape itself.

The trope of recovered memory is indicative of the temporal modes most commonly adopted by the feminist familial novels of the 1980s and 1990s, which were frequently either set in a traumatic historical past, engaged with such traumas through characters' retrospective accounts of past experiences, or both. The most prominent and complex engagements with the traumatic past came to be associated with the mother–daughter novel, a form that rose to prominence with the commercial success and critical industries that have come to surround Tan's *The Joy Luck Club* and Morrison's *Beloved* (1987) in particular. In a fashion similar to *The Color Purple*, Tan's novel presents a temporalized contrast between a more feminist present and a less feminist future but personifies this contrast through the figures of mother and daughter, who come to represent the past and the future respectively. Marked by traumas that the novel associates with a putatively more patriarchal Chinese culture, the mothers sacrifice themselves to grant the daughters access to a feminist future characterized as uniquely American, but the daughters have all been too damaged by their relationships with their mothers to grasp these opportunities for happiness. Although the inability of each daughter to take advantage of her opportunities seems at first to keep feminist futurity out of reach, the transfer of these dilemmas to the family makes a crucial difference. In contrast with the mother's suffering in the past, the daughter's present comes to appear defined by the availability of feminist fulfillment, and, given that the daughter is blocked from this fulfillment by her own emotions, transformation now requires only the daughter's catharsis. Once access to progress hinges only on the daughter's interpersonal relationship with her mother, all the previous difficulties in accessing feminist futurity can be transcended – dissolved in a flood of reconciliatory tears.

While *The Joy Luck Club* was taking part in the creation of the mother–daughter novel as a feminist genre, a host of other novels were engaging in very different, much more formally experimental feminist explorations of the relationship between history and futurity. From Cha's *Dictee* to Gloria Anzaldúa's *Borderlands/La Frontera: The New Mestiza* (1987) to Cisneros's *House on Mango Street* to Acker's *Blood and Guts in High School*, these novels drew on a host of genres, literary and otherwise, to suggest the way in which the rethinking of representation itself was crucially linked to any successful imagination of feminist transformation. In both *Dictee* and *Blood and Guts in High School*, for example, familial relationships remain key but are subject to a form of fragmentation and replication that bars any straightforward genealogies. In Acker's text, poetry, drawings of sex organs and a pornographic revision of Nathaniel Hawthorne's *The Scarlet Letter* combine to document the life of Janey, who is variously the daughter and girlfriend of Johnny, her boyfriend/father. In a much more experimental fashion than in Smiley's novel, *Blood and Guts* intertwines incestuous familial relationships and textual revision, creating a powerful analogy between Janey's heterosexual masochism and her recourse to linguistic representation to explore her life; in both cases, the novel suggests, Janey attaches herself to the very thing that is causing her suffering. Such critiques of what Jacques Derrida famously called "phallogocentrism" are similarly evident in *Dictee*, though in Cha's novel patriarchal experience is complexly intertwined with colonial history. Constructed of multiple languages and genres as well as visual images, Cha's novel utilizes the central metaphor of *dictée*, or the dictation exercises customary in French schooling, to interrogate both the creation of colonial history and the intergenerational transmission of female experience. Through this metaphor, *Dictee* suggests the punitive qualities of the drive for representational coherence, at the same time that it challenges this drive through its own fragmented form. For some critics this strain of experimental fiction constituted a feminist version of postmodernism, sharing with other postmodern novels a suspicion of the totalizing properties of narrative and a critical relationship to received history.

While novels such as *The Joy Luck Club* offered a much more powerful experience of feminist fulfillment than the deliberately vexed and halting gestures toward transformation found in postmodern feminist fiction, much feminist literary criticism has placed a higher value on the formal literary experimentation found in novels such as *Dictee*. In part, such a judgment reflects the value conventionally placed on difficulty and complexity by literary critics, but it also reflects political discomfort with the powerful affective experiences of feminist transcendence offered by novels such as *The Joy Luck Club* or *The Color Purple*. Required to represent not only the capacity for feminist futurity but also the full extent of women's oppression, fictions that err on the side of feminist fulfillment can be charged with offering a novelistic substitute for genuine political change – a kind of literary opiate for the oppressed female masses. And this judgment might be considered justified, given that the 1990s saw the birth of "chick lit," a conservative genre largely devoted to the easy narrative resolution of dilemmas familiar from earlier feminist fiction. Although it remains unclear as yet what twenty-first-century feminist fiction will become central to literary critical discussions – and whether it will make any challenges to the entrenched nature of chick lit in the realm of popular reception – it can be expected that the most groundbreaking forms, both politically and aesthetically, will continue to be those that find new ways to accommodate the contradictory demands that women's oppression be represented as both overriding and subject to change.

FURTHER READING

Elliott, Jane. *Popular Feminist Fiction as American Allegory: Representing National Time*. New York: Palgrave, 2008

Melzer, Patricia. *Alien Constructions: Science Fiction and Feminist Thought*. Austin: University of Texas Press, 2006

Nicholson, Linda J. (ed.). *Feminism/Postmodernism*. New York: Routledge, 1990

Sandoval, Chela. *Methodology of the Oppressed*. Minneapolis: University of Minnesota Press, 2000

Schneir, Miriam. *Feminism in Our Time: The Essential Writings, World War II to the Present*. New York: Vintage, 1994

NOTES

1   Ray Walters, "Ten Years of Best Sellers," *New York Times Book Review*, December 30, 1979: BR3.
2   Rosalind Coward, "Are Women's Novels Feminist Novels?" in Elaine Showalter (ed.), *The New Feminist Criticism: Essays on Women, Literature and Theory* (New York: Pantheon Books, 1985), p. 225.
3   Lisa Maria Hogeland, *Feminism and Its Fictions: The Consciousness-Raising Novel and the Women's Liberation Movement* (Philadelphia: University of Pennsylvania Press, 1998), p. 72. On the convention, see www.columbia.edu/cu/irwag/events/main/jong.
4   *Jezebel* website: http://jezebel.com/376859/erica-jongs-sister-fear-of-flying-has-been-a-thorn-in-my-flesh-for-thirty+five-years.
5   See Fredric Jameson (ed.), *Aesthetics and Politics* (London: New Left Books, 1977).

6 Rita Felski, *Beyond Feminist Aesthetics: Feminist Literature and Social Change* (Cambridge, MA: Harvard University Press, 1989), p. 8.

7 See Kim Loudermilk, *Fictional Feminism: How American Bestsellers Affect the Movement for Women's Equality* (New York: Routledge, 2004).

8 Helen Mary Washington, "Plain, Black and Decently Wild: The Heroic Possibilities of Maud Martha," in Elizabeth Abel, Marianne Hirsch, and Elizabeth Langland (eds.), *The Voyage In: Fictions of Female Development* (Hanover, NH: University Press of New England, 1983), p. 286.

9 Ann Snitow, "Preface to Coming of Age: Civil Rights and Feminism," in Rachel Blau DuPlessis and Ann Snitow (eds.), *The Feminist Memoir Project: Voices from Women's Liberation* (New York: Three Rivers Press, 1998), p. 54.

10 See Susan J. Rosowski, "The Novel of Awakening," in Elizabeth Abel et al. (eds.), *The Voyage In*, pp. 49–68.

11 See Maria Lauret, *Liberating Literature: Feminist Fiction in America* (London: Routledge, 1994), pp. 124–43.

12 See Barbara Christian, *Black Women Novelists: The Development of a Tradition, 1892–1976* (Westport, CT: Greenwood, 1980); Madhu Dubey, *Black Women Novelists and the Nationalist Aesthetic* (Bloomington: Indiana University Press, 1994); Cheryl Wall, *Worrying the Line: Black Women Writers, Lineage, and Literary Tradition* (Chapel Hill: University of North Carolina Press, 2005).

13 See Leslie Bow, *Betrayal and Other Acts of Subversion: Feminism, Sexual Politics, and Asian-American Women's Literature* (Princeton University Press, 2001); Sonia Saldívar-Hull, *Feminism on the Border: Chicana Gender Politics and Literature* (Berkeley: University of California Press, 2000); Katherine Sugg, *Gender and Allegory in Transamerican Fiction and Performance* (New York: Palgrave, 2008); Bonnie Zimmerman, *The Safe Sea of Women: Lesbian Fiction 1969–1989* (Boston: Beacon Press, 1991).

14 Rachel Blau DuPlessis, *Writing Beyond the Ending* (Bloomington: Indiana University Press, 1985).

11

MARTYN BONE

Southern fiction

In 1945, Allen Tate declared that "the Southern literary renascence ... is over."[1] This was a startling claim, not least given its source: as a poet, novelist, and essayist, Tate had been both a creative participant in and critical shaper of the "renascence." Ten years earlier, Tate had argued that "From the peculiar historical consciousness of the Southern writer has come good work of a special order"[2] – literature that, by taking a "backward glance," was "conscious of the past in the present."[3] Between 1929 and 1945, "good work" by Tate, William Faulkner, Thomas Wolfe, Robert Penn Warren, Richard Wright, Zora Neale Hurston, Eudora Welty, Carson McCullers, and others disproved H. L. Mencken's notorious accusation that the South was "almost as sterile, artistically, intellectually, culturally, as the Sahara Desert."[4] Tate's announcement that the Southern Renaissance was over, therefore, seemed premature: that same year, Welty published her powerful novel *Delta Wedding* (1945), while 1946 witnessed the appearance of Warren's opus *All the King's Men*. Furthermore, *The Portable Faulkner* (1946) triggered a rapid revival of interest in Faulkner that culminated with the 1949 Nobel Prize for Literature.

Yet in the 1950s modern Southern literature was, like the South itself, at a crossroads. The region, as both a social reality and a literary subject, was changing in profound ways. The prominent social, economic, and cultural role of what the Nashville Agrarians in *I'll Take My Stand* (1930) termed "the agrarian tradition" was in terminal decline. Between 1940 and 1945, between 20 and 22 percent of the South's agricultural population, more than three million people, had left the land. After such demographic upheaval, Agrarian assumptions that Southern identity was bound up with rural communities rooted in place seemed much less secure. Southern writers and critics were confronted by a series of serious questions: could a changing social reality sustain an identifiably regional literature? Could younger writers maintain the modes and themes of the Southern Renaissance, or should they seek new ground?

For many Southern writers, such dilemmas were compounded by the looming presence of Faulkner. Though Faulkner's major period ended with *Go Down, Moses* (1942), he was still publishing at a prolific rate during the 1950s, and his public profile was far higher following the Nobel Prize. In 1960, Flannery O'Connor wryly observed that "The presence alone of Faulkner in our midst makes a great difference in what the writer can and cannot permit himself to do. Nobody wants his mule and wagon stalled on the same track the Dixie Limited is roaring down."[5] Until her premature death in 1964, O'Connor was more successful than most of her contemporaries in charting a literary landscape distinct from Faulkner's Yoknapatawpha. The vivid Catholic visions of a Christ-haunted South that saturate O'Connor's novel *Wise Blood* (1952) and *A Good Man Is Hard to Find and Other Stories* (1955) targeted modernity's spiritual malaise more directly – and dogmatically – than Faulkner ever did. (For more on O'Connor, see Chapter 15.)

However, the dubious distinction of being compared to Faulkner dogged the earliest work of other Southern writers – especially white men. William Styron's debut *Lie Down in Darkness* (1951) was the first novel to suffer critical comparison with the newly canonical Faulkner, though Styron's style and subject matter – the tribulations of a dysfunctional white Southern family – practically invited comparison with *The Sound and the Fury*. In a review of Cormac McCarthy's first novel, *The Orchard Keeper* (1965), a tragic family tale set in rural Tennessee, the *New York Times* opined that McCarthy employed "so many of Faulkner's literary devices and mannerisms that he half submerges his own talents beneath a flood of imitation."[6] When Mississippi-born Richard Ford published *A Piece of My Heart* (1976), Larry McMurtry scored Ford's "neo-Faulknerism" and complained that "The South – dadgummit – has struck again, marring what might have been an excellent first novel."[7] Both McCarthy and Ford subsequently escaped the shade of Faulkner by displacing their fiction from the Deep South altogether: to the Texan–Mexican borderlands in all five of McCarthy's novels from *Blood Meridian* (1985) via the Border Trilogy (1992–1998) to *No Country for Old Men* (2005), and to suburban New Jersey in Ford's three lavishly praised books (1985–2006) about Mississippi-born sportswriter turned realtor Frank Bascombe.

Other post-Renaissance writers were more successful in clearing their own creative space beyond the shadow of Faulkner while still writing in and about the South. The work of these emerging authors diverged notably from the literature of place, community, and history championed by those academic acolytes of the Agrarians who institutionalized Southern literary studies at universities during the 1950s and 1960s. Indeed, much of the most interesting Southern fiction since 1960 can be read as both a response to the changing social reality of the South and a reaction against the Renaissance canon carved out by neo-Agrarian critics.

A key transitional text between the Southern Renaissance and later "postsouthern" fiction is Walker Percy's debut novel *The Moviegoer* (1961). Winner of the 1962 National Book Award, *The Moviegoer* brought into focus a region ever more immersed in the suburban "masscult" of post-war America. The novel's protagonist and narrator, John Bickerson "Binx" Bolling, lives "the most ordinary life imaginable … selling stocks and bonds and mutual funds."[8] Binx resides in "Gentilly, a middle class suburb of New Orleans," which he prefers to "the old world atmosphere of the French Quarter or the genteel charm of the Garden District" where he was raised.[9] In stark contrast to Faulkner's and Warren's anxious male protagonists, Binx feels no burden of Southern history: he declares the Confederate fortress at Ship Island to be "the soul of dreariness"; for Binx, even 1948 is a "faroff time."[10] At such moments, Binx seems to exhibit the "weakening of historicity, both in our relationship to public History and in the new forms of our private temporality" that Fredric Jameson argues is characteristic of postmodern consciousness.[11] Binx also seems to anticipate Jean Baudrillard's argument that the postmodern "age of simulation … substitut[es] signs of the real for the real itself" when he explains that he experiences time and place primarily through movies.[12] For Binx, New Orleans is only "certified" once he has seen it in the film *Panic in the Streets*.[13]

It would seem, then, that Binx Bolling is the prototypical post-Renaissance character: he feels no particular sense of place or community, and he exhibits little interest in Tate's "past in the present." Yet Binx is a profoundly troubled character, and throughout the novel he ponders "the possibility of a search."[14] Though this "search" is never clearly defined (much less completed) and seems more spiritual than social in nature, it prompts Binx to abandon Gentilly. He eventually returns to the Garden District, sanctuary of his aristocratic aunt Emily Cutrer, who berates Binx for betraying "the only good things the South ever had."[15] As Philip Simmons observes, ultimately "Percy's novel is not postmodern" because "mass culture can still be seen as an alien presence rapidly colonizing the old South."[16] Because "history is [still] visible in the landscape,"[17] albeit in the attenuated form that so disturbed Tate, Binx finds a "way out of mass culture and back into the history of his family's and society's decline."[18]

Though a similar ambivalence toward the emerging "Sunbelt" South informs later novels like *The Last Gentleman* (1966) and *Love in the Ruins* (1971), Percy understood that he and his peers could not simply retreat into a mythic Southern past – or a Renaissance model of southern fiction.

In 1986, Percy wished out loud that contemporary Southern writers would move beyond "Faulkner country ... O'Connor country ... Welty country" and "not try to become a neo-Agrarian."[19] As Lewis P. Simpson was the first to note, Percy's novels map a "postsouthern America."[20] Percy was also the first post-Renaissance writer to make extensive use of parody as a way to negotiate the burden of Southern *literary* history: *Lancelot* (1977) lampoons Old South nostalgia through sly intertextual references to two novels from 1936 – Faulkner's *Absalom, Absalom!* and Margaret Mitchell's *Gone with the Wind*.

Critic Michael Kreyling defines postsouthern parody as a metafictional mode of writing that "adjusts or lightens the burden of southern literariness it must necessarily carry in the presence of 'Faulkner' triumphant." For Kreyling, Barry Hannah's fiction is "aggressively postsouthern" in using parody to get out from under Faulkner.[21] Born in Mississippi in 1944, Hannah was shadowed by critical comparisons to Faulkner from the start of his career, when his ramblingly inventive *bildungsroman, Geronimo Rex* (1972), won the William Faulkner Prize. Hannah's postsouthernism is already evident in *Geronimo Rex*'s parodic primal scene, in which protagonist Harry Monroe kills a peacock called Bayard – a name given to generations of males in Faulkner's Sartoris clan. (The dead peacock also suggests Hannah's response to O'Connor, who was famous for her real and fictional peacocks.)[22] Hannah often expressed chagrin at "lazy" interviewers "asking me what it's like to be an heir to Faulkner, or what it's like writing in the shadow of Faulkner."[23] Yet Hannah's fiction frequently suggests that Faulkner's legacy provides a daunting challenge: in the semi-autobiographical novel *Boomerang* (1991), the narrator notes "All the Confederate dead and the Union dead planted in the soil near us. All of Faulkner the great. Christ, there's barely room for the living down here."[24]

Hannah's two most celebrated books, the short-story collection *Airships* (1978) and the novella *Ray* (1980), challenge Faulkner's representation of the South and the white male Southern hero by reworking a scene from *Sartoris* (1929) in which Confederate heroes "Carolina" Bayard Sartoris and J. E. B. Stuart gallivant through a Union camp. In contrast to Faulkner's Stuart, engaged in anachronistic derring-do, Hannah's Stuart is an exponent of modern total war. The narrator of "Dragged Fighting from His Tomb," a gay Confederate captain called Howard, sets aside his sexual attraction to Stuart to attack the general's military strategy: "You shit. What are we doing killing people in Pennsylvania?"[25] Howard's disgust at Stuart's tactics becomes so pronounced that he deserts, joins the Union, and avenges his misplaced faith in the Confederate cause by killing Stuart. In *Ray*, the eponymous narrator Ray Forrest conflates his memories of flying F-4 fighter planes in Vietnam with fantastical visions of fighting for the Confederacy as part of Stuart's cavalry. Through this post-modern recasting of Tate's "past in the present," Hannah suggests the grim historical continuities between the domestic battlefields of the Civil War and the high-tech total warfare practiced by the US Army in Vietnam. In Ray's Civil War hallucination, it is not Stuart's cavalry but John Pelham's artillery that decimates a Union battalion. Pelham's howitzers foreshadow the dehumanizing technological power of Ray's F-4 plane: "Then the buttons when he got into the middle of the scope. It's so easy to kill. Saw him make the bright, white flower. It's so fucking hard to live."[26] Like Captain Howard, Ray Forrest begins to doubt the Confederate cause, much as many of his (and Hannah's) contemporaries questioned the US Army's presence in Vietnam.

Hannah is not the only Southern novelist born during World War II in whose fiction the Civil War, that mythic crucible of Southern identity, is superseded by the conflict in Vietnam. Bobbie Ann Mason's bestselling debut novel *In Country* (1985) focuses on Sam Hughes, a seventeen-year-old girl whose father was killed in Vietnam and who now lives with her uncle Emmett, a veteran struggling like Ray Forrest to process the trauma of his wartime experiences. But whereas Hannah's Ray retains a Southern historical consciousness (however hallucinatory), in Sam's hometown of Hopewell, Kentucky, residues of regional tradition barely register in a generic late-capitalist landscape of malls and fast food joints. When the Vietnam veteran Tom observes that "Here, everybody's looking backward – to old-timey days. Antiques and Civil War stuff,"[27] it is less an echo of Tate's "backward glance" thesis than a sign that, as Matthew Guinn puts it, "the accoutrements of the past are reduced to the level of kitsch."[28] When a man "wearing a Confederate flag T-shirt that said I'M A REBEL AND DAMN PROUD OF IT" tries flirting with Sam at a mall, "Sam gave him such a mean look that he backed off."[29] The man is an unwitting pastiche of the Confederate military hero romanticized by earlier Southern writers, including Tate and Faulkner. The forlorn lives of Emmett and his fellow Vietnam veterans provide a bleaker but more realistic case study of what it means to fight in and lose a war.

While the war in Vietnam has had a significant bearing on Southern fiction since the 1970s, the impact of the Civil Rights Movement has been even more pronounced. On May 17, 1954, the Supreme Court decision in *Brown* v. *Board of Education* required that racial segregation be dismantled. On December 1, 1955, Rosa Parks refused to give her seat to a white man while riding on a segregated bus in Montgomery, Alabama. Four days later, twenty-five-year-old clergyman Martin Luther King, Jr., was chosen to lead a black boycott of the Montgomery buses. As historian Michael O'Brien has remarked, the emergence of the Civil Rights Movement compels us to rethink the very concept of a Southern Renaissance. Whereas Tate in 1945 articulated "the sense of an ending," for a younger generation the Southern Renaissance could be seen "more as a beginning": "If the culture of the South awoke, Selma is what it awoke to."[30]

Established white Southern authors responded in various ways to the upheavals generated by the Civil Rights Movement. Until his death in July 1962, Faulkner struggled to reconcile his conflicted but essentially moderate (by white Southern standards) views on race with his unwanted post-Nobel status as a spokesman for the South. In 1963, Eudora Welty reacted to the assassination of NAACP field secretary Medgar Evers in her hometown of Jackson by writing the short story "Where Is the Voice Coming From?" Welty later recalled feeling that "Whoever the murderer is, I know him: not his identity, but his coming about, in this time and place."[31] However, when Welty published an essay entitled "Must the Novelist Crusade?" in 1965, her muted answer was "no" – fiction, she argued, should not be a platform for politics.

For certain black Southern writers who came of age during the Civil Rights Movement, separating art and politics was neither possible nor desirable. A key figure here is Alice Walker, born in Eatonton, Georgia, in 1944. In her first published essay, "The Civil Rights Movement: What Good Was It?" (1967), Walker explained how her activism defined her: "To know is to exist: to exist is to be involved, to move about, to see the world with my own eyes. This, at least, the Movement has given me."[32] The movement had also helped Walker identify herself as a Southerner: "when he [King] spoke of 'letting freedom ring' across 'the green hills of Alabama and the red hills of Georgia' I saw again what he was always uniquely able to make me see: that I, in fact, had claim to the land of my birth. Those red hills of Georgia were mine."[33] In turn, this enhanced racial and regional consciousness shaped Walker's relationship to the Southern literary tradition. In the mid-1970s, Walker remembered being "shocked and delighted"[34] by O'Connor's characters but also observed that O'Connor's house in Milledgeville was built by slaves – slaves who might have been her own ancestors: "For a long time I will feel Faulkner's house, O'Connor's house, crushing me."[35] By this time, Walker was educating herself about earlier black women writers. In 1973, Walker located Zora Neale Hurston's unmarked grave in Florida, where she erected a marker bearing the legend "Zora Neale Hurston: A Genius of the South." Walker's crucial role in the rediscovery of Hurston anticipated, even instigated, the wider reinvention of Southern literary studies since the 1980s to encompass black writers past and present.

Although Walker is best-known for her Pulitzer Prize-winning novel *The Color Purple* (1982), her engagement with the Civil Rights Movement and her passionate attachment to the South are most powerfully demonstrated in *Meridian* (1976). Structured as a *bildungsroman* around the experiences of eponymous protagonist Meridian Hill, *Meridian* more broadly explores the complex racial, sexual, and gender dynamics of the movement as black activists lose faith in nonviolent protest and white liberals are marginalized. *Meridian* is especially compelling when depicting the fraught triangular relationship between Meridian, fellow activist Truman Held, and Lynne Rabinowitz, a white Northern student who becomes Truman's wife. In a pivotal sequence, Lynne, estranged from both Truman and the increasingly militant movement, is raped by a black activist named Tommy Odds. In raw scenes like this, Walker uncompromisingly interrogates the ways in which King's concept of Beloved Community was ruptured by tensions between not only blacks and whites, but also men and women. Yet the often harrowing racial and sexual violence that permeates *Meridian* is leavened by lyrical paeans to the South's physical landscape, and a sympathetic portrayal of black Southern Christianity.

The Civil Rights Movement is also a central theme in *The Autobiography of Miss Jane Pittman* (1971), a defining novel in the distinguished career of Ernest Gaines. Gaines was born on the River Lake Plantation in Pointe Coupee Parish, Louisiana, in 1933; by the age of eight, he was working in the cane fields for 50 cents a day. Since the publication of his first short story, "A Long Day in November," in 1958, Gaines has written numerous novels and stories set in the sugarcane country of southwestern Louisiana. But at the height of Black Power militancy, Gaines's intense focus on the local, historical experience of blacks from rural Louisiana was met with some skepticism. When he began writing *Jane Pittman* in 1968, black activists scolded Gaines: "Who wants to hear about a hundred and ten year old woman these days, man? We're talking about what's happening *now*!"[36] Yet *Jane Pittman*'s power derives from Gaines's skill in situating contemporary African American struggles within a broader Southern history. The formal and thematic conceit of *Jane Pittman* is that narrator and protagonist Jane Pittman was born into slavery, is now (1962) 110 years old, and that her story is recorded by a history teacher who edits Jane's oral narrative into the published text. Gaines's novel thus recalls the form and function of both the original slave narratives and the Works Progress Administration's interviews with ex-slaves during the 1930s and 1940s. Jane's longevity allows Gaines to emphasize not only the grim historical continuity of white Southern racism from Reconstruction to the Civil Rights Movement, but also the endurance and resistance of generations of black Southerners. The most recent racist act of violence against a black Southern leader, the murder of local activist Jimmy, recalls the assassination of teacher Ned Douglass at the end of the nineteenth century. But in the very last sentence of the novel, Jane herself leads "the people" past the plantation owner Samson to claim Jimmy's body in nearby Bayonne. Thus Jane, a relatively passive witness to others' lives throughout much of her autobiography, becomes an active participant in a movement that emerges from and empowers "the people."

Gaines's "attention to place and community" and his "awareness of the past in the present" prompted critic Fred Hobson to identify Gaines with "the old power of southern fiction" at a time when white writers like Hannah and Mason seemed immersed in a postmodern world.[37] But as Kreyling warns, there are problems with "[n]ominating Ernest Gaines to redeem southern literary history."[38] Though Gaines has acknowledged that "Faulkner showed me a lot," he has also remarked that "I could no more agree with his philosophy ... than I could agree with [George] Wallace's."[39] Though Gaines follows Faulkner in focusing on a postage stamp of native soil, Gaines's narrative geography is centered on the black quarters. As such, when talking about place in Gaines's fiction, one cannot overlook the quarters' origins in slavery – what Charles Rowell terms "the oppressive elements of the past in the present."[40] If Gaines's characters develop a sense of place, community, or history, they do so within and despite the South's oppressive historical and spatial structures. This is evident in *A Gathering of Old Men* (1983) when the aged cane worker Johnny Paul declares that:

> Sure, one day they will get rid of the proof that we ever was, but they ain't go'n do it while I'm still here. Mama and Papa worked too hard in these fields ... They mama and they papa people worked too hard, too hard to have that tractor just come in that graveyard and destroy all proof that they ever was. I'm the last one left. I had to see that the graves stayed for a little while longer. But I just didn't do it for my own people. I did it for every last one back there under them trees.[41]

Johnny Paul is not simply lamenting the destruction of an agrarian tradition by modern technology. He is reiterating an oral history of the plantation as a locus of black life and death – an intensely local history that must be remembered and passed on. Gaines's gathering of old men embodies the sentiment expressed by Walker in 1970: "What the black Southern writer inherits as a natural right is a sense of *community* ... Nor am I nostalgic ... for lost poverty. I am nostalgic for the solidarity and sharing a modest existence can sometimes bring."[42]

The ambiguities of living a "modest existence" characterize another distinctive area of recent Southern fiction. In 1991, Hobson predicted that "class – now that race and gender are being addressed – will be the next enlivening issue in the consideration of southern letters."[43] This increased alertness to class partly explains why considerable critical attention is being paid to Harry Crews. Crews is now figured as the founding father of "Grit Lit" or "Hick Chic," loaded terms that have been extended to writing by and about white Southerners from working-class backgrounds such as Mason, Jayne Anne Phillips, Larry Brown, and Chris Offutt. Born to tenant farmers in Georgia in 1935, Crews has published a formidable body of work since his first story appeared in *Sewanee Review* in 1963. It is no small irony that Crews's early mentor was Andrew Lytle, the Agrarian who in *I'll Take My Stand* scorned poor whites as "shiftless." While Crews has expressed his appreciation of "Mr. Lytle," he also emphasized that "we were from very different Souths ... His daddy was a planter that never touched a plow ... My family was the white trash way down at the end of the road from the big house."[44]

In his extraordinary autobiography *My Childhood: The Biography of a Place* (1978), Crews observes that "Wounds or scars give an awesome credibility to a story."[45] Throughout Crews's fiction, too, there is a notable focus on his characters' wounds and scars – mental as well as physical. Critics have compared Crews's "grits" with O'Connor's "freaks," but whereas the grotesque in O'Connor's fiction was bound up with spiritual matters, the corporeal concerns of Crews's writing are tied to class and poverty. In novels like *Car* (1972), *Body* (1990), and *Scarlover* (1992), Crews's characters remain obsessed with their bodies in an urbanized and commercialized South where traditional rural labor is largely redundant. In *A Feast of Snakes* (1976), which takes place in Mystic, Georgia, during the annual rattlesnake round-up festival, the only farmer featured in the novel is a kind of ghost of agrarian manhood past. He props up the bar in a shabby roadhouse, "drinking whiskey out of a water glass and never looking up" except to watch, "with no expression at all," the absurd performance of machismo played out by high school football stars Joe Lon Mackey and Willard Miller as they taunt a feeble traveling salesman called Poncy.[46] Throughout the novel, Joe Lon and Willard try to affirm their masculinity through sports and body-building rather than agricultural labor. Eventually, however, Joe Lon's aimlessness and alienation explode into a murderous rampage, the only way that Joe Lon can regain agency over his body and identity: "Christ, it was good to be in control again. He shot the nearest [rattlesnake] hunter."[47]

Dorothy Allison's *Bastard Out of Carolina* (1992) offers a compelling exploration of how class intersects with gender in the young life of Ruth Anne "Bone" Boatwright. Identified on her birth certificate as "a bastard by the state of South Carolina," Bone is saddled with all the stereotypical connotations such a definition brings: "*No-good, lazy, shiftless.*"[48] Yet in Allison's nuanced portrayal of Bone's fractious but close-knit family, we encounter a "trash" version of Walker's "solidarity and sharing a modest existence can sometimes bring." Indeed, Bone's memories of her infant years in 1950s Greenville diverge little from familiar Southern literary images of place, family, and storytelling:

> The world that came in over the radio was wide and far away and didn't touch us at all. We lived on one porch or another all summer long ... listening to stories ... When I think of that summer ... I always feel safe again. No place has ever seemed so sweet and quiet, no place ever felt so much like home.[49]

But Bone recalls her early childhood so fondly because of the trials she has endured since her mother married Glen Waddell, the rogue son of a local businessman. Subjected to violent beatings by her stepfather and shuttled from one rental property to another, Bone becomes increasingly aware of the restrictive roles assigned to women from her family and class. In a scene that doubles as a commentary on the class biases of earlier Southern fiction, Bone realizes just how much the Boatwright women diverge from the dominant ideal of white Southern womanhood:

> Aunt Alma had given me a paperback edition of *Gone with the Wind*, with tinted pictures from the movie, and told me I'd love it. I had at first, but one evening I looked up from Vivien Leigh's pink cheeks to see Mama coming in from work with her hair darkened from sweat and her uniform stained. A sharp flash went through me. Emma Slattery, I thought. That's who I'd be, that's who we were. Not Scarlett with her baking-powder cheeks. I was part of the trash down in the mud-stained cabins, fighting with the darkies and stealing ungratefully from our betters, stupid, coarse, born to shame and death.[50]

Bone later recounts how she was brutally raped by "Daddy Glen," and how her mother abandoned her in favor of her stepfather. Yet this often harrowing coming-of-age novel concludes with Bone defiantly facing down the future with the support of an unconventional role model from within the Boatwright clan: her lesbian aunt Raylene. In the ambiguous final paragraph, Bone affirms that "I would be thirteen in a few weeks. I was already who I was going to be ... someone like her [Raylene], like Mama, a Boatwright woman. I wrapped my fingers in Raylene's and watched the night close in around us."[51]

Perhaps the most striking trend in recent Southern fiction has been the proliferation of novels written about and by recent immigrants to the region. Important books by native authors like Tom Wolfe (*A Man in Full* [1998]) and Cynthia Shearer (*The Celestial Jukebox* [2005]) depict a South populated by immigrants from Asia, Africa, and Latin America. Writers with immigrant backgrounds have begun publishing powerful novels about bicultural identity: Lan Cao's *Monkey Bridge* (1997) offers a fresh angle on the theme of Vietnam in Southern fiction by focusing on Vietnamese immigrants in North Virginia. Meanwhile, major non-Southern American novelists such as Russell Banks (*Continental Drift* [1985]) and Dave Eggers (*What Is the What* [2006]) have charted Haitian and Sudanese immigration to south Florida and Atlanta respectively. It remains to be seen whether this "transnational turn" in fiction will continue in accordance with the exponential rise in immigration to the South. What seems fairly clear is that the neo-Agrarian model of Southern fiction as a regional literature rooted in fixed ideas of place, community, and history has reached the end of the line. In the second decade of the twenty-first century, few novelists writing about the South feel compelled to glance backward – longingly or anxiously – at the receding shadow of the Dixie Limited.

FURTHER READING

Bone, Martyn. *The Postsouthern Sense of Place in Contemporary Fiction*. Baton Rouge: Louisiana State University Press, 2005

Jones, Suzanne. *Race Mixing: Southern Fiction Since the Sixties*. Baltimore: Johns Hopkins University Press, 2004

Jones, Suzanne and Sharon Monteith (eds.). *South to a New Place: Region, Literature, Culture*. Baton Rouge: Louisiana State University Press, 2002

Monteith, Sharon. *Advancing Sisterhood: Interracial Friendships in Contemporary Southern Fiction*. Athens: University of Georgia Press, 2000

Romine, Scott. *The Real South: Southern Narrative in the Age of Cultural Reproduction*. Baton Rouge: Louisiana State University Press, 2008

Taylor, Helen. *Circling Dixie: Contemporary Southern Culture Through a Transatlantic Lens*. New Brunswick: Rutgers University Press, 2001

NOTES

1 Allen Tate, "The New Provincialism," in *Essays of Four Decades* (Chicago: Swallow Press, 1969), p. 535.
2 Allen Tate, "The Profession of Letters in the South," in *Essays*, p. 533.
3 Tate, "New Provincialism," p. 545.
4 H. L. Mencken, "The Sahara of the Bozart," in *Prejudices: Second Series* (London: Jonathan Cape, 1921), p. 136.
5 Flannery O'Connor, "Some Aspects of the Grotesque in Southern Fiction," in *Mystery and Manners: Occasional Prose* (New York: Farrar, Straus, and Giroux, 1969), p. 45.
6 Orville Prescott, Review of Cormac McCarthy's *The Orchard Keeper*, *New York Times*, May 12, 1965: www.nytimes.com/1965/05/12/books/mccarthy-orchard.html.

7   Larry McMurtry, Review of Richard Ford's *A Piece of My Heart*, *New York Times Book Review*, October 24, 1976: 16.
8   Walker Percy, *The Moviegoer* (New York: Vintage International, 1998), p. 9.
9   Ibid., p. 6.
10 Ibid., pp. 129–30.
11 Fredric Jameson, *Postmodernism, or, the Cultural Logic of Late Capitalism* (London: Verso, 1991), p. 6.
12 Jean Baudrillard, *Simulations* (New York: Semiotext[e], 1983), p. 4.
13 Percy, *The Moviegoer*, 63.
14 Ibid., p. 10.
15 Ibid., p. 224.
16 Philip E. Simmons, *Deep Surfaces: Mass Culture and History in Postmodern American Fiction* (Athens: University of Georgia Press, 1997), pp. 25–6.
17 Ibid., p. 26.
18 Ibid., pp. 39–40.
19 Percy, "Novel Writing in an Apocalyptic Time," in Patrick J. Samway (ed.), *Signposts in a Strange Land* (London: Bellew, 1991), pp. 166–7.
20 Lewis P. Simpson, *The Brazen Face of History: Studies in the Literary Consciousness of America* (Baton Rouge: Louisiana State University Press, 1994), p. 269.
21 Michael Kreyling, *Inventing Southern Literature* (Jackson: University Press of Mississippi, 1997), p. 161.
22 Ibid., p. 162.
23 Daniel E. Williams, "Interview with Barry Hannah," in Martyn Bone (ed.), *Perspectives on Barry Hannah* (Jackson: University Press of Mississippi, 2007), p. 185.
24 Barry Hannah, *Boomerang/Never Die* (Jackson: Banner Books, 1994), pp. 137–8.
25 Barry Hannah, "Dragged Fighting from His Tomb," in *Airships* (New York: Knopf, 1978), p. 58.
26 Barry Hannah, *Ray* (New York: Knopf, 1980), p. 64.
27 Bobbie Ann Mason, *In Country* (London: Flamingo, 1986), p. 79.
28 Matthew Guinn, *After Southern Modernism: Fiction of the Contemporary South* (Jackson: University Press of Mississippi, 2000), p. 66.
29 Mason, *In Country*, p. 201.
30 Michael O'Brien, "A Heterodox Note on the Southern Renaissance," in *Rethinking the South: Essays in Intellectual History* (Baltimore: Johns Hopkins University Press, 1988), p. 167.
31 Eudora Welty, "Preface," in *The Collected Stories of Eudora Welty* (Harmondsworth: Penguin, 1983), p. xi.
32 Alice Walker, "The Civil Rights Movement: What Good Was It?" in *In Search of Our Mothers' Gardens: Womanist Prose* (London: The Women's Press, 1984), p. 126.
33 Alice Walker, "Choosing to Stay at Home," in *In Search*, p. 160.
34 Alice Walker, "Beyond the Peacock: The Reconstruction of Flannery O'Connor," in *In Search*, p. 52.
35 Ibid., p. 58.

36 John Lowe, "An Interview with Ernest Gaines," in Lowe (ed.), *Conversations with Ernest Gaines* (Jackson: University Press of Mississippi, 1995), pp. 316–17.

37 Fred Hobson, *The Southern Writer in the Postmodern World* (Athens: University of Georgia Press, 1991), pp. 92–3.

38 Kreyling, *Inventing*, p. 98.

39 Fred Beauford, "A Conversation with Ernest Gaines," in Lowe (ed.), *Conversations*, p. 19.

40 Charles Rowell, "The Quarters: Ernest Gaines and the Sense of Place," *Southern Review*, 21.3 (1985): 745.

41 Ernest Gaines, *A Gathering of Old Men* (New York: Vintage, 1992), p. 92.

42 Alice Walker, "The Black Writer and the Southern Experience" in *In Search*, p. 17.

43 Hobson, *Southern Writer*, p. 20.

44 Erik Bledsoe, "An Interview with Harry Crews," in Bledsoe (ed.), *Perspectives on Harry Crews* (Jackson: University Press of Mississippi, 2001), pp. 153–4.

45 Harry Crews, *A Childhood: The Biography of a Place*, in *Classic Crews: A Reader* (New York: Touchstone, 1993), p. 37.

46 Harry Crews, *A Feast of Snakes* (New York: Scribner, 1998), pp. 103–4.

47 Ibid., p. 176.

48 Dorothy Allison, *Bastard Out of Carolina* (New York: Plume, 1993), p. 3.

49 Ibid., p. 22.

50 Ibid., p. 206.

51 Ibid., p. 309.

12

ALAN NADEL

Fiction and the Cold War

In the "Epilogue" to Ralph Ellison's *Invisible Man*, the anonymous narrator says, "I was never more hated than when I tried to be honest ... On the other hand, I've never been more loved and appreciated than when I tried to 'justify' and affirm someone's mistaken beliefs; or when I've tried to give my friends the incorrect, absurd answers they wished to hear."[1] When juxtaposed with the novel's final line – "Who knows but that, on lower frequencies, I speak for you?" – this statement suggests how much *Invisible Man* functions as a quintessential Cold War narrative, in addition to being, arguably, the definitive novel of pre-desegregation African American literature.[2] Ellison's Epilogue, in other words, gives his modernist representation of African American history and culture a Cold War interpretation, replete with its sense of, and fear about, the ethos of conformity.

That ethos, memorably named other-directedness in David Riesman's 1950 bestselling sociological study, *The Lonely Crowd*, is posited on Riesman's belief that the notion of a social character is more or less accepted fact. A troubling new social character, Riesman argued, was starting to dominate twentieth-century urban America. Cultures ranging from prehistoric Africa and pre-Christian Athens to the pre-Columbian Americas, from the Ptolemaic Dynasty and the Ming Dynasty to contemporary Japan and Italy had shared the *same* social character, which he labeled tradition-directed. In the eighteenth- and nineteenth-century industrialized West, he claimed, an inner-directed social character emerged that consolidated the values of what is usually called the Protestant Ethic. In the mid twentieth century, however, this inner-directed individual was being usurped by other-directed people, whose values come not from what Riesman called an internal gyroscope but rather from external radar.[3]

Although *The Lonely Crowd* provides virtually no evidence for these sweeping generalizations and its assumptions and conclusions are often racist and colonialist, Riesman's study was the canonical work of post-World War II American sociology. From a twenty-first-century perspective, however, *The Lonely Crowd* looks more like a piece of Cold War science fiction that describes a strange planet, one uncannily like Earth, threatened by uncertain demographic shifts that may cede domination to new, strange creatures marked by moral and social uncertainty. The lack of an internal gyroscope made these creatures literally unstable and potentially unbalanced. And they take their directions – like stereotypical "commies" – from others, constantly seeking confirmation from their peers and guided by the social cues those peers give off.

In many ways, *The Lonely Crowd* provides the social fiction that ties *Invisible Man* to J. D. Salinger's *The Catcher in the Rye* (1951), published just one year before *Invisible Man* and one year after *The Lonely Crowd*. For the invisible man, the desire to tell his story becomes by the end of the novel both the speaker's refrain and his motivating passion, one that echoes Holden Caulfield's desire to tell his story as well as to distance himself from the society that produced him as its historian. Like Riesman, both narrators compulsively assault their other-directed society, while constantly betraying how much they, themselves, are other-directed. From the moment when the invisible man overhears his grandfather's deathbed pronouncement, through his experiences at the Battle Royal, in college, at the paint factory, and with the New York City Brotherhood, Ellison's anonymous narrator remains acutely conscious of his behavior, regularly afraid that he has fallen short of what others expect of him or of what he expects from himself. Fear and disappointment thus delimit his search for identity. Caulfield, in exactly the same way, internalizes the mechanisms of surveillance. While astutely noting each nuance of conformity and attendant phoniness in his social surroundings, his sense that his own identity is constructed in the eyes of others remains a structural given of his discourse, such that he cannot describe anything he does without justifying it to some invisible audience in relation to some arbitrary rule or social norm. He even invents rules to normalize his own aberrations.

If Caulfield and the invisible man expose the folly and phoniness of the other-directed people who, according to Riesman, threaten the civilized world, they do so because, at lower frequencies, they speak for readers, who, at the height of the McCarthyist surveillance state, made the term "non-conformist" not merely a pejorative but also a cause of suspicion. An American population emerging from two decades that included a prolonged depression followed by a world war tended to regard "deviance" as potentially subverting the long-awaited return to national normality. Being other-directed thus represented an homage to national consensus; Americans could help win the Cold War by pledging allegiance to the one nation decreed by a 1954 Act of Congress to be "under God." In this context, *The*

Lonely Crowd's imaginary could be seen as invoking the aura of social science to vent this anxiety about the burden of conformity and the ubiquity of its enforcement. Thus, Riesman's own obsessive normativity, drawing on stereotypes of America's western settlers and captains of industry, made the rugged individualist the apotheosis of progress. This inner-directed man was the social face of American exceptionalism, which allowed Reisman's Cold War American reader to remain John Waynes and Gary Coopers at heart while in their normal lives confirming the expectations of others.

One aspect of this phenomenon is a form of literary other-direction in which the postwar generation of writers directly appropriated canonical works and authors, shifting the innovations of Joyce, Eliot, and Pound from the literary avant-garde to lingua franca. Salinger's debt to *Huckleberry Finn*, for instance, has been widely noted. Updike's *Rabbit, Run* (1960) has similarly been regarded as the escapades of a contemporary, suburban Huckleberry Finn, in the same way that Saul Bellow's *Henderson the Rain King* (1959) modernized and resituated Twain's *A Connecticut Yankee in King Arthur's Court*. Ellison, particularly in specific chapters, à la Joyce, rewrites work by Faulkner, Melville, Emerson, and Whitman. Even more blatantly, Saul Bellow's 1947 novel, *The Victim*, appropriates Melville's "Bartleby," updating it to mid-century New York, where Allbee (phonetically "Bartleby" minus the "bart") invades the life and the home of a guilt-ridden copy-editor, Asa Leventhal, a man who, like the anonymous narrator of Melville's story, has always preferred the easiest way of life. Similarly, Norman Mailer's 1967 novel, *Why Are We in Vietnam?* adapts Faulkner's "The Bear" in an attempt to define the cultural lineage that invests American adventurism with its historicity. Mixing, à la Faulkner, the ancestral fantasy and fantastic ancestry of a boy, Ranald "D. J." Jethroe – in this case from Texas rather than Mississippi – not much older than Faulkner's Isaac McCaslin at the time McCaslin went on his fateful bear hunt, Mailer starts with a psychedelic barrage of obscene ventriloquism that articulates, as projected onto the unconscious voice of D. J.'s mother, the ultra-vulgar Oedipal dynamics of Mailer's mid-1960s stoned Texas redneck teen. D. J. and his father, Rusty, "the cream of corporation corporateness," embark on an Alaskan bear hunt that occupies the remainder of the short novel, engaging in the process the full spectrum of patriarchal specters that define for Mailer the cultural masculinity informing American imperialism.[4] If the adolescent rant moves in stages through a pastiche of neo-folk idioms interweaving frontierism and tourism, Huck Finn naivety and pickup-truck, rock-music grit, this initiation tale resolves into the fluid strings of Faulknerian clauses, each successive phrase reasserting the hope for a language that might be ameliorative in its persistent attempt to modify the speaker's present, that is, his history. Mailer's attempt to pass for everything in America that he is not is particularly interesting in light of the fact that Mailer can't seem to do so without taking direction from Faulkner, in much the way that Salinger and Updike do from Twain, or Bellow does from Melville.

The epitome of literary other-directedness, however, might be *Herzog*, both Bellow's 1964 novel and its eponymous central character, Moses Herzog, whose life, bereft of its gyroscope, maintains tenuous balance by producing relentless correspondence, addressed not only to his peers and to the important figures in his life, living and dead, but also to public figures, dead philosophers, and God. These epistles, importantly, structure Bellow's novel as much as they do Herzog's life, making Herzog the medium of Bellow's literary self-consciousness, the character through whom Bellow can channel the intellectual touchstones of Western philosophy and Cold War history to fulfill what we can recognize as Holden Caulfield's need for self-validation or the Invisible Man's desire for visibility. Equally important is the transparency of this ruse, revealed by the disparity between the letters' addressees and their ultimate delivery address, which is Herzog's own briefcase. Not just Herzog but Bellow himself thus comes full circle, making Herzog yet another former employee of the dead letter office, akin to the character Bartleby, upon whom, at the beginning of the Cold War seventeen years earlier, Bellow based *The Victim*.

Herzog underscores the relationship between *identity* and *identification* that represents the fundamental conflict of *The Lonely Crowd*, the fictional world populated by people torn between the desire for inner identity and the demands of social identification. That conflict is equally represented by such ostensibly rebellious writing as Mailer's "The White Negro," a diatribe against a 1950s conformity that Mailer conceives in distinctly Cold War terms. In the aftermath of the Holocaust and the shadow of nuclear annihilation, Mailer felt, "our psyche itself was subjected to the intolerable anxiety that death being causeless, life was causeless as well, and that time deprived of cause and effect had come to a stop."[5] The alternative to this "stop" is the hipster, who models himself on the Negro. Mailer's "Negro," described in hypermasculine terms, is an over-sexed, violent psychopath (Mailer's valorizing term), driven by the desire not for love but for orgasm. The white Negro thus rejects the status quo; he is on the go. Jack Kerouac's *On the Road* (1957), featuring a quintessential white Negro, Dean Moriarty, based on Neal Cassidy (whom Allen Ginsberg, in "Howl," called the "cocksman of Denver"), similarly links identity (especially male identity) to escape. The idea that manhood is at odds with domesticity, asserted by Leslie Fiedler's *Love and Death in the American Novel* (1960) – an influential book of literary criticism providing yet another story of American literature inflected by Cold War values and identifying the Negro as the model of escape from them – attempts to deploy the conflict between identity and identification across a gendered spectrum, one that quarantines female space as it resides in both physical and social geographies. Interestingly, for Mailer, Fiedler, or Kerouac, homosexuality is less threatening to masculinity than are women.

This could be read as post-World War II nostalgia for the wartime homo-social world that, during the war, had defined manliness for over one-third of the American adult male population, through the bonding produced by geographical dislocation, physical danger, martial activity, and casual relationships with the opposite sex. The problem for the Cold War man was that military service had dictated conformity to a set of social conditions almost antithetical to those in postwar America, which valorized the nuclear family instead of dislocated male units, and promoted assembly-line workers and middle-management employees as the appropriate models for manhood.

The conflict in the Cold War period between wartime and postwar models of masculinity informs virtually all the relations in James Jones's 1951 novel *From Here to Eternity*. A consolidating moment, the attack on Pearl Harbor subordinates all domestic agendas to a military courage defined by duty to a requisite spectrum of male bonds. Another 1951 novel about men at war, Herman Wouk's *The Caine Mutiny*, which replaced *From Here to Eternity* on the bestseller list and went on to win the Pulitzer Prize, also bridges the worlds of the wartime and peacetime military so as to value two forms of heroism, that which defies authority and that which privileges conformity rather individual initiative; the mutineers, initially exonerated from seizing control of the USS Caine from the tyrannical and possibly paranoid Captain Queeg, are subsequently renounced by their own defense attorney for their failure to honor the years of peacetime service that earned Queeg his command. The armed services, in both of these postwar novels, is as much a corporate structure as an instrument of warfare. That structure, moreover, encompasses homoerotics with more complacency than it tolerates female authority. While *From Here to Eternity* more explicitly acknowledges homo-sexuality (even though the published version excised some gay sex from the original manuscript), it is not hard to queer some of the relationships among the crew of the USS Caine.

This is just one way in which World War II conformists and postwar non-conformists valorize similar tenets of gender distinction. The intense homo-phobia that McCarthyism promoted, causing numerous resignations from the State Department and more generally making homosexuals official secur-ity risks,[6] reflected profound contradictions; Senator Joseph McCarthy's close advisor, for instance, was the homosexual Roy Cohn, whose attempt to secure privileges from Army officers for his intimate friend, David Schein, led to the Army–McCarthy hearings that brought about McCarthy's downfall.

The hiding-in-plain-sight during the Cold War not just of homosexuality but the full spectrum of sexual desires was foundational to what I have called "containment culture,"[7] a closeted sensibility encompassing not just sexual orientation but any aspect of behavior, belief, or desire regulated by internalized surveillance and manifest by constantly negotiated self-censorship. This sensibility was reinforced by politicians, religious leaders, news media, boards of education, as well as a still active Hollywood Production Code and an even more stringent code for television production. The resulting perversions of representation and consensus of denial suggested tacit acceptance of the idea, for example, that married couples slept in separate beds, that men were the agents of sexual desire that (good) women were responsible for regulating, and that Liberace was one of the most eligible bachelors of the decade.

Although today this era's rigid heteronormativity may seem anything but normal, in the 1950s it gave women a crucial role in postwar reassimilation: they enabled men to marry, start families, and take command of those families, thus helping veterans transition from military victors to breadwinners. Thus charged, women could also obstruct this return to "normalcy" by remaining in the workforce, retaining or advancing upon the corporate or industrial roles they had occupied during the war; they could privilege their own sexual desire beyond its functional relationship to fertility; and they could resist occupying a subordinate role in the masculine chain of command. Lest these become normal options, adult women were somewhat scarce as role models in 1950s American culture. The most pervasive motif in the most popular television sit-com of the 1950s, *I Love Lucy*, was that the ability to love Lucy required regularly disciplining her for exercising any of those adult options. Her infantile bawling, as much a cultural trademark as Marilyn Monroe's baby talk or Audrey Hepburn's waif-like innocence, helped confine the range of possibilities in Cold War America for mature female agency.

The adulation of women to the extent that they remained tacitly puerile, sexually naive, and professionally unambitious is ruthlessly satirized in Vladimir Nabokov's *Lolita*. Everything about the 1950s – from its relentless normativity, its self-serving worship of young girls (and women who emulated them), its dogmatic belief that father knows best, its thirst for kitsch, to its blindness to closeted behavior and its trust in the concepts of progressive education – made it paradise for the novel's narrator, Humbert Humbert, a delusional European pederast, who possessed good looks, a second-rate education, and a knack for fulfilling the fantasies of a middlebrow society informed chiefly by the clichés of popular magazines, self-help books, tourist guides, and Hollywood films. The novel's hero arrives in America harboring an insatiable desire to replicate his affection for a lost childhood love, a young girl who was, herself, he believes, the replica of Annabel Lee, the fictitious child love of Edgar Allan Poe's poetic imagination. What the unbalanced Humbert discovers, however, is a country generally as deluded by Poe's romanticism as he is. If Humbert encounters very little trouble passing for normal in 1950s middle-class America, even more astonishing is how easily the twelve-year-old Lolita is taken for the fictitious child that mass culture wants to adulate, instead of what she actually is: sexually active, inarticulate, and vacuous.

By juggling several disparities – between Lolita in actuality and as she exists in Humbert's imagination, between Humbert and the public perception of him, between the nation and its perception of itself – Nabokov impales Cold War America on a satiric skewer. Neither her poor hygiene, addiction to comic books and bubble gum, nor love of slang dislodges Lolita's status in Humbert's purple prose and gothic plots. He persists, willfully oblivious to the fact that Lolita is no nymphette. Society is equally blind: constantly Humbert hears she is an exceptional child, although her teachers think her social development, as indicated by her interactions with the opposite sex, is somewhat retarded. Only the perverted playwright, Quilty, has any suspicion of her sexual relationship with Humbert, a relationship that Humbert insists on seeing as grounded in romantic passion, despite the evidence to the contrary, which, at times, he cannot avoid revealing.

These revelations periodically punctuate Humbert's satiric ridicule of such aspects of Americana as motel names, interior decorating hints, educational curricula, or extracurricular activities, creating a pattern of irony, deprecation, self-deprecation, revelation, and denial that allows a particularly arch interpretation of Humbert's confession, late in the novel, that "It had become gradually clear to my conventional Lolita during our singular and bestial cohabitation that even the most miserable of family lives was better than the parody of incest, which in the long run was the best I could offer the waif."[8] Like the invisible man, at lower frequencies, Humbert here speaks for his audience, the people who fetishize childhood and adore screen waifs, infantile homemakers, and baby-talking blondes. These middle-class readers take pride in their nuclear families that substitute "the parody of incest" for any developmental community aimed at intellectual maturation and sexual adulthood.

Ironically, the phrase "parody of incest" also applies to Grace Metalious's 1956 bestseller, *Peyton Place*, written a year after *Lolita* but published in the United States a year before Nabokov's novel. A crucial event in Metalious's story of life in a small New Hampshire town in the 1930s is the repeated rape of Selena Cross by her alcoholic stepfather, Lucas, who, in Metalious's original manuscript, was Selena's father. Forced to turn Lucas into Selena's stepfather (Humbert's relationship to Lolita), Metalious told a friend "They've ruined my book. Now it is trash rather than tragedy."[9] If Nabokov turns "trash" into parody instead of tragedy, more significantly, both novels include sexual abuse of a young girl (Lolita is twelve, Selena thirteen) by her stepfather in order to grapple with a conformist culture profoundly uncomfortable with mature female sexuality. *Peyton Place* begins in 1939, the same year that Humbert immigrated to the United States and concludes in 1944, three years before Humbert's first fateful summer with Lolita. Both books, however, reflect strongly the prism of the 1950s, particularly the strict social norms of the surveillance state, as those norms regulated gender roles. If Humbert's fear that he is being followed parodies the mentality of Cold War citizens – he actually is being followed for a portion of the novel – it also shares the other-directed concerns of Allison MacKenzie, the pubescent girl whose high school years organize *Peyton Place*'s chronology. Certainly no Lolita, Allison nevertheless articulates concerns about female sexuality and female agency for which Cold War America has no appropriate label. Her mother, Constance, having secretly had Allison out of wedlock, projects her own sexual desires onto Allison and then vigorously attempts to constrain Allison's sexual license. Constance thus makes Allison the medium of her own sexual self-discipline. Constance's behavior reflects as much a need to conform to the socially defined role of mother as to renounce her youthful affair with a married man. The social codes of Cold War America, in other words, suggest that the mother of a teenaged girl – even though that mother is still in her mid-thirties – should focus her energies upon raising her child instead of meeting her own personal or professional needs. In her ostensible frigidity, Constance MacKenzie is thus conforming to the role that society prescribes and that the paradigmatic surveillance state of small-town America enforces.

A central motif in *Peyton Place*, however, is that the enforcement is as perpetually ineffective as the role is inadequate. These facts of life in Peyton Place are hidden everywhere in plain sight, manifest through Selena's impregnation by her stepfather, her mother's madness that culminates in suicide, the alcoholism or insanity that infects an array of townspeople, and the persistent legal abuse of power and physical abuse of women. Because sexual repression in the town equates so strongly with respectability, at least two characters – Norman, Allison's quasi boyfriend, and Reverend Fitzgerald – can be read as closeted homosexuals who would rather sublimate their sexual desires than acknowledge them. (During World War II, Norman receives a medical discharge from the Army because he is "mentally unfit.")[10] In this environment, Allison, like Holden Caulfield, delineates the dimensions of social confusion while nevertheless being increasingly confused by them. Late in the novel, she, like Caulfield, has a psychological breakdown, ostensibly from having found Selena's mother, Nellie, hanging in the closet, but more fully from having succumbed to the cumulative power of a society that economically, socially, and psychologically forecloses the options for the women of Peyton Place.

Published seven years after *Peyton Place* and set six years earlier, Mary McCarthy's *The Group* (1963) recounts the postgraduation experiences of several 1933 Vassar graduates. Despite the differences in class and education, McCarthy's women have many experiences and concerns similar to those of Allison MacKenzie and her peers, suggesting the ways that *The Group*, like *Peyton Place*, reflects Cold War America gender distinctions, as much as, if not more than, the social milieu of its historical setting. Allison's affair with a married editor, near the end of *Peyton Place*, is echoed by the experience of *The Group*'s Polly. Certainly the frankness of *Peyton Place* helped change publishing norms in ways that made possible McCarthy's explicit, clinically detailed examination of female experience. Accompanied by a set of instructions on the practice of sexual intercourse, Dottie loses her virginity, experiences her first orgasm, and receives postmortem explanations of her reactions from her initiator (named Dick) who then orders her to be fitted for a diaphragm. What typifies *The Group* is that it describes the sexual intercourse, the medical examination, and the fitting as though they were interchangeable – comparable procedures performed on a woman's body, personal and physically intimate, but hardly erotic. Throughout, *The Group* details women's lives with unflinching precision, shunning euphemism and keeping metaphor to a minimum – Dottie describes her orgasm as "a series of long, uncontrollable contractions that embarrassed her, like hiccups" – and avoiding romantic imagery, such that the book becomes a topography of women's body parts, deployed across a social and historical landscape.[11] The professional workplaces and domestic arrangements of 1930s New York City become the sites at which the mouths, the breasts, the vaginas of these women are considered, engaged, and explored. The analysis, always clinical in tone, emanates from the array of perspectives – e.g., Freud, Kraft-Ebbing, behavioral psychology, aesthetics, Marxism, socialism – that constitute the authoritative intellectual parameters of these Vassar graduates' social world.

In this light, *The Group* can be read as making women's bodies the site of the battle between inner-direction and other-direction. Libby's concern, for instance, when she finds herself unable to consummate her first sexual encounter, is how the man could have thought she was not a virgin and, equally, how he could have figured out that she was. Even Libby's thoughts about masturbating are filtered through the eyes of others:

> Libby … sometimes made love to herself … She always felt awful afterward, sort of shaken and depleted and wondering what people would think if they could see her, especially when she took herself what she called "Over the Top." She stared at her pale face in the mirror, asking herself whether Nils could have guessed: was that what made him think she was experienced?[12]

A chapter devoted to Priss's difficulties breastfeeding similarly situates her body at the intersection of conflicting social and clinical discourses:

> She was doing "the most natural thing in the world", suckling her young, and for some peculiar reason it was completely unnatural, strained, and false, like a posed photograph. Everyone in the hospital knew it; that was why they were all talking about her nursing and pretending that it was exciting, when it was not, except as a thing to talk about.[13]

Reflecting a preference for formula less typical of the 1930s than of the postwar period (which was a difficult time for women to demonstrate even biological agency), the chapter concludes with Priss's belief that her "baby's voice was rising to tell her" that breastfeeding was "horrid" and "making a natural request in this day and age; it was asking for a bottle."[14] Like every other aspect of these women's lives – mental illness, extra-marital affairs, politics, sexual orientation, house cleaning, budgeting, and toilet training their children – the issues are informed by the quintessential Cold War question: what is normal?

The question of normality haunts James Baldwin's *Another Country* (1962), about a group of white writers and artists in the aftermath of the suicide of their friend Rufus, a black musician in his late twenties. In his stunning "Notes of a Native Son," the title essay of his 1955 bestselling collection, Baldwin identified his father's irrational, even paranoid hatred of America as the trait that most made his father an American. To experience the irrationality of racial prejudice, to suppress rage or to fail to, as Baldwin's interactions with his father and with the white world demonstrated, was the trait he most shared with his father and that they both shared with most Americans. His father's mental illness, therefore, was not only a normal response to racism but also a mirror of the racism that was the American norm.

In many ways Rufus is the logical extension of Baldwin's (as opposed to Richard Wright's) "native son." Deranged by guilt over the mental breakdown and institutionalization of his white girlfriend, Rufus wanders the city aimlessly, unable to differentiate his anger from his shame, unable to distinguish the external anger he has turned against himself from the sense of inadequacy that he projects outward. Racial prejudice corrupts all perceptions, not just for Rufus but for all the characters in the novel, including Rufus's best friend, a white aspiring novelist, Vivaldo, and Rufus's sister, Ida, with whom Vivaldo begins an intimate relationship after Rufus's suicide. Moving back and forth between Greenwich Village and Harlem, the novel recounts the sexual interactions among a small group of friends – Ida, who moves in with Vivaldo; Richard and Cass, a married white couple; and Eric, a gay actor whose boyfriend, Yves, is in Paris – as they analyze and reformulate their pairings and allegiances, making racism an intimate rather than a social problem. In this light, Rufus is the logical extension of an American insanity, in which the subject self-destructively absorbs the norms it most detests.

If racism represents every form of both hatred and self-hatred, the novel's portrayal of heteronormativity reinforces racial divides. Eric thus stands in contrast with the other characters. Before leaving for Paris, Eric had been Rufus's (only male) lover; upon returning, Eric has a passionate affair with Cass, and eventually makes love to Vivaldo (who otherwise considers himself straight). Unlike the conflicted sexual couplings in the novel, all those with Eric produce an unqualified love for him, comparable to the love he feels for Yves, who is coming to America to join him. For the characters in *Another Country*, Eric is Eros, the means by which they convert hatred to love, exactly the conversion urged as a patriotic necessity in the conclusion to "Notes of a Native Son," because that conversion makes it possible to embrace the nation's flawed patriarchs. If, in this regard, Baldwin echoes the invisible man's argument in the Epilogue, he is also queering that argument by exposing the vast corrupting extent of the regulatory functions of normality.

The reconfiguration of norms lies at the center of Joseph Heller's *Catch-22*, a book as obsessed with sanity as is *Another Country* and even more relentlessly critical of norms that are presented as so irrational that conformity itself becomes quintessential insanity. This World War II novel about fliers in a bombardier squadron stationed on an island off the coast of Italy covers their experiences from basic training through the last weeks of the European campaign. In direct contrast to *From Here to Eternity* or *The Caine Mutiny*, which use the military structure as a justification for the efficacy (and morality) of an other-directed social code, *Catch-22* uses that structure to expose the duplicitous authority that gives the Other its directions. The directions, themselves, demonstrate the fallacy of logical systems and deductive reasoning by showing repeatedly that in *Catch-22* the major premise in the syllogistic structure upon which logical systems depend is a null set, symbolized most acutely by the character Major Major Major Major, whose rank, the result of a punning IBM machine, is purely nominal. So is his authority; an officer whose office is empty, he may only be seen when he is not there.

The central character, Yossarian, rejects deductive reasoning for inductive, giving him a set of premises at odds with those produced by the normal chain of command. He defines "enemy," for instance, as anyone who is trying to get him killed, thus not distinguishing the Germans who shoot at him from the American officers who place him in their line of fire. The world of *Catch-22* precludes mental breakdown "because nothing could be more insane than following the norm – continuing to fly missions – especially when the norm set by Colonel Cathcart was abnormal."[15] The term "catch-22" thus represents the circular logic that renders authority simultaneously absolute and absolutely relative: "Even when the norm is abnormal and arbitrary, any aberration from the norm, according to 'catch-22', signifies sanity and therefore is not an excuse for deviating from the norm. A breakdown of the sort Holden Caulfield had, in other words, would not take him out of the war but prove his sanity and hence his fitness for combat."[16] (In the same way, perhaps, Humbert Humbert's pedophilia could be viewed a sign of his fitness for American citizenship in the 1950s.) With *Catch-22*'s prolific explosion of dualities – such as the soldier who sees everything twice, Milo's selling everything twice, the second bombing run over Ferrara, the two "Washington Irving/Irving Washingtons," and the recurrent motif of déjà vu – the novel explodes the ostensible singularity of purposes and beliefs that Cold War conformity had asserted.

Thus, Yossarian's belief that people are trying to kill him is equally a paranoid deduction and an empirical fact:

> "Then why are they shooting at me?" Yossarian asked.
> "They're shooting at *everyone*," Clevinger answered. "They're trying to kill everyone."
> "And what difference does that make?"[17]

The trajectory of Cold War literature, in other words, could be viewed as repositioning paranoia from a psychological malady to a social condition. With the waning of McCarthyism and the blacklist, the erosion of the sexual double-standard, and the diminishing power of the Hollywood Production Code, the other-directed person starts to look less like a failed individual than an individual in a faulty social order.

Two important novels, Thomas Pynchon's *The Crying of Lot 49* (1967) and Joan Didion's *Play It as It Lays* (1970), reflect this shift. Both novels focus on women whose marriages are coming apart and who appear to have lost (or to be losing) their grips on "reality," although the women's response may be less aberrant than the society to which they are responding. The consciousness of Pynchon's heroine, Oedipa Maas, starts to expand when she becomes executrix of the multi-million-dollar estate of her former lover, Pierce Inverarity, who had tentacles throughout American life, from aerospace to television, such that his estate resembles America itself, especially in its vast incomprehensibility. Oedipa, a marginalized woman created by a male author, nevertheless discovers that all narrative strains intersect in her consciousness. Accepting that she is paranoid but wondering – in the paranoiac *coup de grâce* – if her paranoia has been induced, Oedipa finds no sign apart from her story. Despite her inability to understand her role or articulate her position, Oedipa remains at the center of narrative power. For the paranoid, everything applies.

In contrast, for Maria Wyeth, Didion's nearly catatonic heroine who is confined to a mental institution, as she repeatedly says, "nothing applies." At eighteen, Maria was sent to New York by her parents to become a model. After her parents died, she married Carter Lang, a movie director, moved to California and had a child who was institutionalized with some form of brain damage. Maria's tenuous relationship with her husband becomes further strained by his prolonged absences – shooting on location in the desert – and by her pregnancy as the result of an extra-marital affair. Threatening to deny her rights to see her daughter, Carter coerces Maria into having an (illegal) abortion and then into a divorce. When she keeps BZ – her friend and Carter's producer – company while he takes a lethal dose of pills, she is declared mentally unfit and put in the asylum that frames her story.

Unable to correlate cause and effect, Maria, the creation of a female author, unlike Oedipa, is cut off from any coherent narrative, including her family history: parents dead, child institutionalized, husband estranged, fetus aborted. The word "cut" forms a motif in the novel, relating her psychological detachment to her forced abortion and, as well, to the cinematic process of editing, in which images are cut together with the same ease as they are cut apart. While both Pynchon and Didion suggest that a cinematic consciousness has replaced Cold War norms in shaping cultural dictates, for Pynchon this means identifying with the film editor who is burdened with turning the proliferation of images into a coherent narrative; for Didion it means identifying with the individual cinematic frame, the image that is reduced to two dimensions and has no control over the narrative that will contain or omit it.

In both novels, however, paranoia no longer signifies that identity constructed in some form of contested relationship with a knowable set of social norms, the same kinds of norms that Riesman required to determine who was inner- and other-directed. Nor does either novel understand nonconformity in hypermasculinist terms. Rather, they both point toward a period when the juxtaposition of cause and effect, of foreground and background, of subject and object will treat privileged metanarratives as a set of pliable fictions and arbitrary frames. Nothing could be more antithetical to the worldview of which *The Lonely Crowd* was instrumentally symptomatic.

FURTHER READING

Briar, Evan. *A Novel Marketplace: Mass Culture, the Book Trade, and Postwar American Fiction*. Philadelphia: University of Pennsylvania Press, 2009
Cornis-Pope, Marcel. *Narrative Innovation and Cultural Rewriting in the Cold War and After*. New York: Palgrave, 2001
Schaub, Thomas Hill. *American Fiction in the Cold War*. Madison: University of Wisconsin Press, 1991
Whitfield, Stephen. *The Culture of the Cold War*. Baltimore: Johns Hopkins University Press, 1991

NOTES

1 Ralph Ellison, *Invisible Man* (New York: Random House, 1995), p. 573.
2 Ibid., p. 581.
3 David Riesman, *The Lonely Crowd: A Study of the Changing American Character* (New Haven, CT: Yale University Press, 1965), pp. 16–31.
4 Norman Mailer, *Why Are We in Vietnam?* (New York: Henry Holt, 1967), p. 29.
5 Mailer, "The White Negro," in *Advertisements for Myself* (New York: G. P. Putnam's and Sons, 1959), p. 338.
6 David K. Johnson, *The Lavender Scare: The Cold War Persecution of Gays and Lesbians in the Federal Government* (University of Chicago Press, 2004).
7 Alan Nadel, *Containment Culture: American Narratives, Postmodernism, and the Atomic Age* (Durham, NC: Duke University Press, 1995), p. x.
8 Ibid., p. 287.
9 Ardis Cameron, Introduction in Grace Metalious, *Peyton Place* (Boston: Northeastern University Press, 1999), p. xii.
10 Metalious, *Peyton Place*, p. 307.
11 Mary McCarthy, *The Group* (New York: Harcourt, 1963), p. 41.
12 Ibid., p. 285.
13 Ibid., p. 316.
14 Ibid.
15 Nadel, *Containment*, p. 167.
16 Ibid., p. 168.
17 Joesph Heller, *Catch-22* (New York: Dell, 1961), p. 17.

13

JOHN N. DUVALL

Fiction and 9/11

In the last decade, American fiction has articulated important political, aesthetic, and psychological contexts for understanding the wounds of September 11, 2001. This body of work does so in one of two ways: by directly representing the terrorist attacks or by displacing the attacks historically, allegorically, or metafictionally. This chapter first examines the former representational method before taking up the latter narrative strategy.

Fiction that directly addresses 9/11 and its aftermath focuses almost exclusively on the attack on the World Trade Center. The symbolic impact of the Twin Towers' destruction, televised as it was around the world, has made New York City the nexus of the 9/11 imagination for many novelists as they depict the lives of New Yorkers who were the victims, the survivors, or the witnesses of the devastation. These narratives of individual trauma and loss, however, have been deemed a failure on a number of fronts. Indian author Pankaj Mishra expresses disappointment that American novelists have retreated "to the domestic life" and have struggled "to define cultural otherness" of Islam.[1] Richard Gray notes that much of the American fiction about the terrorist attacks emphasizes "the preliminary stages of trauma."[2] His assessment, however, echoes Mishra's: American fiction that directly engages 9/11 "adds next to nothing to our understanding of the trauma at the heart of the action. In fact, it evades that trauma" by its focus on domestic issues and personal lives, rather than "facing the [Islamic] other."[3]

If one retrospectively applied Mishra's and Gray's perspective to fiction after World War I, one might be forced to say that Virginia Woolf's *Mrs. Dalloway* (1925) and Ernest Hemingway's *The Sun Also Rises* (1926) were failures of the imagination for not treating the root cause of a historical trauma, since Woolf's Septimus Smith and Hemingway's Jake Barnes depict the private traumas of war veterans. And what, after all, does Clarissa Dalloway's party planning do to help us understand Gavrilo Princip's anger at Austria–Hungary? Hemingway and Woolf, on this view, should have attempted to face the Serbian Other.

To complain that 9/11 novels encompass domestic issues is a little like faulting a sonnet for taking up the matter of love. Domesticity has always been one of the primary subject matters of the novel: coming of age, marriage, family, adultery, illness, and death all play out against the backdrop of an individual's home, whether grand or mean. The question one might ask instead is whether a novel is *merely* domestic.

Admittedly, some recent 9/11 fiction never transcends the domestic. Chief among these are Jay McInerney's *The Good Life* and Claire Messud's *The Emperor's Children*, both published in 2006 and focused on the lives of well-heeled Manhattanites. McInerney turns the days after 9/11 into a backdrop for his characters' marriages and affairs. The shock of the terrorist attack serves simply to underscore something the characters already knew – that their status-seeking materialism is shallow. In the end, 9/11 merely functions as an event that urges us to try to be a bit better in our personal lives and interpersonal relations. If the firefighters who ran into the World Trade Center made the ultimate sacrifice, McInerney's novel implies, then surely comfortable Manhattanites can think of their children and not leave their spouses to join their adulterous lovers. Messud's comedy of manners hardly focuses on 9/11, since it details the characters' lives in the months leading up to the event. The terrorist attacks merely form the occasion for the novel's denouement. Witnessing the burning towers, an older famous writer is struck with concern for his wife and ends his affair with his daughter's best friend. The writer's nephew, presumed to have died in the attack, uses the moment to escape both his mother's interference and his uncle's disdain in order to create a new identity in Florida.

Ken Kalfus's *A Disorder Peculiar to the Country* (2006) equally cannot move past a contextualizing of 9/11 within the disintegration of the nuclear family. This satirical novel, however, is wonderfully premised: Joyce and Marshall are going through a messy divorce when the towers collapse. Each should have died on 9/11 but Marshall, whose office was in the south tower, manages to escape before the building falls, and Joyce, who was to have been on United flight 93, doesn't board when she gets a call telling her that her meeting in Berkeley has been canceled. On learning that the other has presumably been killed, both Joyce and Marshall can barely contain their joy. This depiction of human wish-fulfillment fantasies casts an ironic glance at the patriotic correctness that characterized the commemoration of the dead in the months following 9/11.

The early promise of Kalfus's novel, however, never is fulfilled. The detailed scene of Marshall's escape from the south tower – which includes his witnessing the gruesome deaths of two people – fails to serve as anything more than a set piece. Marshall never subsequently seems traumatized by this experience. If the novel begins with naughty personal wish-fulfillment, it ends by abruptly taking wish-fulfillment into the realm of political fantasy: American troops find weapons of mass destruction, Iraqis fully embrace their liberation and quickly form a new government that allows American troops to leave the country, and Osama bin Laden is captured, which leads to a spontaneous mass celebration at the site of the destroyed towers. While Kalfus's depiction of the extreme legal negotiations of the divorce proceedings is at times quite funny, in the end the point of the novel's satire has been obscured. Who or what is the target – the Bush administration's political naivety, American jingoism more broadly, or those who opposed the War on Terror?

Specifying trauma: Foer, DeLillo, Walter

Other novelists, however, have depicted post-9/11 domesticity against larger issues of history and culture, taking up the specificity of trauma in ways that challenge the notion that the terrorist attacks form the basis of a new collective American identity.

In Jonathan Safran Foer's *Extremely Loud and Incredibly Close* (2005), Oskar Schell, the precocious nine-year-old protagonist and narrator, bears a particularly heavy burden following the destruction of the towers. On the morning of 9/11, he listens as his father leaves several messages on the family's answering machine while trapped in the Windows on the World restaurant in the north tower of the World Trade Center. Despite his intelligence, Oskar has no idea how to cope with the loss of his father. He resents his mother's new boyfriend and bruises himself as punishment for not picking up the phone when his father called. While Foer's novel may look at the specificity of a son's loss of his father, it does so, however, with a historical consciousness that forces the reader to see 9/11 not as a unique event that creates a heretofore unimagined collectivity but as one that resonates with attacks on other cities and civilians during the twentieth century in which the United States was more perpetrator than victim.

While Oskar is the main narrator, both his grandfather and grandmother also narrate portions of the novel. We read excerpts of the grandfather's series of unmailed letters to the son he never meets, as well as portions of the grandmother's autobiography that she began writing shortly after she married. Against Oskar's story of grief, then, one sees slowly revealed the traumatized relationship of the boy's grandmother and grandfather, survivors of the firebombing of Dresden in the waning days of World War II. The grandparents' stories serve to historicize trauma. As a teenager, Thomas Schell had loved Anna Schmidt, who becomes pregnant with his child. She, however, is killed in the Dresden bombing. Both Thomas and Anna's sister independently emigrate to America. Thomas's traumatic response has been to lose the ability to speak and communicate only by writing phrases in a notebook. One day, these two meet by chance in New York and marry. Thomas does not want to bring children into the world, and when his wife becomes pregnant in 1963, he leaves. Only after 9/11 does Thomas return to his wife after learning that his son had been killed.

In one of the letters to his son from 1978, Thomas recounts the horrific firebombing of Dresden by British and US planes in 1945 that killed around 40,000 people:

> I saw humans melted into thick pools of liquid, three or four feet deep in places, I saw bodies crackling like embers, laughing, and the remains of masses of people who had tried to escape the firestorm by jumping head first into the lakes and ponds, the parts of their bodies that were submerged in the water were still intact, while the parts that protruded above water were charred beyond recognition.[4]

While this bombing occurred in the context of war, the citizens of Dresden could only experience the firestorm as terrorism. In Foer's narrative, the Schmidt family is hiding a Jewish neighbor from the Nazis, but this indiscriminate Allied bombing did not make any moral distinctions in its mass killing of civilians.

Foer also invokes the specter of the US atomic bombing of Japan. In the chapter immediately preceding his grandfather's lengthy and horrific account of the Dresden bombing, Oskar (at nearly the center of the novel) gives a report in school on the after-effects of the atomic blast in Hiroshima. Once again, the disorientation of the citizens, many of whom are looking for lost loved ones, recalls that of New Yorkers in the days following the terrorist attack. Moments such as these push the novel beyond its domestic framework and remind the reader that 9/11 is but the latest instance of mass trauma. Just as Oskar must lose his childhood innocence in the face of his father's death, Foer asks his American readers to relinquish their political innocence that might lead them to believe in the inerrancy of the US moral compass.

Like Foer, Don DeLillo resists the notion that 9/11 has constructed a new collective American identity based on trauma. DeLillo's *Falling Man* (2007) also begins with a domestic premise. After escaping from the north tower, Keith Neudecker makes his way to the apartment of his estranged wife, Lianne. Through this couple's attempted reconciliation, DeLillo stages the effects of individual trauma. Readers hope that Keith and Lianne will successfully make their marriage work, that this reunification will provide the Shakespearian happy ending that will offer a kind of symbolic healing of the wound of 9/11. This hope, however, is frustrated. Lianne may find the strength to go on alone in a return to the forms of her long-forgotten Catholic faith; Keith, in contrast, is left with a belief that the last best hope for free will lies in the turn of the card at professional poker tournaments in Las Vegas.

In *Falling Man*, DeLillo explores a subject matter that he had previously taken up in *Mao II* (1992) – the way that art might still vie with terrorism in shaping the American imagination, only this time there is an uncanny sense in which terrorist acts, such as those of 9/11, resonate with performance art. DeLillo builds this correspondence into the very structure of his novel. The three major sections of *Falling Man* are each named for a man, but the names fail to identify correctly or fully: each points to mistaken, secret, or double identity. The first, "Bill Lawton," is simply a misunderstanding, how Keith and Lianne's son and his friends mishear the name "Bin Laden." The middle section, "Ernst Hechinger," is the real name of the art dealer who now goes by Martin Ridnour, an alias that leads to speculation regarding the extent of his involvement with a left-wing movement that protested against fascist elements in the West German government during the late 1960s and early 1970s. The final section, "David Janiak," is the actual name of the performance artist known as Falling Man. In the names of the three main sections, then, we have a terrorist, a political radical turned art dealer, and an artist. DeLillo's truest subject matter is less domestic than it is an examination of the relationship between terrorism and art. If the terrorist has succeeded in politicizing aesthetics, what might the artist now learn from the terrorist?

DeLillo's depiction of the performance artist known as Falling Man attempts to address this question. Shortly after the destruction of the towers, a performance artist begins staging falls throughout Manhattan that recall the people who fell to their deaths from the towers. His unannounced falls are arrested by ropes and harnesses so that he hangs suspended in the attitude of freefall. With the trauma of 9/11 so fresh, Falling Man's art is an outrage. One might say that Falling Man is a terrorist of perception.

In the aftermath of 9/11, a number of visual artists tried to represent the particular horror evoked by those who jumped from the towers rather than burn to death. The contemporary response to these artistic meditations was quite negative, sometimes leading to the censoring or removal of certain artwork.[5] People who found this art objectionable felt that the subject matter was taboo. DeLillo's depiction of David Janiak seems to respond to this public urge to police artistic expression. Janiak's art also depends on the 9/11 jumpers as an intertext, but his art is not primarily representational; rather, it carries with it an element of witness precisely because of its effect on his unsuspecting audience: Janiak's art, in other words, allows his viewers themselves to become witnesses of the horror. Rather than simply represent what happened when people jumped from the World Trade Center, Janiak's art extends 9/11 into the present. By doing so DeLillo suggests that his imagined performance artist creates an art commensurate with the tragedy.

Lianne twice happens to see Falling Man's performances. The first time she does not actually see him fall but only notices him dangling in his safety harness. Seeing only the result, she finds it insignificant. The second time, however, Lianne witnesses all of Falling Man's unannounced performance, one that she does not initially understand to be a performance. This time, Janiak's art removes for Lianne all distance between re-enactment and the actual horrific moment when people chose to jump rather than burn to death. Watching him prepare to jump for an audience that will consist mainly of commuters on a passing train, Lianne experiences an almost unbearable foreknowledge of the horrified responses of those who will not have seen Falling Man attach his safety harness, yet her helpless compulsion will not allow her to look away. After Janiak's fall, Lianne panics and runs in terror. For her, then, witnessing Falling Man's full performance is not a representation of the horror of 9/11, it is the horror of 9/11 itself.

In the disturbing, transgressive art that DeLillo's performance artist Falling Man produces, an art that invokes (and perhaps transcends) AP photographer Richard Drew's iconic image of a 9/11 death known as "Falling Man," the possibility for a degree of healing arises. In imagining Janiak's art, DeLillo is metafictionally commenting on the limitations of, and his desire for, his own narrative art. Janiak's art, like DeLillo's, does not produce a final healing of the wound of 9/11 but probes at hidden recesses of our memories. For Lianne, Falling Man's art ultimately provides a small bit of solace. After experiencing the terror of Janiak's performance, Lianne finds she is able to forgive her father for his decision to commit suicide when he learned that he had Alzheimer's.

What Falling Man's performance and Lianne's reception underscore is the gap between the artistically mediated response to trauma and the individual reception of such a work of art. Even if the work of art (Falling Man's performance) bypasses representation and functions as a form of witness, the individual (such as Lianne) who encounters the work of art is still an individual, not a collectivity. As such, the individual is not solely constituted by some collective trauma but is already the bearer of previous private traumas. Because our multiple traumas interact (overlap, reinforce, or diverge), any particular artist's response to 9/11 or viewer's reaction to such art is radically unpredictable. This is why, even if there is such a thing as collective trauma, there will never be any work of art that can collectively heal this trauma.

Given its satire and paranoid plot and characters, Jess Walter's *The Zero* (2006) seems like the novel that DeLillo or Thomas Pynchon might have written twenty years ago. The title refers to Ground Zero, the site where the World Trade Center towers collapsed. The novel opens with New York City police officer Brian Remy, who shoots himself in the head (an act that may be an accident or an attempted suicide) a few days after 9/11. His visceral response to the disorientation of shooting himself parallels that of his being present when the towers collapsed. This opening underscores Walter's exploration of trauma: the specificity of Brian's head wound is a baseline against which to measure the extent to which all of America has been traumatized.

The narration comes from a limited third-person perspective in which Brian provides the angle of vision, but it is an impaired perspective because, as a result of his head wound, Brian is quite literally of two minds. The reader directly follows only those events of which Brian is conscious. Brian's wound is apparently not serious and he is soon recruited to join an intelligence agency that seeks to uncover new terrorist threats. This agency is neither the FBI nor the CIA, but Brian finds himself in competition with agents of these other two agencies. Brian's bigger problem, however, is that he suffers from trauma-induced gaps in memory and consciousness.

It is never clear if Brian's memory loss stems from psychological (9/11) or physical (head wound) trauma. He finds himself in situations (meetings, lover's trysts, hostage interrogations) where he has no idea how he got there or what exactly he has done. Since he has no access to what he does during these periods of unknowing, neither does the reader. But there are intimations that his actions are unethical, violent, and potentially criminal – or at least they would be if this weren't happening under an American administration that sanctioned torture in the name of homeland security.

Against this larger plot, there is a backdrop of domesticity. Brian's ex-wife lives with their teenage son, Edgar, and her new husband. Early in the novel, Brian is called into a family discussion because Edgar has been telling everyone at school that his father died in the collapse of the towers. In a hilarious scene that recalls the debates between Jack Gladney and his teenage son Heinrich in DeLillo's *White Noise* (1985), Edgar argues for the validity of grieving for his dead father, even while conversing with Brian, his obviously still-living father:

> I suppose you'd rather I behave like everyone else and grieve *generally*. Well, I'm sorry. I'm not built that way. General grief is a lie. What are people in Wyoming really grieving? A loss of safety? Some shattered illusion that a

lifetime of purchases and television programs had meaning? The emptiness of their Palm Pilots and SUVs and baggy jeans? ... Generalized grief is a fleeting emotion, like lust. It's a trend, just some weak shared moment in the culture, like the final episode of some TV show everybody watches.[6]

Even though Walter here expresses the matter from a ludic postmodern position, he confirms DeLillo's and Foer's suspicion about an overly facile application of a notion of collective trauma. Although people throughout the country had a sense of immediacy of the collapse of the towers, the trauma of someone who experienced the moment through the mediation of television has not had the same experience as someone who survived the destruction or someone who lost a loved one in the attack. If the experience is not identical, such fiction seems to ask (and to answer in the negative), can the event produce a trauma that is constitutive of a new collective American identity?

The climactic moment of Walter's plot works within the logic of postmodern paranoia. The supposed sleeper cell that Brian has been tracing (even though he is largely unaware that he is doing so) turns out to be composed entirely of informants who work for competing US intelligence agencies. When these agencies converge to make the big bust, things turn violent. But the man whom Brian has been handling is spooked before he arrives at this meeting (where all the other "terrorists" are killed) and escapes with a bomb, which he then detonates. Essentially, the US government – in its zeal to ensure America's safety – becomes complicit in a new terror attack.

Displacing trauma: Auster and Roth

If the writers in the previous section emphasize the individual wounds of 9/11, other authors address the political fallout of the attacks, which may in the long run be recognized as the real trauma to American national identity. A politics of fear, a manufactured war in Iraq, the suspension of habeas corpus, extraordinary rendition, justifications for torture by State Department attorneys, and the widening polarization between Red and Blue states characterize the United States during the Bush years. These tensions in the body politic are thematized through the narrative strategy of postmodern metafiction in both Paul Auster's *Man in the Dark* and Philip Roth's *The Plot Against America*. In a political climate in which to voice dissent with American foreign policy was to be identified with supporting terrorism, both Auster and Roth imagine alternative American histories as a way to critique the Bush administration's strategy of pre-emptive war and regime change in Iraq and the general movement to the political right in the United States following 9/11.

Auster's novel imagines an aging writer named August Brill who suffers from insomnia. To pass one sleepless night, Brill creates an America in which Owen Brick wakes up to find himself trapped in a hole. The hole is a kind of portal between the world of post-9/11 America and a world in which 9/11 did not happen. America is still at war, but not with Iraq; rather, America is involved in a second civil war. As a result of George Bush's disputed election in 2000, the political process breaks down and New York secedes from the union. After Federal troops attack the state and bomb New York City, the Blue states that had supported Al Gore, one by one, join New York to form the Independent States of America.

When he is pulled from the hole, Brill discovers that he is a conscript taken from his world to serve in the armed forces of the Independent States. Owen wonders if "he has suffered some debilitating trauma that has blacked out large portions of his brain" and feels "trapped inside some supernaturally lucid dream, a dream so lifelike and intense that the boundary between dreaming and consciousness has all but melted away."[7] Auster allegorizes America as a house divided against itself, and Brick's disorientation speaks to the anxiety and disbelief that half of the American electorate felt during Bush's presidency. Brick's assignment is to assassinate the man responsible for the civil war, an aging writer named August Brill, whose very story is what instigates the conflict in this parallel world. In fact, the only way Brick can return to his world is by killing Brill. Brick, however, is a failure as an assassin, and Brill violently kills Brick off two-thirds of the way through the novel.

The violence of Brill's story, however, cannot match that of the Iraq War in his own world. The novel returns to the grounds of domesticity in the final third. Brill's granddaughter, who cannot sleep either, joins him in his dark room. She is grieving for Titus, a boyfriend whom she had broken up with shortly before his death. When she drifts off to sleep, Brill remembers Titus, who went to Iraq to work for a company that provided the kind of services that Halliburton (of which Dick Cheney was the CEO before becoming Bush's vice president) did for US troops. Titus is kidnapped and executed; his beheading, posted on the Internet, is far more graphic in its details than the death Brill imagines for Brick.

In September 2004, a month before the publication of *The Plot Against America*, Philip Roth's novel of alternative history, the author wrote an essay for the *New York Times* about his forthcoming novel in which he warns:

> Some readers are going to want to take this book as a roman à clef to the present moment in America. That would be a mistake. I set out to reconstruct the years 1940–42 as they might have been if Lindbergh, instead of Roosevelt, had been elected president in the 1940 election. I am not pretending to be interested in those two years – I am interested in those two years.[8]

Roth is correct in saying that *The Plot Against America* is not a *roman-à-clef*. Incidents and characters do not line up simplistically; however, his novel resonates as much with the time he wrote the novel as the historical period he depicts. The title itself is the first marker of this resonance. The plot against America in the world of the novel results from the surprising victory of a populist, America First Republican following eight years of Franklin Delano Roosevelt's Democratic administration. Lindbergh's upset of FDR produces a new administration that makes its peace with Adolf Hitler and, as a result, sees the United States drift toward anti-Semitism. But in its contemporary moment, the plot against America simultaneously suggests the terrorist attacks of 9/11 and the plot of the Bush administration to use falsified intelligence to lead the country into a costly and unnecessary war. In the novel, to question the decision to stay out of war was to be labeled by the government as un-American, while in the contemporary moment of the novel's publication, to question the rationale for the Iraq War was to be similarly branded.

Roth unfolds this frightening political shift in the early 1940s through the domestic situation of a largely assimilated Jewish American family, the Roths, as narrated by a family member named "Philip," who is looking back from the present to this troubled time in the America of his boyhood. The author Roth is clearly interested in the past, and his Postscript to his novel lays out short, accurate biographies of the major and minor historical figures that appear or are referred to in the novel. But the question remains whether Roth is only interested in the past.

The final, much briefer section of the Postscript is titled "Some Documentation," and Roth there reproduces a speech – "Who Are the War Agitators?" – that Lindbergh gave in Des Moines, Iowa, on September 11, 1941. In the speech Lindbergh identifies American Jews as the main internal force that wants to draw the country into war with Hitler. Roth, however, subverts the Postscript's documentary impulse in the novel proper, since in chapter 1, he has Lindbergh give this speech two years earlier, a fictional move that helps establish the aviator as a plausible Republican candidate in the 1940 presidential election. Through this play between fiction and history, Roth effectively makes Lindbergh's presidency a post-9/11 event (whether the year is 2001 or 1941).

Even his *New York Times* essay, in which Roth appears to limit in advance the possible ways his novel might be read (effectively telling us "Don't think of the Bush administration when you read my book"), the penultimate paragraph turns precisely to the present:

> And now Aristophanes, who surely must be God, has given us George W.
> Bush, a man unfit to run a hardware store let alone a nation like this one, and

who has merely reaffirmed for me the maxim that informed the writing of all these books and that makes our lives as Americans as precarious as anyone else's: all the assurances are provisional, even here in a 200-year-old democracy. We are ambushed ... by the unpredictability of history.[9]

Roth then turns to a quotation from his new novel as a way to illuminate his sense of American ills in the Bush administration, essentially doing himself what he has told his readers they may not do, namely, use *The Plot Against America* to read contemporary America. Roth's move here makes his essay a ludic (even metafictional) context in which to read his metafictional historical novel. In *The Plot Against America*, Lindbergh wins the hearts and minds of people for his stance on the war by donning his pilot's outfit, flying across the country, and giving a speech about peace and American freedom. Even if unintended, this moment in Roth's novel seems an uncanny double to George Bush's infamously theatrical landing on an aircraft carrier on May 1, 2003 in which he emerges in full fighter-pilot regalia from the co-pilot's seat of a Navy jet and announces the end of hostilities in Iraq under a banner reading MISSION ACCOMPLISHED. Like Lindbergh's fictional speech, Bush's also emphasizes peace and American liberty. Whatever Roth's intentions for his novel were, it speaks as much to the moment of its production as it does to the American past.

The dismissal of American 9/11 fiction for being only about domestic issues, as I have argued, misses the ways in which the political often arises out of the domestic. There are, however, equally problematic claims in criticism that finds merit in this fiction. Totalizing claims about this body of work often achieve rhetorical coherence only by excluding particular novels. David Wyatt, for example, tells us that 9/11 fiction by American writers is marked by "a turn toward 'seriousness,' a turn away from modern irony and the lightness of the postmodern turn."[10] Wyatt's assertion may seem correct if one focuses on DeLillo's and Foer's novels but misses the mark when one considers Kalfus's and Walter's satiric fiction. Alternatively, Kristiaan Versluys's humanistic articulation creates a narrow canon of "those few novels" that "affirm the humanity of the befuddled individual groping for an explanation" and "suggest the impact of shock – the immediate shock that causes panic or the slower realization that things have been altered beyond repair."[11] Because Versluys is primarily interested in narratives that directly represent the immediate trauma of the terrorist attack and the possibility of novelistic discourse as a first step toward healing, Auster's and Roth's books do not count as 9/11 novels. Although Wyatt and Versluys offer nuanced readings of particular texts, their efforts (as well as my own) suggest that we are still learning how to tell the story of the American fictional response to 9/11.

FURTHER READING

DeLillo, Don. "In the Ruins of the Future." *Harper's*, December 2001: 33–40

Duvall, John N. and Robert P. Marzec (eds.). "Fiction After 9/11." Special issue of *MFS: Modern Fiction Studies* 57.3 (2011)

Gray, Richard. *After the Fall: American Literature Since 9/11*. Oxford: Wiley-Blackwell, 2011

Keniston, Ann and Jeanne Follansbee Quinn (eds.). *Literature after 9/11*. New York: Routledge, 2008

Martin, Randall. *9/11 and the Literature of Terror*. Edinburgh University Press, 2011

Melnick, Jeffrey. *9/11 Culture: America under Construction*. Oxford: Wiley-Blackwell, 2009

Simpson, David. *9/11: The Culture of Commemoration*. University of Chicago Press, 2006

NOTES

1 Pankaj Mishra, "The End of Innocence," *Guardian*, May 19, 2007: www.guardian.co.uk/books/2007/may/19/fiction.martinamis.

2 Richard Gray, "Open Doors, Closed Minds: American Prose Writing at a Time of Crisis," *American Literary History*, 21.1 (2009): 130.

3 Ibid., p. 135.

4 Jonathan Safran Foer, *Extremely Loud and Incredibly Close* (Boston: Houghton Mifflin, 2005), pp. 211–12. The red circles that mark punctuation errors have not been reproduced here.

5 See Anne K. Swartz, "American Art after September 11: A Consideration of the Twin Towers," *symplokē*, 14.1–2 (2006): 81–97.

6 Jess Walter, *The Zero* (New York: Harper Perennial, 2006), p. 34.

7 Paul Auster, *Man in the Dark* (New York: Picador, 2008), p. 4.

8 Philip Roth, "The Story Behind 'The Plot Against America'," *New York Times*, September 19, 2004: http://query.nytimes.com/gst/fullpage.html?res=9500E7DB1338F93AA2575AC0A9629C8B63&sec=&spon=&pagewanted=3, 15 January 2010.

9 Ibid.

10 David Wyatt, "September 11 and Postmodern Memory," *Arizona Quarterly*, 65.4 (2009): 140.

11 Kristiaan Versluys, *Out of the Blue: September 11 and the Novel* (New York: Columbia University Press, 2009), p. 13.

PART III

Major authors

14

NICOLE A. WALIGORA-DAVIS

Ralph Ellison

"Consciousness and conscience," admonished Ralph Ellison, "are the burdens imposed upon us by the American experiment."[1] Penned just months before Lyndon Johnson signed the 1964 Civil Rights Act, Ellison's characterization of a peculiarly American civic obligation undoubtedly reflected his own experience with a Jim Crow that steadily crept to the frontier he called home – Oklahoma. His words were certainly a response to a global struggle for decolonization and to the political unrest and hope inspired by the nation's ongoing revolution in race relations. By May 1964, Ellison, like all Americans, had experienced (if only through newspaper accounts and televised reports) events that are now recognized as crucial to the Civil Rights Movement: the bravery of the "Little Rock Nine," who helped usher in the judicially mandated desegregation of public schools; the brutal lynching in Mississippi of fourteen-year-old Emmett Till, who had supposedly flirted with a white woman; the year-long bus boycotts spurred by the defiance of Rosa Parks; the march led by Martin Luther King, Jr. on the nation's capital; and the Sunday morning church bombing that killed four girls in Birmingham, Alabama. Ellison's call to "consciousness and conscience" reveals his commitment to the nation's experiment in democracy and offers a slogan capturing the moral aesthetics suffusing his work. He was convinced that writing was "an ethical instrument," and that American writing, in particular, "might well exercise some choice in the ethic it prefers to support."[2] For this recipient of the Medal of Freedom (1969), America's highest civilian honor, the ethical choice included demanding respect for African Americans' humanity and cultural contributions, as well as supporting the project of freedom wherever it took hold.

Ellison authored the award-winning *Invisible Man* (1952) and posthumously published *Juneteenth* (1999), two volumes of collected essays titled *Shadow and Act* (1964) and *Going to the Territory* (1986), short stories compiled in *Flying Home and Other Stories* (1996), and numerous contributions to anthologies, periodicals, and newspapers. He received a fellowship from the National American Academy of Arts and Letters (1955–1957), the Chevalier de l'Ordre des Arts et des Lettres (1970), and the National Medal of Arts for *Invisible Man* (1985); was elected vice-president of the prestigious American PEN (1964); served as vice-president of the National Institute of Arts and Letters (1967); and was a member of the National Arts Council and Carnegie Commission on Educational Television. Despite Ellison's insistence that he was "not primarily concerned with injustice, but with art," whether one reads him on jazz, representational politics, segregation, American literary history, folklore, or tradition, his prose implicitly (if not explicitly) engages the concept of freedom.[3] Rejecting the well-worn mythologies of American literature, including demands by figures like Irving Howe that all black writing model Richard Wright's protest fiction, Ellison shifted the debate over black literature. He insisted: "The real questions seem to be: How does the Negro writer participate *as a writer* in the struggle for human freedom? … What values emerging from Negro experience does he try to affirm?"[4] Waged in letters, Ellison's five-decade-long civil rights campaign underscored two crucial tenets: (1) a fundamental connection between equality and the legal and social recognition of the individual as a human being, and (2) culture as a critical terrain where any campaign for racial parity and democracy must be waged. Ellison recognized how culture influences socioeconomic and political relations. He was convinced that tradition, ritual, and myth formed the substance of human life through which individuals were governed and, importantly, through which they might also find the sustenance to survive. His work acknowledged the discontinuity between the modern black experience and nation-state conceptualizations of History as a progressive movement toward equality.

Ellison remained haunted by a summer train ride into Decatur, Alabama, in June 1933. Eager to accept his Tuskegee music fellowship, but without sufficient funds to pay his fare from his native Oklahoma to the Institute, Ellison hoboed. A relatively uneventful ride abruptly changed in Decatur: armed with nickel-plated .45 revolvers, railroad detectives forcibly removed Ellison along with forty-plus black and white illegal riders from the L&N line. Sixty miles from Scottsboro, Alabama, the scene of the 1931 arrest of nine African American males for the alleged rape of two white women, Ellison entered Decatur, a town "undergoing a siege of lynch-fever" amid the Scottsboro defendants' retrial.[5] Although he remained elusive and glossed the events that transpired as an incident from which he "escaped unharmed," biographer Lawrence Jackson suggests that Ellison's student photograph, taken shortly after arriving at Tuskegee, contradicts this account.[6] His youthful gleam is marred by the visible "open gash alongside his right eye" and the bandage partially covering his forehead.[7] Decades later Ellison recounted this moment when he became the "sacrificial scapegoat," the role that he feared his skin color automatically assigned him, writing "that scrape with the law – the fear, the horror and sense of helplessness before legal injustice – was most vivid in my mind, and it has so remained."[8] His first short story, "Hymie's Bull" (1937), figuratively returns to the scene of the crime. The repeated reference to "drifting" captures the hopelessness and vulnerability of black Americans whose only certainty amid a national depression is that they will remain unemployed: "We were just drifting ... having long ago given up hopes of finding jobs. [Just drifting, ten black boys on an L&N freight.]."[9] The vulnerability announced by their age ("ten *boys*"), by their homelessness ("just knocking around the country"), and by their tenuous circumstances increases when these young vagabonds confront the brute force employed by "bulls" – railroad detectives. Readers quickly sense the dehumanizing effects produced during these excessively violent encounters between black riders and railway "bulls": furnished with gun and "loaded stick," railway authorities pummel the skulls of defenseless black youths with a ferocity resembling "a man cracking black walnuts with a hammer."[10] The bulls' torture expertise extends to every anatomically weak spot. "They know all the places to hit to change a bone into jelly," cautions Ellison's narrator.[11] Capturing a brutal racial antipathy held by some police, institutional authorities, and white supremacists, more generally, toward black bodies, "Hymie's Bull" represents Ellison's earliest attempt at what would become a life-long effort to distill the conditions of black life in a "segregated democracy."[12]

Humor offered a salve for the wounds of segregation. He records, "we were compelled to buffer the pain and negate the humiliation by making grotesque comedy out of the extremes to which whites would go to keep us in what they considered to be our 'place.'"[13] For Ellison, "the blackness of *Afro-American* 'black humor' is not black, it is tragically human and finds its source and object in the notion of 'whiteness.'"[14] Black folklore "taught the preservation of one's humanity by masking one's motives and emotions, just as it prepared one to be unsurprised by anything that whites might do, because a concern with race could negate all human bonds, including those of shared blood and experience."[15]

Ellison was born in 1914, in the frontier state that inspired Bessie Smith to sing of the promise and possibilities that "Goin' to the Nation, Goin' to the Terr'tor'" held for African Americans in the wake of a post-Reconstruction South. Between the 1890s and the turn of the twentieth century, the black population in Oklahoma Territory climbed from 3,000 to 19,000.[16] Reminding readers of the neocolonial conditions effectively renewing slavery in the South, E. P. McCabe, founder of the *Langston City Herald* and proponent of an all-black Oklahoma, encouraged blacks to emigrate: "What will you be if you stay in the South? Slaves liable to be killed at any time, and never treated right: but if you come to Oklahoma you have equal chances with the white man, free and independent."[17] It is likely that the reflections Mama shares with her young son, James, in Ellison's quasi-autobiographical story, "Boy on a Train," resemble the sentiment Ellison's own parents held as they fled the South for the western territory: "We traveled far, looking for a better world, where things wouldn't be so hard like they were down South," recites the grief-stricken widow, Mama.[18] The early essays collected in *Shadow and Act* reflect the passion of a man born within a space relatively unique with respect to the segregated South or "the deceptively 'free' Harlem": in Oklahoma it was still possible for blacks to dream, at least until they hit "reality."[19] These essays outline Ellison's blueprint for black writing. They identify what he perceived as the primary obligations and the key failings of contemporary fiction and its authors. In short, with the exception of William Faulkner, twentieth-century writers lacked the moral purpose and political and social responsibility that anchored the work of Herman Melville, Mark Twain, and Ralph Waldo Emerson. Woefully divorced from the sociopolitical, economic, and racial crises marking their inscription, novels by white twentieth-century writers capitulated to the status quo and singularly advanced the writer's "personal freedom" over that of the reader or society.[20] "It is not accidental that the disappearance of the human Negro from our fiction," Ellison accused, "coincides with the disappearance of deep-probing doubt and a sense of evil."[21] He railed at the cowardice of American writers who opted for Spain and its ongoing battle with fascism over the lynched black American body in a discussion on ritualized violence, who willfully ignored and shielded themselves from the very real drama of racial tyranny devastating their native soil. Essays like "Twentieth-Century Fiction and the Black Mask of Humanity" offer more than an indictment of the limits and outright failures of twentieth-century American literature. Defining an alternative and deeply humanist aesthetic, these pieces place in relief the instrumental role culture plays in civil society. "Richard Wright's Blues" (1945) offers his most succinct and culturally nuanced definition of the blues: "The blues is an impulse to keep the painful details and episodes of a brutal experience alive in one's aching consciousness, to finger its jagged grain, and to transcend it, not by the consolation of philosophy but by squeezing from it a near tragic, near-comic lyricism."[22] Writing provided Ellison what the blues gave to the musician: an arsenal for railing against a racialized system that adversely shaped his material world and that aggressively sought to influence his psychological outlook toward himself and his community.

Five years after the Senate failed to pass the 1935 Costigan–Wagner anti-lynching act into federal law, Ellison published "The Birthmark" (1940) in *New Masses*, a story partially based on the unsuccessful attempt to lynch Kentuckian James McMillian.[23] In little more than a page, Ellison reorients the landscape of lynching narratives. He shifts attention away from the events precipitating the ritualized mob killing that is commonly featured in this genre. Instead readers are confronted by a family's agonized attempt to identify the disfigured remains of their loved one and an elaborate ruse orchestrated by a patrolman and a coroner to conceal this murder. By Ellison's measure, the crimes committed during a lynching exceed the murder and include the collusion of state officials in covering up the crime (effectively guaranteeing immunity to the assailants) and the intimidation of surviving family members. Here the victim's brother and sister risk certain death if they refuse to still their tongues and blind their eyes to the lynching of their sibling, Willie:

> "He's telling you right, boy," the coroner said, "he was hit by a car. Feller saw him laying longside the road and called us."
> "And you better remember that nigger," the patrolman said. "And your sister better remember that, too. 'Cause a car might hit *you*. Understand what I mean?"[24]

Ellison's sustained critique of extralegal violence, racial discrimination, and judicial malfeasance in his early stories ("Slick Gonna Learn" [1939], "A Party Down at the Square" [n.d.], "The Black Ball" [n.d.]) and essays ("Judge Lynch in New York [1939], "A Congress Jim Crow Didn't Attend" [1940]) was shaped by his investment in black leftist politics. Harlem figured integrally in the "new social consciousness" marked by mass demonstrations, increased unionization, and "a sharp leftward turn in American politics" that arose during the Depression.[25] Arriving in Harlem on July 4, 1936, Ellison entered one of America's largest black urban spaces, and an intellectual scene where, according to a former Communist Party member, "75% of black cultural figures had Party membership or maintained regular meaningful contact with the Party."[26] On July 8 Ellison met Alain Locke, author of "The New Negro" (1922), a constitutive text of the Harlem Renaissance, and Langston Hughes. A champion of the Scottsboro boys, President of the League of Struggle for Negro Rights, and contributing editor for George Padmore's *The Negro Worker*, Hughes deepened Ellison's political sensibilities: he introduced the young writer to Marxism, shared his copies of socialist Cecil Day Lewis's *A Hope for Poetry* (1934), John Strachey's *Literature and Dialectical Materialism* (1934), and André Malraux's *Man's Fate* (1934), and encouraged Ellison to study other Left publications including *Partisan Review*.[27] Hughes gave Ellison entry into Harlem's black Left, introducing him to artists and intellectuals, including sculptor Richard Barthé, Communist Party member Louise Thompson, and the *Daily Worker*'s Harlem division head, Richard Wright.[28]

"Ellison's encounter with Wright's committed Marxism radicalized him," insists Jackson.[29] He read this rising star's essays and manuscript-in-progress, *Native Son*, as pages poured from Wright's typewriter. Wright's troubled relationship with the Communist Party lent Ellison a bird's-eye view of the internecine battles waged among members and Party officials.[30] Ellison's Federal Writer's Project pieces on slave rebellion and black history (1938–1942) reflect a larger trend in publications on black history and insurrectionism during the late 1930s by figures like Hughes, W. E. B. Du Bois, and C. L. R. James. His essays mirror the National Negro Congress's cultural nationalist push to preserve black culture and to engage culture itself as the terrain for democratic possibility. Five years after Wright printed Ellison's first publication, a review of Waters Turpin's *These Low Grounds* (1937) in *New Challenge* and encouraged him to turn his talents toward fiction, the Oklahoman was managing editor for Angelo Herndon's *Negro Quarterly*. Featuring the writing of poets, literary critics, historians, heads of state, philosophers, and political activists, the *Quarterly* concretely worked to promote black culture and history, democracy, and sensitivity to global politics.

Ellison's "In a Strange Country" (1944) and "Flying Home" (1944) address the psychological costs of military service for African Americans. In Ellison's words, theirs is "an archetypal American dilemma."[31] Simply, "How could you treat a Negro as equal in war and then deny him equality during times of peace?"[32] These stories affirm the military desegregation A. Philip Randolph and Bayard Rustin demanded as they threatened to march on Washington in 1941. Engaging the unsettling psychological question of diminished self-perception and self-worth that remained the under-acknowledged casualty of racial discrimination, Ellison deepened the debate on black disaffection and dispossession within the military and society. These stories, like the others gathered in *Flying Home*, reflect Ellison's commitment to democracy, to elevating individual and social consciousness, and to acknowledging black Americans' integral role in American history and culture.

Ellison's opening line to his 1952 masterpiece is unforgettable: "I am an invisible man."[33] Marrying the traditions of the African American migration narrative, the African American folktale, and the black autobiography, *Invisible Man* engages black radical politics and philosophy, psychoanalysis, existentialism, and history to address black Americans' relationship to

American culture and society. *Invisible Man* is among the most important, rigorous, and exhaustive accounts of the modern black experience. A manuscript that took five years to write, *Invisible Man* earned Ellison the National Book Award in 1953, when he was aged thirty-eight. Among the estimated 10,000 books published between 1945 and 1965, a poll of 200 writers, critics, and editors in 1965 heralded *Invisible Man* the most distinguished novel.[34] Arranged according to what Ellison characterizes as Kenneth Burke's tripartite structured principle of moving from "purpose to passion to perception,"[35] *Invisible Man* is a memoir chronicling an eponymous protagonist's journey toward self-awareness.

A retrospective where the story's beginning prefigures its end, *Invisible Man* is a cautionary tale outlining the psychosocial costs to individuals and the material consequences for society that arise from a world shaped by racism. Ellison's worldly-wise protagonist unapologetically traces his transformation from racial naivety (which made him hold faith in white philanthropy as a sufficient antidote to Jim Crow and which caused him to believe that blind obedience to the demands of others guaranteed success)[36] to a more sophisticated New York social activism. The Invisible Man, however, quickly becomes frustrated with, and is later spurned by, the Brotherhood, a hierarchical social organization resembling the Communist Party that refuses input and disregards the needs of the communities it professes to serve. Having progressed from student to "would-be-politician and rabble rouser and orator to writer," the Invisible Man's memoir becomes, for Ellison, a "social act," a means of explaining "reality as it really exists rather than in terms of what he had assumed it to be."[37]

Written in the aftermath of World War II, *Invisible Man* advances key debates emerging as this global conflict drew to an end: (1) the appropriate strategy for achieving black civil rights, and (2) the nature of freedom in an industrial world where the profitability of colonialism and segregation continued to outweigh and outvalue a global commitment to human and civil rights. While it is admittedly not a war novel, *Invisible Man* nonetheless stages another kind of war: a war over ideas and visions of reality. That is, over the biopolitical power of racial stereotypes. For Ellison, the pain caused by his restricted mobility under Jim Crow paled in comparison to the routine assault from the racial stereotypes sustaining segregation:

> I found it far less painful to have to move to the back of a Southern bus, or climb to the peanut gallery of a movie house … than to tolerate the concepts which distorted the reality of my situation or my reactions to it. I could escape the reduction imposed by unjust laws and customs, but not that imposed by ideas which defined me as no more than the sum of those laws and customs.[38]

Assuring readers that he is neither phantasm nor "one of your Hollywood-movie ectoplasms" but rather "a man of substance, of flesh and bone, fiber and liquids – and ... might even be said to possess a mind," the Invisible Man, Ellison's symbol for black America, is instead the victim of willed ignorance: "I am invisible, understand, simply because people refuse to see me."[39] This novel is preoccupied with Maurice Wallace's "spectragraphia":[40] a visual hegemony circumscribing blackness to a hypervisibility that renders all that blackness signifies – peoples, cultural practices, and ways of knowing and being – invisible. Underlying the Invisible Man's opening rant is a fundamental question regarding the status of blacks in the United States, particularly the status of blacks' humanity. The obsessive references to vision, perception, recognition, and apprehension throughout the novel are nodal points within a larger discourse on the politics of recognition, history, and American citizenship that sit at the heart of this seminal study on the modern black experience.

Ellison addresses the costs of racialized sociopolitical recognition for a world avowedly committed to peace, marred by global poverty, and stubbornly wed to colonialism amid civil unrest. Within the brutal social calculus of racism, invisibility equals facelessness – a depersonification affecting every aspect of the social, legal, and political order. Invisibility, Ellison notes, challenges black Americans' right to citizenship and questions their humanity:

> as far as many whites were concerned, not only were blacks faceless, but that facelessness made the idea of mistaken identity meaningless, and the democratic assumption that Negro citizens would share the individual's recognized responsibility for the welfare of society was regarded as subversive.
>
> In this denial of personality (sponsored by both law and custom) anti-Negro stereotypes served as an efficient and easily manipulated instrument of governance.[41]

The Invisible Man's forced migration from the South to the North mirrors black emigrants' route during the Great Migration (1910–1930), while symbolizing a concurrent psychological reversal: in *Invisible Man*, Ellison diagnoses the damaging psychology of stereotypes and seeks to reverse the psychologically damaging effects of racial caricature on the communities they claim to represent. Published the same year, Ellison's novel moves in lock-step with Frantz Fanon's seminal psychoanalytic study of racialized colonial neuroses in the French Antilles, *Black Skin, White Masks* (1952). With diagnostic precision, Ellison partially lists symptoms suffered by the black American psyche from the visual hegemony of race: (1) "you often doubt if you really exist" and (2) "you ache with the need to convince yourself that you do exist in the real world."[42] Read in this sense, the Invisible Man's involuntary lobotomy shortly after arriving in the North takes on new meaning.

Shortly after he is hired at Liberty Paints, the Invisible Man is injured in an explosion caused by his older African American supervisor who feels threatened by the new hire. At the factory infirmary the Invisible Man is shuttled from chair, to cot, and finally to a glass and nickel box. His confinement signifies the mental prison erected when an individual blindly assumes, rather than knowingly constructs, an identity or social role for him/herself. Ellison describes his titular character as both confined and confused: "I discovered now that my head was encircled by a piece of cold metal like the iron cap worn by the occupant of an electric chair."[43] Dazed and amnesiac following this painful procedure, Ellison's unwitting patient quickly suspects that his hospital release remains contingent on his being able to recall his identity: his name, his mother, his birthplace, and his folk heroes. The series of questions posed by the psychiatrist to Ellison's lobotomized protagonist suggests that identity surpasses simple name recognition and is instead a marker for history. Here, the connection between freedom and identity central to this tale are explicit. The progressive staging of the psychiatrist's questions dramatize the link between self-awareness and history: the physician's prompts shift from identificatory queries to racialized cultural markers: "What is your name?"; "WHO … ARE … YOU?"; "WHAT IS YOUR MOTHER'S NAME?"; "Where were you born? Try to think of your name"; "WHO WAS YOUR MOTHER?"; "WHO WAS BUCKEYE THE RABBIT?"[44] If the task of remembering his identity demands an understanding of the self predicated on a sense of personal and, as the litany of questions posed by the psychiatrist suggests, cultural history, then freedom hinges on an understanding and (self-) consciousness about history – personal and otherwise.

"[I]t is worth remembering," Ellison cautioned, "that the past … is never past."[45] Slavery, its history and legacies, permeates this novel. Ellison's references to slavery and its cultural byproducts – slave auctions, incest, manumission papers, black folklore, and minstrelsy – critique the disconnect between modern nation-state conceptualizations of History as a movement toward equality and the modern black experience. As writing on behalf of and from the "lower frequencies," the Invisible Man's memoir documents "the void of faceless faces, of soundless voices, lying outside history."[46] Offering an underground history – the subterfuge of black life/life on the margins – Ellison challenges History: a filtered record sustaining the institutionally powerful: "it is only the known, the seen, the heard and only those events that the recorder regards as important that are put down [in history], those lies his keepers keep their power by."[47]

Similarly, Ellison's unfinished novel, *Juneteenth*, interrogates the meaning of Emancipation for a country continuing to wrestle over black civil rights. Affixed by Ellison's literary executor, John Callahan, the title locates the story within the space of slavery, emancipation, and belated news. Here Ellison describes the annual memorialization of this day as "The celebration of a gaudy illusion."[48] Ellison began writing *Juneteenth* in 1954, the year the US Supreme Court ruled against the constitutionality of the "separate but equal" provision in *Brown* v. *Board of Education of Topeka*, sounding the death knell to legislatively sanctioned segregation. Influenced by the Civil Rights Movement, *Juneteenth* locates racial intolerance, forgiveness, care and protection, and interdependency among humans within the larger sphere of the human condition. *Juneteenth* charts the shared histories of an orphaned, biracial child-preacher-turned-politician who fled the black community that cared for him, and the itinerant black preacher, Rev. Hickman, charged with the painful task of raising this child. In a novel grappling with the costs of love across the color line, which includes the pain of black nursemaids raising white children who later spurn them because of their blackness, Ellison reimagines the terms of human decency in his portrait of Hickman. For Hickman this child's presence triggered a series of losses: Hickman's mother dies prematurely after his brother, Robert, is lynched following a false rape allegation by the infant's mother, an allegation used to protect her lover and conceal the sexual indiscretion that left her pregnant. Only hours removed from the double funeral, Hickman is confronted by this pregnant mother in labor demanding that he help deliver her baby. In this moment of misery and anger, Ellison offers a lesson in forgiveness, kindness, and love: Hickman delivers and is later left to care for this child who is abandoned by a mother quickly transformed into a social pariah because she dared to love a black man. Hickman's question to his now grown "adopted" son who has been passing for white – "What goes on in that darkness I create when I refuse to see?"[49] – dilates a conversation on the injuries levied from disavowing relationships because of race, of permitting race to mean more than the value of a human life: "Who reaches out to whom within that gulley, under that lid of life denied?"[50]

Ellison's writing demanded a deeper consciousness about and conscientiousness toward the world we live in and our social interactions with others. For him, literature was a vehicle for engaging in a "comparative study of humanity," and necessarily enabled us to imagine better, even ideal worlds. Ellison challenged himself and us to imagine the post-equality world, to conceive of how blacks and America will need to equip themselves to succeed when equality is no longer at stake. "What part of Negro life," he asked, "has been foisted on us by Jim Crow and must be got rid of; What part of Negro life, expression, culture do we want to keep?"[51]

FURTHER READING

Bradley, Adam. *Ralph Ellison in Progress: From Invisible Man to Three Days Before the Shooting ...* New Haven: Yale University Press, 2010

Ellison, Ralph. *Three Days Before the Shooting ... The Unfinished Second Novel.* John F. Callahan and Adam Bradley (eds.). New York: Modern Library, 2010

Morel, Lucas E. (ed.). *Ralph Ellison and the Raft of Hope: A Political Companion to Invisible Man.* Lexington: University of Kentucky Press, 2006

Rampersad, Arnold. *Ralph Ellison: A Biography.* New York: Vintage Books, 2007

Rankine, Patrice D. *Ulysses in Black: Ralph Ellison, Classicism, and African American Literature.* Madison: University of Wisconsin Press, 2006

Watts, Jerry Gafio. *Heroism and the Black Intellectual: Ralph Ellison, Politics, and Afro-American Intellectual Life.* Chapel Hill: University of North Carolina Press, 1994

Wright, John. *Shadowing Ralph Ellison.* Jackson: University Press of Mississippi, 2006

NOTES

1 Ralph Ellison, "Introduction," in *Shadow and Act* (New York: Vintage International, 1964), p. xxiii.

2 Ralph Ellison, "Twentieth-Century Fiction and the Black Mask of Humanity," in *Shadow and Act*, p. 44.

3 Ralph Ellison, "The Art of Fiction: An Interview," in *Shadow and Act*, p. 169.

4 Ralph Ellison, "The World and the Jug," in *Shadow and Act*, p. 113.

5 Ralph Ellison, "An Extravagance of Laughter," in *Going to the Territory* (New York: Vintage International, 1986), p. 167.

6 Ibid., p. 166.

7 Ralph Ellison, "Perspective of Literature," in *Going to the Territory*, p. 325; Lawrence Jackson, *Ralph Ellison: Emergence of Genius* (New York: John Wiley and Sons, 2002), pp. 93–4.

8 Ellison, "Perspective of Literature," p. 325.

9 Ralph Ellison, "Hymie's Bull," in John F. Callahan (ed.), *Flying Home and Other Stories* (New York: Vintage International, 1998), p. 82.

10 Ibid., p. 82, emphasis added.

11 Ibid., p. 83.

12 Ralph Ellison, "On Being the Target of Discrimination," *New York Times*, April 16, 1989: AS6.

13 Ellison, "An Extravagance," p. 171.

14 Ibid., p. 178.

15 Ellison, "An Extravagance," p. 180.

16 George O. Carney, "Oklahoma's All-Black Towns," in Monroe Lee Billington and Roger D. Hardaway (eds.), *African Americans on the Western Frontier* (Niwot: University Press of Colorado, 1998), p. 148.

17 Ibid., p. 150.

18 Ralph Ellison, "Boy on a Train," in Callahan (ed.), *Flying Home and Other Stories*, p. 18.

19 Ellison, "Introduction," in *Shadow and Act*, pp. xii, xvi.

20 Ellison, "Twentieth-Century Fiction and the Black Mask of Humanity," pp. 33, 38–40.

21 Ibid., p. 35.

22 Ralph Ellison, "Richard Wright's Blues," in *Shadow and Act*, pp. 78–9.

23 Jackson, *Ralph Ellison*, p. 233.

24 Ellison, "The Birthmark," *New Masses* July 2, 1940, p. 16.

25 Robert A. Bone, *The Negro Novel in America* (New Haven: Yale University Press, 1965), p. 112.

26 Mark Naison, *Communists in Harlem During the Depression* (Urbana: University of Illinois Press, 2005), p. 193.

27 Jackson, *Ralph Ellison*, pp. 170–1, 175.

28 Ibid., p. 178.

29 Ibid., p. 179.

30 Ibid., p. 185.

31 Ellison, "Introduction," in *Invisible Man*, preface by Charles Johnson (New York: Modern Library, 1994), p. xxiii.

32 Ibid.

33 Ellison, *Invisible Man*, p. 3.

34 John Corry, "An American Novelist Who Sometimes Teaches," *New York Times*, November 20, 1966: SM15.

35 Ellison, "The Art of Fiction," pp. 176–7.

36 Ibid., p. 177.

37 Allen Geller, "An Interview with Ralph Ellison," in Maryema Graham and Amritjit Sing (eds.), *Conversations with Ralph Ellison* (Jackson: University Press of Mississippi, 1995), p. 76.

38 Ellison, "The World and the Jug," p. 122.

39 Ellison, *Invisible Man*, p. 3.

40 Maurice Wallace, *Constructing the Black Masculine: Identity and Ideality in African American Men's Literature and Culture, 1775–1995* (Durham, NC: Duke University Press, 2002), p. 6.

41 Ellison, "An Extravagance," p. 175.

42 Ellison, *Invisible Man*, p. 3.

43 Ibid., p. 228.

44 Ibid., pp. 235–7.

45 Ellison, "The Art of Fiction," p. 173.

46 Ellison, *Invisible Man*, p. 432.

47 Ibid.

48 Ralph Ellison in John F. Callahan (ed.), *Juneteeth: A Novel* (New York: Random House, 1999), p. 115.

49 Ibid., p. 164.

50 Ibid.

51 Harold Issacs, "Five Writers and Their African Ancestors," in Graham and Sing (eds.), *Conversations*, p. 68.

15

JAY WATSON

Flannery O'Connor

Born March 25, 1925, in Savannah, Georgia, Flannery O'Connor was an only child and a cradle Catholic in one of the most Protestant areas of the United States, the Deep South. Her father's declining health forced O'Connor and her mother to move to the latter's hometown of Milledgeville, Georgia in 1938, where O'Connor began high school as a writer and illustrator for the student newspaper. Three years later her father died, at the age of forty-four, of disseminated lupus, an incurable autoimmune disease. The following year O'Connor entered Georgia State College for Women in Milledgeville, majoring in sociology and English, writing fiction and poetry for the college literary magazine, and contributing satirical cartoons to the yearbook. Her vivid visual sense and gift for caricature would inform her mature fiction, in striking depictions of rural and urban landscapes and deft, often devastating physical portraits of her characters.

After graduating in 1945, she went on to study journalism at the University of Iowa but soon joined the Writers' Workshop, the first program in the country to offer the MFA degree in creative writing. Guided by Workshop director Paul Engle and a series of mentors including John Crowe Ransom, Robert Penn Warren, Andrew Lytle, and Austin Warren – some of the founding figures in American New Criticism – she enjoyed almost instant success as a fiction writer, publishing her first story in 1946 and placing work with *Mademoiselle* and *Sewanee Review* the following year. After completing the MFA and relocating to New York, she appeared to be well under way with a promising career when health problems forced her home to Milledgeville late in 1950. The return would prove permanent: O'Connor was suffering from lupus, and except for brief reading or lecture tours, occasional trips to visit friends, and a two-week pilgrimage to Lourdes, France, in 1957, she would remain in Milledgeville for the rest of her life, under the care of her mother at the family farm, Andalusia. Blood transfusions and experimental drugs kept her illness under control for over a dozen years, but early in 1964, an operation reactivated the lupus, and she succumbed to complications from the

disease on August 3. Her weakened condition undoubtedly limited her literary output, but the fiction she did publish during her lifetime is of remarkable originality, depth, and quality: two novels, *Wise Blood* (1952) and *The
Violent Bear It Away* (1960); two story collections, *A Good Man Is Hard to
Find and Other Stories* (1955) and *Everything That Rises Must Converge*
(1965); and a handful of tales that remained uncollected until 1971.

Critics have given O'Connor an unusual amount of authority to dictate
the terms according to which she is read. In occasional writings and her
correspondence, she presented her artistic vision first and foremost as an
expression of her Catholic worldview. Boiled down to its theological essen-
tials, that vision rested on two elements. The first was a cosmological and
epistemological emphasis on mystery, a conviction that the workings of the
universe were ultimately unknowable, exceeding the limits of human perception and reason. The second was a deep belief in the radical incompleteness
and dependence of humanity, a condition of ontological lack remediable only
by and through otherness, an outside agency she identified with God's grace.
That human beings characteristically disavow their vulnerability and limitations, preferring to see themselves as self-actuating, coherent, and in control,
was merely another symptom of their brokenness and imperfection.

O'Connor's protagonists invariably reject these twin articles of faith.
Supremely confident in their self-sufficiency, their place in the world, and
their high opinion of themselves, they fancy themselves in possession of all
the answers and fundamental truths concerning their lives. This spiritual
arrogance takes one of two forms. Many of O'Connor's most memorable
characters are self-styled intellectuals who are ultimately under-served by
their intelligence and education. As products of "the popular spirit" of the
modern age, these characters labor under the misguided assumption "that
the mysteries of life will eventually fall before the mind of man."[1] The other
large cohort of O'Connor protagonists consists of middle-class figures, usually women, whose exaggerated sense of social self-importance leads them
to equate human legitimacy and worth with superficial aspects of ancestry, breeding, manners, and class status and thus to look down with willful
obtuseness on everyone around them. Their confidence in their ability to fix
others in the South's social hierarchies goes hand in hand with the pride of
place they so smugly assign themselves in that class structure.

The paradigmatic O'Connor narrative sets these self-absorbed, self-
deceiving figures down in a realistically rendered social landscape, a postwar
South characterized by dynamic transformation: new forms of movement
and tension between country and city, accelerating class mobility and racial
activism, and the breakdown of traditional hierarchies and codes. In this
fluid, unpredictable, rapidly modernizing environment, O'Connor's secular

intellectuals and complacent class snobs experience unsettling encounters with a rogue's gallery of subaltern figures no longer content to dwell silently on the periphery of Southern social existence: angry poor whites; backwoods prophets; idiots, amputees, and sideshow freaks; assertive blacks and European refugees; drifters, conmen, sociopaths, and juvenile delinquents. The effect of these collisions is to shatter the narrow, self-congratulatory worldview of the principals, to overturn their guiding fictions and cherished assumptions and thus to offer them a chance to see their world anew and aright, to open themselves to mystery, acknowledge their insufficiencies, and admit the healing, completing action of grace.

O'Connor referred to this crucial moment in her tales – a moment of anguish, disillusionment, and profound spiritual possibility – as the anagogical gesture, drawing her terminology from the category of medieval scriptural exegesis that concerns "the Divine life and our participation in it." This gesture results, she explains, from a character's action that "was both totally right and totally unexpected; it would have to be one that was both in character and beyond character; it would have to suggest both the world and eternity. The action or gesture I'm talking about would have to be on the anagogical level … It would be a gesture which somehow made contact with mystery."[2]

And with violence as well. Every O'Connor narrative turns upon an interior rupture that manifests itself in profound psychological – and often physical – violence. Her protagonists suffer bodily penetration and breakdown: they are shot, stabbed, drowned, infected, felled by heart attacks and strokes, crushed by farm equipment, gored by a bull. Their homes, farms, and families are overrun by alien forces that they are powerless to stop. They are insulted, humiliated, made laughing-stocks, victimized by comic uncrownings and the scouring, unmasking function of language that John May calls "the pruning word."[3] The redemptive element of these stories lies precisely in such fundamental displacements, in a breaching of subjective borders that John Desmond describes as a "complexification of consciousness."[4]

"Greenleaf," a mid-career story that won the O. Henry Prize for the best American short story of 1956, beautifully exemplifies this narrative paradigm. The protagonist, Mrs. May, is a farm widow with two grown sons who struggles to keep her dairy operation running in orderly fashion. She is assisted and obstructed in this effort by her semi-reliable hired man, Mr. Greenleaf, and his wife, an obese fundamentalist given to rolling in the dirt while conducting prayer healings for the afflicted.[5] The scandal of Mrs. May's life is that her own boys have neither the desire nor the initiative to make anything of themselves, whereas the Greenleafs' twin sons, O. T. and E. T., are moving up in the world, leaving their working-class origins behind.

As World War II veterans, O. T. and E. T. enjoy government pensions, subsidized educations, and financial assistance with their dairy farm.[6] They have married classy French wives, started thriving families, and are sending their children to Catholic school to be "brought up with manners." The May bloodline, by contrast, seems destined to grind to a halt with Wesley and Scofield, perennial bachelors who still live with their mother and never meet any "nice" girls.

The Greenleaf boys' meteoric rise up the economic ladder unsettles Mrs. May's bourgeois notions of social class. The criteria distinguishing respectable, property-owning families like her own from the trashy Greenleafs are no longer reliable. She lives in fear that her uncomprehending sons will "marry trash and ruin everything [she has] done" with the farm,[7] even as the Greenleafs knock at the door of the middle class:

> "And in thirty years," Mrs. May asked Scofield and Wesley, "do you know what those people will be?"
> "*Society*," she said blackly.[8]

The twins' success and prosperity feels like a usurpation.

Things come to a head when a "scrub bull"[9] escapes from the Greenleaf farm and begins hanging around Mrs. May's pastureland. The immediate threat is that the bull will "ruin the breeding schedule" at the dairy[10] and mix his inferior stock with Mrs. May's prize herd – much as the "scrub-human" Greenleafs seem to be mounting their own assault on good breeding and the middle-class gene pool.[11] As the bull's threatened transgressions merge with the Greenleafs' own in her imagination, containing its threat – by penning up the animal, returning it to the twins, or shooting it – becomes a way to insure that on her farm, at least, things will remain in their designated places. So when Mr. Greenleaf proves as half-hearted about catching the bull as his sons are about reclaiming it, Mrs. May takes charge. Ignoring repeated warnings that the animal is violent and unpredictable, she marches out to do battle, "exhilarat[ed]" at her own command over the situation.[12] As she zeroes in on the bull, however, it turns on her, "racing" across the pasture to bury "his head in her lap, like a wild, tormented lover."[13] Suddenly the hybridizing, contaminating force she has fought to keep at bay descends upon her person in the most horrifyingly intimate way and the body-trauma brings an attendant psychological rupture, a radical defamiliarization of vision:

> She continued to stare straight ahead but the entire scene in front of her had changed – the tree line was a dark wound in a world that was nothing but sky – and she had the look of a person whose sight has been suddenly restored but who finds the light unbearable.

Mr. Greenleaf was running toward her from the side with his gun raised and she saw him coming though she was not looking in his direction. She saw him approaching on the outside of some invisible circle.[14]

At the center of this circle, in the focal place that she has always assigned herself in the larger scheme of things, Mrs. May is radically *displaced*, her world turned upside-down. To make oneself central, as she so haughtily does, is to risk becoming a target, a human bull's-eye. Yet the moment is infused with possibility as well as gruesome finality: as the story closes, the dying woman seems "to be bent over whispering some last discovery in the animal's ear."[15]

What gives this moment an anagogical dimension is the way O'Connor invests the Greenleaf bull with a spiritual significance exceeding its overt role as biological interloper and class transgressor. On its first appearance in the story, it is likened to "a patient god come down to woo" Mrs. May,[16] with a hedge-wreath encircling its horns "like a menacing, prickly crown."[17] Mrs. May would seem a most unlikely beloved for this "god," since she associates religion primarily with social rather than spiritual opportunities: "If you would go to church," she tells her sons, "you would meet some nice girls."[18] She is particularly unnerved to discover Mrs. Greenleaf, in the midst of a healing, groaning, "Oh, Jesus, stab me in the heart!"[19] Mrs. May's distaste for such spiritual passion is explicit, reflecting her preoccupation with assigning words and feelings, much like classes of people, to their proper social sphere: "She thought the word, Jesus, should be kept inside the church building like other words inside the bedroom. She was a good Christian woman with a large respect for religion, though she did not, of course, believe any of it was true."[20] Despite her cynicism, however, she is shaken by the intensity of Mrs. Greenleaf's prayer, which she finds "so piercing that she felt as if some violent unleashed force had broken out of the ground and was charging toward her" – the psychological equivalent of a rampaging bull. The pieces are in place, then, for the story's denouement, when the widow's patient god and suitor, having eluded her best efforts to expel him from her domain, charges in to stab her in the heart and overturn her interior landscape. It is as bizarre a spiritual fate as can be imagined: gored by god. Perhaps the widow's final whispered words are a prayer of thanksgiving she offers to the intrepid force that ravishes and completes her.

This sort of theologically driven reading has dominated O'Connor criticism for forty years, framing her tales as backhanded conversion narratives about reluctant believers and their ultimately unsuccessful efforts to resist a spiritual calling (see, for instance, in "Further Reading" the works by Giannone, Montgomery, and Wood). In the novels, that call is explicitly to prophecy. Hazel Motes of *Wise Blood* returns from World War II to deliver a godless gospel to the citizens of Taulkinham as part of his intentionally blasphemous "Church without Christ." Preaching from atop his Essex automobile, the secular symbol that props up his shaky faith in liberal humanism and self-help ("Nobody with a good car needs to be justified"),[21] Haze is outraged to discover that the urban populace outdoes him in its vulgar materialism and pleasure-seeking. When a highway patrolman relieves him of his ideological crutch by pushing the Essex off an embankment, he blinds himself with lime, redirecting his spiritual gaze inward, to the ragged figure of Jesus that has stalked him throughout the novel from the back of his own mind. In a similar fashion, Francis Marion Tarwater of *The Violent Bear It Away* tries to escape the spiritual influence of his grandfather, a backwoods prophet in the fiery Old Testament mold, by fleeing to the city upon the old man's death and moving in with his uncle, an arid intellectual named Rayber. Intent on demonstrating his nihilism (to himself above all) and on lashing out against his uncle's oppressive efforts to remake the boy in his own image, young Tarwater hits on the idea of drowning Rayber's idiot son, Bishop, only to find himself, to his horror, uttering the words of the baptism as the dying child struggles beneath the water. Sexually assaulted by a stranger on his way back to his ancestral home, Tarwater is consumed by a spiritual hunger so acute "he could have eaten all the loaves and fishes after they were multiplied."[22] So he prepares to return to the city once more, not to evade his call this time but to answer it, to carry the Word "where the children of God lay sleeping."[23]

To focus so strictly on O'Connor as a crafter of Christian parables, however, is ultimately to do a disservice to her work. She was also an incisive observer of the contemporary social, cultural, racial, and political scene in postwar America, and a writer whose work was in active and often inventive dialogue with US literary history. One native tradition on which she indisputably left her mark, for instance, was the school of vernacular dialect writing known as southwestern humor. As originated in the nineteenth century by Augustus Baldwin Longstreet, George Washington Harris, and others, southwestern humor was the nation's first true movement in humor writing, pitting the unrefined antics and exuberant vernacular language of backwoodsmen, tricksters, mountaineers, and other marginal Southern whites against a series of urbane, genteel, middlebrow, Whiggish narrators in a narrative structure that both reflected and interrogated the political and class dynamics of Jacksonian America. As Louis D. Rubin, Jr. and Robert Brinkmeyer, Jr.[24] have noted, the influence of this genre on O'Connor's work is profound. Her stories are filled with confrontations between characters enjoying the social or intellectual advantages of the Eastern-bred, Easterneducated narrators of southwestern humor, and characters from the regional white underclass. The former have learning, etiquette, status, and verbal elegance on their side; the latter have native wit, energy, and resourcefulness on theirs. Indeed, it often falls to these vernacular figures to deliver the lacerating verbal verdict that punctures the bombast and self-indulgence of the protagonists to open a space for interior transformation. When philosophy PhD Hulga Hopewell is hoodwinked out of her wooden leg by a seemingly innocent bible salesman and stammers out in disbelief, "Aren't you just good country people?", the salesman, Manley Pointer, delivers this withering reply: "Yeah. But it ain't held me back none. I'm as good as you any day of the week."[25] A moment later he takes the atheist Hulga down another peg: "You ain't so smart. I been believing in nothing ever since I was born!"[26] Something similar happens in "The Life You Save May Be Your Own," when a one-armed drifter named Shiftlet swindles a farm woman out of an old automobile and her feebleminded daughter. After ditching the daughter at a roadside diner, Shiftlet picks up a hitchhiker and launches into a treacly tribute to his mother, whereupon his passenger, fed up with this windy insincerity, sneers, "My old woman is a flea bag and yours is a stinking pole cat!" before tumbling out of the moving vehicle and leaving Shiftlet to ponder his own hypocrisy.[27]

But the vernacular voice that O'Connor inherited from southwestern humor is also capable of saying things like this:

> Jesus was the only one that ever raised the dead ... and he shouldn't have done it. He thrown everything off balance. If He did what He said, then it's nothing for you to do but to throw away everything and follow Him, and if He didn't, then it's nothing for you to do but enjoy the few minutes you got left the best way you can.[28]

Or these words, spoken by a hermaphrodite at a tent show:

> God made me thisaway and if you laugh He may strike you the same way. This is the way He wanted me to be and I ain't disputing His way. I'm showing you because I got to make the best of it ... I never done it to myself nor had a thing to do with it but I'm making the best of it. I don't dispute hit.[29]

Here the vernacular becomes a vehicle of spiritual reflection, inquiry, commitment, and even doubt. This is an accent entirely missing from the tradition as practiced by the antebellum humorists or by later figures like Mark Twain, Erskine Caldwell, and William Faulkner, all of whom stressed social, political, and economic concerns over religious ones. Alongside the deep if homely thinking that O'Connor's dialect figures do on spiritual matters, the intellectual cynicism or pious self-righteousness of her more privileged characters seems thin and unsatisfying – a wake-up call to the modern secular readership O'Connor anticipated for her work. O'Connor, then, is taking an established American literary genre with a decidedly secular emphasis and *spiritualizing* it, charging it with new energy and intensity to give it what she liked to call an added dimension. In returning southwestern humor to its native ground in middle Georgia (where Longstreet invented the genre in the 1830s), she also broadens and complicates it, dramatically expanding its resonance and range. More than just an heir to this tradition, she is an innovator in it as well.

She brought an equally innovative sensibility to the depiction of her own era. All of O'Connor's major fiction was published between 1952 and 1965, the peak years of the Cold War between the United States and the Soviet bloc. This period was characterized by a stark oppositional mindset in American culture and politics, and by a pair of distinct yet related national anxieties: the fear of communist infiltration and the fear of nuclear war. These fears combined to erode civic confidence in the home, the family, the heartland, and other home-front formations supposedly beyond the clamor of military and ideological conflict. Nuclear war, after all, was waged on cities: Hiroshima and Nagasaki were graphic historical reminders that atomic weapons observed no distinction between military and civilian targets, and with the development of intercontinental ballistic missiles in the 1950s, the Cold War battlefront could be extended, in a matter of minutes, to any point on the global map. There were ultimately no safe havens, no sanctuaries, in this new and frightening world.

At the same time, the ideological menace of communism threatened homeland security in more subtle ways. Vigilance was felt by many to be crucial lest un-American ideas and values slip into the national community unnoticed and spread among friends and loved ones like some sort of exotic contagion. This crisis of faith in the integrity of the domestic realm prompted a variety of distinctive and often extreme responses. Cold War Americans built bunkers and fallout shelters and conducted air-raid drills at schools and workplaces. They reported suspicious activities by neighbors and co-workers and flocked to B-movies featuring sensationalistic invasion scenarios. And they developed a cultural obsession with the so-called nuclear family and its ostensibly *non*fissile suburban home.

Many twenty-first-century Americans accept this paranoia, this rigid, dug-in siege mentality, as indicative of a wider cultural inertia that ruled the period. O'Connor offers a different view. Her great insight into her place and time was that it was characterized not by cultural and social sclerosis as much as by dynamic transformation and movement, by new forms of interaction and encounter that pointed forward, beyond fixity and fear, to more genuinely diverse and democratic possibilities for the nation. Two of her signature motifs as a writer can be seen as implicit critiques of Cold War-era insularity and conservatism: the fractured family, and the plotline that Jon Lance Bacon dubs "the invaded pastoral."[30]

It is emblematic that O'Connor's first great story, "A Good Man Is Hard to Find," features an unremarkable family of middlebrow city-dwellers being systematically wiped out by a murderous trio of prison escapees. For the rest of her career, the nuclear family would be a rare item indeed in her work. Nowhere to be found in the novels, it occasionally surfaces in the stories – in the enervated Ashfield household of "The River," for example, or the racist Shortley clan of "The Displaced Person" – but in only two cases does it seem to receive a tentative endorsement from the author: the Pitts family in "A View of the Woods" and the thriving families headed by the Greenleaf twins. Far more common are nonnuclear configurations: single-parent households headed by working women; grown children who have never left the nest; old men raising grandsons or moving in with adult daughters; widowers taking in nephews or adopting orphans. It is conceivable, of course, that, having lost her father so young, and being compelled by illness to spend her adult life in her mother's care, O'Connor was temperamentally unsuited to give the nuclear family a starring role in her fiction. But she may have intentionally devised her fragmented family structures in order to challenge the reigning domestic ideology of her day – to suggest that the family unit, as a putative source of stability and security, is always already compromised, thereby exposing the Cold War love affair with the nuclear family as a cultural overreaction to contemporary geopolitical insecurities.

Similar insecurities come under scrutiny in the stories O'Connor set on working farms. There, as Bacon points out, "one narrative pattern predominates. Someone or something enters the pastoral setting and disrupts or destroys the lives of its residents."[31] Bacon identifies this "invaded pastoral" scenario as "a subspecies of the Cold War narrative" in which "the agrarian setting ... function[s] as a synecdoche for the United States," rural life in general nostalgically symbolizes the American way, and fear "of Soviet treachery" supplies "the psychological subtext" of the plot.[32] The invading figure typically exhibits alien or directly antagonistic ways of thinking about authority, private property, self-reliance, and other values dear to postwar America. For example, in "A Circle in the Fire," Mrs. Cope's farm is assailed and eventually torched by a trio of delinquent boys from Atlanta, whose urban landscape of soulless high-rises evokes specters of Soviet-style government housing: "The only way you can tell your own is by smell," says one of the boys. "They're four stories high and they're ten of them."[33] No less ominous are the boys' redistributionist notions about Mrs. Cope's property. Rejecting her premise of ownership, they alternately declare the land to be "Gawd's,"[34] their own, and "nobody['s],"[35] before their ringleader steps in with a Marxist account of the relation between private property and oppression. "If this place was not here anymore, you would never have to think of it again," he observes before reaching for his matches. Moreover, the McIntyre farm of "The Displaced Person" is *doubly* invaded: by the Guizac family, refugees from an Eastern European nation – Poland – under postwar Soviet control; and by a Catholic priest, mouthpiece for an alien European ideology that many conservatives linked with communism in the 1950s. To make matters worse, the Guizacs bring with them some disturbingly progressive ideas about race relations: Mr. Guizac is ready to arrange a marriage between his teenaged cousin and one of Mrs. McIntyre's African American hired hands, if it will get the cousin out of the internment camp where she has been mired for three years. Mrs. McIntyre's outraged reaction only underscores the extent to which her farmstead signifies as a regional as well as national space, a "segregated" as well as invaded pastoral,[36] marked by explicitly undemocratic attitudes toward class and race. This insight – that the postwar Southern farm is "anything but Edenic"[37] – becomes the basis of O'Connor's critique of the pastoral as a Cold War archetype for an endangered national culture. Inasmuch as the corruption of this realm "precedes invasion,"[38] "external threats" cannot be held responsible for the misfortunes that befall it. Indeed, invasion may even turn out to be a "fortunate" event "that benefits the invaded"[39] by challenging them to revisit outmoded or exploitive assumptions about race, class, and society from a more generous, democratic perspective.

In O'Connor's South, the postwar period also saw the rise of what was then called "massive resistance": organized white opposition to the 1954 *Brown* v. *Board of Education* decision by the US Supreme Court and the impending desegregation of the region's schools and other institutions. And when you stop and think about it, "massive resistance" isn't a bad way to describe the basic mentality, the psychological orientation, of O'Connor's fictional protagonists. All of them attempt to resist – massively, strenuously – the coming of change to their lives, change in all its forms: social, economic, racial, and spiritual. Late in her career, however, O'Connor began to examine the phenomenon of massive resistance in more historically and culturally specific contexts, by explicitly locating the action of her tales in the slowly and fitfully desegregating social spaces of the post-*Brown*, post-Montgomery order. "Everything That Rises Must Converge" (1961) takes place on a Southern city bus, where an elderly white paternalist and her racially liberal, yet elitist son both run aground on the complications attending an increasingly porous color line. "Revelation" (1963) gets under way in a doctor's waiting room, the sort of once-segregated realm beginning to be transformed by new social and racial arrangements; and sure enough, a violent encounter in the midst of this space forces protagonist Ruby Turpin to re-examine her sense of racial and class entitlement – and to question her God in the bargain. O'Connor's final story, "Judgment Day" (1965), is set in an integrated apartment building in the urban North, where an elderly Southern expatriate struggles to accommodate himself to new racial realities and interracial protocols. These stories directly record the destabilizing impact of Civil Rights-era confrontations on the values and sensibilities of whites, a dawning, discomfiting sense that traditional models of social and racial privilege are no longer viable. Indeed, John Duvall has observed that the anagogical "moment of grace" in O'Connor often doubles as a "moment of *race*,"[40] in which her stiff-necked whites must confront their own cultural blackness and thereby grapple with their historical and ontological entanglement with the region's, and nation's, paradigmatic figure of alterity.

Massive resistance followed by fundamental displacement: this is the arc of O'Connor's fiction, where dispossession signals the potential for spiritual progress. It is an insight she gleaned from her Southern and American milieu as well as from her Catholic faith. The explosiveness of her fiction is a testament to the energy, fluidity, and possibility she associated with her era. Her major contribution to the literature of that era was to recognize, and tap into, its constitutive volatility and movement.

FURTHER READING

Asals, Frederick. *Flannery O'Connor: The Imagination of Extremity*. Athens: University of Georgia Press, 1982

Di Renzo, Anthony. *American Gargoyles: Flannery O'Connor and the Medieval Grotesque*. Carbondale: Southern Illinois University Press, 1993

Giannone, Richard. *Flannery O'Connor and the Mystery of Love*. Urbana: University of Illinois Press, 1989

Gordon, Sarah. *Flannery O'Connor: The Obedient Imagination*. Athens: University of Georgia Press, 2000

Montgomery, Marion. *Why Flannery O'Connor Stayed Home*. La Salle, IL: Sherwood Sugden, 1981

O'Connor, Flannery. *The Habit of Being: Letters*, ed. Sally Fitzgerald. New York: Farrar, Straus, and Giroux, 1979

Prown, Kathleen Hemple. *Revising Flannery O'Connor: Southern Literary Culture and the Problem of Female Authorship*. Charlottesville: University Press of Virginia, 2001

Rath, Sura P. and Mary Neff Shaw (eds.). *Flannery O'Connor: New Perspectives*. Athens: University of Georgia Press, 1996

Wood, Ralph C. *Flannery O'Connor and the Christ-Haunted South*. Grand Rapids, MI: William B. Eerdmans, 2004

NOTES

1 Flannery O'Connor, *Mystery and Manners*, ed. Sally Fitzgerald and Robert Fitzgerald (1969; reprinted New York: Farrar, Straus, and Giroux, 1981), p. 158.
2 Ibid., p. 111.
3 John R. May, *The Pruning Word: The Parables of Flannery O'Connor* (University of Notre Dame Press, 1976).
4 John Desmond, *Risen Sons: Flannery O'Connor's Vision of History* (Athens: University of Georgia Press, 1987), p. 110.
5 Flannery O'Connor, *The Complete Stories* (1971; reprinted New York: Farrar, Straus, and Giroux, 1981), pp. 316–17.
6 Ibid., p. 318.
7 Ibid., p. 315.
8 Ibid., p. 318.
9 Ibid., p. 311.
10 Ibid., p. 314.
11 Ibid., p. 317.
12 Ibid., p. 322.
13 Ibid., p. 333.
14 Ibid., pp. 333–4.
15 Ibid., p. 334.
16 Ibid., p. 311.
17 Ibid., p. 312.
18 Ibid., p. 320.
19 Ibid., p. 317.
20 Ibid., p. 316.
21 Flannery O'Connor, *Wise Blood*, 2nd edn. (1962; reprinted New York: Farrar, Straus, and Giroux, 1985), p. 113.
22 Flannery O'Connor, *The Violent Bear It Away* (1960; reprinted New York: Farrar, Straus, and Giroux, 1984), p. 241.
23 Ibid., p. 243.
24 Louis D. Rubin Jr., *A Gallery of Southerners* (Baton Rouge: Louisiana State University Press, 1982), pp. 121–33; Robert H. Brinkmeyer, Jr., *The Art and Vision of Flannery O'Connor* (Baton Rouge: Louisiana State University Press, 1989), pp. 45–50.
25 O'Connor, *The Complete Stories*, p. 290.
26 Ibid., p. 291.
27 Ibid., p. 156.
28 Ibid., p. 132.
29 Ibid., p. 245.
30 Jon Lance Bacon, *Flannery O'Connor and Cold War Culture* (New York: Cambridge University Press, 1993), pp. 8–40.
31 Ibid., p. 9.
32 Ibid., p. 17.
33 O'Connor, *The Complete Stories*, p. 182.
34 Ibid., p. 186.
35 Ibid., p. 192.

36 Bacon, *Flannery O'Connor*, p. 88.
37 Ibid., p. 81.
38 Ibid., p. 48.
39 Ibid., pp. 81–2.
40 John N. Duvall, *Race and White Identity in Southern Fiction: From Faulkner to Morrison* (New York: Palgrave Macmillan, 2008), p. 65.

16

BRIAN JARVIS

Thomas Pynchon

Thomas Pynchon is perhaps best known for knowing a lot and not being known. His novels and the characters within them are typically engaged in the manic collection of information. Pynchon's fiction is crammed with erudition on a vast range of subjects that includes history, science, technology, religion, the arts, and popular culture. Larry McMurtry recalls a legend that circulated in the 1960s that Pynchon "read only the *Encyclopaedia Britannica*."[1] While Pynchon is renowned for the breadth and depth of his knowledge, he has performed a "calculated withdrawal" from the public sphere.[2] He has never been interviewed. He has been photographed on only a handful of occasions (most recently in 1957). Inevitably, this reclusion has enhanced his cult status and prompted wild speculation (including the idea that Pynchon was actually J. D. Salinger). Reliable information about Pynchon practically disappears around the time his first novel was published in 1963.

While Pynchon the author is a conspicuous absence in the literary marketplace, his fiction has a commanding presence. His first major work, *V.* (1963), has a contrapuntal structure in which two storylines gradually converge. The first line, set in New York in the 1950s, follows Benny Profane and a group of his bohemian acquaintances self-designated the "Whole Sick Crew." The second line jumps between moments of historical crisis, from the Fashoda incident in 1898 to World War II and centers on Herbert Stencil's quest for a mysterious figure known as "V." Pynchon's second novel, *The Crying of Lot 49* (1966), is arguably his most accessible work and has certainly been the most conspicuous on university syllabi. Oedipa Mass, a suburban Californian housewife, is asked to act as executrix to the will of her former lover and real-estate mogul Pierce Inverarity. Subsequently she appears to uncover a secret organization – the Tristero – although the novel leaves open the key question of whether this cabal is real, a hoax, or merely Oedipa's paranoid fantasy. Pynchon's most approachable fiction was followed by his most challenging: *Gravity's Rainbow* (1973). Tony Tanner sums up the consensus among many literary critics that *Gravity's Rainbow* is "one of the great historical novels of our time and arguably the most important literary text since *Ulysses*."[3] The initial focus in the text is an American lieutenant, Tyrone Slothrop, stationed in London during the Blitz. A map of his sexual conquests appears to predict precisely where German V2 rockets are going to hit the city. The explanation for this uncanny coincidence leads to an explosive proliferation of conspiracies and characters that may lead the reader to repeat the epigraph from section four of the novel: "'What?' Richard M. Nixon."[4]

A collection of short stories, *Slow Learner*, was published in 1984 but it was seventeen years before Pynchon's next novel appeared. *Vineland* (1990) is set mainly in California and jump-cuts between the rampant conservatism of the Reagan 1980s and the promissory but frustrated radicalism of 1960s counterculture. *Mason & Dixon* (1997) centers on the astronomer Charles Mason and the surveyor Jeremiah Dixon as they attempt to fix the boundary line between Pennsylvania and Maryland. The tale of the Mason–Dixon line is narrated in a stylized eighteenth-century prose by one Reverend Cherrycoke and includes numerous fantastic digressions into a world of mechanical ducks and were-beavers, giant cheeses, and a druggy George Washington. *Against the Day* (2006) sweeps magisterially from the Chicago World Fair of 1893 to the wake of World War I. It passes through a host of locations both real and fantastical and features a vast gallery of historical and fictional characters that includes anarchist bombers and capitalist bosses, miners and mathematicians, scientists and shamans. *Inherent Vice* (2009) is set in Los Angeles in 1970 and follows a hippie "private gumshoe, or do I mean gumsandal" called Larry "Doc" Sportello as he becomes embroiled in the malevolent machinations of a sinister corporation known as the Golden Fang.[5]

Admittedly, the preceding précis are necessarily reductive. A defining feature of Pynchon's fiction is the way it vigorously resists summation due to its scope, complexity, and openendedness. Aside from the deceptively slim *Lot 49*, Pynchon's novels are lengthy affairs that teem with characters and rhizomic plot structures shooting off into sub-plots and sub-sub-plots. The encyclopedic range, structural entanglement, and tantalizing indeterminacy of Pynchon's writing are frequently commented on by his critics. Pynchon criticism is almost as vast and variegated as the author's own writing. One online bibliography of Pynchon criticism lists over 3,500 published items that includes over fifty monographs and essay collections, guides and companions to particular novels, journal articles, and reviews.[6] While it is impossible here to map all of the subjects addressed by Pynchon criticism, this chapter surveys six key areas: the postmodern, the historical, the geographic, the scientific, the political, and the spiritual.

Pynchon is routinely referred to as a quintessentially postmodern writer. Many of the formal signatures of his fiction are central to definitions of postmodern culture: the prominence of pastiche and eclectic combinations of genre, style, and tone; the splicing of high art and popular culture; the frenetic intertextuality and self-reflexivity. Collectively, the Pynchon canon resembles a veritable catalogue of literary and paraliterary genres and styles: travel and quest narratives, detective and spy stories, historical fiction and magic realism, comic book and burlesque, psychedelic noir and gothic science fiction, Jacobean revenge tragedy and Menippean satire, surrealism and the absurd, the picaresque and the pornographic. This archive is supplemented by a range of extraliterary discourses from the scientific (thermodynamics and ballistics) and mathematical (vectors and quaternions) to the philosophical (behaviorism and determinism) and theological (Puritanism and Manichaeism). To the list of genres that defines the hypergeneric Pynchonesque we must also add Pynchon himself. Pynchon texts often repeat people, places, and terms from other Pynchon texts. So, for example, one of the *Chums of Chance* novels referenced in *Against the Day* is "*The Wrath of the Yellow Fang*."[7] This fictional children's adventure story represents a proleptic auto-citation (the Yellow Fang reappear in Pynchon's next novel, *Inherent Vice*) as well as a contribution to the text's rampant and retro- hypertextuality. *Against the Day* weaves a patchwork pastiche of genres from the era in which it is set: the adventure stories of Tom Swift, the Hardy Boys, and the 1895 edition of *Surprising Adventures of Baron Munchausen*; the pulp westerns of Zane Gray; the *fin-de-siècle* science fiction of Jules Verne and H. G. Wells; the Victorian gothic of Bram Stoker, Arthur Machen, and Robert W. Chambers; the spy fiction of Joseph Conrad and John Buchan; the exploration memoirs of Henry Morton Stanley and the erotic adventures of Leopold von Sacher-Masoch. Alongside the incessant literary allusions in Pynchon's fiction, one finds countless references to film, television, and music. Often, high and popular culture will be conjoined, as for example in *Gravity's Rainbow* when "André Omnopon, of the feathery Rilke moustaches and Porky Pig tattoo on stomach," performs a (fake) Haydn Quartet on the kazoo.[8]

Wild modulations in tone are another trademark of the postmodern and the Pynchonesque. Passages of apocalyptic terror are intercut with daft limericks, vaudevillian show tunes, raunchy romps, and anarchic toilet humor (often literally involving privies). Language games are central to Pynchon's postmodern comic sensibility and typically involve giddy puns along with absurd appellations and acronyms. Thomas Ruggles Pynchon, Jr. clearly finds names funny and accordingly infects the whole process of nomenclature with sophomoric silliness: a native American called "Defecates-with-Pigeons," a reverend called "Lube Carnal," or a Viennese operetta called "*The Burgher King.*" In *Against the Day*, Gottlob Frege points out that the "English word 'pun,' upside down, is ... 'und'" – an observation which niftily couples Pynchon's passion for playful paronomasia *and* connectives.[9] "And" is arguably the most important word in Pynchon. More than any American writer since Whitman, Pynchon's work is founded on expansive lists and a fierce sensitivity to the nexus between each and all.

In *Gravity's Rainbow*, Pynchon describes paranoia as the "leading edge, of the discovery that *everything is connected*, everything in the Creation."[10] Everything in Pynchon's fictional creations is connected by paranoia, conspiracies, and "master cabal[s]" at every level, from the historical and political to the galactic and subatomic.[11] Paranoia in Pynchon is seen to be both a legacy of the "Puritan reflex of seeking other orders behind the visible" and a survival strategy for the subjects of modernity.[12] The metastasis of powerful global organizations, information glut, and omnipresent surveillance technologies provide the material conditions in which paranoid fantasy can flourish. However, it is worth noting that in Pynchon paranoia is almost always justified: there *are* huge conspiracies and people *are* being controlled and duped and surveilled. Consequently, as Leo Bersani notes, paranoid thinking in Pynchon, "at least in the traditional sense of the word – [is] really not paranoid at all."[13] This key term is also problematized by its very ubiquity. Again, as Bersani inquires: "since when do paranoids label themselves paranoid?"[14]

In Pynchon's novels everything appears to be intricately connected in baroque and burgeoning structures. Often his plots are about the activity of *plotting* itself. The Pynchonian protagonist, enmeshed in cabals and conspiracies, struggles to make sense from an endless bombardment of cryptic signs, images, and texts. Herbert Stencil in *V.* forlornly attempts to interpret and integrate innumerable references to V. Similarly, in *Lot 49*, Oedipa Maas is confronted by the will of Pierce Inverarity, a series of stamps, a painting, a Jacobean drama, letters, acronyms, and graffiti on a toilet wall. Quite simply, these protagonists model reading and interpretation and thus serve as the reader's double. The metafictional dimension to Pynchon's work was vigorously pursued by deconstructive criticism from the mid-1980s.

While deconstructionists have placed Pynchon's fiction in the fun house of self-reflexive semiotic shenanigans, other critics have prioritized his importance, first and foremost, as a historical novelist. *Mason & Dixon* offers some of Pynchon's most explicit commentary on what Hayden White terms "metahistory," or the "deep structure of the historical imagination":[15]

> Facts are but the Play-things of lawyers ... History is not Chronology ... not a Chain of single Links ... – rather, a great disorderly Tangle of Lines, long and short, weak and strong, vanishing into the Mnemonick Deep ... History is hir'd, or coerc'd, only in Interests that must ever prove base. She is too innocent, to be left within the reach of anyone in Power ... She needs rather to be tended lovingly and honourably by fabulists and counterfeiters, Ballad-Mongers and Cranks of ev'ry Radius.[16]

History, here, is a fiction manufactured by the powerful and based on the illusions of "Fact," linearity, coherence, and progression. Pynchon aligns himself instead with the tradition of crafting counterhistories that are dialectical and discontinuous. Like Walter Benjamin, Pynchon aims to "blast open the continuum of history"[17] and he is motivated by the conviction that "*even the dead* will not be safe from the enemy if he wins."[18]

Pynchon keeps himself secret and his historical imagination is animated by a sense of hidden networks existing between disparate events. In *Against the Day*, for example, the following historical strands are intricately interwoven: contemporary scientific speculation regarding the Æther, the "hollow earth" hypothesis, and a quarrel in late Victorian mathematics divided between Vectorists and Quaternionists; the "War of the Currents" between Tesla and Edison, experiments with Iceland Spar and Hollywood in the silent era; railroad networks in the American West and across Europe; labor battles in the Colorado mining industry and political upheavals in Mexico; anarchist and espionage activities across America and Europe; Shamanic mythology in Central Asia, the mysterious Tunguska event, and World War I. It is important to recognize the extent to which Pynchon's novels also offer a history of the present. Thus, for example, the "Anarchist question"[19] in *Against the Day* offers a thinly veiled commentary on political violence and terrorism in the twenty-first century. Khachig Tölölyan and other critics have observed that Pynchon's World War II novel, *Gravity's Rainbow*, hardly mentions Hitler or the Holocaust.[20] However, as Dale Carter illustrates, Pynchon's history deftly imbricates the formation of the Nazi Rocket State in the 1930s and 1940s with the subsequent Cold War and nuclear terror, the permanent arms economy, the NASA space program, the Vietnam War, and Watergate.[21]

Pynchon's historiography triangulates then and now to produce a third space: "the realm of the Subjunctive."[22] History, in this process, is spatialized: "Time is the Space that may not be seen."[23] The historical and the geographical imagination in Pynchon are inseparable. Unlike the West of

Cormac McCarthy, or Paul Auster's New York, there is no one distinctive Pynchonian place; instead, frenetic travel between multiple locations is his geographical trademark. Pynchon's fiction is relentlessly migratory and his characters are typically involved in quests (for V, the Tristero, the Rocket, Shambhala). In the process Pynchon travels beyond US national boundaries more frequently and widely than any other American writer. In *Against the Day*, Pynchon's wanderlust achieves epic proportions as the reader is propelled across the United States and Mexico, Europe and Central Asia, beneath the desert sands, through a hollow earth, and off toward a "Counter-Earth" on the far side of the sun. Pynchon's "World-Narrative" is characterized not only by its geographical diversity, but also by an insistence on intimate global *connectivity*.[24] Various "trans-national plexuses"[25] evolve in his work from the economic and military (multinational corporations and a borderless Rocket State in *Gravity's Rainbow*) to the environmental and mystical (the spiritual afterglow of the Tunguska event experienced at different points across the globe in *Against the Day*). For Pynchon, "geography is as much spiritual as physical."[26] At the centerpoint of Pynchon's spatial imagination lies the possibility of crossing over into "territories of the spirit" beyond and beneath the everyday landscapes of capitalism.[27] These mystical locations assume various forms – Vheissu in *V.*, the Yurok Land of the Dead in *Vineland*, Shambhala in *Against the Day*, Lemuria in *Inherent Vice* – but are always associated with the utopian yearning for an end to exile. In this scheme, America is not only the fallen world, "a very Rubbish-Tip for subjunctive Hopes," but also, still, a space "for all that *may yet be true*."[28]

In *Mason & Dixon*, the thwarted promise of the New World is viewed in relation to cartography: "the West ... seen and recorded, measur'd and tied in, back into the Net-Work of Points already known ... winning away from the realm of the Sacred, its Borderlands one by one, and assuming them unto the bare mortal World that is our home, and our Despair."[29] Maps are a striking motif in Pynchon's work: *Gravity's Rainbow* begins with the uncanny doubling of two maps and *Against the Day* abounds with Foreign Office maps and maps of battlefields, mines and railroads, and invisible cities. Typically, the map in Pynchon is an instrument of imperial power. Even the "Sfinciuno Itinerary,"[30] a map to the mystical Shambhala, may in fact be pointing the way "to unexplored reserves of gold, oil, Plutonian wealth."[31] The eponymous cartographers in *Mason & Dixon* come to realize that their map-making is not a purely scientific exercise, but one that intersects with capitalism and colonialism, slavery and Indian removal. In place of the violence of a Cartesian cartography that inscribes lines of power on places and people, Pynchon practices a counterhegemonic "Parageography ... alternative Maps of the World superimpos'd upon the more familiar ones."[32]

Pynchon's commitment to putting new and even white spaces back on the map should be read as part of his general hostility toward the Enlightenment project with its "Gospels of Reason" that produce a systematic disenchantment of the world.[33] Science is a key component in this process and an indispensable ingredient in the Pynchon novel. Entropy, both thermodynamic (to do with energy and "the decline of the animate into the inanimate") and informational (as a measure of uncertainty in communication), is a recurrent concern.[34] Engineering features prominently in *V.*, *Gravity's Rainbow* (alongside rocketry, chemistry, calculus, probability theory, and behavioral science), and *Against the Day* (alongside math and physics). Science, in Pynchon, is the enemy when it serves the controlling interests of business, military, and government. At the same time, he valorizes the scientific imagination when it is not subjected to the "Disciplines of Control,"[35] but aspires instead to the condition of art or religion. In *Against the Day*, for example, Æther, light, and electricity are treated as quasi-mystical phenomena and the clash between Vectorists and Quaternionists has the devotional intensity of ecclesiastical factionalism. As well as offering a challenge to general standards of scientific literacy, Pynchon also resists the division of the humanities and science into what C. P. Snow in 1956 famously termed "two cultures."

A similarly dialectical comprehension is evident in Pynchon's approach to technology. His early fiction concentrates largely though not exclusively on the threat and increasing autonomy of the mechanical. *V.* delineates the reciprocal process whereby machines become increasingly animate (the cyborgs SHOCK and SHROUD) while humans become increasingly robotic in their behavior and have the inanimate grafted onto their bodies. In parts of *Gravity's Rainbow*, technology is deified as the driving force behind history: "this War was never political at all, the politics was all theatre … secretly it was being dictated by the needs of technology."[36] Alongside the apocalyptic Rocket, however, there is the serio-comic allegory of "Byron the Bulb": "an old, old soul" trapped in a "glass prison."[37] The technophobic and Luddite tendencies in Pynchon are tempered in places by a technological romanticism that rejoices in fantastical contraptions: a "mechanickal Duck" in *Mason & Dixon*, or the airships, "paramorphoscope[s]" and "Integroscope[s]" of *Against the Day*.[38]

The redemptive possibilities for science and technology in Pynchon are inversely proportional to their intimacy with money. Capitalism in Pynchon assumes multiple forms but is always the enemy: a "dusty Dracularity, the West's ancient curse."[39] In *Mason & Dixon* the East India Company is depicted as the prototype of the multinational corporation: "richer than many a Nation, yet with no Boundaries"[40] and with designs on "total

Control over ev'ry moment of ev'ry Life."[41] The same goal drives the Vibe Corporation in *Against the Day*, and in *Gravity's Rainbow* interlocking cartels (IG Farben, Shell) transcend nation-states and threaten to make them obsolete. Global conflict itself is deemed to have been manufactured by the needs of capital: "the real business of the War is buying and selling ... The true war is a celebration of markets."[42] In *Inherent Vice* the Golden Fang represents a comic book incarnation of a global capitalist order that throughout Pynchon's work is associated with social conflict and environmental devastation.

In *Gravity's Rainbow* the American businessman Lyle Bland speculates that "Earth is a living critter, after all these years of thinking about a big dumb rock."[43] Environmental politics and eco-spirituality emerge as a possible counterforce to the deathly alliance of money and machines. Tyrone Slothrop apologizes to a grove of trees for the fact that his family made their fortune from the paper industry and is offered the following penance by a pine: "Next time you come across a logging operation out here, find one of their tractors that isn't being guarded, and take its oil filter with you."[44] The eco-mystical epiphanies in the final stages of *Gravity's Rainbow*, such as Geli Tripping's vision of the Titans, resurface in Pynchon's subsequent fiction. Following the Tunguska event in *Against the Day*, Kit Traverse watches in wonder as "[t]wo small black birds who had not been there now emerged out of the light ... Kit understood for a moment that forms of life were a connected set."[45] Sentient animals form a connected set in Pynchon that underline, often in magic-realist visions, his eco-political sentiments: *Against the Day* features Siberian wolves who quote scripture, talking reindeer, and a dog who reads Henry James; *Mason & Dixon* includes the Learned English Dog and a were-beaver who enters a tree-cutting contest; in *Vineland*, Desmond runs off with a pack of "ghost-dogs"; and in *V.* we meet a rat, named Veronica, who wants to be a nun.

In *Against the Day*, a homosexual spy achieves Veronica's aspiration by becoming a postulant after a miraculous sex change. Pynchon has been criticized for a dated and even reactionary sexual politics (Cyprian Westwood's mystical gender reassignment might appear to reinforce homophobic stereotypes). It has been suggested that he indulges in pornographic fantasy and subscribes to sexist cliché. A casual glance at his most recent novel, *Inherent Vice*, might tend to reinforce this suggestion as "Doc" Sportello drools over a succession of receptionists and stewardesses and "oriental cutie[s]"[46] all with "unquestionably alluring ass[es]"[47] and "exquisite ... no-bra tits, their nipples noticeably erect."[48] It might be countered, however, that such descriptions are a reflection of the novel's milieu (pre-second-wave feminism) and that Pynchon has a distinguished track record of parodying patriarchal stereotypes (in *V.*, for example, where V, precisely, is not a woman so much as a series of feminine archetypes constructed by Stencil), of critiquing phallocentrism (in the sexual symbolism of the rocket throughout *Gravity's Rainbow*), and of offering a number of strong and complex female characters, such as Oedipa Maas, Frenesi Gates, and Yashmeen Halfcourt.

A key component in Pynchon's sexual politics is his depiction of sex. Sexuality is polymorphous in Pynchon – threesomes and orgies, striptease and spankings, fetishes and flagellation, bestiality, coprophagia, and pedophilia – but it tends to push in one of two directions. Sex is depicted in a carnivalesque mode as liberatory and life-affirming, or it becomes a sinister sadomasochistic spectacle at the interface between desire and power. S&M is typically gendered by Pynchon in accordance with classical psychoanalysis. Most of his gallery of sadists (Blicero, Brock Vond, Zarpazo, Adrian Prussia) are male and many of his masochists are female (Frenesi Gates and Shasta Fay Hepworth). There are, of course, exceptions (for example, the submissive role-play of General Pudding in *Gravity's Rainbow* and Cyprian Lockwood in *Against the Day*), but in general terms while Pynchon recognizes political problems with masochism he unequivocally identifies sadism as the enemy. Sadism is linked to oppressive control and forms of colonialism both geographical and biological: *Gravity's Rainbow* integrates the sexual decadence of German imperialism in Africa with behavioral psychology and Slothrop's fear that his "programmed" penis is "a colonial outpost … another office representing Their white Metropolis far away."[49] Psychoanalytically, self-consciousness in Pynchon often teeters on the brink of Freudian farce, but the coupling of rocket and phallus in *Gravity's Rainbow* offers a deadly serious critique of violent eroticism as mechanized death-wish. Like Walter Benjamin, Pynchon sees the sadist as one who is "bent on replacing the human organism with the image of machinery. Sade is the offspring of an age that was enraptured by automatons."[50]

In general terms Pynchon's political sensibility is founded on an opposition, often melodramatic, between "Them" (the powerful sadists) and "Us" (their) victims. On one side there are the capitalists, states, governments, bureaucracies, and technocracies. "They" can assume different guises but are united by their desire for power. "They" aim to replace love and sex with violence, nature with technology, the animate with the inanimate and ultimately life with death. Aligned against these apocalyptic forces Pynchon assembles a rag-bag of likable losers, dopers and drifters, surfers and schlemiels, the preterite and the lost. Pynchon is politically motivated by visions of justice for the oppressed and disinherited but is often skeptical about the possibility of organizing a collective counterforce. His characters are typically more concerned with avoiding power than obtaining it for themselves en masse. Consequently, his fiction leans toward alternative rather than oppositional cultures and micro-political moments of spontaneous rebellion and personal liberation as opposed to structured programs for social change. There are numerous points at which Pynchon's politics intersect with a left-wing perspective. All of his novels are passionately opposed to capitalism, and labor history features in *Mason & Dixon* (General Wolfe and the Stroud Weavers' strike of 1756), *Against the Day* (the Ludlow massacre and Linderfelt's Company B), and *Vineland* (the IWW and Hollywood blacklisting). At the same time, Pynchon tends to favor forms of anarchism (anarchists appear in most of his novels and are central to *Against the Day*) and countercultural subversion rather than the programmatic collective action and political organizations traditionally favored by the Left.

Issues of race and empire have always been integral to Pynchon's politics. In a review of *Mason & Dixon*, Louis Menand claimed that "nearly everything Pynchon has written is, essentially, a lament over colonialism – political, economic, cultural, sexual."[51] In *V.* the focal point for these interests is the Herero tribe in South-West Africa. Pynchon documents the history of the Herero and Hottentot Rebellion and its brutal suppression by General Lothar von Trotha between 1904 and 1907. During the Herero Uprising of 1922, von Trotha's exploits are recreated by Foppl on his plantation in a violent and murderous orgy. The Herero genocide is returned to in *Gravity's Rainbow* where political and psychosexual conflicts are mapped onto the relationship between the Nazi Captain Blicero and the half-Herero Oberst Enzian. Black and white are the key colors in *Gravity's Rainbow*, or rather white fantasies of blackness are projected onto subjects, signs, and spaces ranging from Enzian's *schwarzcommandos* to King Kong. As in Herman Melville's *Moby-Dick*, the novel to which *Gravity's Rainbow* is most often compared, whiteness becomes the color of terror. The director of the Nazi rocket program, Blicero (the "bleacher") is also Weissmann (the "white man"), while the Pavlovian Pointsman directs sinister experiments in behavioral psychology at "The White Visitation."

Michael Harris has connected the representation of the Herero in *Gravity's Rainbow* to the Native Americans in *Mason & Dixon* and the genocide of the Yurok tribe in *Vineland* as evidence of Pynchon's postcoloniality.[52] Toward the end of *Vineland*, Jess Traverse reads a passage from Ralph Waldo Emerson that promises "Divine Justice" for the lost and dispossessed. This extract is taken from *The Varieties of Religious Experience* and "variety" is precisely what characterizes Pynchon's engagement with the mystical. His fiction swells with spiritualities: Puritanism features prominently (and perhaps unsurprisingly given Pynchon's Puritan ancestry); Protestantism is similarly ubiquitous (and often aligned with a rationalist and de-sacralizing modernity); Manichaeism receives its most explicit and extensive representation in *Against the Day* alongside Islam, Buddhism, and Shamanism; Judaism, the Kabbalah, and eco-spirituality figure in *Gravity's Rainbow*; Jesuits and Quakers are important to *Mason & Dixon*; while paganism, animism, Native American beliefs, and New Age mysticism are similarly significant in *Vineland*. Alongside ultra-modern scientific and technological discourses, in a Pynchon novel the reader will encounter a theological lexicon that can be quite arcane. Tony Tanner suggests that the religious in Pynchon "usually takes the form of a yearning or a sense of absence" and in this context his fiction might be read as a form of "hierophany" (a term he uses in *Lot 49*) – an attempt to manifest the sacred and thus re-enchant the profane landscapes of modernity.[53]

Some critics have lamented the parabolic curve of Pynchon's career with the rise to *Gravity's Rainbow* followed by a falling off. It would, however, be hard to find many novels that were not left trailing in the flight path of Pynchon's *magnum opus*. Other critics have remarked disparagingly on the tonal shift in Pynchon's fiction away from the gothic and apocalyptic shadings toward day-glo comedy, whimsy, and soft-focus sentimentalism. Nevertheless, Pynchon has been ahead of the critics for half a century: he was mercilessly parodying phallocentrism during the rise of second-wave feminism; he was addressing issues of empire, colonialism, globalization, and whiteness before the advent of postcolonial theory; he was blending history and fiction before new historicism; he was practicing eco-theory *avant la lettre*; he was examining the "Disciplines of Control"[54] and surveillance before Foucault's work was popularized in the academy; and challenging all forms of binary logic long before deconstruction became de rigueur. For the influence he has had on the academy and across the arts, for his peerless erudition, for his indefatigable questioning and lyrical achievement, Pynchon has to be engaged with by anyone with a serious interest in contemporary fiction.

FURTHER READING

Abbas, Niran. *Thomas Pynchon: Reading from the Margins*. London: Associated University Presses, 2003

Green, Geoffrey (ed.). *The Vineland Papers*. London: Dalkey Archive Press, 1994

Hinds, Elizabeth Jane Wall (ed.). *The Multiple Worlds of Pynchon's Mason & Dixon: Eighteenth-Century Contexts, Postmodern Observations*. New York: Camden House, 2005

Tanner, Tony. *Thomas Pynchon*. London: Methuen, 1982

Weisenburger, Steven C. *A Gravity's Rainbow Companion: Sources and Contexts for Pynchon's Novel*. Athens: University of Georgia Press, 1988

www.thomaspynchon.com (an excellent source for information about Pynchon's works, including wikis on each novel)

NOTES

1 Larry McMurtry, *Walter Benjamin at the Dairy Queen* (New York: Simon & Schuster, 1999), p. 128.
2 Thomas Pynchon, *The Crying of Lot 49* (London: Picador, 1979), p. 101.
3 Tony Tanner, *Thomas Pynchon* (London: Routledge, 1982), p. 75.
4 Thomas Pynchon, *Gravity's Rainbow* (London: Picador, 1975), p. 617.
5 Thomas Pynchon, *Inherent Vice* (London: Jonathan Cape, 2009), p. 239.
6 "A Thomas Pynchon Bibliography of Secondary materials": www.vheissu.name/biblio/alles.php (accessed March 2010).
7 Thomas Pynchon, *Against the Day* (London: Penguin, 2006), p. 1019.
8 Pynchon, *Gravity's*, p. 711.
9 Pynchon, *Against*, p. 62.
10 Pynchon, *Gravity's*, p. 703.
11 Pynchon, *V.* (London: Picador, 1975), p. 91.
12 Ibid., p. 188.
13 Leo Bersani, "Pynchon, Paranoia and Literature," *Representations*, 25 (1989): 101.
14 Ibid., p. 179.
15 Hayden White, *Metahistory: The Historical Imagination in Nineteenth-Century Europe* (Baltimore: Johns Hopkins University Press, 1973), p. ix.
16 Thomas Pynchon, *Mason & Dixon* (New York: Picador, 1997), pp. 349–50.
17 Walter Benjamin, "Theses on the Philosophy of History," in *Illuminations* (New York: Schocken, 1969), p. 262.
18 Ibid., p. 255.
19 Pynchon, *Against*, p. 37.
20 Khachig Tölölyan, "War as Background in *Gravity's Rainbow*," in Charles Clerk (ed.), *Approaches to Gravity's Rainbow* (Columbus: Ohio State University Press, 1983), p. 56.
21 Dale Carter, *The Final Frontier: The Rise and Fall of the American Rocket State* (London: Verso, 1988).
22 Pynchon, *Mason*, p. 543.
23 Ibid., p. 326.
24 Pynchon, *Against*, p. 1023.
25 Ibid., p. 936.
26 Ibid., p. 165.
27 Thomas Pynchon, *Vineland* (London: Little, Brown & Company, 1990), p. 317.
28 Pynchon, *Mason*, p. 345.
29 Ibid.
30 Pynchon, *Against*, p. 425.
31 Ibid., p. 631.
32 Pynchon, *Mason*, p. 141.
33 Ibid., p. 359.
34 Pynchon, *V.*, p. 6.

35 Pynchon, *Gravity's*, p. 238.

36 Ibid., p. 521.

37 Ibid., p. 648.

38 Pynchon, *Mason*, p. 372; *Against*, pp. 249 and 1061.

39 Pynchon, *Against*, p. 263.

40 Pynchon, *Mason*, p. 140.

41 Ibid., p. 154.

42 Pynchon, *Gravity's*, p. 105.

43 Ibid., p. 590.

44 Ibid., p. 553.

45 Pynchon, *Against*, p. 782.

46 Pynchon, *Inherent*, p. 76.

47 Ibid., p. 60.

48 Ibid., p. 170.

49 Pynchon, *Gravity's*, p. 285.

50 Walter Benjamin, *The Arcades Project* (Cambridge, MA: Belknap Press, 2002), p. 386.

51 Louis Menand, "Entropology," *New York Review of Books*, June 12, 1997: www.nybooks.com/articles/1159.

52 Michael Harris, "Pynchon's Postcoloniality," in Niran Abbas (ed.), *Thomas Pynchon: Reading from the Margins* (London: Associated University Presses, 2003), pp. 199–214.

53 Tony Tanner, *Thomas Pynchon* (London: Routledge, 1982), p. 50.

54 Pynchon, *Gravity's*, p. 238.

17

LINDEN PEACH

Toni Morrison

Born in Lorain, Ohio, in 1931, Toni Morrison was awarded the Nobel Prize for Literature in 1993, the first African American woman to be so honored. A major focus of her work is the reinterpretation of key events and periods in African American women's history. Within this framework, her fiction explores themes such as race, gender, redemption, reconciliation, forgiveness, love, and desire. To date, she is the author of nine novels, including one of the most significant trilogies in modern American literature.

Morrison's trilogy, consisting of *Beloved* (1987), *Jazz* (1992), and *Paradise* (1997), spans 150 years of African American history. While the conventional historical saga usually charts a sequential narrative through generations of the same family, Morrison's trilogy consists of three very different novels, each located in an important period in black history. In its scope and form, *Beloved* is generally regarded as her most ambitious refocusing of history, in this case an exploration of slavery in nineteenth-century America from a black woman's perspective. But to fully understand this aspect of Morrison's work, it is important to recognize the way in which her novels juxtapose events from different periods of history and weave literary and historical allusions, myths, fables, and cultural anecdotes together.

Ostensibly, the trilogy appears to move from the mid nineteenth century to the mid-1970s, but the structures of the individual novels disrupt this linearity. Set in a black community near Cincinnati, Ohio, the "present" of *Beloved* is 1873, but the memories of three generations of women broaden the novel's historical scope, encompassing the Middle Passage and, in more detail, slavery in Kentucky. *Jazz* is set in Harlem in the 1920s and, as Eusebio Rodrigues argues, "jazzifies the history of a people."[1] Once again, the book moves backward in time, through the memories of a woman who helped bring up a mixed-race child, to the post-Civil War American South and the post-Reconstruction black migration to the North. *Paradise* is set in Oklahoma in the 1970s, in the wake of the Civil Rights Movement; however, characters recall black westward migration and the foundation of all-black townships in the Midwest from the 1870s and the 1940s.

The trilogy exemplifies how a black history of America has different priorities and emphases than the dominant narratives of white America. But it also approaches significant periods in black history from fresh perspectives. Thus, the trilogy rewrites the history of African American slavery from the perspective of black women, revises the black cultural iconography of Harlem through focusing on the violent underside of the city, and displaces the westward movement in white American history by the equally significant black migration to the Midwest. But through its flashbacks and memories, it also encourages the reader to engage with a nonlinear view of history. As I have pointed out elsewhere, the image of the quilt at the end of *Beloved* is important in this respect.[2] The squares that are added sequentially to the quilt assume, within the quilt as a whole, a new spatial simultaneity that suggests the nature of black historical consciousness as well as Morrison's own approach to composition.

Throughout Morrison's fiction, the reinterpretation of black history interweaves an external-facing examination of the complex relationship between white and black America with an inward-facing analysis of the heterogeneity of black identity and community. In examining African America's presence in white America's consciousness, Morrison's fiction often suggests that white America is largely established on a fear of black America. In her critical book *Playing in the Dark* (1992), completed while she was working on *Jazz*, Morrison argues: "What rose up out of collective needs to allay internal fears and to rationalize external exploitation was an African Americanism – a fabricated brew of darkness, otherness, alarm, and desire that is uniquely American."[3] This thesis is evident in each of the books of the trilogy. *Beloved*, in which a female slave is haunted by the ghost of a daughter she murdered to prevent her being taken as a slave, invokes a plantation tradition arising from the fear of slave insurrection in which slaves were told ghost stories to dissuade them from escaping. In *Jazz*, the story of the mixed-race child brought up by the grandmother of one of the central protagonists portrays the fear of mixed-race people by both whites and blacks. And the way in which whites projected their fears, as Morrison argues, onto black people is encapsulated in the violent deaths of approximately 100 African Americans in the 1917 East St. Louis Riots. Scapegoating and projection are key themes in all three novels, including *Paradise* where the men who run the black township project their fears onto the women of the Convent, seventeen miles away, and also onto mixed-race people.

Morrison's trilogy is clearly indebted to the mid-twentieth-century understanding of history as a narrative involving selection, prioritizing, editing, and occlusion, developed by numerous modernist writers such as Virginia Woolf and William Faulkner, on whom Morrison wrote her Masters thesis at Cornell University in 1955. From them she derived her multiperspective, nonlinear narratives that cryptically interweave personal and cultural stories. In this regard, too, the trilogy has much in common with the novels which preceded it, *The Bluest Eye* (1970), *Sula* (1973), *Song of Solomon* (1977), and *Tar Baby* (1981), and with the two works that have followed it, *Love* (2003) and *A Mercy* (2008). The first sentences of *Beloved*'s three major sections each open with the number of the house, 124, in which the book's "present" is located, but these sections are divided into smaller chapters separated only by breaks in the text.[4] And in *Jazz*, the interweaving of personal and cultural histories is equally complex. Chapters have neither titles nor numbers, but flow into one another where the first line of one section picks up, as in a jazz composition, the last line of the previous section. In its narrative structure, *Paradise* is closer to the adaptation of modernist techniques from Woolf and Faulkner than Morrison's first two novels, *The Bluest Eye* and *Sula*, although the individual stories constituting the narrative are more enigmatic than in these earlier books. Consisting of nine chapters titled with the name of the characters through which each is ennunciated, the novel recalls Faulkner's *As I Lay Dying*, which, through fifty-nine chapters, each of which is allocated to one of fifteen narrators, relates a family's journey to bury their matriarch among her own people.

The trilogy, which is the centerpiece of Morrison's oeuvre, has not simply evolved from but invites re-readings of her other novels. The dysfunctional family, the oppressive nature of class, and the domination of black women by black men, highlighted in the trilogy, are themes that recur in Morrison's fiction as lenses through which African American history is reinterpreted. The subsections of her first novel, introduced by lines reprinted without the punctuation from the Dick and Jane American Primer, stress the disjuncture between the white middle-class values of the Primer and the values of a poor African American family, the ironically named Breedloves. The black lower classes are also the focus in *Jazz*, which implies a comparison with the black middle classes who, outside this particular text, frequent representations of the Harlem cultural and literary renaissance. As in *The Bluest Eye*, the form of the novel (in this case the flow, twists, and turns in the text mirroring a jazz composition) is the means by which the disenfranchisement and experiences of the poorer African Americans are explored. The allusion in *Jazz* to a photograph by the African American photographer, James Van Der Zee, who had a studio in Harlem in the 1920s, is ironic given that he photographed the emergent black middle class, often touching up their portraits to enhance their (white-defined) respectability.

Historical and cultural discourse

The trilogy shares with Morrison's first two novels a concern with the way in which particular historical narratives are kept alive in the public consciousness through multilayered webs of cultural reference. World War I enters *The Bluest Eye*, set in 1940–1941, cryptically through, for example, the names of the three whores, Poland, China, and the Maginot Line. The Maginot Line is not only a reference to the war in a general sense but is an allusion, like Poland and China, to one of the fronts, as it was a line of resistance between France and Germany.[5] As such, it underscores the novel's concern with the boundary between African American and white culture, where the former is perceived as being consumed by the latter. In *Sula*, the name Shadrack is equally cryptic, derived from Shadrach in the Book of Daniel, one of three young men thrown into a furnace by Nebuchadnezzar for refusing to worship an idol. The war is the equivalent of Nebuchadnezzar's furnace, but Shadrack, unlike Shadrach, does not emerge unscathed, although he also demonstrates courage in refusing to compromise his identity as a black man.

The cryptic technique demonstrated by these two examples from Morrison's early novels is employed, as in Woolf's fiction, to mirror the way in which cultural discourses encapsulate and convey meaning through subtle codes and codified behaviors that can almost go unnoticed. The embodiment of meanings in everyday discourses and objects is a recurring motif in the trilogy. For example, the statue of a kneeling black boy, bearing the words "At Yo Service," at Miss Bodwin's back door in *Beloved* encapsulates the Southern myth of the plantation social system in which everyone had, and knew, their place.[6] The inscription "At Yo Service" not only mimics black vernacular, but also mocks black (seemingly) respectful discourse as envisaged by the white-dominated South. Its codified subservient message, mirroring the way in which black slaves and servants paid lip-service to their white masters and mistresses, has an obvious absent presence, the cruel way in which Miss Bodwin treats her black servant. This, in itself, stands in contrast to the kindness that Miss Bodwin shows Denver.

Avoiding realist conventions of chronology, character, and plot, Morrison's fiction appears skeptical of traditional narratives, whether historical or literary, as a means of ascertaining and communicating truth. Indeed, *Sula*, her second novel, is an interesting example of African American, nonrealist, experimental fiction. In covering the period from 1919 to 1965, it mirrors Woolf's longer novel, *The Years* (1937), concerned with English history from 1880 to 1937. Each is organized through chapters that, on a cursory glance, appear to have randomly selected years for their titles. On close reading, it becomes clear that the years have been deliberately chosen in the creation of a new history based, in Woolf's text, on what was important to women, and in Morrison's novel, what was significant to black women. In each novel, the rechronologizing of history to reflect new priorities and emphases is interwoven with the way individual chapters and years echo and re-echo each other. In a movement that is cyclical rather than simply chronological, *Sula* begins not with the war years as such but with the aftermath of the war. In many respects, 1919 is more significant to African American history than the war years themselves because African Americans who had fought in the war, who saw their comrades slaughtered and were sometimes honored, returned home to racist violence and lynchings. The book's chapters both invoke and undermine the traditional historical novel, reminding us that historical moments acquire their significance from larger narratives that interpret them according to particular cultural perspectives and vested interests. But the novel also challenges the way in which history tends to use years as boundaries, imposing a structure, such as the years of World War I, on experiences whose beginning and ending are not so easily defined. Although *Sula* describes Shadrack's injury in battle, it is mainly concerned with his deteriorating mental condition and descent into madness following the war. Another black veteran, Plum, becomes a heroin addict. Although the novel is concerned with World War I, the reader, especially bearing in mind when the novel was published, cannot but notice the relevance of what is said about World War I to the Vietnam War and the similarities between Shadrack and Plum and black Vietnam War veterans.

Before embarking on the trilogy, Morrison deepened and broadened her understanding of how African American history is preserved in a range of codified discourses through writing her third and fourth novels, *Song of Solomon* and *Tar Baby*. In *Song of Solomon*, the spiritual rebirth of its central protagonist, Milkman Dead, is dependent upon the rediscovery and reclamation of a black cultural identity and history embedded in black folk stories, black myths (such as the story of a slave who flew back to Africa), and a collective, oral black history that includes tales of atrocities. These mythical references, which Jacqueline de Weever argues reflect the inadequacy of the realist mode to encapsulate black experience, are integrated in the narrative.[7] The story is framed by the African American fable of a slave who flew back to Africa, and the variant of this Gullah folk tale that Pilate sings at Milkman's birth anticipates his leap at the end of the novel.

The trilogy and *Song of Solomon* share an obvious excitement at the variety of cultural references constituting black consciousness and at the reclamation of significance in what appears, at first, to be random cultural and historical fragments. *Beloved* is based on the story of the slave mother,

Margaret Garner, who killed her child; *Jazz* is based on a photograph of a black girl in her coffin taken by James Van Der Zee, mentioned earlier; and *Paradise* is built on two sources, a tract inviting African Americans to come west to settle in all-black communities and a story, which Morrison heard, of the massacre of a convent of Brazilian nuns who had practiced an African Brazilian religion. They, too, become the basis of narratives that are used to revise key moments in black history. The extent to which Morrison is interested not in cultural references as such but in the narrativization of these references is particularly evident in *Beloved*, which is actually based on a particular version of the Margaret Garner story, "A Visit to the Slave Mother Who Killed Her Child," written by the Reverend P. S. Bassett, and published in the *American Baptist*, February 12, 1856.

Joe Trace's attempt to find his feral blood mother in *Jazz*, leading to his obsession with what appear to be track marks on a young girl's face,[8] might be read as a metaphor for the creative process that unites the trilogy: writing a narrative inspired by cultural fragments. Joe takes the name "Trace" because, on hearing that his parents disappeared "without a trace," he assumed that he was the "trace" that they left behind. In other words, in searching for his mother, he constructed his history on the fragment, the trace, which kept it alive.[9] In the trilogy, African American history is developed from "traces" of black events, narratives, and myths that dominant Euro-American historical discourses have left displaced. For example, the African American South was displaced by white interpretations of the South as historical romance, woven around stock motifs that are deconstructed by the story of Golden Gray: miscegenation, the abandoned child, concealed paternity, and the power of white culture. While the Southern romance did not invent the South, it transformed a rural, largely illiterate region into a mythologized geographical and racial entity.[10] The language, style, and mythological nature of the sections of the novel concerned with the South parody the romance narrative. Here, Morrison's demythologizing of the South is spatially connected to the way *Beloved* subverts the myth of Southern paternalism in which the slave owners were envisaged as presiding over an extended and subservient family of both blacks and whites.

Many of the key symbols of the trilogy focus on the issue of interpretation such as the whip scars on Sethe's back in *Beloved*, which are described as a tree by her lover rather than the clumps of flesh that she imagines, and the disorienting crucifix in *Paradise*. Reflecting the tension between the male-dominated Black nationalist movements of the 1960s and the more openly critical spaces created by black feminist thinkers and writers, *Paradise* suggests that the black township of Ruby is the product of fixed ideologies of race, gender, and continuity, against which many black women had to struggle. The central image of the Convent, the white painted crucifix without a crucified Christ, is disorienting for a number of reasons. The displacement of one of the dominant symbols of Euro-American culture encourages reflection not only on its ambivalence, as sacred symbol and signifier of common punishment, but also on the voided whiteness that is left when the discourses that have sustained it are removed. In this regard, the image signifies the wider possibility of the void of any meaning, ideology, and continuity at all.

In *Paradise*, the principal opposition of the two communities, Ruby and the Convent, is mirrored by the antagonisms within them. The Convent is indebted to an American genre of separatist writing that can be traced back to Adela Orpen's *Perfection City* (1897), which dramatized the hypocrisy, selfishness, and apathy of members of separatist communities. The influence of this genre on *Paradise* can be seen in the conflict between Mavis and Gigi in the Convent; how Connie at times despairs of the people under her roof; and how, on finding a box concealed in the bathroom wall, Gigi plans to keep any valuables it may contain herself.

New versions of black history

In its depiction of rivalry within African American communities, and particularly between black women, the trilogy can once again be seen as evolving from the novels that preceded it and as providing a lens through which Morrison's other novels may be read. This aspect of Morrison's fiction is complicated because it is concerned not only with race but also gender as constituting oppressive discourses. The history that is preserved through the relations between generations of women is both emboldening for African Americans and restrictive, as Jadine, an African American, art history graduate of the Sorbonne, and a model, discovers in *Tar Baby*. But in this novel, there is tension between race (Jadine seeks to lighten her skin color in order to be a successful model) and gender as the more significant oppressive force for women. This is evident in the oppressive attitudes of the men whom Jadine meets, including Son, a violent, contemptuous fugitive from a small all-black town in Florida. This dialectic between race and color is more pronounced when we return to the novel after reading *Jazz*, where mixed-race characters, who, as Hazel Carby has argued, betray particular social practices, reflect the black obsession with "passing" for white in Harlem.[11] Or after reading *Paradise*, where the township has been founded by men exiled from a community by lighter-skinned black people but the female voices, in which the narrative is enunciated, make it difficult (if not impossible) for the reader to identify black and white female characters.

The relative significance of skin color, class, and gender is an issue that Morrison further develops in the first novel after the trilogy, *Love*. At one level, this book reflects the shift in ideological emphasis in the 1960s from segregationalism to integrationalism, to which Shirley Ann Stave has drawn attention in regard to *Paradise*.[12] It is primarily concerned with Bill Cosey, who, before the end of segregation with the Civil Rights Act of 1964, owned one of the prestigious resorts for middle-class African Americans on the east coast. Despite all the benefits of desegregation, what African Americans lost were cultural centers where black Americans could meet and develop a sense of communal identity. But *Love* rather cryptically engages with the Civil Rights Movement in other ways, too. It focuses not so much on Bill Cosey but on the many women who surround him. These include his second wife, Heed, whom he married when she was eleven (which brings to mind Cholly's rape of Pecola in *The Bluest Eye*), and his granddaughter, Christine. In this regard, the novel cryptically mirrors the gender construction of the Civil Rights Movement, which in turn reflects the gender and class politics within the African American community. During the time that *Love* depicts, the role of black women in the Civil Rights Movement had not adequately been recognized. Indeed, Rosa Parks, whose refusal to give up her seat on a bus sparked the Montgomery bus boycotts, was one of the few women whose role in the Civil Rights Movement was celebrated during this period and in the immediate decades that followed. In this regard, the Civil Rights Movement reflected wider African American society as a whole. Admittedly, the wives of the principal leaders enjoyed some visibility, but they mirrored the way in which the wives of public figures had a role dependent upon their husbands' achievements rather than their own. The Civil Rights Movement was patriarchal even though it was often black women and girls who constituted the majority of protesters.

The approach to Morrison's fiction that I have been recommending in this chapter, reading the trilogy in the light of Morrison's other novels and her other novels through the trilogy, is exemplified in a juxtaposition of her two works focused upon slavery, *Beloved*, from the trilogy, and her most recent novel at the time of writing, *A Mercy*. The latter is set much earlier than any of Morrison's other novels, taking us back to the origins of slavery in late-seventeenth-century America. However, it has a number of parallels with the trilogy. For example, while *Beloved* concerns a mother who kills her daughter, *A Mercy* involves a mother abandoning her child. Like *Jazz*, it involves characters who have no family roots and, like each of the novels in the trilogy, although set in a defined present *A Mercy* covers a much wider temporal and geographical space through the stories of its different protagonists.

Although the chronology of Morrison's work has moved backward, as it were, *A Mercy* encourages the reader to reflect upon what was to come in time. Thus, it can be seen as picking up a point about slavery suggested but not fully developed in *Beloved*. In *Beloved*, the white, working-class "slave," Amy, reminds us of the slavery endured by poor working-class whites, whose treatment at the hands of their masters was not so dissimilar from Sethe's. The allusion to the Cherokee Indians who befriended runaway slaves signals how the Indians were also taken as slaves but, prone to European diseases, they were less robust than their African and West Indian counterparts. *A Mercy* reminds us that slavery did not begin as a black project. Florens is a young black woman who was sold by her mother to settle a debt. But her owner's wife, Rebekka, an English refugee who came to the colonies to escape religious persecution, was originally bought by him. The other slaves are Lina, an American Indian who has seen her tribe wiped out by smallpox, and the mixed-race daughter of a sea captain, Sorrow. There are also two white male indentured servants who are part of a system at that time whereby servants sold their labor for a period in return for clothes, food, tools, and land.

That whites, blacks, and other races constituted the slave population in the colonies is well documented in American history. What is original in *A Mercy* is Morrison's exploration of the emergent discourses that led to a society so dependent upon African and West Indian slaves. In this regard, the novel encourages the reader to think about how what happened in early modern America led to the plantation system of *Beloved* and the mythologization of the South. Much of the novel is concerned with the commodification of people as agents of economic exchange. This is epitomized in Florens's name, which cryptically suggests small change but is also evident in the money Vaark has paid for his wife.

During the time in which *A Mercy* is set, a number of different future possibilities were still available to America. Vaark's acceptance of Florens in payment of a debt is a further step along the road to a slave-based economy on which he set out when he advertised for a wife. Although this is symbolic of the direction in which the country as a whole was heading, it is his decision to become involved in the slave economies of the West Indians that proves really significant, an act analogous to America's decision to become a society dependent upon mass slave labor. The fact that Vaark and his wife become victims of smallpox, the disease that wiped out Lina's tribe, suggests, like the sound of pent-up anger made by the slaves in the yard when Vaark takes Florens, that slavery will enslave and destroy those in control as well as those that are controlled. The new laws which are introduced, banning African Americans from assembly and giving whites the power to shoot blacks, reflect white fear of the African American, but Morrison's text questions the relationship between this economic "othering" and the simultaneous cultural construction of blackness as "other," and suggests that whiteness itself subsequently became a creation of this "othering."

The similarities and differences between the approaches to slavery in *Beloved* and *A Mercy* and to the Civil Rights Movement and concepts of segregation and integration in *Paradise* and *Love* suggest that Morrison's work is best viewed as a single, ongoing project in African American sociopolitical history, culture, and identity rather than simply a collection of individual novels. While it might be argued that the work of other authors featured in this book might be read in the same way, in Morrison's case such an approach is encouraged by the continuities in theme, language, and symbolism across the various texts. The novels explore topics such as race, gender, redemption, suffering, forgiveness, and love within an overarching reinterpretation of African American and American history. Avoiding many of the conventions of the realist novel, under the influence of modernists such as Woolf and Faulkner, Morrison's novels are multilayered and multiperspectival. However, her ongoing project is not exclusively an aesthetic one, though aesthetics and experimental narrativization are important to her composition. In many respects, the form of her novels is determined by her overriding concern to reinterpret African American and white American histories. Taken in its totality, Morrison's project is impressive in its originality as much as the individual novels are aesthetically engaging and innovative in their narrative techniques. Her fiction repeatedly refocuses white and African American conventional wisdoms, for example, in looking at slavery from a black woman's perspective and from previously obscured contexts, re-envisioning Harlem, and reclaiming the black westward movement. But it also breaks new ground in its understanding of how African American and white cultural discourse operate through codified symbols and representations. The trilogy, at the center of Morrison's oeuvre, shares with all her work a concern with how African American histories, like those of the white lower class and other ethnicities, have been occluded, displaced, or distorted by dominant white political and cultural narratives. But the trilogy develops her increasingly complex understanding, as in *Song of Solomon*, of how black consciousness is constituted of a mixture of historical fact, narrative, tradition, custom, myth, and anecdote. It focuses on how African American truths have been preserved in, and can be released through, the fragments, traces, and pieces displaced by dominant African American and white discourses.

FURTHER READING

Duvall, John N. *The Identifying Fictions of Toni Morrison: Modernist Authenticity and Postmodern Blackness*. New York: Palgrave Macmillan, 2000

Harris, Trudier. *Fiction and Folklore: The Novels of Toni Morrison*. Knoxville: University of Tennessee Press, 1991

Kolmerten, Carol A., Judith Bryant Wittenberg, and Stephen M. Ross (eds.). *Unflinching Gaze: Morrison and Faulkner Re-Envisioned*. Jackson: University Press of Mississippi, 1997

Matus, Jill. *Toni Morrison*. Manchester University Press, 1998

Peach, Linden (ed.). *Toni Morrison: Contemporary Critical Essays*. New York: St. Martin's Press, 1998

Peterson, Nancy J. (ed.), *Toni Morrison: Critical and Theoretical Approaches*. Baltimore: Johns Hopkins University Press, 1997

Rigney, Barbara Hill. *The Voices of Toni Morrison*. Columbus: Ohio State University Press, 1991

NOTES

1 Eusebio Rodrigues, "Experiencing *Jazz*," *Modern Fiction Studies*, 39 (1993): 742.

2 Linden Peach, *Toni Morrison* (Basingstoke: Palgrave Macmillan, 2000), p. 118.

3 Toni Morrison, *Playing in the Dark: Whiteness and the Literary Imagination* (Cambridge, MA: Harvard University Press, 1992), p. 38.

4 Wen-ching Ho, Preface in *Beloved*, trans. Wen-ching Ho (Taipei: Commercial Press, 2003), p. iv.

5 Ágnes Surányi, "*The Bluest Eye* and *Sula*: Black Female Experience from Childhood to Womanhood," in Justine Tally (ed.), *The Cambridge Companion to Toni Morrison* (Cambridge University Press, 2007), p. 12.

6 Toni Morrison, *Beloved* (1987; reprinted London: Picador, 1988), p. 255.

7 Jacqueline De Weever, *Mythmaking and Metaphor in Black Women's Fiction* (New York: St. Martin's Press, 1991), p. 4.

8 Carolyn M. Jones, "Traces and Cracks: Identity and Narrative in Toni Morrison's *Jazz*," *African American Review*, 31 (1997): 483.

9 Shirley Ann Stave, "*Jazz* and *Paradise*: Pivotal Moments in Black History," in Justine Tally (ed.), *The Cambridge Companion to Toni Morrison*, pp. 62–3.

10 Peach, *Toni Morrison*, p. 150.

11 Hazel Carby, "'On the Threshold of Woman's Era': Lynchings, Empire and Sexuality in Black Feminist Theory," *Critical Inquiry*, 12 (1985): 274.

12 Stave, "*Jazz* and *Paradise*," p. 68.

18

LAURA BARRETT

Don DeLillo

In Don DeLillo's first novel, *Americana* (1971), David Bell abandons his role as a network television executive and takes to the road to make a film only to confront "the thick paragraphs and imposing photos, the gallop of panting adjectives" that have preceded his vision of the nation.[1] The novel adumbrates many of the themes that inform DeLillo's later works: the often embattled relationship between words and images, the human need for systems in the seeming absence of a divine plan, the competing paradigms of contingency and conspiracy, the limits of knowledge and the desire for mystery, the responsibility of the artist to take stock of the world, and the erasure of subjectivity in an increasingly mediated century. Noting that he "had almost the same kind of relationship with [his] mirror that many of [his] contemporaries had with their analysts,"[2] David confesses that his "whole life was a lesson in the effect of echoes, that [he] was living in the third person."[3]

Describing DeLillo as a "postmodern Henry Adams," David Cowart has noted both authors' interest in "gauging 'the track of the energy' that makes or transforms a civilization," but the connection between DeLillo and Adams goes further.[4] Adams's ironic use of a third-person perspective in an autobiography certainly speaks to a crisis of identity engendered by a classical education ostensibly unsuitable for a modern world run by machines. *The Education of Henry Adams* marks the moment not only when the dynamo supplants the virgin, but also when it overwhelms history and subjectivity, when "the supersensual universe ... could be known only as unknowable."[5] The particular machines in DeLillo's garden are no longer the generators of the World's Columbian Exposition; they are, instead, ATMs and televisions, supermarket scanners and satellites, our dei ex machina whose mechanisms are ubiquitous, invisible, timeless, and seemingly consecrated.

DeLillo's novels simultaneously chronicle history's effacement in the second half of the twentieth century and insist on its importance as a cultural force, the last of which is easily overlooked in *Americana*. David recalls the end of his cross-country journey, driving to the airport via downtown Dallas: "I turned right at Houston Street, turned left onto Elm and pressed my hand against the horn. I kept it there as I drove past the School Book Depository, through Dealey Plaza and beneath the triple underpass. I kept blowing the horn all along Stemmons Freeway and out past Parkland Hospital."[6] The image of "lost innocence"[7] that inspired *Americana* is shattered by the assassination of John F. Kennedy, at which point, DeLillo argues, America "entered a world of randomness and ambiguity, ... a natural disaster in the heartland of the real, the comprehensible, the plausible."[8] The novel ends with a remembrance of one of the greatest national tragedies juxtaposed with the seemingly incongruous and frivolous detail about the type of credit card David uses to buy an airline seat back to New York. Of course, the name of the card – American Express – could not be less arbitrary. DeLillo's novels provide a ride on the American Express, a vehicle that prizes the ideal consumer above the ordinary citizen but whose efforts to enforce conformity are occasionally resisted by unexpected sparks of agency.

Although *Americana* took DeLillo four years to complete, it convinced him to quit his copywriting position at a Madison Avenue advertising agency and devote himself full time to his fiction. His next five books – *End Zone* (1972), *Great Jones Street* (1973), *Ratner's Star* (1976), *Players* (1977), and *Running Dog* (1978), published within seven years – span a range of topics and genres from football to physics and stock markets to rock and roll, but all circle around the central issue of human design, our attempts to control a world that increasingly surpasses our powers of comprehension or representation. Science, finance, war, art, even games, provide examples of human systems invented to control chaos.

Nowhere are those attempts more visible than in language, which can shape reality as well as reflect it, a central preoccupation of DeLillo's 1982 novel *The Names*, considered by many to be the author's "'breakthrough' book"[9] because of its ambition in terms of structure, theme, and scope. *The Names* offers what is perhaps DeLillo's most thorough and troubling engagement with language, while at the same time introducing what will become an essential element of many of his later and most accomplished novels – an examination of world politics. James Axton, an American insurance risk analyst stationed in Greece, chronicles his adventures with a group of American and British expatriate bankers, insurers, and archeologists connected by their common exploitation of foreign territories.

While James assumes that his work in Greece is motivated by private sector profit, he learns in the last pages of the novel that his profession has been more political than financial, as it is revealed that Axton has unwittingly been spying for the CIA. Here, as in *Americana*, even the most privileged

Americans, those who assume they are in control, are pawns of a corporate culture and are guilty by virtue of a refusal to be politically and historically engaged. Andreas Eliades, a Greek activist in the novel, comments on how "Americans choose strategy over principle every time and yet keep believing in their own innocence."[10] That innocence is an American imperative, a legacy that breeds fecklessness, as James confesses: "I began to think of myself as a perennial tourist ... To be a tourist is to escape accountability. Errors and failings don't cling to you the way they do back home. You're able to drift across continents and languages, suspending the operation of sound thought."[11]

The novel's many conspiracies, ranging from the petty and personal to the profound and political, simultaneously represent attempts to assert individual agency and to be incorporated into a larger body. American banker David Keller, his wife Lindsay, and James briefly toy with the idea of boarding a drunken American on a plane to Tehran, never considering the dire consequences of their childish prank. On the other end of the spectrum, members of a particularly macabre underground cult, known to its members as The Names, select victims whose initials match the initials of the geographical locations in which they are found and killed. Owen Brandemas, the manager of an archeological dig, becomes implicated in the murders when he elects to keep the cult's secret. Language in *The Names* is, then, a means of control. James, like many of DeLillo's characters, protects secrets, refusing to dilute their potency by sharing them, a lesson he has learned from Andahl, a cult member, who claims that a "secret name is a way of escaping the world. It is an opening into the self."[12] The expatriates soon realize that power lies in linguistic fluency but an even greater power is gained by concealing that fluency. Feeling subservient to the hotel staff because of his inadequate Greek, James begins to lie to the doorman about his destination, offering "a place that had a name I could easily pronounce."[13] His justification sounds eerily similar to the logic of the murderous cultists: "What a simple, even elegant device this seemed. Let the nature of the place-name determine the place."[14] His sense of "something metaphysically disturbing" about the lies, a "grave misplacement" rests in a feeling that he is "tampering ... with the human faith in naming ... Could reality be phonetic, a matter of gutturals and dentals?"[15] Such a reality would, of course, utterly efface history, which is precisely what the cult members attempt to do by choosing as their home a place that is not "full of associations." "No gods, no history ... A place where it is possible for men to stop making history. We are inventing a way out."[16]

The false binaries – self or world; language or history – engender characters who retreat from reality. That retreat may be as innocent as a childish secret language like "Ob," which Katherine Axton and her son, Tap, play-fully speak, or as sinister as a cult which employs a secret code to choose its victims. The novel, however, seems to suggest that the distance between innocence and guilt is less than one might think. Ob's name mirrors the ini-tials of Owen Brandemas, a character whose own obsession with languages stems from traumatic childhood memories of his community's Pentecostal church, where the congregants spoke in tongues. In fictionalizing his own story, Owen wonders if speaking in tongues is "the language of innocence," "a coming out of stasis."[17] The "terrible holy gibberish"[18] may rescue us from "the fallen wonder of the world,"[19] the language of expulsion, but its invi-tation to prelapsarian bliss is also an impediment to community; the price for spiritual and linguistic "ecstasy" is an unraveling of the ego, in which "[n]ormal understanding is surpassed, the self and its machinery obliterated."[20] While DeLillo has commented on "the secret aspiration" of writers – "You want to lose yourself in language, become a carrier or mes-senger. The best moments involve a loss of control. It's a kind of rapture"[21] – he also recognizes the importance of being in the world: "I don't think that a writer can allow himself the luxury of separating himself from the crowd, even if he is by definition a person who spends much of his life alone in a room."[22] In contrast to Owen's bloodless pursuit of knowledge and bloody implication in the cult is "The Prairie," Tap's fictionalized account of Owen's bewilderment, which is translated by Tap into a new language; his "spirited misspellings made [the words] new again," revealing "how they worked, what they really were" – "ancient things, secret, reshapable,"[23] an obser-vation about language's ability to awaken and inspire without obliterat-ing subjectivity, without eliding history, which is corroborated by DeLillo's belief that "it's possible for a writer to shape himself as a human being through the language he uses."[24]

The notion that language shapes people and experiences is at the heart of DeLillo's best-known novel, *White Noise* (1985), whose main character, Jack Gladney, Professor of Hitler Studies at the College on the Hill, is a man in search of an identity. On the advice of a chancellor, Jack gains weight and changes his name to J. A. K. Gladney. Becoming "the false character that follows the name around," Jack cannot establish how he feels without the confirmation of a medical expert.[25] Characters gauge their responses to environmental catastrophes on the basis of media reports, and tourists travel to the "most photographed barn in America" to see *pictures* of the barn.[26] *White Noise* is a comic appraisal of the rise of mediation in the twen-tieth century, a clear-eyed assessment of the postmodern condition that is simultaneously hilarious and unnerving. The survivors of a flight that nearly crashed, for example, find themselves entranced and consoled by the story of their own near-death experience, a narrative confirming and reframing what they had endured. While mediation proves comforting, the absence of media in Iron City provokes the comment that "[t]hey went through all that for nothing," suggesting that experience is unreal unless caught on camera.[27]

Language's ability to shape the world, however, does not rescue it from near incoherence. The mutating descriptions of the chemical spill that forces the evacuation of Blacksmith – "a feathery plume," "a black billowing cloud," "an airborne toxic event" – reflect media attempts to control the level of alarm.[28] Similarly, an airline crew ameliorates passenger anxiety through use of the term "crash landing": "After all, the difference between [crash and crash landing] is only one word. Didn't this suggest that the two forms of flight termination were more or less interchangeable?"[29] The purported power of a noun, here, is tantamount to a desire for linguistic control over death, an ultimately unrealizable desire since death is the one experience that cannot be mediated or rehearsed, the only event we all suffer whose representations are sheer speculation, as much fantasy as living on the moon and traveling in time. DeLillo's alternative title, "The American Book of the Dead," suggests that the novel is in part a funerary text not unlike the Tibetan and Egyptian books of the dead, a guide to the afterlife for a culture whose postmortem gateway is a supermarket, whose divinity resides in ATMs and televisions, and whose religious leaders feign belief.

Notwithstanding the increasing secularization of society, Americans in DeLillo's text hunger for a transcendent experience, searching for it in the tabloids and hearing echoes of it in brand names and meaningless jargon. Jack, who suffers from a pathological fear of death, resigns himself to an acceptance of uncertainty and indeterminacy that may either be fatal (since he stops taking calls from his doctor) or life-affirming. The novel's last scene in a supermarket, whose merchandise has all been relocated, may represent a bleak picture of the afterlife, one robbed of any warmth and sense, or it offers an odd secular spirituality that acknowledges the essential isolation of humans as mysterious and sacred, what DeLillo would call "radiance in dailiness."[30] In *White Noise*, that radiance is described in linguistic terms. Before Jack and his neighbors file into the supermarket, they stand at the overpass and watch the sky take on "content, feeling, an exalted *narrative* life,"[31] its "spell, powerful and *storied*."[32] However imprecise and comically bumbling language may be, its absence would make the world an even more alien place. Wilder's "mystically charged" trek across the "modernist" highway, then, bodes well, partly because he has finally entered the world of language with all its disappointments and victories: "Stunned, he made the decision to cry ... The women began to call once more ... And he seemed, on his seat in the creek, profoundly howling, to have heard them for the first time."[33]

If *Americana* signals DeLillo's interest in the assassination of President John F. Kennedy, *Libra* (1988) becomes the author's full-scale investigation into "the seven seconds that broke the back of the American century."[34] The novel's chapters alternate between a rather straightforward biography of Kennedy's assassin, Lee Harvey Oswald, and DeLillo's speculations about the competing plots of various intelligence agencies and criminal organizations that interact beyond the intentions of any one group to produce the event in Dallas of November 22, 1963. Like the comic Jack Gladney, the tragic Lee Oswald is a hollow figure, constructed more by external agents and the media than by ego, taking his cues from films and magazines: "He saw himself writing his story for Life or Look, the tale of an ex-Marine who has penetrated the heart of the Soviet Union."[35]

The tale that is eventually written about Lee's life is far less flattering – or even readable – than he had imagined. Paradoxically, an attempt "to regain our grip on things"[36] and the "Joycean Book of America ... in which nothing is left out,"[37] the Warren Commission *Report* is a book "lost to syntax and other arrangement,"[38] a compilation of noise so overwhelming and distracting that its mere presence prevents a coherent story from unfolding. Ironically, the superfluity of information in the *Report*'s twenty-six volumes – which includes films, documentaries, transcripts, autopsies, as well as "floor plans, home movies ... [b]aptismal records, report cards ... photos of knotted string,"[39] "feature films and documentaries ... transcripts of panel discussion and radio debates"[40] – does not include all the information. DeLillo's fictive premise, then, is that the CIA charges one of its analysts, Nicholas Branch, to write the secret history of the assassination, but the Agency, Branch surmises, is not telling him everything. Like a novelist trying to the weave the threads of various plots together, Branch finds himself inundated by data as he seeks the missing puzzle pieces, thus making clear the novel's own preoccupation with plots. The political and narrative intrigues invented by humans in the absence of divine plans are marked by desperation. In *Libra*, anxious male characters stalk the pages with even more determination and disorientation than in other DeLillo works. Lee, more pawn than player, "a fiction living prematurely in the world," cannot even seem to impose a pattern on his own life, as his radicalism is literally co-opted by the very forces he wishes to overthrow.[41] Branch, meanwhile, attempts to unearth the truth from the mountain of data and detritus, facts and factoids, wisdom and whimsy cluttering his rooms, but the document that he writes is not for public consumption. It is the "secret history of the assassination."[42]

The contingency of language and the danger of formulaic plots haunt many of DeLillo's characters, but *Mao II* (1991) confronts the increasing irrelevance of the writer in a world where information is delivered by streams of words that scroll across the bottoms of television screens or the "band of glowing letters" that encircles One Times Square.[43] Author Bill Gray, another in the long line of DeLillo's disoriented male protagonists, has sequestered himself in the foothills of upstate New York in an effort to preserve his authenticity from overwhelming media attention following the success of a "slim novel" early in his career. Notwithstanding his refusal to be "incorporated" and his rejection of mass culture, Bill allows himself to be photographed, hoping that the resulting images will dispel the aura engendered by his isolation. Paralleling the decreasing influence of writers is the increasing power of the image in an age of digital reproduction. The novel's cover, including a reprint of Andy Warhol's Mao series, 1972–1974, and its reproduced photographs of the Tiananmen Square massacre, a Unification Church mass wedding at Yankee Stadium, the soccer tragedy at Hillsborough stadium in Sheffield, and Khomeini's funeral testify to its preoccupation with images and their association with crowds. The most pervasive cultural influence, however, is the rise of terrorism, which, according to Bill, has usurped the novelist's role as shaper of meaning. A more accurate view, however, seems to be that Bill, in surrendering his role as a cultural critic by refusing to be seen or heard, represents the failed artist figure in DeLillo's work. Bill's desire to re-enter the messy fray of the world comes too late to save himself or his current project and certainly too late to influence the culture. Fittingly, he dies on a ferry to Junieh, en route to help a poet kidnapped by Lebanese terrorists. His pockets picked clean by a passer-by, Bill Gray will become the identity of someone willing to pay for his stolen identification. *Mao II* contends that the withdrawal of the novelist from public life can only augment the seeming irrelevance of literature. As Mark Osteen notes, an alternative artist figure, one engaged with the world, is Britta Nillson, the photographer hired to usher Bill back to the land of the living.[44] Britta is a forceful critic of cultural paradigms, rejecting both the American myth of individualism embodied by Bill and the totalitarianism and eradication of identity demanded by Abu Rasid, the leader of a Lebanese terrorist organization.

Underworld (1997), DeLillo's *magnum opus*, begins at a baseball stadium in the Bronx, a setting just across the Harlem River from *Mao II*'s opening scene in Yankee Stadium. Six years after his previous novel's publication, DeLillo is less the ironist bemused by the irreverent use of an American icon – a baseball stadium – for such anti-American ends – a mass wedding – and more the democratic poet, fulfilling his boyhood dreams of making visible a baseball game. Still, it is difficult to read the prologue as full-on nostalgic reverie given its title: "The Triumph of Death," a reference to the reproduction of Bruegel's painting which appears in *Life* magazine and whose shredded remnants contribute to the confetti after Bobby Thomson's home run at the Polo Grounds on October 3, 1951, that clinches the National League pennant for the New York Giants. Indeed, the entire prologue is a study in contrasts: the various interpretations of "the shot heard round the world," and the subsequent headlines warring for attention in the *New York Times* after the Giants' victory and the detonation of one of the first Soviet atomic bombs; the ballgame experienced so differently by Jackie Gleason and J. Edgar Hoover, Russ Hodges and Nick Shay, and especially an impoverished fourteen-year-old African American boy, Cotter Martin, and a middle-aged white architect, Bill Waterson, whose unlikely camaraderie disintegrates when they struggle to possess the ball that Thomson hit. That pairing, the genesis of the black-and-white motif that DeLillo will carry throughout the novel, adumbrates the racial tensions that will tear the country apart in the following decades and challenges the idyllic depiction of 1950s America.

The novel traces the lineage of Bobby Thomson's home-run ball to connect a remarkable number of people in the forty or so years after the history-making game. Central to the narrative is fifty-seven-year-old Nick Shay, a Dodgers fan who, we discover, was listening to the game from the roof of his Bronx apartment building in the summer of 1951. Shay, a waste disposal engineer still trying to come to terms with his abandonment by his father fifty years earlier, believes that he "live[s] responsibly in the real,"[45] a position undermined by his relocation of his mother from the "daily drama of violence and lament and tabloid atrocity" of the Bronx to Phoenix, Arizona, a mythical city where "history did not run loose ... They caged it, funded and bronzed it, they enshrined it carefully in museums and plazas and memorial parks."[46] Like David Bell, Shay recognizes the inevitable "third-person" perspective of contemporary citizens: "I noticed how people played at being executives while actually holding executive positions. Did I do this myself? You maintain a shifting distance between yourself and your job ... You're pretending to be exactly who you are";[47] however, he yearns, like Jack Gladney, to experience history as a "single narrative sweep, not ten thousand wisps of disinformation,"[48] but his voice stutters, cluttered with distractions and digressions, desultorily shifting among a hodgepodge of topics.

The novel's achronological structure, staccato rhythm, and host of characters, both literary and historical, argue against history as a "single narrative sweep." Sister Edgar, a Catholic nun whose austere attire, critical eye, and punitive hand remain unaffected by Vatican II, Klara Sax, a young wife whose affair with seventeen-year-old Nick Shay ironically initiates her career as an artist of found materials, and Marvin Lundy, collector of memorabilia, mingle with J. Edgar Hoover, Jackie Gleason, and Lenny Bruce.

As in E. L. Doctorow's *Ragtime* (1974), the effect is to privilege the private histories of characters whose lives we follow for forty years. Cotter Martin's desire to see a baseball game sets the stage not only for a legendary home run but also for the second act in the drama of twentieth-century America. "Longing on a large scale is what makes history,"[49] says the narrator of *Underworld*'s prologue, the rare second-person narrative voice that tells the "people's history."[50] Not unlike Klara Sax, who works with discarded materials, turning abandoned aircraft into landscape art, DeLillo wants to recuperate "the ordinary life behind the thing."[51] The Thomson ball becomes less an enchanted object than a connective tissue linking unlikely partners. For Nick, the ball "commemorate[s] failure,"[52] a homage to loss in a novel preoccupied with renunciation, desolation, and waste, whose characters, salvage artists, conscientious recyclers, or disposal agents, specialize in detritus, or, like Sister Edgar and J. Edgar Hoover, view the world as a germ-ridden rubbish heap. Indeed, the title of the novel recalls the literal world beneath New York City, a world of rat-infested sewer lines and subway tracks – the homeless, the rejected, the preterite of Thomas Pynchon's world. In *Underworld*, these are "[w]orking people, shopkeepers, ... drifters and squatters, ... charismatics, ... tublike women, reedy men in dreadlocks" who seek spiritual consolation and see the image of a murdered twelve-year-old girl, Esmeralda Lopez, on a Minute Maid billboard.[53]

That lost world is recovered through the accumulation of individual stories, "word passing block to block, moving through churches and superettes, maybe garbled slightly, mistranslated here and there, but not deeply distorted."[54] As Father Paulus teaches Nick, language recuperates: "You didn't see the thing because you don't know how to look. And you don't know how to look because you don't know *the names*."[55] Yoking the mundane to the historic, the pedestrian to the sublime, Father Paulus lectures Nick: "[E]veryday things lie hidden. Because we don't know what they're called ... Quotidian things. If they weren't important, we wouldn't use such a gorgeous Latinate word ... An extraordinary word that suggests the depth and reach of the commonplace."[56] The Jesuit priest ends his lesson by warning Nick to take seriously his own name, which he has mindlessly affixed to a petition in support of Joseph McCarthy. Nick returns to his room determined to "look up words," because this "is the only way in the world you can escape the things that made you,"[57] a sentiment confirmed by Marvin Lundy, a character forgetful of words and stumbling through the novel in search of stories to organize his paranoia, his specious vocabulary providing the foundation for a life of misunderstanding.

Language is less a quasi-mystical vehicle to transcendence in DeLillo's recent novels. In *The Body Artist* (2001), Lauren Hartke, a performance artist who is "always in the process of becoming another,"[58] deals with the foreignness of her body after the suicide of her husband, a filmmaker whose work in "landscapes of estrangement" is the visual equivalent of the characters' alienation from their voices, which are pilfered by mimics and tape recorders.[59] Confronting identity crisis on a national level, *Cosmopolis* (2003) channels the language of Hart Crane's "Proem" *The Bridge*, whose shadow haunts a culture that values only money and speed, ensuring that "time is a corporate asset" and words are merely the antiquated vestiges of obsolete concepts.[60] Seemingly driven by the notion that "numbers behave, words do not,"[61] characters in *Falling Man* (2007), DeLillo's 9/11 novel, engage in mathematical rituals – counting backwards by seven, playing Texas Hold'em, and speaking monosyllabically – to make sense of the nation's tragedy. Here the novel's circularity signifies the nation's stagnation and promises the continuation of the rituals and routines that help us "organize time until [we can] live again."[62] In *Point Omega* (2010), Richard Elster, an architect of America's war in Iraq, retires to the California desert to talk about "transcendence, paroxysm, the end of human consciousness" only to end his days in near silence, his "grand themes funneled down to local grief" when his daughter disappears.[63]

If these recent novels seem to wallow in the inadequacy of language – their relative brevity a response to *Underworld*'s epic size and themes – the reader is faced with the irony that the failure of words can only be communicated by words, a paradox not unlike Lianna's Zen koan in *Falling Man*: "God is the voice that says, 'I am not here.'"[64] DeLillo's tolerance for ambiguity and contradiction certainly testifies to his "first-rate intelligence," a concept F. Scott Fitzgerald defined as "the ability to hold two opposed ideas in the mind at the same time, and still retain the ability to function."[65] What Tom LeClair calls DeLillo's "double view of American life" that encompasses "an appreciation of its rich potentialities and an ironic sense of its excessive failures" describes DeLillo's view of language as well.[66] David Bell's "literary venture" is also DeLillo's: the creation of "a squeamish thesis on the essence of the nation's soul,"[67] a proposition of immanence and transcendence, history and eschatology, agnosticism and mysticism disclosed in a fractured idiom that is both "the fallen wonder of the world"[68] and "the revelation yet to come."[69]

FURTHER READING

Cowart, David. *Don DeLillo: The Physics of Language*. Athens: University of Georgia Press, 2002 (2nd rev. edn., 2003)

Dewey, Joseph. *Beyond Grief and Nothing: A Reading of Don DeLillo*. Columbia: University of South Carolina Press, 2006

Duvall, John N. (ed.). *The Cambridge Companion to Don DeLillo*. Cambridge University Press, 2008

Lentricchia, Frank (ed.). *Introducing Don DeLillo*. Durham, NC: Duke University Press, 1999

NOTES

1 Don DeLillo, *Americana* (New York: Penguin, 1989), p. 349.
2 Ibid., p. 11.
3 Ibid., p. 58.
4 David Cowart, *The Physics of Language* (Athens: University of Georgia Press, 2002), p. 8.
5 Henry Adams, *The Education of Henry Adams* (New York: Vintage Books, 1990), p. 420.
6 DeLillo, *Americana*, p. 377.
7 Adam Begley, "The Art of Fiction CXXXV: Don DeLillo," in Thomas DiPietro (ed.), *Conversations with Don DeLillo* (Jackson: University of Mississippi Press, 2002), p. 88.
8 Don DeLillo, "American Blood: A Journey Through the Labyrinth of Dallas and JFK," *Rollling Stone* (December 8, 1983): 22–3.
9 Tom LeClair, *In the Loop: Don DeLillo and the Systems Novel* (Urbana: University of Illinois Press, 1987), p. 180.
10 Don DeLillo, *The Names* (New York: Vintage, 1989), p. 236.
11 Ibid., p. 43.
12 Ibid., p. 210.
13 Ibid., pp. 102–3.
14 Ibid., p 103.
15 Ibid.
16 Ibid., p. 209.
17 Ibid., p. 307.
18 Ibid.
19 Ibid., p. 308.
20 Ibid., p. 305.
21 Begley, "The Art of Fiction CXXXV," p. 91.
22 Maria Nadotti, "An Interview with Don DeLillo," in DiPietro (ed.), *Conversations with Don DeLillo*, p. 110.
23 DeLillo, *The Names*, p. 313.
24 Thomas LeClair, "An Interview with Don DeLillo," in DiPietro (ed.), *Conversations with Don DeLillo*, p. 7.
25 Don DeLillo, *White Noise* (New York: Penguin, 1985), p. 17.
26 Ibid., p. 12.
27 Ibid., p. 92.
28 Ibid., pp. 112, 113, 117.
29 Ibid., p. 91.
30 Anthony DeCurtis, "'An Outsider in This Society': An Interview with Don DeLillo," in DiPietro (ed.), *Conversations with Don DeLillo*, pp. 70–1.
31 DeLillo, *White Noise*, p. 324 emphasis added.
32 Ibid., p. 325, emphasis added.

33 Ibid., pp. 322–3.
34 Don DeLillo, *Libra* (New York: Penguin, 1991), p. 181.
35 Ibid., p. 206.
36 Ibid., p. 15.
37 Ibid., p. 182.
38 Ibid., p. 181.
39 Ibid.
40 Ibid., p. 442.
41 Ibid., p. 179.
42 Ibid., p. 60.
43 Don DeLillo, *Mao II* (New York: Penguin Books, 1991), p. 185.
44 Mark Osteen, *American Magic and Dread: Don DeLillo's Dialogue with Culture* (Philadelphia: University of Pennsylvania Press, 2000), p. 212.
45 Don DeLillo, *Underworld* (New York: Scribner, 1997), p. 82.
46 Ibid., p. 86.
47 Ibid., p. 103.
48 Ibid., p. 82.
49 Ibid., p. 11.
50 Ibid., p. 60.
51 Ibid., p. 77.
52 Ibid., p. 97.
53 Ibid., p. 820.
54 Ibid., p. 818.
55 Ibid., p. 540, emphasis added.
56 Ibid., pp. 541–2.
57 Ibid., p. 543.
58 Don DeLillo, *The Body Artist* (New York: Scribner, 2001), p. 107.
59 Ibid., p. 31.
60 Don DeLillo, *Cosmopolis* (New York: Scribner, 2003), p. 79.
61 DeLillo, *The Names*, p. 208.
62 DeLillo, *Body*, p. 39.
63 Don DeLillo, *Point Omega* (New York: Scribner, 2010), p. 98.
64 Don DeLillo, *Falling Man* (New York: Scribner, 2007), p. 236.
65 F. Scott Fitzgerald, *The Crack Up*, ed. Edmund Wilson (New York: New Directions, 1993), p. 69.
66 LeClair, *In the Loop*, p. 14.
67 DeLillo, *The Names*, p. 52.
68 Ibid., 308.
69 DeLillo, *Americana*, p. 117.

JESSICA PRESSMAN

Conclusion: Whither American fiction?

The death of the book is good for literature. At least, one can draw this conclusion from contemporary American fiction. The threat or promise of an increasingly paperless society prompts innovation through interaction with digital technologies and, as a result, reinvigorates literature in both print and digital formats. To assess where American fiction is and where it is going, I examine a few case studies of recent print and digital literature that share a commitment to pushing literature's boundaries by experimenting with its media. My focus is cutting-edge, avant-garde literature because these works blaze the paths others will follow. Instead of withering away, such works show how fiction finds new sources of inspiration in and from digital technologies and networked reading practices. So, at the intersections of new media and traditional literary practices, whither American fiction?

An examination of recent literary engagements with the digital exposes two significant trends: fiction that embraces new media to experiment with ways of representing digitality, and fiction that retreats from the digital through acts of aestheticizing and fetishizing the printed book. These trends are not opposites but are mutually dependent, and their dialectical relationship, I argue, revolves around the concept of remediation. Jay David Bolter and Richard Grusin define remediation as "the representation of one medium in another," and they see remediation as "a defining characteristic of the new digital media."[1] Building upon Marshall McLuhan's famous claim that the medium is the message, that, in other words, the content of any medium is another medium, Bolter and Grusin put forward a theory of media evolution that focuses on the interactions between older and newer media forms. As we will see in the examples that follow, contemporary fiction turns the media theory of remediation into an aesthetic practice.

Of course the novel genre has always engaged with other media forms. The act of repurposing other genres in fact could be identified as the novel's primary defining trait. Yet, the remediation at work in contemporary fiction, I would like to suggest, takes this tradition in new directions. Contemporary novels not only consume other genres and media formats but also, as we will see, configure their bodies within an actual network of other media forms that often include the Internet. In other words, remediation serves to extend the reader's gaze beyond the text to larger systems in which it exists and operates. Katherine Halyes reminds us that all contemporary print literature is marked by digital practices so thoroughly that "intermediation" is the status quo and "digitality has become the textual condition of twenty-first century literature."[2] This new literary situation demands that we approach the age-old novelistic technique of remediation with new-found attentiveness. In what follows, I focus on literary acts of remediation that represent and enable examination of how digitality affects literature in the contemporary moment of medial shift.

We begin with the most obvious instance of contemporary fiction that embraces digitality: electronic literature, born-digital works that are made on the computer and read on the computer. Electronic literature encompasses diverse genres from hypertext to dynamic poetry, generative narrative to interactive fiction, virtual reality to augmented and locative narrative. What unites these works is the fact that they appear as a processural performance across codes and circuitry within the computer and in response to interactions from the reader. For these reasons and more, electronic literature challenges traditional notions of what it means to read as well as what defines a literary text. Yet electronic literature often seeks alignment with the print tradition, both to provide inspiration for digital adaptations and to validate the newer creations through alignment with the more canonical. An exemplary instance of electronic literature that both remediates the printed page and the literary canon is in the online, Flash-based animations of Young-hae Chang Heavy Industries (YHCHI). Within the first few seconds of the first flashing screens, you know you are seeing something new but also familiar. All of YHCHI's works share a simple but sophisticated style: sleek text in capitalized Monaco font flashes onscreen, speeding in synchronization to jazz or electronic music.

As the soundtrack speeds up, so does the text. There are no control buttons, no options to pause or slow the work. Readers find themselves glued to the screen, unable to look away for fear of missing something, and undeniably spellbound. This is why YHCHI is one of the most popular and critically acclaimed collaborations in digital literature and web art. Their work generates buzz on blogs and bulletin boards across the Web; it is taught on university syllabi and inspires scholarly articles. This is in part due to the fact that YHCHI's work appeals to multiple audiences; it is a merger of high art, with its serious or "heavy" affect, and popular culture inflected with the mass-production of "industries." Their work is available free of charge and

THE ALL NEW AND IMPRØVED
YØUNG-HAE CHANG
HEAVY
INDUSTRIES
PRESENTS

Figure 1 Screenshot from YHCHI's Flash animation *Close Your Eyes*. Used with permission from the artists.

in a variety of languages online, and a visit to the artists' website imparts a sense that their oeuvre speaks to a globally networked, multilingual readership, one created by and for the Internet. But as the Internet increasingly develops social-networking capabilities and functionalities that allow consumers to become content producers, YHCHI remain steadfast in retaining a minimalist aesthetic that rejects interactivity. This rejection is a motivating force of their work and expresses their alignment with the print literary tradition. Although they build their works in the Flash authorware, the standard proprietary platform for creating Web content, YHCHI use only a nominal percentage of the software's capacity. What little they use, they use to pursue a retro-aesthetic that foregrounds typography and narrative content over flashy design or interactivity. Their innovation is dual: they retain tight control over the pace of their animation and thus refuse readerly control of works that are accessed within the interactive environment of the Web; they also retain a minimalist aesthetic of text onscreen that remediates print media and earlier literary forms.

While digital writers like YHCHI remediate print literature into electronic literature, some authors strive to appropriate the digital into the pages of print fiction. Mark Z. Danielewski's *Only Revolutions* (2006) is a print novel that revels in its book-bound form but is deeply informed by the Internet. The narrative follows two young lovers, Hailey and Sam, who are "allways [sic] sixteen," as they pursue a picaresque road trip across the United States and across time. Their first-person perspectives depict the same actions told differently, from different sides of the page and from different moments from American history. The two perspectives that constitute the narrative are printed at opposite ends of the page, and a publisher's note suggests that one read eight pages from one narrator before turning the book around to read the other narrator on the other side of the page. Dizziness is produced by rotating the book and from the overwhelming amount of information contained on its pages. For example, along the spine of the book, dates and events from American history are interspersed with poetic lines whose decontextualized presentation produces a database aesthetic – the sense that this content is the result of a search-engine query.

Only Revolutions bears the imprint of the collaborative, social-networking environment that is Web 2.0. The novel incorporates emails from readers of Danielewski's first novel, *House of Leaves* (2000) – another ambitious work of experimental fiction that stretches across media formats. On August 17, 2005, Danielewki sent a message to members of the *House of Leaves* Bulletin Board (a large and vibrant online discussion space) titled "THAT." The posting began, "Yes, it's about time for something new/ but before bringing their long run to a close/it makes sense first to turn to you."[3] Readers and fans of *House of Leaves* dedicated enough to join the Bulletin Board knew that "THAT" referred to the much-anticipated work-in-progress, *Only Revolutions*. The message asked readers to identify important dates in history as well as favorite types of animals, plants, and cars. Some of the responses were incorporated into the pages of *Only Revolutions*, but Danielewski does not clearly demarcate the labor of his readers. A reader approaching the book without knowledge of "THAT" would have no reason to assume that the extraordinarily experimental typography (including the large, bolded, colored words that appear in the middle of lines) represents and traces the communication process between author and readers across the digital network. The digital is enfolded into the book's pages in ways that situate the novel in a digital network of reader/writers via the Internet. Yet, only a reader who accesses the *Only Revolutions* website (connected to the *House of Leaves* Bulletin Board) will discover the specific details of intermediation in this novel's publication history. It takes an innovative and *digitally* literate reader to move between book and Internet and back to the book in ways that illuminate the novel's layers of medial complexity. The text's bolded words retain traces of the Internet and act as metaphoric hyperlinks that connect the book-bound novel to the digital network while also animating the novel's title by showing that all trajectories return to – or revolve around – the book. Thus, while *Only Revolutions* engages with and, to some extent, remediates the Internet, it also exemplifies the other trend in contemporary fiction emerging at the nexus of print and digital media. *Only Revolutions* retreats from its engagement with the digital into its book-bound form and fetishizes the codex as a reading technology. Reading is shown to be an act of rotating the book, of learning to drive the now-defamiliarized reading machine, and of navigating the content of its printed interface. This work of contemporary print fiction displays how engagement with digitality transforms print literature and promotes its evolution and refashioning. The novel's title expresses the circularity of remediation and presents the dialectical relationship between print literature and new media as a central tension in contemporary fiction.

Contemporary digital literature also participates in this exchange between older and new media by remediating bookish forms and adapting print-based reading practices for the screen. Some works remediate lined notebook paper and hand-drawn scribbles as backdrops for extensive Flash-animated narratives (Jason Nelson's "Game, Game, Game, and Again Game" [2007]) or use the computer's folder icons (which themselves remediate paper objects) as a literary device for creating and containing narrative fragments (Jeremy Douglass's "Eight Was Where It Ended" [2005]). Other works remediate the aesthetic of paper crafts and genres such as scrapbooking and postcard epistles (Travis Alber's "30 Days of Rain" [2005] and "Who Is Flora?" [2007] respectively). And, as we saw with YHCHI, digital literature also takes inspiration for narrative content from print literature. Mark C. Marino's *Marginalia in the Library of Babel* (2007) embraces all of these aspects of remediation as aesthetic strategy: it imitates a print media form for presenting text, references an older reading practice, and takes as its narrative inspiration a work from the print literary canon.

Marino's work serves as an excellent example of electronic narrative literature that uses Web 2.0 applications to expose and aestheticize the overlap between digital literature and the print tradition it both extends and transforms. As the title implies, *Marginalia in the Library of Babel* is inspired by Jorge Luis Borges's short story "The Library of Babel" (1941). Borges's story about a universe that is an infinite library has been retrospectively admired for its prescient depiction of a cyberspace-like archive of infinite information. But "The Library of Babel" is actually a story about books; the Internet-like universe consists entirely of codices, and an obsession with them is central to Borges's story and to Marino's digital adaptation of it. *Marginalia* exists on the Web as a web of marginalia; its narrative is contained in remediated Post-it notes injected onto webpages created by others through an Internet annotation application called Diigo. This parasitic narrative attaches to

Figure 2 Close-up of screenshot from the online hypertext *Marginalia in the Library of Babel* by Mark C. Marino. Used with permission from the author.

webpages created by others with Post-it notes that contain rambling commentary and personal confessions of an insomniac narrator as he weaves a web around the short story that stimulated his Internet search. "It starts with Borges," the work begins; "It always starts with Borges" (n.p.). Like Borges's narrator, Marino's roams the infinite library, searching in solitude for answers that lead him back to questions about himself: "At night, I search for Borges, alone, hunched in the solitary chamber of an internet browser ... If I were not seeking him, I would be seeking myself."[4] The work promotes a meta-awareness that reading is always partly an act of reading over the shoulder of a previous reader, and that electronic literature, with all its novelty, still relies on the humanistic and even voyeuristic desires that prompt readers of fiction to follow their narrators and the narratives they leave behind.

Marginalia is both new in its digital form yet also deeply engaged with older literary traditions and media. It is a hypertext narrative built from marginalia, exemplary of Web 2.0's social-networking practices, but it uses the Diigo web-application to encourage readers to recall the pleasures of hypertext. Hypertext is a literary genre that produces nonlinear narrative through a link-and-node structure of chunked text (called lexias) connected through hyperlinks. Shelley Jackson's *Patchwork Girl* (1995) and Michael Joyce's *afternoon, a story* (1987) are examples of classic electronic hypertexts, and both have been included in literary anthologies (including the Norton print edition of *Postmodern American Fiction* [1998]) and thus enfolded into the literary canon. Yet, hypertext has been largely displaced by shorter Flash-based works (such as YHCHI's oeuvre), and Marino's remediation refashions this earlier electronic literary form even as it also adapts the codex-based culture of annotation that has its roots in early modern manuscripts. With its remediation of Post-it notes, its foregrounding of annotation, and its intertextual adaptation of Borges's bibliophile story, *Marginalia* exemplifies both trends I have been charting here: the embrace of and retreat from digital technologies in contemporary fiction. In so doing, Marino's *Marginalia* shows that the technology supposedly threatening to books – the Internet – can actually serve to turn the reader's attention back to them.

Approaching literature by focusing on the intersection of print and digital media provides opportunities to reflect upon what we consider to be the more traditional aspects of literature. For example, in foregrounding annotation, Marino highlights the materiality of the literary object and its capacity to be altered in interactions with readers; *Marginalia* thus challenges the idea of a stable or transcendental text. Incorporating readers' submissions into his narrative, Danielewski seems to subvert the author function in a work whose vast complexity paradoxically reinstates the need for an author capable of explaining it. The collaboration that is YHCHI challenges the notion of a single author and of a national identity for fiction: is their oeuvre American literature, Korean literature, or something other? Moreover, YHCHI adopt a guise of anonymity that they claim is constitutive of the Internet and, thus, consciously challenge the efficacy of nationality as a meaningful category in a global, networked world.[5] These works also challenge the genre of fiction. YHCHI's works are, after all, both prose and poetry. Text is choreographed to produce a poetic rhythm and generate line-breaks while presenting a linear narrative. Similarly, the cover of *Only Revolutions* proclaims it "a novel," but its pages – the visual arrangement of text on the page, the line breaks and structures – reveal it to be poetry. But pushing the envelope is what the avant-garde does, right? So, how does a focus on remediation at the cutting edge of fiction inform more traditional and mainstream print fiction? To answer this question, I turn to a popular print novel, a bestseller of middlebrow variety that seems to have nothing whatsoever to do with digital technologies or their effect on literary practices. Upon closer examination, however, it exemplifies my argument that print fiction engages with the digital and the threat it presumably poses to books as a means of reinventing and reasserting the stakes and significance of fiction.

The Guernsey Literary and Potato Peel Pie Society (2008) by Mary Ann Shaffer and Annie Barrows is trade paperback fiction that topped the *New York Times* bestseller list and spent forty-three weeks on the list. A favorite of book clubs around the country, the novel centers on a female journalist in London, Juliet Ashton, who, in the aftermath of World War II, learns about a book club formed in the Channel Islands during the war and begins writing to the people involved in it. The eponymous book club was formed in an act of subterfuge by inhabitants of Guernsey during the Nazi invasion as a means of escaping punishment for a breached curfew. This act of "self-defense," as one reviewer aptly calls the genesis of the literary society,[6] can also be understood as a metacritical effort by a work of fiction to assert the power of print in a moment wherein the dominant threat is not the Nazis but Google. This is a novel about books, and it begins when the protagonist receives a letter from a stranger in Guernsey: "I have an old book that once belonged to you … Your name and address were written inside the front cover."[7] Juliet responds, "I wonder how the book got to Guernsey? Perhaps there is some secret sort of homing instinct in books that brings them to their perfect readers. How delightful if that were true."[8] Readers become writers in this novel as they correspond with Juliet in written letters about their experiences in the wartime literary society. It is an epistolary novel and is thus composed from the dead (or dying) art of letter-writing, a genre killed by computing and email. Although digital technologies never enter into the novel, it is, I suggest, a book about fiction in the digital age. It imagines the scenario wherein books unite people and produce a web of social networking in print and on paper. The novel thus shows how the aesthetic of remediation – which involves exploring and exploiting the boundary between print and digitality – is not limited to the avant-garde, but penetrates mainstream American fiction. To answer the question posed by this chapter's title, then, the place to look for the continuing evolution of American fiction is wherever print and digital media interact and produce innovation. Rather than withering, literature revives when it engages head-on with digital technologies and Internet reading practices.

FURTHER READING

Danielewski, Mark Z. *House of Leaves*. New York: Pantheon Books, 2000
Electronic Literature Collection, Vol. 1 (October 2006). Online: http://collection.eliterature.org
Halyes, N. Katherine. *My Mother Was a Computer: Digital Subjects and Literary Texts*. University of Chicago Press, 2005
Pressman, Jessica. "*House of Leaves*: Reading the Networked Novel." *Studies in American Fiction*, 34.1 (2006): 107–28
  "The Strategy of Digital Modernism: Young-hae Chang Heavy Industries' *Dakota*." *MFS* 54.2 (2008) 302–26

NOTES

1 Jay David Bolter and Richard Grusin, *Remediation: Understanding New Media* (Cambridge, MA: MIT Press, 1999), p. 45.

2 N. Katherine Halyes, *Electronic Literature: New Horizons for the Literary* (South Bend, IL: University of Notre Dame Press, 2008), p. 186.

3 Mark Z. Danielewski, username "MZD," "THAT." Post to HouseofLeaves.com (August 18, 2005, 12:27 a.m.): www.houseofleaves.com/forum/showthread. php?t=3967 (accessed December 10, 2010).

4 Mark C. Marino, *Marginalia in the Library of Babel* (2007), online: http://bunk-magazine.com/diigo (accessed December 10, 2010).

5 Thom Swiss, "'Distance, Homelessness, Anonymity, and Insignificance': An Interview with Young-Hae Chang Heavy Industries" (2002), *Iowa Review Web*: www.uiowa.edu/~iareview/tirweb/feature/younghae/interview.html.

6 Norah Piehl, "*The Guernsey Literary and Potato Peel Pie Society* Review," *Book Reporter*: www.bookreporter.com/reviews2/9780385340991.asp.

7 Mary Ann Shaffer and Annie Barrows, *The Guernsey Literary and Potato Peel Pie Society* (New York: Dial Press, 2008), p. 9.

8 Ibid., p. 10.

INDEX

Cambridge Companions to ...

AUTHORS

TOPICS